Diversity, Culture
and Counselling

Diversity, Culture and Counselling

A Canadian Perspective

SECOND EDITION

Edited by
M. Honoré France
María del Carmen Rodríguez
&
Geoffrey G. Hett

Brush Education Inc.
Edmonton, Alberta, Canada
www.brusheducation.ca

Library and Archives Canada Cataloguing in Publication

Diversity, culture and counselling : a Canadian perspective / edited by M. Honoré France, María del Carmen Rodríguez, & Geoffrey G. Hett.
— 2nd ed.

Includes bibliographical references.
Issued also in electronic format.
ISBN 978-1-55059-441-6

1. Cross-cultural counseling — Canada. 2. Minorities — Counseling of — Canada. I. France, Honoré II. Rodríguez, María del Carmen III. Hett, Geoffrey

BF636.7.C76D59 2013   158.3   C2012-906859-4

Printed and manufactured in Canada
Copyediting: Leslie Vermeer
Design and Layout: Donald Ward

Produced with the assistance of the Government of Alberta, Alberta Multimedia Development Fund. We also acknowledge the financial support of the Government of Canada through the Canada Book Fund for our publishing activities.

Government
of Alberta ■

Canadian   Patrimoine
Heritage   canadien

Dedications

To my loving wife Lorraine; my children Shawna, Jordan, Tannis, and Bradly; their spouses Sandra, Mark, and Rebecca; my grandchildren Meghan and Zake, Linzy and Russ, Ryan, Dallin, Nathan, Tessa, Courtney, Kirsten, Brooke, Victoria, Madison, Luke, Daniel, Bree, Chloe, Lily, Lannie, and Noah; and my great grandchildren Emma, Aliza, and Jude

— Geoff

To our wonderful triplets: Alonzo, Morana, and Xochitl

— Carmen & Honoré

Contents

Preface

IN THIS, THE SECOND EDITION of *Diversity, Culture, and Counselling*, we have revised all of the chapters and added a few new ones that reflect the current state of diversity in Canadian counselling. Our rationale for redeveloping this book is to bring more Canadian content to our course on diversity, culture and counselling. It has been eight years since the first edition came out, and we have been delighted that the book has been adopted by a number of Canadian colleges and universities. For years, most students taking courses at Canadian universities have had to use American textbooks in an area where much of the materials were mostly irrelevant from a Canadian perspective. Also important for us was the opportunity to give voice to the people multicultural counsellors work with — the various cultural groups that make up Canadian society. Therefore, we have a myriad of professional counsellors — from those of African-Canadian descent talking about counselling in their communities to counsellors who are Buddhists, Christians, Jews, Muslims and Sikhs talking about dealing with specific aspects of counselling related to their faiths. Each chapter has been written by or in collaboration with a person from the ethnic group the author is writing about or a practitioner with specific expertise in the method that is described. In addition, because we have included chapters on various culturally related approaches, we have Indigenous people talking about the use of traditional helping and healing methods as well as counsellors who advocate the use of nature to assist in the helping relationship or the use of yoga in therapy. For us, such scope is one of the best features of this book, giving it more authenticity than it might otherwise have.

Finally, because we believe in diversity and the importance of culture, we believe that multicultural counselling offers an effective approach to working with people from different ethnic, racial, sexual orientation and religious backgrounds, thus moving the profession to another dimension of effectiveness. Racism and prejudice are major areas of concern in every society and must be addressed. Understanding the causes and costs of stereotypes and biases is vital if counsellors are to bridge the ethnic and racial divide.

There are important factors that can help or hinder effective counselling across cultures and differences; consequently, knowing how to enhance communication becomes not only vital but also necessary. Being secure in one's own identity, culturally and racially, can only help to ensure that people accept and respect individual and collective differences. Multiculturally effective counsellors must remember that, as helpers, they are working not just with individuals but with groups of people with collective orientations.

We also recognized as we completed each of the chapters that there was more we would have liked to say or include, but alas, we had to let go of our desire to be totally complete or perfect and send our manuscript to the publisher. We are grateful to Brush Education for accepting our idea and promoting the second edition of this book. We want to always remind ourselves of the words of Geronimo: "Let us put our heads together and do what is best for our children. . . ."

M. Honoré France
María del Carmen Rodríguez
Geoffrey G. Hett

May 2012

Part I

Issues in Diversity, Culture and Counselling

A TRULY MULTICULTURAL CANADIAN SOCIETY would encompass all ethnic and racial groups, including the original founders of the Canadian state – English and French immigrants. While these two formally dominant groups have made way for new groups of immigrants, such as the growing population of Asian Canadians, the English and French languages continue to dominate. The term *multiculturalism* was introduced to the Canadian public in 1971 by Prime Minister Pierre Elliott Trudeau, but did not become government policy until the mid 1980s. The original idea behind multicultural policy was to deal with the tensions between English and French Canadians, resulting in a number of strategies to unite these two communities while at the same time changing "racist" immigration policy. However, the term *multicultural* still carries the stigma of political policy that is exclusive and for some people (e.g., First Nations) unacceptable. In the counselling literature, however, the word *multicultural* has been adopted to refer to culturally sensitive counselling. We have adopted this usage although what we are really talking about is how diversity, culture and counselling merge. Thus, in using the word multicultural, we include all people, not only visible minorities but majority groups too. In this way, the idea of multiculturalism is used to address the issues of culture, oppression and a host of other factors that influence the counselling process.

The focus of the chapters in Part I of this book is on celebrating cultural differences, exploring world views and developing culturally sensitive counselling skills. As counsellors, we believe in the need to embrace and encourage in our profession cultural diversity as being enriching and protective. As a human condition, people around the world tend to be distrustful of those who are different. However, the truth is that, regardless of one's language, race or culture, communities are interdependent. We profoundly believe that when a community discriminates against and marginalizes people for being different, instability occurs and everyone suffers.

The changing trends in Canadian immigration are having a major impact on how counselling services are offered. The multicultural reality in Canada is changing and necessitates a shift from the dominant Eurocentric counselling theories and practice, which favour the white, middle-class population, to approaches that emphasize diversity and a new world perspective. As counsellors, we need to recognize the importance of language and communication in counselling diverse groups of people. We believe that multicultural experiences can enhance a counsellor's personal growth and overall communication skills. When we work with diverse groups, our behaviour and language greatly influence the communication process and counselling outcome. Further, we live in a time that warns us that our very survival may depend on our ability to communicate effectively on a multicultural level. Counsellors are in a unique position to model culturally sensitive behaviour and language and help challenge the issues of discrimination and racism as part of counselling practice. Frequent contact with different cultures is particularly important in achieving this goal.

The cornerstone of counselling with diverse clients is an understanding of world view and how it relates to developing multicultural skills. No matter where we live on the globe, we modify our perception of the world by understanding, experiencing and making meaning of an array of customs dissimilar to our own, unique in their own right and indispensable while interacting with others in a culturally diverse setting. This need to modify our world view goes beyond cultural legacies (i.e., folklore, customs, traditions and rituals), allowing us to pursue an understanding of the values, beliefs, attitudes and affective perceptions that constitute the life of a population and its members. In addition to these aspects, normative standards of subsistence, communication, technology and political ideas also come to form part of our new world view.

As Canada has evolved, immigration has reshaped the population of the country, making it one of the most diverse in the world. The impact of this shift in immigration is significant for counsellors. The multicultural reality of Canadian society will challenge counsellors in a time when universities are slow in providing multicultural training for the helping professions. As most Canadian counselling theories and practices originate from European models, counsellors are at a disadvantage when providing services to people who hold a different world view. We encourage counsellors to seek out experiences, training and competencies necessary to support people who hold different world views and cultural values. Gaining multicultural counselling skills is necessary, and doing so is the only ethical way to proceed if we are to move beyond a Eurocentric position and empower all clients, regardless of their culture, race, abilities, sexual orientation or religious beliefs.

1

Counselling across Cultures

Identity, Race and Communication

M. Honoré France

How have Torontonians gone from around 3% visible minorities in the early 1960s to more than 50% now without any major disruption, while the people of Los Angeles, experiencing about the same degree of change over the same period, felt the need to burn down parts of their city not once but twice?

— Gwynne Dyer (2001, p. 45)

Nega Mezlekia's novel *Notes from the Hyena's Belly* (2000), which won the Governor General's Literary Award, begins with a metaphor of a donkey and a hyena. A lion, leopard, hyena and donkey come together to discuss why their land is in such poor state. In turn, they explain that the turmoil is due to a sin that has displeased God. Each animal, except the donkey, tells a story of attacking another animal and eating it, but each animal is told that eating an animal is an animal's nature, so it is not wrong. When it is the donkey's turn, he relates that while his human master was busy talking with another man, the donkey went off the trail and ate some grass. The other animals become enraged and tell the donkey that he is the one who has caused the problems by going off the path and eating the grass; they attack the donkey, kill him and eat him. Mezlekia concludes by saying that "we children lived like the donkey, careful not to wander off the beaten trail and end up in the hyena's belly" (p. 7).

Moving away from one's routines and traditions has a price; dangers are always present, and change is a constant. There is a subtle warning too in the metaphor: being different, like the donkey, can be dangerous. Mezlekia's metaphor is an apt warning not to take risks while at the same time showing that undertaking new challenges is a part of being human. Despite our best-laid plans, there are dangers in the world and down the street. Since the terrorist bombings on New York City and the fallout from the war in Iraq, the challenge for counsellors is that new tensions and new alliances abound. For counsellors, these new tensions and new alliances emerge from working in the reality of the multicultural, multi-ethnic and multilingual society that is Canada today.

The rapid changes in this society need to be addressed in a realistic yet positive manner, in which differences are not homogenized but celebrated because diversity is beautiful and strengthening. Being accepting and open to differences is often elusive. But why is this so? According to Baron, Kerr and Miller (1992), it is "the human tendency to disparage, distrust and dislike groups other than our own" (p. 134). One tendency of societies in general is that people exclude others who are different. In fact, it is not uncommon for people from the majority cultural and racial group to see someone different as being a stranger in their midst. Diller (2003) relates the story of someone of Asian extraction whose family has been living in North America for over a hundred years being taken as a foreign visitor because the country is seen as a country of European immigrants. People who are different "are deeply disturbed by their second-class citizenry" (Diller, 2003, p. 26). In Canada, people of colour who are not from the original founders of the Canadian state are called *visible minorities*; this label includes the original inhabitants — First Nations people. Visible minorities is a distinctive Canadian term that is often used as a shorthand to describe racial minorities who are not of European origin and who have physical characteristics that distinguish them from Canada's traditional mainstream of English and French peoples (Labelle, 2007).

The changing nature of society makes the argument for or against multiculturalism moot; but if society is to avoid cultural and racial misunderstanding, then the institutions of society need to adapt to the new realities. For counsellors, this adaptation may mean adopting a frame of reference in which counselling can be described as a working alliance. In other words, the counsellor creates a common ground with clients by establishing an avenue to resolution rather than first building on the idea of a trusting relationship. For people from some racial or ethnic backgrounds, trust of the counsellor may not be inherent, nor can it be established in the traditional manner that theoreticians like Carl Rogers suggested.

So, how does one establish a trusting relationship? Adopting the idea of a working alliance, counsellors and clients work in a collaborative way to accomplish clients' goals. Furthermore, we must consider that all counselling is potentially multicultural in one way or another, because it always deals with a range of variables that may be contradictory from situation to situation. Sciarra (1999) provides the following example: "the personalismo of the Latino culture can require a less formal and more affective counsellor, whereas these same counsellor characteristics may be alienating to some Asian clients"

(p. 10). Adapting the process to suit the situation is fundamental, therefore, because there will always be some cultural differences between clients and counsellors.

Rationale for Diversity and Multicultural Counselling

The rationale for multicultural counselling arises in part from the growing multicultural factor in everyday life and from the increasingly small world brought about by more efficient communication and transportation systems. In early 2003, as the war in Iraq began, tensions between Christians and Muslims increased, along with more tensions between the developed and developing world, which only highlights cultural differences that divide people around the world. Waging war when differences are greater may be easier and more acceptable. In counselling, the challenge is to understand differences and enhance communication across cultures. More importantly, cultural differences exist not just between one group of people in the West and another group in the Middle East, but within the borders of Canada. Therefore, Canadians have no choice but to face the challenge of diversity issues and the changing mosaic of the Canadian nation.

Do societies made up from a variety of ethnic backgrounds experience more ethnic conflict than those that are more homogeneous? Certainly; and cultural differences in a counselling group usually stem from issues in the way the members communicate with one another. In the post 9/11 political environment, the issues of culture and religious values have been important factors in how terrorism and the invasion of Iraq have been dealt with in the media and everyday life. North American society cannot close its eyes to the issue of culture, race and language. In a world where most people are not Westerners, Caucasian or Christian — and in a world that is growing smaller — becoming multicultural is not only enriching but also protective. Everyone must be aware that humanity, as a community, has the power to destroy our world through nuclear war and pollution. War has its genesis in society's disrespect for people who are different. People have to learn not only how to control their willingness to harm those who have different customs and views, but also how to live in harmony with others and the environment.

Regardless of our language, race or culture, every community is interdependent with others. Therefore, when society discriminates, marginalizes and ostracizes people because they are different, everyone suffers. Society has come a long way in being more accepting of differences among people, yet it has a long way to go in creating a society that respects diversity. According to Suzuki, Ponterotto, Alexander and Casas (2009), when cultural aspects are added to the counselling process, the following rules have to be considered in order to be sensitive to different people:

1. A tolerance for logical inconsistency and paradox suggests a subjective definition of knowledge to supplement the more familiar rules of objective, rational logic;
2. The primary importance of relationships and collectivism contrasts with the more familiar bias toward individualism;
3. The implicit or explicit differentiation between modernization and Westernization ignores the possibility that other cultures may have good solutions to our problems;
4. The implicit assumption that change and progress are good must be challenged by clients having to deal with change as both good and bad at the same time;
5. The metaphor of a natural ecological setting reminds us of the many unknown and perhaps unknowable mysteries of the relationships among people and their environments;
6. The absolute categories of problem and solution and success and failure must be brought into question as inadequate;
7. The need to apply familiar counselling concepts to less familiar multicultural settings must be emphasized;
8. The need for new conceptual and methodological approaches to deal with the complexities of culture is apparent; and
9. The need for a grounded theory of multicultural counselling is essential to all counsellors and is not an exotic or specialized perspective. (p. 23)

The world is changing swiftly where ethnic boundaries are changing. In the past, European cultural groups made up the vast majority of new immigrants in North America, whereas today Asian groups top the list. According to the Canadian Census Bureau (cited in Cohen, 2012), two-thirds of the country's population growth is now fuelled by immigration. More than half of those immigrants are from Asia, particularly from China and India, with fewer immigrants from Europe. In addition, the Aboriginal population increased by 3.4 per cent during the period between 1996 and 2001, and if current trends continue, Aboriginal people "may well be heading to majority status in many cities within the next 25 to 50 years" from Saskatchewan to northwestern Ontario (Dyer, 2001, p. 49). The Census Bureau has also estimated that by 2030 the province of British Columbia will have a majority non-white population. Already many urban areas of Canada are composed largely of racial minorities. What is making a remarkable impact, however, is the large number of immigrants settling in North American cities. This trend can already be seen in cities like Vancouver, Toronto and Montreal, where more than 70 per cent of immigrants settle. The multicultural reality is also evident in North American schools, where large numbers of students do not come from the "founding" ethnic groups. However, the issue goes much deeper than accommodating the new multicultural fact to changing the structures of our schools that were initially designed for a homogeneous population. The multicultural reality has changed the nature of a Eurocentric counselling theory and practice that fits a homogeneous population into a system that emphasizes diversity and a world perspective. Lorde (in Siccone, 1995) says, "it is a waste of time hating a mirror or its reflection instead of stopping the hand that makes glass with distortions" (p. xvi).

The Cost of Racism

It is hard to understand a culture that justifies the killing of millions in past wars, and is at this very moment preparing bombs to kill even greater numbers. It is hard for me to understand a culture that spends more on wars and weapons to kill, than it does on education and welfare to help and develop. It is hard for me to understand a culture that not only hates and fights his brothers but also even attacks nature and abuses her. (George, 1994, p. 38)

The pain and sorrow in Chief Dan George's words in describing the cultural misunderstandings between First Nations people and "white" people typifies like nothing else the nature of prejudice and racism. Diller (2003) suggests that helpers need to understand important elements of racism in order to help people work together in a multicultural society. First, racism is a universal phenomenon that exists in all societies around the world among all races. Secondly, most people are uncomfortable with talking about racism and even deny that it exists. There is a difference between prejudice and racism. Prejudice is an unfair and negative belief about the inferiority of a group of people, often based on faulty knowledge and a generalized view of others who are different. Racism "involves the total social structure where one group has conferred advantage through institutional polices . . . it is a social construction based on sociopolitical attitudes that demean specific racial characteristics" (Robinson & Howard-Hamilton, 2000, p. 58). It is not a natural response, but one learned from societal norms and observations of parents, friends and neighbours. Not surprisingly, prejudice does not result from constant negative experience with someone who is different, but through occasional contacts and reinforcement, such as a negative experience in a bar or an ethnic joke.

In Canada, minorities have been subjected to three forms of discrimination: individual racism, institutional racism and cultural racism. The most obvious forms of individual racism involve personal expressions that one race is superior to another. Institutional racism is communicated through established practices that perpetuate inequities, while cultural racism involves believing in the inferiority of one culture over another. The Government of Canada established the residential school system in order to "help" Aboriginals assimilate into majority society; however, the result was very different and demonstrates the cost of racism to individuals and communities:

> Social maladjustment, abuse of self and others and family breakdown are some of the symptoms prevalent among First Nation Babyboomers. The "Graduates" of the "Ste. Anne's Residential School" era are now trying and often failing to come to grips with life as adults after being raised as children in an atmosphere of fear, loneliness and loathing.
>
> Fear of caretakers. Loneliness, knowing that elders and family were far away. Loathing from learning to hate oneself, because of repeated physical, verbal or sexual abuse suffered at the hands of various adult caretakers. This is only a small part of the story. (in Milloy, 2001, pp. 295–96)

The reason for discriminating against others is not really complex. Consider that when people are faced with evidence of prejudice, they tend to reject it: "I'm not prejudiced against Indians, but most of them want to live on government assistance." There is of course some cognitive dissonance going on, because prejudice and racism are difficult to admit. It is easy for a society to judge situations in other nations as racist or oppressive, such as Apartheid in South Africa or the practices of the Israeli occupation forces on the West Bank. Some might respond by saying, "It's their fault that their culture has disintegrated." While this is not an uncommon response, it is a curious one, because it blames the victim for being victimized. Aboriginals are penalized for being culturally different, because of a system that neither allowed them citizenship nor allowed them to practice their language and culture. Chief Dan George (in de Montigny, 1972) said:

> Do you know what it is like to have your race belittled. . . ? You don't know for you have never tasted its bitterness. . . . It is like not caring about tomorrow for what does tomorrow matter? It is having a reserve that looks like a junk yard because the beauty in the soul is dead. . . . Why should the soul express an external beauty that does not match it? It is like getting drunk for a few brief moments, an escape from the ugly reality and feeling a sense of importance. It is most of all like awaking next morning to the guilt of betrayal. For the alcohol did not fill the emptiness but only dug it deeper. (pp. 162–163)

The dehumanization of "enemies" can clearly be observed when examining the emotional demonstrations of Arabs shouting "Down with America" or the indifference of American leaders to the welfare of civilians during the first and second Gulf wars. In the war against Iraq, American President George W. Bush constantly compared Iraqi President Saddam Hussein with Stalin and other despots, ignoring the fact that millions of people in the

Middle East regarded Hussein as a hero, a symbol of defiance, for standing up against the firepower of the US military. In war, the enemy has to be dehumanized in order to sustain hate; this dehumanization occurs in all wars. Such an image certainly helps to alleviate any guilt one nation may feel for waging war against another. In the same way, accepting stereotypes about a people, such as those voiced by Chief Dan George, can justify actions such as war, colonization and the establishment of residential schools. These rationalizations are really a façade for an attitude that allows one to treat the in-group differently than the out-group. Conversely, co-operative activities can reduce racial tension if both parties work in a strategic alliance. According to Baron, Kerr and Miller (1992), "cooperation may break down group boundary lines (the 'us versus them' mentality) to some degree" (p. 150). People must become cognizant of the effect of prejudice on others.

Ethnic stereotypes create a problem when they are inaccurate and produce a negative evaluation of other people. In a multicultural society, such stereotypes bring a sense of exclusiveness that can result in a strong feeling of superiority. Interestingly, research evidence suggests that individuals need to maintain a sense of group distinctiveness (Berry, Poortinga, Segall & Dasen, 2002). Sometimes people refer to this as "group pride," but why does pride hinge on a feeling of superiority? Pride in doing things well or in a feeling of solidarity with one's ethnic group is beneficial, but when it evolves into superiority, it is destructive. There also seems to be a relationship between prejudicial attitudes and people who have a disposition towards authoritarianism. People who are overly submissive, feel inadequate or are overly suspicious seem to be more prone to prejudice than others. While these examples suggest how racism may be used to deprive others of their human qualities, the process is similar for sexism, ageism, religious bigotry and homophobia.

The kind of prejudice experienced by ethnic and racial minorities, intentionally or unintentionally, is the essence of the challenge of an open society, and an insidious aspect of racism is the manner in which it is reinforced by society's institutions. The scope of the issue is associated with integrating the culturally different into society, however: "According to a Leger Marketing poll, Canadians are divided on whether racism poses a problem for them: 52 per cent say it's significant while 47 per cent consider it to be insignificant" (Song, 2011). These results are not comforting.

The Causes of Conflict and Prejudice

There has been a good deal of research examining what creates conflict and gives birth to prejudice. Is it a part of the human experience? Are people born feeling prejudice? Consider that when people compete for scarce resources, they form groups to help them get ahead. Often, these groups are based on similarities within the group, which becomes the in-group. Those who are different become the out-group. Differences could be based on a number of factors including group norms, language, race, religion or even goals. On a smaller scale, even people who are similar but who have different goals become frustrated with others whose goals are different. According to Baron, Kerr and Miller (1992), however, people become less aggressive, and thus more cooperative — thereby reducing prejudice — if goals are mutual. In fact, friendships develop and differences of colour or race are minimized when goals are mutual. Generally, people from one group are more generous or overcompensate for those in their group; at the same time, they may be less generous and under-compensate for those from another group. In other words, people from one cultural group will be more forgiving of those in their group and less forgiving of those from another group. For some reason, there is a tendency to exaggerate similarities with the in-group while exaggerating differences with other groups. People react to each other based on their group membership. Since they do not know the others, viewing the others as faceless and interchangeable is common. It is easy to see others in a different light than we ourselves and so differences become exaggerated (e.g., others don't value human life the way we do).

Is it human nature to try to simplify the environment, despite the fact that most day-to-day interactions among people are positive? A good question. One bias is that members of one group will "naturally" see themselves as acting responsibly, but see the other group and its members as being irresponsible. According to Baron, Kerr and Miller (1992), this bias is a factor of the human experience. For whatever reason, people also tend to promote negative views about others who are distinct and different. Thus, the bias is reinforced with each "negative" experience one has. In the end, one's attitude becomes more rigid and ideological, part of one's cultural norm. This outcome means, for example, that if one's attitudes are negative towards the police, one will see examples that reinforce this bias more often than if one does not have the bias.

There is also the reciprocity rule, or the notion of "tit for tat," in which if one "wrong" is done, the harmed party retaliates, causing a series of behaviours that reinforce one's beliefs. Social comparison is also a factor in creating a sense of anger, prejudice and aggression. And finally, if there is a "triggering" event, people may react on the basis of emotion and do something that produces a chain of events that can last for decades. Consider, for example, the Kosovo situation in which Serbs fought Albanians. Historical "wrongs" were enmeshed within the differing groups' attitudes about each other. The Turkish invasion during the sixteenth century continues to be played out in the twenty-first century. People adopt these historical attitudes and make them part of their behaviour, thus creating another myth that reinforces prejudice.

Cultural Influences

Culture is a human necessity, because it is the way people establish and maintain a relationship with their environment. As people of understanding interact with those who are culturally different, they must explore the socialization forces that affect behaviour, values and language. For example, notice the dichotomy between the ways of understanding the relationship of people with nature: control and good/bad versus harmony and good. The stress of control over nature produces a feeling of seeing other people in terms of good and bad, which corresponds exactly with how humanity ought to be treated. If people are not good or consistent with societal norms, then they need to be controlled. Taking this attitude one step further, people may also seek to control the urges they feel within themselves. Even in a relatively homogeneous population, there are cultural differences that are easier to be aware of in others than in the self. According to many social scientists, culture is both a critical aspect of a person's lifestyle and an essential element of human behaviour. While the clothes people wear and the attitudes they voice may reflect the dominant culture they inhabit, it is their cultural background that shapes their thinking and feelings, as is reflected in the expression "blood is thicker than water." There are strong indicators that cultural conditioning reflects how people communicate with others (Pedersen, Draguns, Lonner & Trimble, 2002).

The biological force is universal: no matter who people are or where they are from, they are human beings. Some biological differences include age, shape, size, colour and gender. With few exceptions, these differences do not change nor can they be manipulated. In all societies biological differences have produced attitudes relating to behaviour and how people interact with others. For example, someone large is viewed as powerful and possibly aggressive; as a result, more deference may be shown towards that person. A big and muscular person may be seen as a brute, a lean and slight person as effeminate, someone with rough features as unrefined; in some groups, plumpness is healthy while in others it is negative. The cultural norms that dictate reactions to biological differences are infinite, with each group having its own interpretation about the meaning of physical and biological characteristics.

All cultures are affected psychologically by various influences on the group. People in the group are continuously subjected to pressures to conform to the norms of the group. In this respect, personality is to a large extent formed through group norms. The family, as a primary socializing agent, is responsible for the basic values people exhibit. This is particularly true of Asian cultural values of respect for authority, tradition and learning. Exposure to significant others, relatives, friends, teachers and peers enhances one's repertoire, inculcating the social mores and behaviours of the entire culture. This trait is obvious if we compare the ways people feel, think and act in different cultures. For example, according to Salagame (2011), people from different places in the world have a different construct of self:

> It is observed, in general, the Western Concept of Self is of an individual who is separate, autonomous, and atomized (made up of a set of discrete traits, abilities, values, and motives, seeking separateness and independence from others). In contrast, in Eastern cultures relatedness, connectedness, and interdependence are sought, rooted in a concept of the self not as a discrete entity, but as inherently linked to others. The person is only made "whole" when situated in his or her place in a social unit. (p. 133)

Behaviour may also be affected by ideology or one's characteristic manner of thinking (e.g., assertions, theories or aims). The ideological foundation of an individual's culture will, to a large degree, have an impact on his/her behaviour. It is from such foundations that people derive religious, social and political beliefs that direct and govern their behaviour. Being born in a certain culture occasions the display of certain characteristics that are behaviourally right for that culture. In other words, people have a cultural or national way of thinking and seeing the world, which is reflected in their language, values and beliefs, norms, socio-political history and the like. The ideological differences can be observed in the behaviour of group members who come from different ethnic groups.

The ideology of a nation dictates to people certain attitudes, beliefs and ways of thinking that frame their existence. Beliefs about life, death and marriage, for instance, determine relationship behaviours. People tend to respond to their environment in consistent ways that are dictated by the attitudes of their society. Minorities have partially adopted the ideology of the dominant culture in order to survive, but the adoption may or may not be fully ingrained in their personality. Consider that even after three generations of living in the United States, some Mexican-American adolescents modified their basic cultural characteristics in only a few small ways (cited in France, 2001). Yet such minorities are also dissimilar to the cultures of their origin. For example, African-Canadians and Arab-Canadians may have more in common with one another than with people in Ethiopia or Jordan. This dissimilarity creates a strain for visible minorities who can feel that they are neither here nor there. It is also true that some beliefs and values are more affected by gender than cultural differences — for instance, that men have more freedom of choice regardless of culture. Finally, ecological forces refer to how the environment has influenced culture and behaviour. Someone born on an isolated island may develop a different view of the world than someone born on a large continent. Climate, terrain, prosperity and population density can also play a role in developing distinct cultural norms. People born in highly populated areas may have to be more assertive because that is the only way to survive, while someone born in a less populous area may be more relaxed and quiet.

Class, Language and Diversity

As a primary form of communication, language is of great importance to people in groups. Language patterns reflect people's culture or subculture (Berry, Poortinga, Segall & Dasen, 2002). Even when people are speaking the same language, there may be misunderstanding because of individual differences. Thus, it becomes easy to imagine why people who do have different cultural and linguistic backgrounds misunderstand each other. An inaccurate picture of another person's issue formed from verbal responses — or in some cases formed from what is not said — produces real conflict. Certain phrases in one language may be un-interpretable in another or, if translated literally, may not convey the many dimensions the phrase encompasses.

Some words, phrases or expressions might have negative meanings that are acceptable to some people from a cultural group but not to others. For example, many high school and professional sports teams have names and logos like "Braves," "Indians" and "Redskins." First Nations communities have protested such names on the basis that they reinforce negative stereotypes, use Aboriginal images and icons in a disrespectful manner, and trivialize their ethnic background. A recent incident in greater Vancouver created controversy when the Musqueam name *Spull'u'kwuks* was proposed for a school. Authorities felt the name, meaning "place of bubbling waters," could be used in a negative way because of the potential for rhyming with "the F word" or "sucks" or so on. The response from the Musqueam First Nation was "it was their language . . . and . . . it should be celebrated, not made the subject of humour" (France, 2002).

Even non-verbal gestures are relatively different from culture to culture. According to Matsumoto and Juang (2012), "being unaware of these differences can definitely cause problems" (p. 352), because each culture develops unique patterns of non-verbal communication. Eye contact and personal space, for example, differ from culture to culture. In North America, people are taught that eye contact communicates closeness and attention, while lack of eye contact communicates dislike, lack of interest or disrespect. Arabic societies gaze even longer than North Americans do (Matsumoto & Juang, 2012), but the degrees of eye contact may have different implications for different cultures. According to Sue and Sue (2007), white middle-class people, when speaking to others, look away (eye avoidance) approximately 50 per cent of the time. When whites listen, however, they make eye contact with the speaker over 80 per cent of the time. But blacks make more eye contact when speaking and infrequent eye contact when listening. This difference reinforces the idea that we should be careful when we try to attribute reasons for the amount of eye contact we encounter. Eye contact is not necessarily related to aggressiveness, shyness or inattentiveness but rather may depend on cultural patterns.

Physical distance is another cultural variable. Francophones touch more in conversation and kiss those they feel close to, while Anglophones touch far less and rarely kiss both cheeks in greeting. In North America, proximity is closely related to relationships. In an intimate relationships, people may come within 0 to 1.5 feet of one another; in a personal relationship, from 1.5 to 4 feet; in a social consultative relationship from 4 to 8 feet; and in a public relationship up to 10 feet. According to Matsumoto and Juang (2012), Latinos feel more comfortable in close proximity than those of European ancestry.

According to Pedersen and Carey (2003), socio-economic factors affect the way people communicate and interact. For example, groups with members from lower economic and educational levels appear to prefer more concrete and structured activities. These people may want direct advice or at least a chance to talk in terms of concreteness and tangible outcomes. In general, those in the lower socio-economic spheres report that counselling activities are "all talk and no action." In addition, people from different cultures may be unfamiliar with the dynamics of groups, which may be incongruent with what they expect. This inexperience may in turn block their progress in counselling groups.

As counsellors, we must be aware of and able to identify the values of different people that we work with. All people tend to project their cultural values in their behaviour, and verbal and emotional expressions. Obviously, these differences may create distances between people. Individuals from some cultural groups may be reluctant to disclose their feelings because their culture places a high priority on restraint in expressing feelings and thoughts, particularly to strangers. If one misinterprets the reasons behind the reluctance to self-disclose, the results may produce a block of communication, severe anxiety and extreme discomfort.

Another important cultural value is the family relationship. People of European ancestry and those acculturated by this ancestry tend to centre on personal responsibility; their decisions may be made based on the good of the individual. Other cultures emphasize the family or the collective good. If someone from a culture that emphasizes family involvement in decision-making makes a personal decision, the family might block attempts to achieve the individual's goals. One Asian-Canadian client, for example, stated, "Whenever I disagreed with my mother, it seemed to her that I was questioning her character" (France, 2002, p. 220). In this client's family, the authority of the parents is paramount and not to be questioned by the child. When the client made a decision without consulting her family, her mother felt hurt and angry. The client loved her mother but felt a desire to assert her individuality, and this desire produced many conflicting feelings. There are also positive aspects to cultural values in which adult children make important choices only after consulting with their parents. For example, a Brazilian woman, aged 30, said that she and her husband felt it necessary to ask her parents whether their decision to buy a particular apartment was a good one. Upon hearing her, a Canadian male responded that, if he asked his parents what they thought, the response would be, "You're an adult now; decide what you think is best."

Cross-Cultural Communication Difficulties

When people encounter cultural differences as sojourners, they find "that adjustment problems were greatest at the beginning and decreased over time" (Berry, Poortinga, Segall & Dasen, 2001, p. 409). Interestingly, there is a "honeymoon period" in adjustment in which the sojourner is enthusiastic; this is followed by anxiety, frustration, and adjustment difficulties. However, these dissipate as the sojourner develops new coping mechanisms. This experience is sometimes referred to as the U- or W-shaped curve, as cultural adjustment occurs. But what are some of the blocks that challenge people in cross-cultural communication? To be sensitive to and aware of another person's frame of reference is elementary, but it is particularly significant with those of diverse cultural backgrounds. In some ways the following list of stumbling blocks applies to almost any group but is especially pertinent in cross-cultural groups (France, 2002).

Language: Vocabulary, syntax, idiom, slang and dialect can create problems of understanding. The problem is the tenacity with which people cling to "the" meaning of a word or phrase in the new language, regardless of its connotation or the context.

Non-verbal areas: People from different cultures employ different non-verbal sensory words. They see, hear, feel and smell only that which has some meaning or importance for them. They extract whatever significance fits their personal world of recognition and then interpret it through the frame of reference of their own culture.

Tendency to evaluate: Some people from different cultures need to approve or disapprove the statements and actions of others, rather than to try to comprehend the thoughts and feelings expressed. This bias prevents the open-minded attention needed to look at attitudes and behaviour patterns from others' frame of reference. This is heightened when feelings and emotions are deeply involved. Yet this is the time when listening with understanding is most needed. As counsellors, we especially need to examine values that are negatively evaluative towards those who are different.

High anxiety: This stumbling block is not distinct but underlies and compounds the others. Its presence is very common because of uncertainties present when people function in a foreign language where the normal flow of verbal and non-verbal interaction cannot be sustained. There is a sense of threat by the unknown knowledge, experience and evaluation of others, therefore bringing the potential for scrutiny and rejection by the self. There is also the added tension of having to cope with the differing pace, climate and culture. Self-esteem is often intolerably undermined unless people employ defences such as withdrawal into their reference group or into themselves, thus screening out or misperceiving stimuli, rationalizing, overcompensating or even showing hostility. (p. 219)

Cross-Cultural Communication

Multicultural experiences can enhance a counsellor's personal power and improve overall communication skills not only with culturally different clients but with clients in general. What counsellors say and do can either promote or reduce their credibility and effectiveness with others. Their style of self-disclosure, perceived trustworthiness and counselling style emphasize just a few of the variables. In this regard, the cultural background of counsellors is not as important to how effective they are as the way their credibility, attractiveness and trustworthiness are perceived by clients. In studies on evaluating the effects of counsellors' race and ethnic background on perceived effectiveness in communication, people were affected by the person's race and ethnic background either negatively or positively (cited in France, 2002). In counselling situations, the evidence suggests that, for culturally different people, the issue of expertise is raised more often than whether the person has a similar cultural or racial background (Pedersen & Carey, 2003). This finding suggests that group members will have to be sensitive and develop strategies that will attenuate or eliminate this effect, particularly if the effect is negative. In other words, using appropriate communication skills and strategies that are congruent with the client's values is more important than race or ethnic background. There seems to be no particular communication strategy that proves more successful with specific populations. Yet the approach used by group members from the majority culture must be consistent with those from other cultures' lifestyles, along with flexibility for individual differences within a culture: not all people with a similar cultural background behave in the same way.

On the other hand, equal treatment in communication may be discriminatory treatment. If group members proceed on the basis that everyone is the same without recognizing differences, this approach may have a negative effect. If we could all be more aware and appreciate other cultures' different attributes, perhaps we could be more accepting of cultural differences in others.

The Process of Cultural Adjustment

The process of adaptation is a universal phenomenon that everyone experiences in growing from infancy to adulthood within a given cultural milieu. According to Sciarra (1999), "counselors working with clients from non-dominant cultural backgrounds need to assess their acculturative levels and the amount of stress resulting from living in a different environment" (p. 25). Okun, Fried and Okun (1999) emphasize that cultural adaptation and "development can be considered as a series of fluctuations between agency or the ability to carry out one's purpose or function and communion or the ability to connect with another" (p. 24). Such is the challenge of being oneself while being able to connect with others who may be different. How one does this can determine how safe one feels in any different cultural situation. However, three categories of processes of adaptation have been identified:

- Unidirectional, or adapting to one culture and away from another;
- Bidirectional, or adapting by moving back and forth between two cultures while feeling at home in both;
- Multidirectional, or adapting to other cultures but feeling positively grounded in one's own culture.

In the example of the war in Iraq, there was much talk about the evils of terrorism, and Islam was sometimes portrayed as the root cause of the terror. Terms like "regime change" conveyed the idea that somehow the invasion of Iraq was a positive endeavour; such language dehumanizes the "other" side. Dyer (1999) argues that each nation invents the myths of nationhood just as each country decides what is "good" or "bad." In effect, reasons behind various national policies are subjective. But reality is subjective: it looks different from an Arab perspective compared to an American perspective. Each side views the other as either an "Axis of Evil" or the "Big Satan," when in fact, both sides are made up of human beings who love their children.

Many of the issues that have divided people historically are still unchanged. Over time the enemy changes, but the process of dehumanizing stays the same; for instance, the Russians are now like us, while Muslims are seen very differently. Despite openness to new ideas, people in North America may be quite ignorant of other world literature, customs and languages. The more people foster the notion that there are multiple explanations or sides to an issue, the less the chance that we will be ignorant and fear the unknown. Fear, after all, is the culprit behind racism.

Encouragement of Cultural Identity

All people want acceptance from others, yet regardless of how they adapt to new cultural situations, their cultural roots bind them and this binding in turn affects how they feel about themselves and are perceived by others. Sciarra (1999) stresses that "attitudes and behaviors are the result of complex cognitive and emotional processes around the relationship people have to their own cultural group" (p. 47).

Racial–ethnic identity development may be defined as pride in one's racial, ethnic and cultural heritage. People who have strong cultural identities seem to have a greater sense of control over their lives. Sue and Sue (2007) suggest that counsellors' cultural identity can adversely affect how they interact with clients by reinforcing negative self-esteem if the client is experiencing dissonance about his/her cultural development. Helms (2010) proposes two models of identity development to describe how minorities form their identity compared to the majority group. There are six stages in the Majority Racial Identity Development Model:

1. Lack of awareness: A person has no sense that there are any differences in cultures simply because he/she has no contact.
2. Contact: A person has contact with someone who is different. This stage is characterized by curiosity and the recognition that there are differences among people — colour, race, language, and so on.
3. Conflict: Once differences are identified, there is a great chance for conflict. Differences become exaggerated and "war" is inevitable. People become frustrated and differences create fear; people may become defensive and sometimes aggressive.
4. Pro-minority stance: Once people understand that conflict is not a positive option, they begin to reach out to others. In their desire to connect, members of the dominant group embrace minority characteristics and values (e.g., language, dress, etc.). However, this strategy is bound to fail because those reaching out can never be minority members because they cannot change their complexion or culture.
5. Pro-majority stance: This stage occurs when the pro-minority stance is not accepted. Members of the dominant group embrace an attitude that is not diverse or accepting of others (that is, they support only their own).
6. Internalization: At this stage, people accept themselves as coming from a certain ethnic group and accept others in the same way. They have a good sense of their own boundaries and those of others, and recognize that their ethnic identity is a part of themselves and is built on a positive foundation. They accept others who are different and value others based on their behaviours, not on their colour.

In the Minority Identity Development Model, Helms (2010) suggests that if counsellors want to understand minority people, they must understand the individual's identity development. If there are problems, they may have something to do with the person's identity development. The model consists of five stages:

1. Conformity: The acceptance of majority standards and values at the cost of one's own ethnic identity.

2. Dissonance: The person perceives a difference between what he/she feels and what he/she experiences.

3. Resistance: Based on their sense of dissonance, people revolt. A sense of power and even exclusiveness takes place (e.g., "Black Power").

4. Introspection: Based on the sense that resistance doesn't always accomplish what one wants, the individual looks for reasons for the whys and hows. What happens is an examination of everything.

5. Synergistic articulation and awareness: This stage occurs when one accepts oneself.

What about mixed race people? The National Film Board video *Domino* (1990) relates stories of growing up biculturally. Biracial identity development, however, is a much more complex and undefined process. Poston (in France, 2002) developed the Biracial Identity Development Model to address the inherent weakness of the previously mentioned models and to recognize the increasing numbers of biracial youth. Admittedly, this progressive, developmental model is tentative and based on the scant research on biracial individuals and information from support groups. Nevertheless, the following five-stage model does have implications for personal identity constructs (e.g., self-esteem) for biracial youth:

1. Personal identity: Biracial children tend to display identification problems when they internalize outside prejudices and values. Young children's reference-group observation attitudes are not yet developed, so their identity is primarily based on personal factors such as self-esteem and feelings of self-worth within their primary reference group.

2. Choice of group categorization: Youth at this stage are pushed to choose an identity, usually of one ethnic group. Numerous factors can influence the individual's identity choice (e.g., status, social support, personal appeals). It is unusual for an individual to choose a multi-ethnic identity because this choice requires a level of knowledge of multiple ethnicities, races and cultures and a level of cognitive development beyond what is characteristic of this age group.

3. Enmeshment or denial: This stage is characterized by confusion and guilt at having to choose one identity that is not fully expressive of one's background. Biracial youth may experience alienation at the Choice stage and make a choice even if they are uncomfortable with it.

4. Appreciation: Individuals at this stage begin to appreciate their multiple identities and broaden their reference group orientation. They might begin to learn about their racial/ethnic/cultural heritage, but they still tend to identity with one group.

5. Integration: Individuals at this stage experience wholeness and integration.

They tend to recognize and value all of their racial and ethnic identities. At this level, biracial youth develop a secure, integrated identity.

This model is similar to the previously mentioned models in that it integrates a lifespan focus. Yet this model is different in that it underscores the uniqueness of biracial identity development. In addition, it recognizes that the most difficult times of adjustment and identification confusion are during the Choice stage and Enmeshment/Denial stage. Helping professionals who understand and accept the five stages will be better prepared to assist biracial youth in their identity development.

It is vital for the practitioner to be in sync with the client and to facilitate movement toward the client's goals (Sue & Sue, 2007). The practitioner's goal should be to help clients to develop functional environmental mastery behaviours that lead to personal adjustment and optimal mental health, with the operational therapeutic objective of helping these clients empower themselves for environmental mastery and competence. Many helping professionals, however, assume that all people from a specific ethnic or cultural group are the same and that one theoretical orientation is universally applicable in any intervention effort. Such an assumption is just as harmful for biracial youth as it is for youth from any specific ethnic background. Professionals with this perspective may approach clients not as distinct human beings with individual experiences, but rather merely as cultural stereotypes.

Social ostracism and racism continue to direct stressors on many interracial couplings even though most legal barriers to interracial marriage and coupling have been abolished. A greater acceptance of interracial unions exists today than even 15 to 20 years ago (Matsumoto & Juang, 2012). This increase in acceptance is reflected in the steady growth in the number of interracial couples and their offspring. Helping professionals therefore need to be cognizant of and prepared to address this increasing population in their professions. Matsumoto and Juang (2012) say that studies of intercultural marriages have

> shown that conflicts arise in several major areas, including the expression of love and intimacy, the nature of commitment and attitudes towards the marriage itself, and approaches to child rearing when couples have children. Other potential sources of conflict include differences in perceptions of male–female roles, differences in domestic money management, differences in perceptions of relationships with extended family and defences in the definition of marriage itself. (p. 419)

Interestingly, "anecdotal evidence suggests intercultural marriages are not necessarily associated with higher divorce rates than intra-cultural marriages" (p. 421). Thus, the factors that contribute to a successful intercultural marriage are the same ingredients that make for successful multicultural counselling. That is, the ability to compromise flexibly and a commitment to the relationship, as well as the ability to negotiate differences existing within the relationship, the willingness to make compromises and the desire to stay together regardless of the challenges.

Conclusion

Queen Noor (2003) of Jordan recalls how shocked and insulted she was when US President George Bush, during the first Gulf War, said he would not allow Saddam Hussein to control 25 per cent of the "civilized" world's oil. Queen Noor's story reflects how Arabs are perceived by people in other parts of the world, particularly in North America. It is possible, though, that there was a cultural misunderstanding in Bush's expression, thus underscoring the importance of meaning and language in communication. All counsellors working with people who are different need to realize how behaviours and words influence the communication process. People, like nations, have a tendency to look at the outside world from their own perspective. This is natural and perhaps necessary, for all people are "prisoners" of a particular space and time. A global view of the group is that everyone is a stranger, just as everyone is a neighbour. In fact, at one time all of us were foreigners, outsiders, perhaps even outcasts. The challenge for counsellors is to be more culturally sensitive yet maintain a sense of their own cultural identity.

According to Berry, Poortinga, Segall and Dasen (2001), "a common core to psychotherapeutic practices may exist, but with different historical and cultural roots, and with highly varied cultural expression" (p. 441). In other words, while there may be some universals in regards to counselling, the way in which they are perceived and used is influenced by culture. A multicultural orientation has tremendous implications for counselling practice because being knowledgeable and sensitive to cultural diversity makes all the difference between success and failure. Multicultural counselling is concerned with the usual developmental issues, but with the added element of cultural differences. We live in a society in which the world is represented by our major cities, which demand that we become engaged in intercultural communication for our survival. If the interaction is to be significant, and if cross-cultural communication and multiculturalism are to foster increased understanding and cooperation, then counsellors must be aware of the factors that may affect how we relate to others. Counsellors must not only avoid actions that hinder effective communication, but must be actively engaged in helping others deal with diversity issues. It is axiomatic to suggest that the success of cross-cultural communication may well depend on the attitudes and philosophies people adopt. The way in which people in a group relate to each other often reflects their larger philosophy towards life and themselves.

Counsellors must be models for promoting the acceptance of diversity and for encouraging others not only to be culturally sensitive but also to fight discrimination and racism. All people are capable of change from day to day and from situation to situation, but counsellors who work with people from different cultures have a unique opportunity to act as agents of change. Siccone (1995) reminds us, "Every bigot was once a child free of prejudice" (p. 133); therefore, celebrating diversity must begin early. Many attitudes and behaviours are deeply ingrained in people's psyches and many of them are subject to ethnocentrism. The challenge for counsellors is to help people become grounded in their cultural identity, develop an appreciation for others who are culturally different, and look for ways of reaching out to others who are different. The changes required are not simple, nor are they easy. They require that people possess a willingness to communicate, show empathy toward foreign and alien cultures, tolerate views that differ from their own and develop a more open approach to communication with others from different cultural groups. In order to increase acceptance of people who are different, more contact with minorities is particularly important (Berry, Poortinga, Segall & Dasen, 2002). If people have the resolve to adapt their behaviours and attitudes and the desire to overcome ethnocentrism, they may begin to know the feelings of exhilaration that come when they have made contact with those from cultures far removed from their own sphere of experience. This willingness to realize interdependency is voiced eloquently by McGaa (1990):

> Our survival is dependent on the realization that Mother Earth is a truly holy being, that all things in this world are holy and must not be violated, and that we must share and be generous with one another. . . . Think of your fellow men and women as holy people who were put here by the Great Spirit. Think of being related to all things. (p. 208)

References

Baron, R.S., Kerr, N.L., & Miller, N. (1992). *Group process, group decision, group action*. Pacific Grove, CA: Brooks/Cole.

Berry, J., Poortinga, H., Segall, M., & Dasen, P. (2002). *Cross-cultural psychology* (2nd ed.). London, UK: Oxford Press.

Cohen, T. (2012, February 8). Canada census 2011: Immigrants and newcomers drive population growth. Retrieved from http://news.nationalpost.com/2012/02/08/canada-census-2011-immigrants-and-newcomers-drive-population-growth/

de Montigny, L. (1972). Racism and Indian cultural adaptations. In Waubageshig (Ed.), *The only good Indian* (pp. 97–111). Toronto, ON: New Press.

Diller, J. (2003). *Cultural diversity: A primer for human services* (2nd ed.). Pacific Grove, CA: Brook/Cole.

Dyer, G. (2001). Visible majorities. *Canadian Geographic*, 121(1), 44–55.

France, M.H. (2002). *Nexus: Transpersonal approach to groups*. Calgary, AB: Detselig Enterprises.

George, D. (1994). *My heart soars*. Surry, BC: Hancock House Publishers.

Helms, J.E. (2010). An update of Helms's white and people of color racial identity modes. In J.G. Ponterotto, J.M. Casas, L.A. Suzuki & C.M. Alexander (Eds.), *Handbook of multicultural counseling* (3rd ed., pp. 181–198). Thousand Oaks, CA: Sage.

Labelle, M., (2007). *Challenge of diversity in Canada and Quebec*. Policy Options (March–April), 88–93.

Matsumoto, D., & Juang, L. (2012). *Culture and psychology* (5th ed.). Belmont, CA: Wadsworth.

McGaa, E. (1990). *Mother Earth spirituality: Native American paths to healing ourselves and the world*. San Francisco, CA: Harper.

Mezlekia, N. (2000). *Notes from the hyena's belly*. Toronto, ON: Penguin Books.

Milloy, J. (1999). *A national crime: The Canadian government and the residential school system*. Winnipeg, MB: University of Manitoba Press.

Noor, Queen. (2003). *Leap of Faith: Memoirs of an unexpected life*. New York, NY: Miramax Books.

Okun, B., Fried, J., & Okun, M. (1999). *Understanding diversity: A learning-as-practice primer*. Pacific Grove, CA: Brooks/Cole.

Pedersen, P., & Carey, J. (2003). *Multicultural counseling in schools* (2nd ed.). Boston, MA: Allyn & Bacon.

Pedersen, P., Draguns, J., Lonner, W., & Trimble, J. (2002). *Counseling across cultures* (5th ed.). Thousand Oaks, CA: Sage.

Robinson, T.L., & Howard-Hamilton, M.F. (2000). *The convergence of race, ethnicity and gender*. Upper Saddle River, NJ: Merrill.

Salagame, K. (2011). Ego and ahamkāra: Self and identity in modern psychology and Indian thought, In K.M.M. Cornensen, G. Misra, & S. Varma, *Foundations of Indian psychology, concepts and theories*, Vol. I, New Delhi, India: Longman, Pearson Education.

Sciarra, D.T. (1999). *Multiculturalism in counseling*. Itasca, IL: P.F. Peacock Publishers.

Siccone, F. (1995). *Celebrating diversity: Building self-esteem in today's multicultural classrooms*. Boston, MA: Allyn and Bacon.

Song, V. (2007, January 15). Racism in Canada: Tolerance. Retrieved from http://cnews.canoe.ca/CNEWS/Canada/2007/01/15/3383862.html

Sue, D., & Sue, D.W. (2007). *Counseling the culturally diverse: Theory and practice* (5th ed.). New York, NY: Teachers College.

Suzuki, L., Ponterotto, J., Alexander, C., & Casas, J.M. (2009). *Handbook of multicultural counselling* (3rd ed.). Alexander, VA: ACA Press.

2

Exploring World View

María del Carmen Rodríguez

What we make of people, and what we see in the mirror when we look at ourselves, depends on what we know of the world, what we believe to be possible, what memories we have, and whether our loyalties are to the past, the present or the future.
— Theodore Zeldin

THE NOTION OF WORLD VIEW deals with a culture's orientation and relationship to ideas such as man, nature, spiritual beliefs, the universe and other philosophical issues concerned with the concept of being. Our world view helps us locate our place and rank in the universe and influences our beliefs, values, attitudes, uses of time and other aspects of culture. This construct is ample and complex since it deals with the condition of being human and thus comprises more than just philosophical foundations; it also involves the understanding of socio-cultural components, anthropological conceptions and even psychological behaviours.

Historical Roots

The use of world view has often been conceived from one specific perspective. Scofield (1991), for example, states that the "Old World" (meaning Europe) was more advanced than the "New World" in terms of the fusion of cultural values and complex social structures into what is called civilization. This is a Eurocentric perspective since the inhabitants of the Americas also had social structures and cultural values, as well as knowledge about how the cosmos and thus life was perceived, understood and lived. *Cosmovisión*, a Spanish word that means "vision of the cosmos," describes life-encircling indigenous folklore, myths, legends, philosophy and sky-knowledge. According to Malinowski (cited in Erdoes & Ortiz, 1984) "myth in its living, primitive form is not merely a story told but a reality lived" (p. xv). Thus myths favour the portrayal of diverse social functions, in that they "are magic lenses through which we can glimpse social orders and daily life: how families were organized, how political structures operated . . . how religious ceremonies felt to the people who took part, how power was divided between men and women . . . how honour in war was celebrated" (Erdoes & Ortiz, 1984, xv). Sky-knowledge was fundamental to farming, and owning the knowledge of weather patterns and seasonal changes was crucial for survival.

There is more to a culture's cosmic understanding (or world view), however, than just sky-knowledge, folklore, myths and legends. Cosmovisión also embraces the wisdom, the learning and the emblems of a culture, giving concrete form to a set of beliefs and traditions that link people living today to ancestors from centuries past. While some of these connections might prevail, other views and perceptions of the world develop and unfold as the result of an ever-changing existence. A culture's normative modes of subsistence, political ideas, ways of life, values, attitudes, affective perceptions, modes of communication and even technological advancement give origin to new world views.

Every culture around the world has its own view that reflects the nature of its world (e.g., African, Chinese, Indian, European, Amerindians and so forth). North American educational practices are rich in the philosophical schemes of a world view that stems from Egyptian, Greek, Roman and European traditions; in the latter, the notion of truth or *aletheia*, as Heidegger (1967) calls it, is understood as an active process of unveiling reality through the sharing of personal interpretations and the resulting fusion of individual horizons. If we disregard that Asian, African and Indigenous views were not included in Heidegger's notion, his ideas are rich in describing world view. Historically, world view derives from the German word *Weltanschauung*. Heidegger (1988) explains Weltanschauung as ingrained in a philosophical tradition, which always includes a view of life. He argues that it is a way of being that requires conviction if the world view is to guide the person in times of pressure.

Philosophical Perspectives

A world view originates out of a natural standpoint of the world, out of a range of conceptions and personal understandings, as the result of the possession of a particular horizon; it expands as one becomes more knowledgeable of the world and experiences life in all its unique dimensions. The concept of world view is complex and broad as it encompasses much more than personal reflections and understandings about one's values, beliefs, assumptions, behaviours, rules for interactions and so forth. World view also consists of what people make with such understandings, how they interact and behave with/in the world. According to Gadamer (1986), when we come into the world, we arrive in a physical place and in a tradition that is being lived by our family members and their friends. Those around us live in a particular context at a particular moment in history; they speak a particular language, express religious and philosophical beliefs and have preferred ways of acting socially and ethically. In learning the patterns of tradition of the significant others in our lives during our formative years, we lay the founding grounds for interpreting future experiences. Gadamer (1986) says that tradition is not learned but rather is an experience that occurs as the result of social interaction; it is a particular style of carrying oneself in life, a unique way of possessing and interpreting one's being-in-the-world. Montgomery, Fine and Myers (1990) define world view as "a structure of philosophical assumptions, values, and principles upon which a way of perceiving the world is based" (p. 38).

Socio-Cultural Definition

World view refers to the outlook or image we have concerning the nature of the universe, the nature of humankind, the relationship between humanity and the universe, and other philosophical issues or orientations that help us define the cosmos and our place in it. These orientations are tied directly to the ideological, historical, philosophical and religious dimensions of a culture. Culture has been defined as a set of implicit norms, values and beliefs that influences the attitudes, behaviours and customs of a group (Gushue, 1993). The culture of a family, for example, affects individual behaviours, child-rearing practices, discipline and the importance of achievement and education. Such sets of norms often determine its form and functioning including the type of family, its size and its shape (McGill, 1983; McGoldrick, Giordano & Pearce, 1996); culture defines boundaries, rules for interaction and communication patterns between family members and within the community (Falicov & Brudner-White, 1983; McGill, 1997; McGoldrick et al., 1996; Preli & Bernard, 1993). The roles of family members and the means of defining problems and outlining specific coping skills are determined by culture (Schwartzman, 1983). Falicov (1995) defines culture as a set of shared world views, meanings and adaptive behaviours derived from simultaneous membership and participation in a variety of contexts including language, age, gender, race, ethnicity, religion, socio-economic status, education and sexual orientation. Both definitions of culture indicate that cultural values define behaviours and therefore establish norms for attitudes and behaviours within families and in the larger cultural groups (e.g., religious affiliation, academic community and so forth). Families serve as the primary agent for transmitting cultural values and world view to their children, and parents and extended family help children to learn, internalize and develop an understanding of culture through both covert and overt means

(Preli & Bernard, 1993). Through cultural socialization, families must teach both positive and negative messages of their particular cultural group as well as those of other cultures (Preli & Bernard, 1993).

Every world view is determined by cultural environment: folkways, lore, system, race, class and stage of culture (i.e., family history and specific culture, social expectations, working habits and so forth). Through the interaction of these countless events, culture provides people with a view of themselves, the rest of the world, the universe and individuals' relationship to such events. World view manifests itself in the psychological, sociological and technical aspects of a society, influencing its social organization, the use of tools and instruments, situational behaviour and even language. World view so conceptualized provides a mechanism to understand how ethnicity, culture, socio-political history and lifestyle affect people's life choices and decision-making ability. It is the mediating variable that makes knowledge of a specific cultural group and knowledge of culture-consistent and culture-specific techniques meaningful. Without the world view as a mediating variable, such knowledges may be misapplied, leading to ethical violation and cultural oppression, particularly within a multicultural setting (Ibrahim, 1991).

Sire (1976) states that our world view consists of the presuppositions and assumptions that we hold about the world, while Horner and Vandersluis (1981) maintain that because world views are culturally based variables, they influence the relationships between people and they way in which they interact. Our world view directly affects and mediates our belief system, assumptions, modes of problem solving, decision-making and conflict resolution (Ibrahim, 1991). Seltzer, Frazier and Ricks (1995), in their review of multiculturalism, race and the educational system, indicate that knowing about differences in world views can enhance one's ability to manipulate an environment that includes others from diverse cultures.

Anthropological Contexts

Within anthropology, these general views of the world have been described by a number of terms, including patterns, themes, ethos and value orientations (Agar, 1996; Kearney, 1984). Also termed cultural models, folk models and schema, these specific views of the world encompass a multitude of more circumscribed domains related to various aspects of living. Because of the multiplicity of specific domains, anthropologists have not specified a single set of dimensions; instead, to investigate specific views, they have selected those that are salient within a particular area of interest. According to Kearney (1984), world view systems consist of dynamic, interrelated views. For example, within the general domain of interpersonal relationships (Kluckhohn, C., 1951, 1956), specific views might include understandings about marriage, commitment, companionship, emotions and interpersonal conflict (D'Andrea, 1992; Quinn, 1985; White, 1983). Traditionally, world view has been viewed solely as encompassing the broad, general understandings of the world. Within contemporary anthropology, however, culture is viewed as intricately related to all aspects of personal experience, within both general (shared experiences) and specific (unique experiences) domains of life activity. Thus recent work may more accurately reflect the nature of culture and the individual (Schwartz, 1992).

Cross-Cultural Foundations

According to Hall (1976), in the past, individuals did not need to be aware of the structure of their behavioural system because their interactions occurred in limited settings with people who possessed similar outlooks on life. However, more recently, because of broader interactions and expansion, it has become necessary for individuals to transcend their own culture by making explicit the rules by which it operates. Interactions across cultures can enhance or lessen the perceptions one has of oneself and others as the result of the fusion of the values, beliefs and traditions inherited from our parent culture. Value orientations and world view are so much a part of what we perceive to be "real life" that the philosophical division between existential postulates and normative acceptances becomes blurred. It would be too ambitious to attempt to scrutinize the value orientations of other cultural groups without first beginning to accept one's own.

In a multicultural society, cross-cultural encounters are inevitable and require the understanding of, or at least the ability to conceptualize, cultural variables in order to hinder prejudice. Since multiculturalism is rooted in philosophical views of human nature and people's place in the universe (Atkinson, Maruyama & Matsui, 1978), world view is a significant contribution to multicultural counselling.

Defined as our basic perceptions and understandings of the world (Howard & McKim, 1983; Kearney, 1984), this construct was first introduced into the literature on cross-cultural affairs by Sue (1978), who highlighted the importance of world view in multicultural encounters. Sue defined world view as an individual's perception of his or her relationship with the world (i.e., nature, things, institutions and people) and asserted that the knowledge of an individual's socio-political history and racial, cultural and ethnic background can be helpful in identifying the ways in which he/she perceives the world, therefore providing insight for a counselling approach based on such perceptions.

A Rationale for Using World View Assessment

According to Lonner and Ibrahim (1996), when two people from different cultures communicate, they each need to understand the other's world view in order to establish trust and rapport. Ibrahim (1984, 1985) acknowledged the relevance of the construct of world view in cross-cultural counselling, in order to understand culturally diverse clients, and proposed a broader conceptualization to clarify basic human concerns that are pan-cultural. The theory uses world view and cultural identity as mediational forces in an individual's life (Ibrahim, 1985a; Ibrahim & Schroeder, 1987). Ibrahim suggests the inclusion of an analysis of the cultural identities of the parties — ethnicity, culture, gender, age, life stage, beliefs, values and assumptions — in order to establish effective communication. Once clarified, the world views must be placed in a socio-political context, considering the history of migration, acculturation level (comfort within the mainstream assumptions and values) and languages spoken. Even though Ibrahim developed the Scale for Assessing World View (SAWV) primarily as a counselling tool for initial assessment and understanding the client's world view and cultural identity, we have found it to be a useful resource in a variety of situations — for example, when helping people from different cultures work together more effectively, each having an understanding of the other's world view enhances communication and cooperation. In higher education, where students from different countries study in a second country (i.e., as foreign students), learning about differing world views can assist in cultural adjustment. It can also be used in higher education to facilitate the development of appropriate process and goals based on a student's cultural assumptions. Without the world view as a mediating variable, knowledge of specific cultures and culture-specific techniques can be misapplied, leading to miscommunication. For example, world view provides a mechanism for those in government, education and counselling to understand how ethnicity, culture, socio-political history and lifestyle affect one's life choices and decision-making ability.

Ibrahim (1984, 1985a), Ibrahim and Schroeder (1987, 1990), and Sue (1978) have offered three major suggestions to ease the process of multicultural counselling. Such recommendations include an understanding of world view, knowledge of specific cultures and knowledge of culture-specific verbal and non-verbal skills to facilitate such encounters. At the general level, world view dimensions that are helpful in cross-cultural counselling meet three criteria:

- the dimensions are comprehensive (they capture a broad range of human experience);
- they are applicable across cultural groups;
- they are relevant to encounters across cultures.

The Scale to Assess World view (SAWV) developed by Ibrahim and Kahn (1984, 1987) taps the five existential categories found in the Kluckhohn–Strodbeck (1961) research model. According to Ibrahim and Kahn (1987), the use of the SAWV helps those working with culturally diverse individuals to accomplish an understanding of specific world views, beliefs, values and assumptions, given that an individual's world view is in direct relationship with his/her cognitive, emotional and social perceptions and interactions with the world. Further, it helps in clarifying an individual's world view as compared with his or her primary cultural group (Ibrahim, 1985; Ibrahim & Schroeder, 1990).

Interestingly, as multiculturalism has become government policy around the world, there are few assessment measures that can help clarify cultural identity and world view. With additional information regarding one's socio-political history (e.g., groups that the student identifies with, history of migration, impact of gender from a minority or majority cultural perspective), personal experiences (e.g., family life/cycle history, religion), and primary and secondary identification with another culture (e.g., acculturation level, language[s] spoken), one can develop a clearer comprehension of the concerns of someone from a different culture.

Principles

Results from anthropological studies can be used to demonstrate that the cultures of the world can be arranged into two contrasting categories in which the self is defined, conceptualized and articulated (Bateson & Mead, 1942; Brown & Lundrum-Brown, 1995; Gaines & Reed, 1995; Geertz, 1983; Shweder, 1991). The categories are *relational* or *high-context* cultures (Triandis, 1994; Matsumoto, 1996) and *analytical* (Geertz, 1983; Shweder, 1991) or *low-context* cultures (Triandis, 1994; Matsumoto, 1996). Each category has a different outlook on constructs such as self, autonomy, concept of time, personal control, understanding of mind and body, and construction of morality, among others (see Table 1). However, these classifications should not be interpreted as opposing or definitive. Rather, I believe that they may exist in a continuum, as cyclical aspects, within each other or even in fragments. In a continuum, as cultures change, high-context cultures could become low-context ones (as paradoxical as this change might seem). As cyclical aspects, the change from high-context culture to low-context would appear a return to the original state or mode of being.

Existing within each other would imply that a high-context culture exists within a low-context culture and vice versa. For example, contrast a poor area in a developing country with an area in the same country where technology, health services, jobs, and education opportunities are available for most people. This scenario is possible in developing countries where access to education, health services and other social goods is unequally distributed; in such a setting, value preference and value orientation might differ. High-context and low-context cultures may also exist as fragments; this means that a particular cultural group might exhibit a mixture or combination of preferences that will vary depending on changing variables according to circumstances. Thus, characteristics of both categories (high/low-context cultures) will be present in some specific populations. Such an interpretation could give shape to an extensive combination or amalgamation of possibilities in the way people understand the world.

Some perceptions could be considered more central to a person's world view. These perceptions involve abstract, core understandings of the world, including broad domains of life such as human nature, interpersonal relationships, nature, time and activity, as proposed by Kluckhohn and Strodtbeck in 1961. Their research framework takes the following philosophical and psychological dimensions of existence into account.

What is man's assessment of innate human nature? This category addresses the perception of self and others. There are three dimensions in which this category can be viewed: a) human nature is good; b) human nature is a combination of good and bad parts; c) human nature is bad. The need to understand how the self and others are viewed provides insight into the quality of one's own life and the meaningfulness of relationships or how much a person might experience alienation from the self and others, experience that might in turn engender negative attitudes. The understanding of this ontological dimension can also be representative of the objective-materialist or subjective-spiritual realms. Contrary to the dominant American orientation that humankind has an essentially evil but perfectible nature, may non-Western cultures assume human nature to be essentially good or a mixture of good and evil. Two of the forces present in the universe are good and evil. Since humanity is part of the universe, these forces are also present in humankind. The view of the good and evil in humanity extends to the position that people cannot eliminate evil because it is a natural and necessary part of the universe.

What is man's relation to nature? This category addresses a person's relationship to the natural environment. Some cultures emphasize living in harmony with nature; others highlight subjugating and controlling it; still others recognize the power of nature and the frailty of humans. When the relationship between man and nature is ignored, people fall prey to oversimplification. It is necessary to understand the meaning that the environment holds for individuals. The relationship can be harmonious, where individuals are an integral part of the environment, using it only for survival purposes. In a world where man, as the supreme life form on earth, controls and exploits the natural environment for personal profit and the benefit of society, the relationship to nature is one of domination. In this frame of thought, all natural phenomena have a logical or scientific explanation. Another type of relationship is that of subjugation, where people are helpless and at the mercy of nature. This view is found primarily among less-developed cultures where everyday life is an ongoing struggle just to survive. Extreme climatic conditions, scarcity of food and water and a limited level of technological development situate such cultures at the mercy of nature. Hence, nature is seen as an active, often capricious, force beyond human control that must be appeased. Such views lead to volcano worship, sun worship and the like. The cooperative view is perceived as a working relationship, where people live in harmony with nature; this view is closely tied to respect for the environment. Many cultures consider nature as a divine creation in which the spirit of God resides. Nature and all living things are sacred, and no one has the right to destroy or be the master of nature.

What is the temporal focus of life? This category refers to people's perception and value(s) of time. Hall (1976) divides time into *polychronic* and *monochronic*. In polychronic cultures, people are engaged in several activities at a time and are more spontaneous; the emphasis is on people and not schedules. In the monochronic cultures, people experience time as a continuum that is linear, fixed and tangible. Time is spoken of metaphorically as lost, crawling, made up, accelerated, invested, slowed down or running out. Different cultures perceive and understand the concept of time in different ways, focussing on the past (tradition bound), the present (situational) or the future (goal oriented). According to Ibrahim (1993), "the capacity to relate to time is a uniquely human characteristic" (p. 33).

What is the group's principal mode of activity? This category refers to a culture's dominant forms of activity. Individuals may describe their existence in the world in terms of *doing* or *being-in-becoming*. Being-in becoming is a preference that underscores activities where the goal is the spontaneous development of all aspects of the self as an integrated being, including the spiritual dimension. This is a more passive, process-determined and focussed orientation. Doing, in contrast, is a preference for initiating activity in pursuit of a specific goal. It appears in societies where reward and status are awarded on the basis of productivity and accomplishment. This approach takes universal concerns into account before moving into the specifics of understanding a person as a cultural entity (Ibrahim, 1993). The way in which different views towards work and activity manifest themselves in different cultures is reflected in the following anecdote from Sitaram and Codgell (1976):

> If you ask a Hindu why he got only ten bags of corn from his land while nearby farmers got much more, he would say it was the wish of God. An American farmer's answer to the same question would be: "Because I did not work hard enough." (p. 51)

What is the modality of the group's relationship to others? This classification pertains to people's relationships to other people. Social relations can be described as *collateral-mutual*, in which primacy is given to the goals and welfare of lateral extended groups and the self is enhanced through mutual relationships; or *individualistic*, in which the individual's own goals are primary to the fulfillment of those of the family, the group or society. This classification also refers to the patterns of social relationships in a society, the society's organization and the hierarchical system of the society or social group. Although Western cultures have well-defined hierarchies, there is a prevailing belief (sustained by occasional examples of accomplishment) that through industry and hard work, one can move freely to higher levels. This freedom creates greater mobility between social levels and the idea that anyone can attain high status. On the other hand, social status in Eastern cultures is more static, with birth position tending to predict status; static cultures tend to have greater respect for persons of high status because of limited social movement. Another aspect of social organization is affiliation to groups. Americans tend to be joiners, members of many groups based on forms of activity. However, the depth of commitment to these groups and their members is very weak, and the memberships and people move freely from group to group. In many Eastern cultures, people belong to only a few groups and membership is virtually a lifetime commitment.

Beyond these outlooks, researchers have described other dimensions that focus on ways of knowing, ways of thinking and the concept of self (Brown & Lundrum-Brown, 1995; Oyserman, Coon & Kemmelmeier, 2002). In terms of ways of knowing — epistemology, or how individuals grasp meaning — the realms are cognitive versus affective; the ways of thinking — logic — are linear versus circular; and the concept of self may be defined as individual versus extended (see Table 1). In the epistemological realm, we might affirm that there is a philosophy behind the way of life of every individual and of every relatively homogeneous group at any given point in their histories. This view gives, with varying degrees of explicitness or implicitness, some sense of coherence or unity to living, in both the cognitive and affective dimensions. Each personality gives the philosophy an idiosyncratic colouring, and creative individuals markedly reshape it. However, the main outlines of the fundamental values, existential assumptions and basic abstractions have only exceptionally been created out of unique biological heredity and peculiar life experiences.

The ways of thinking (logic) are consequential (cause-effect) or circular. Almost every cultural group agrees that their culture follows natural processes and that human nature, if not essentially rational, possesses a rational dimension. However, the image or concept of what is rational is subject to cultural variation. The term refers to reaching logical and valid conclusions from the information at hand and from the metaphysical assumptions prevalent in the culture. To understand the rationality in any culture, we must understand the premises on which it is based. American and European cultures tend to follow a system of logic based on Aristotelian principles; other cultures follow such principles as Yin and Yang (balance). Awareness of the principles, premises and assumptions manifest in other cultures enables us to understand different lines of reasoning and logic processes.

The dimension of self is partially defined as culturally bounded by individualistic or extended associations. All cultures reflect a dominant pattern that specifies the cultural location of self within this dimension. Oyserman et al. (2002) found that collectivism is related to a sense of self based on socially oriented variables, sensitivity to rejection, the need for affiliation and a sense of self-worth based on family life. In most Western societies, the self is defined in relationship to the individual him/herself and there little or no association with the members of any other group (e.g., family, neighbours, colleagues); conversely, in most non-Western societies, the group is the primary social entity and the ultimate goal is its well-being (Kearney, 1984; Schwartz, 1992; Samovar & Porter, 1995; Oyserman et al., 2002). Under this doctrine, individuals have significance within the context of the group, which provides them with the necessities of life in return for certain obligations undertaken to assist in the support and maintenance of the group. Moreover, in some cultures, the importance of the self is never emphasized so that the ego does not impose on others and does not interfere with an individual's pursuit of life. According to Ibrahim, Roysircar-Sodowsky & Ohnishi (2001), a person's orientation towards individualism or collectivism affects the way he/she views the helping relationship, the dilemmas he/she faces and the means by which psychological relief can be achieved.

It is these perspectives that have formed the basis of much of the work to date on world view in cross-cultural counselling. Therefore, the discernment of these existential dimensions about a person's world view is essential to understanding those who are different within a given mainstream.

Applications for Multicultural Counselling

The Kluckhohn and Strodtbeck (1961) model of existential dimensions is based on the perception and orientation individuals have of their world; it offers the possibility for exploring personal assumptions and understandings of one's world view. Given that an individual's world view is in direct relationship with his/her cognitive, emotional and social perceptions and interactions with the world, the framework is a significant contribution to multicultural counselling as it is rooted in philosophical and sociological views of human nature and people's place in the universe. Since value orientations and world view are a substantial part of what we perceive to be "real life," it is easy to overlook other people's perspectives, particularly in cross-cultural encounters, which require the understanding of — or at least the ability to conceptualize — cultural variables in order to hinder prejudice. This framework, then, becomes a standpoint from which the world

Table 1

WORLD VIEW PERSPECTIVES

Culture Classification

Value Preference	Analytical/ Low Context	Relational/ High Context
Activity (psychological/ behavioural)	Doing	Being
Relation to Nature	Mastery/Domination	Harmony/ Communion
Time	Monochronic	Polychronic
Social Interaction/ Autonomy (ethos)	Independent/ Individual	Interdependent/ Collective
Human Nature (ontology)	Objective/Materialistic	Subjective/Spiritual
Concept of Self	Individualistic/ Referential	Interdependent/ Extended
Logic (ways of thinking)	Linear	Circular
Epistemology (ways of thinking)	Cognitive	Affective
Axiology (social values)	Competition	Cooperation

(Adapted from Brown & Lundrum-Brown, 1995; Geertz, 1983; Kluckhohn & Strodtbeck, 1961; Matsumoto, 1996; Shweder, 1991; Triandis, 1994)

may be seen and interpreted, determined by a particular time in history, a particular time in culture and a particular orientation toward reality. While the framework is presented as an apparent dichotomy of the ways in which one perceives the world (either/or; see Table 1), it is important to remember that these categories may co-exist within individuals, communities and the world at large.

Within multicultural counselling, the use of the world view framework can help counsellors, clients and others in helping professions learn about themselves, expand their cultural visions, appreciate the relativity of their own reality and acknowledge the validity of other frames of reference and standpoints. Additionally, it is useful as a foundation to analyze one's own values, beliefs and assumptions, as well as a tool to inquire about the construction and validity of diverse types of knowledge (i.e., cultural, social, political, historical and so forth). It is the awareness and the examination of personal perceptions and understandings that allows for constant organization or re-patterning of one's world view, thus leading to an openness in our interactions with one another. Therefore, the use of a world view framework, which examines five existential dimensions and value orientations, might assist in eliminating the risk of oppression due to cultural misconceptions and misunderstandings; concerns regarding the potential stereotyping that occurs when intergroup differences are generalized to all members of a particular group (Myers, Spreight, Cox, Highlen & Reynolds, 1991); and the perpetuation of cultural myths when applying culture-specific information, knowledge and skills in interacting with others. If we recognize the multiple causes of influence (e.g., ethnicity, gender, social class, religion) on the development of world view as well as the examination, assessment and understanding of individual and group world views, we will greatly enhance our inquiry in multicultural counselling, not only as a means to have a more in-depth understanding about individual differences but also as a crucial variable to facilitate these processes.

The framework of value orientations developed by Kluckhohn and Strodtbeck in 1961 has been adapted and adopted across disciplines, proving its strength as a research approach that calls forth the need to examine, analyze and ponder personal standpoints in relationship to an individual's world view. While other investigators (Ibrahim 1984; Ibrahim & Schroeder, 1997; Mikaylo, 1991; Ibrahim & Kahn, 1994; Kohls, 1994; Sue & Sue, 2007) have modified the original research scheme, the five initial existential dimensions or categories continue to be the foundation. As consistent and employed as the framework has been, it does not escape scrutiny, however. In its original format, the questions posed referred only to the dichotomized nature of values as conceptualized by Kluckhohn and Strodtbeck (1961). The outcomes revealed the preferences from people with regards to the existential dimensions; what was absent were the underlying principles, or at least the clarification about such choices. The subjective nature of experience that enriches qualitative studies was not present. Therefore, the data from their study is raw and reflects only partial realities. The foundations and the variations of this framework offer a perspective that was developed 40 years ago; yet it has expanded and evolved into different schemes that are being employed to this date. Some benefits that the framework offers can be summarized as follow:

- It is rooted in philosophical and sociological views of human nature where cultural values constitute cultural knowledge.
- It encourages the development of awareness through the exploration of values, assumptions, traditions, beliefs and ways of knowing, behaving and thinking across cultures, thus promoting and facilitating the understanding of differing world views.
- It provides an understanding of world view and its impact on identity, philosophy and modes of interaction with the world (problem solving, conflict resolution and decision making).

- It promotes the examination of individual world view construction, deconstruction and reconstruction by determining how one's own cultural values, beliefs, perspectives and frames of reference influence personal development and transformation.

Conclusion

The way in which one perceives, experiences and makes meaning of life's driving forces varies from individual to individual over a lifespan. My father always reminds me that everything in this world is relative and circumstantial; and the more I learn about myself and others, the more I am inclined to believe this perspective is true. From the early 1950s until recently, researchers have extensively designed and defined cultural paradigms to describe the dimensions along which cultural groups may differ (Kluckhohn, 1951; Sue, 1978; Ibrahim, 1981, 1984; Ibrahim & Kahn, 1984; Brown & Lundrum-Brown, 1995; Axelson, 1999; Diller, 1999; Okun, Fried & Okun, 1999). Yet it seems that the assumptions, traditions, attitudes, values, beliefs and ways of knowing, behaving and thinking — all of which comprise a world view — have more in common across cultures than one might presume. Still, we cannot deny that there is no substitute for direct, meaningful and comprehensive lived experience; nor can these be identical for any two human beings. The meaning and insight gained when one chooses and ventures to experience the world thus, becoming vulnerable by opening to others, is priceless and irreplaceable. It is only directly that we may experience the everyday world with all its changes and accommodations, all its evolutions and revolutions.

Today, because of broader interactions and expansion, it has become necessary for people to transcend their own culture by making explicit the rules by which it operates; interactions across cultures can enhance or lessen the perceptions one has of oneself. Such perceptions are the result of the fusion of the values, beliefs and traditions inherited from one's parent culture.

The construct of world view is as ancient as the history of humankind. Plato and Socrates, like Parmenides and Heraclitus, evaluated their own lives by constantly reviewing the way in which they saw themselves and thus interacted with/in the world. Socrates' axiom "An unexamined life is not worth living" teaches us about the importance of self-evaluation and self-discovery in everyday life and is perhaps the prelude to Thomas Mann's affirmation that "No one ever remains the same after having seen himself."

This chapter has examined the construct of world view from various perspectives, seeking to bring forth some insight about the ways in which people perceive, experience and make meaning of the world. Philosophically, a world view originates out of a natural standpoint, out of a range of conceptions and personal understandings that arise from life experiences and the experience of developing a conceptual system about the world. It is a conscious way of apprehending a universe of things, and so it always includes a view of life. A world view grows out of an "all inclusive reflection on the world . . . and this happens in different ways, explicitly and consciously in individuals or by appropriating an already prevalent world view" (Heidegger, 1988, p. 3). The mode in which world view is constructed involves the ongoing development and maturation of diverse understandings: understanding of the world, of others and of self. It is a standpoint given by a person's experience through which the world is seen and interpreted from a location determined by a particular time in history, a particular time in culture and the individual's orientation toward reality. Sociologically, every individual's world view is determined by cultural environment: folkways, lore, system, race, class and stage of culture (e.g., family history and specific culture, social expectations, working habits and so forth). Through the interaction of these countless events, culture provides people with a view of themselves, the rest of the world, the universe and the self's relationship with these elements.

Within anthropology, these general views of the world have been described by a number of terms, including patterns, themes, ethos, value orientations, cultural or folk models, and schema (Agar, 1996; Kearney, 1984); they encompass a multitude of more circumscribed domains related to various aspects of living. Distinct cultural groups have developed particular modal patterns for understanding the world; as a result, there are multiple sources of variation within cultures that influence the formation of a given individual's world view. Cross-culturally, Sue (1978) defines world view as an individual's perception of his/her relationship with the world (i.e., nature, things, institutions and people) and asserts that the knowledge of an individual's socio-political history, or racial, cultural and ethnic background can be helpful in identifying the ways in which the world is perceived.

However, world view research needs yet to be unearthed for there is much to be discovered not only in terms of cultural differences but, more importantly, in terms of perspectives, understandings and tolerance of one another. An important area for additional investigation involves instrumentation. Some instruments to assess world view have been extensively developed but not tested across cultures, whereas others have been investigated cross-culturally but are still in need of additional development and improvement. Thus, it is apparent that continued work is needed to adopt the world view notion in cross-cultural situations, for not only does the word view concept appear to be a viable unifying construct for understanding change within cross-cultural education, psychology and counselling, but also it provides a powerful way for understanding others. In a multicultural society, cross-cultural encounters are inevitable and require the understanding of, or at least the ability to conceptualize, other people's world view in order to hinder prejudice and promote acceptance and inclusion. Wurzel (1988) complements these ideas by stating, "the multicultural person questions the arbitrary nature of his or her own culture and accepts the proposition that others who are culturally different can enrich their experience" (p. 10).

References

Agar, M. (1996). *Language shock: Understanding the culture of conversation.* New York: Morrow.

Atkinson, D.R., Maruyama, M., & Matsui, S. (1978). The effects of counsellor race and counselling approach on Asian American's perceptions of counsellor credibility and utility. *Journal of Counselling Psychology, 25*, 76–83.

Axelson, J. (1999). *Counselling and development in a multicultural society* (3rd ed.). Pacific Grove, CA: Brook/Cole.

Bateson, G., & Mead, M. (1942). *Balinese character: A photographic analysis.* New York, NY: New York Academy of Sciences.

Brown, M.T., & Lundrum-Brown, J. (1995). Counsellor supervision: Cross-cultural perspectives. In J.P. Ponterotto, J.M. Casas, L.A. Suzuki & C.M. Alexander (Eds.), *Handbook of multicultural counseling* (pp. 263–287). Thousand Oaks, CA: Sage.

D'Andrea, M. (1992). The violence of our silence. *Guidepost, 35*(4), 31.

Diller, J. (1999). *Cultural diversity: A primer for human services.* Pacific Grove, CA: Brook/Cole.

Erdoes, R., & Ortiz, A. (1984). *American Indian myths and legends.* New York, NY: Pantheon Books.

Falicov, C.J. (1995) Training to think culturally: A multidimensional comparative framework. *Family Process, 34*, 373–388.

Falicov, C.J., & Brudner-White, L. (1983). Shifting the family triangle: The issue of cultural and contextual relativity. In J.C. Hansen & C.J. Falicov (Eds.), *Cultural perspectives in family therapy: The family therapy collections* (pp. 51–67). Rockville, MD: Aspen.

Gadamer, H. (1986). *Truth and method.* New York: Crossroad Publishing Company.

Gaines, S.O., Jr., & Reed, E. (1995). Prejudice. *American Psychologist, 50*, 96–103.

Geertz, C. (1983). *Local knowledge.* New York: Basic Books.

Gushue, G.V. (1993). Cultural-identity development and family assessment: An interaction model. *The Counselling Psychologist, 21*, 487–513.

Hall, E.T. (1976). *Beyond culture.* New York: Anchor/Doubleday.

Heidegger, M. (1967). *Being and time.* New York: Harper & Row.

Heidegger, M. (1988). *The basic problems of phenomenology.* Bloomington: Indiana University Press.

Horner, D., & Vandersluis, P. (1981). Cross-cultural counselling. In G. Althen (Ed.), *Learning across cultures* (pp. 30–50). Washington, DC: National Association for Foreign Students Affairs.

Howard, M.C., & McKim, P.C. (1983). *Contemporary cultural anthropology.* Boston: Little, Brown.

Ibrahim, F. (1984). Cross-cultural counselling and psychotherapy: An existential-psychological perspective. *International Journal for the Advancement of Counselling, 7*, 559–569.

Ibrahim, F. (1985). Cross-cultural counselling training. In McFadden, J. (Ed.). *Transcultural counselling: Bilateral and international perspectives* (pp. 23–58). Alexandria, VA: American Counselling Association Press.

Ibrahim, F. (1985a). Effective cross-cultural counselling and psychotherapy: A framework. *The Counselling Psychologist, 13*, 625–638.

Ibrahim, F. (1991). Contribution of cultural world view to generic counselling and development. *Journal of Counselling and Development, 70*, 13–19.

Ibrahim, F. (1993). Existential world view theory: Transcultural applications. In J. McFadden (Ed.). *Transcultural counselling: Bilateral and international perspectives* (pp. 23–58). Alexandria, VA: American Counselling Association Press.

Ibrahim, F., & Kahn, H. (1984). *Scale to assess world view (SAWV)*. Rockview, CT: Schroeder Associates.

Ibrahim, F., & Kahn, H. (1987). Assessment of world views. *Psychological Reports*, 60, 163–176.

Ibrahim, F.A., Roysircar-Sodowsky, G., & Ohnishi, H., (2001). World view: Recent developments and needed directions. In J.G. Ponterotto, J.M. Casas, L.A. Suzuki & C.M. Alexander (Eds.), *Handbook of multicultural counseling* (pp. 425–456). Thousand Oaks, CA: Sage.

Ibrahim, F., & Schroeder, D.G. (1987). Effective communication with multicultural families. In J. McFadden (Ed.), *Transcultural counselling: Bilateral and international perspectives* (pp. 23–58). Alexandria, VA: American Counselling Association Press.

Kearney, M. (1984). *World view*. Novato, CA: Chandler & Sharp.

Kluckhohn, C. (1951). Values and value orientations in the theory of action. In T. Parsons & E. Shiles (Eds.). *Towards a general theory of action*. Cambridge, MA: Harvard University Press.

Kluckhohn, C. (1956). Towards a comparison of value-emphasis in different cultures. In L.D. White (Ed.), *The state of social sciences*. Chicago: University of Chicago Press.

Kluckhohn, F., & Strodtbeck, F. (1961). *Variations in value orientations*. Evanston: IL. Row Paterson.

Kohls, R. (1994). *Developing intercultural awareness: A cross-cultural training book*. Yarmouth, ME: Intercultural Press.

Matsumoto, D. (1996). *Culture and psychology*. Pacific Grove, CA: Brooks/Cole.

McGill, D. W. (1983). Cultural concepts for family therapy. In J.C. Hansen & C.J. Falicov (Eds.), *Cultural perspectives in family therapy: The family therapy collections* (pp. 108–121). Rockville, MD: Aspen.

McGoldrick, M., Giordano, J., & Pearce, J.K. (1996). *Ethnicity and family therapy* (2nd ed.). New York: Guilford.

Montgomery, D.E., Fine, M.A., & James-Myers, L. (1990). The development and validation of an instrument to assess an optimal Afrocentric world view. *Journal of Black Psychology*, 17, 37–54.

Myers, L.J., Spreight, S.L., Highlen, P.S., Cox, C.I., Reynolds, A.L., Adams, E.M., & Henley, C.P. (1991). Identity development and world view: Toward an optimal conceptualization. *Journal of Counselling and Development*, 70, 54–63.

Mykailo, M. (1991). Cross-cultural awareness in the foreign language class: The Kluckhohn model. *The Modern Language Journal*, 75, iv.

Lonner, W., & Ibrahim, F. (1996). Research about effectiveness. In P. Pedersen, J. Draguns, W. Lonner & J. Trimble (Eds.), *Counselling across cultures* (4th ed., pp. 323–352). Thousand Oaks, CA: Sage Publications.

Okun, B., Fried, J., & Okun, M. (1999). *Understanding diversity: A learning-as-practice primer*. Pacific Grove, CA: Brook/Cole.

Oyserman, D., Coon H.M., & Kemmelmeier, M. (2002). Re-thinking individualism and collectivism: Evaluation of theoretical assumptions and meta-analysis. *Psychological Bulletin*, 128, 3–72.

Preli, R., & Bernard, J.M. (1993). Making multiculturalism relevant for majority culture graduate students. *Journal of Marital and Family Therapy*, 19(1), 5–16.

Quinn, N. (1985). 'Commitment' in American marriage: A cultural analysis. In J.W.D. Dougherty (Ed.), *Directions in cognitive anthropology* (pp. 291–320). Urbana, IL: University of Illinois Press.

Samovar, L.A., & Porter, R.E. (1995). *Communication between cultures*. Belmont, CA: Wadsworth Schelling.

Schwartz, T. (1992). Anthropology and psychology: An unrequited relationship. In T. Schwartz, G.M. White & C.A. Lutz (Eds.), *New directions in psychological anthropology* (pp. 324–349). Cambridge, UK: Cambridge University Press.

Schwartzman, J. (1983). Family ethnography: A tool for clinicians. In J.C. Hansen & C.J. Falicov (Eds.), *Cultural perspectives in family therapy: The family therapy collections* (pp. 122–135). Rockville, MD: Aspen.

Scofield, B. (1991). *Day-Signs: Native American astrology from Ancient Mexico.* Amherst, MA: One Reed Publication.

Seltzer, R., Frazier, M., & Ricks, I. (1995). Multiculturalism, race, and education. *Journal of Negro Education*, 64, 124–140.

Sire, J.W. (1976). *The universe next door.* Downers Grove, IL: Intervarsity.

Sitaram, K.S., & Codgell, R.T. (1976). *Foundations of intercultural communication.* Columbus OH: Charles E. Merrill.

Shweder, R. (1991). *Thinking though cultures.* Cambridge, MA: Harvard University Press.

Sue, D.W. (1978). Eliminating cultural oppression in counselling: Toward a general theory. *Journal of Counselling Psychology*, 25, 419–428.

Sue, D.W., & Sue, D. (2007). *Counselling the culturally different: Theory and practice* (5th ed.). New York: John Wiley and Sons.

Triandis, H.C. (1994). *Culture and social behaviour.* New York: McGraw-Hill.

White, A. (1983). A factor analysis of the Counselling Orientation Preference Scale (COS). *Counsellor Education and Supervision*, 23, 142–148.

Wurzel, J. (1988). *Toward multiculturalism: A reader in multicultural education.* Yarmouth, ME: Intercultural Press, Inc.

3

Developing Multicultural
Counselling Skills

M. Honoré France, Geoffrey G. Hett
& María del Carmen Rodríguez

Others envisage Canada as a cultural and linguistic pressure cooker. A political entity constructed around the principle of consultation and compromise, Canada is depicted as a potpourri of two unequal charter groups, coupled with a vanquished but increasingly assertive aboriginal population and an ever-expanding racial and ethnic minority sector equally intent on staking claims. (Fleras & Elliott, 1992, p. 1)

The cultural reality of Canada, and North America, has changed drastically in the last fifty years, not only in the numbers of minorities but also in the attitude of the general population. It isn't that Canada is less racist. Rather, as the makeup of the world population has changed, national boundaries are no longer ordered in clear ethnic group-ings but instead have become so enmeshed that a generalized view of what a Canadian is has changed. In the past, European cultural groups made up the vast majority of new immigrants in North America, whereas today, Asian groups top the list of new immigrant groups, particularly in British Columbia and Ontario. The multicultural reality is evident in Canada's schools, where large numbers of students do not come from European ethnic groups such as English and French. According to Statistics Canada (2002), the minor-ity population of Canada presents a picture of a growing visible minority group (Table 1). What is more significant is the clustering of visible minorities in the North, where the majority or a significant minority are First Nations people. Also, the large cities of

Canada, such as Toronto, Vancouver and Montreal, are made up of large groups of visible minorities. However, the new face of Canada can be seen in provinces such as British Columbia; including First Nations people, 21.7 per cent of the population of BC are visible minorities. And the vast majority of the minority people in BC, other than First Nations people, live in the lower mainland. That means that the chances of meeting a minority person in BC are more than 1 in 5. Consider the following joke making the rounds in British Columbia:

"Do you know what separates China and India?" asks my friend, in the precisely modulated English spoken by graduates of New Delhi's elite private schools.

"The Himalayas," I venture.

"It's the Fraser River. Surrey is all Punjabi. Richmond is all Chinese." (Das, 2000, p. A6)

Table 1

MINORITY POPULATIONS IN CANADA

Total of Canada — Population groups   31,241,030

Group	Population
White	24,920,465
Chinese	1,168,485
South Asian	1,233,275
Black	696,800
Filipino	389,550
Latin American	304,245
Southeast Asian	231,425
Arab	265,550
West Asian	156,700
Korean	138,425
Japanese	60,415
Aboriginal	1,146,025

Source: Citizenship and Immigration Canada, 2011

The significance of this change for counsellors is that developing and maintaining multicultural counselling skills is imperative if counsellors are to provide adequate assistance to the clients they are charged with serving. The multicultural reality of Canadian society challenges counsellors in a time when universities are just beginning to recognize the importance of multicultural instruction. Generally, out of a program of nine to twelve graduate courses, only one or two focus on multicultural topics. Most of the course work in counselling graduate programs is still Eurocentric, using training interventions that are European in origin. Counsellors and counsellor educators "need to be aware and recognize their cultural encapsulation and work to overcome it" (Vinson & Neimeyer, 2000, p. 177). The purpose of this chapter is to outline the counselling outcomes of the model proposed by Helms and Cooks (1999) and to summarize the multicultural competencies as proposed by Sue, Arrendondo and McDavis (1992).

Fundamental Assumptions of Multicultural Counselling

The current literature illustrates how contemporary service delivery is still failing not only [First Nations people] but other ethnic groups as well. . . . Most providers are trained only in delivering services to the majority/dominant population. Usually [counsellors] are unaware of the life experiences of the ethnic minority patient. (Duran & Duran, 1995, p. 8)

The very nature of counselling — that is, the theories and practice — is based on values and world views that have European models. The dominant theories of counsellor training and practice, including all of the major assessment tools, according to Duran and Duran (1995), perpetuate colonialism and the domination of people with different world views. However, there is growing awareness of the changing realities of the ethnic composition of Canada, and more holistic and non-Eurocentric counselling approaches are finding acceptance by practitioners. While there is "increased attention to diversity and multiculturalism in the counselling profession" (Walden, Herlihy & Ashton, 2003, p. 109), there is still much to be done to move counselling towards a "post-colonial" approach — in other words, moving the counselling profession toward more openness to diversity and a greater acceptance of other world views and culturally different counselling practices.

Helms and Cook (1999) state that ultimately, the outcomes of the counselling process are the result of what both counsellor and client bring to the interaction, which to a large extent is influenced by racial or cultural factors. Helms and Cook outline four main components:

- the input of psychological, race, cultural and distal reactions of clients and therapists;
- the social role, involving therapist skills and theoretical orientation, and client reactions, preferences and expectations;

- process variables, including racial matching and identity levels; and
- the outcome phase, which is marked by distal and psychological factors such as attrition, service utilization, symptom remission, racial development and cultural congruence. (p. 66)

Much has been written in regard to what makes a multiculturally sensitive counsellor. One of the most comprehensive models is the Cross-Cultural Competencies Model proposed by Sue, Arrendondo and McDavis (1993). This multi-dimensional model is divided into three domains: attitudes/beliefs, knowledge and skills. It is based on the counsellor's awareness of his/her personal cultural values and biases, and the client's world view, in order to develop culturally appropriate intervention strategies.

Counsellor Awareness of Assumptions, Biases, and Values

Attitudes and Beliefs

The starting point of multicultural counselling is with the counsellor, in that to be effective in working with people from different cultures, the counsellor must become aware of his/her values, biases and beliefs. "Know thyself": this Delphic slogan is at the heart of being aware of and sensitive to one's own cultural heritage. It means recognizing that differences exist and that if one is to operate within multiple cultures, it is important to value and respect such differences. Along with one's cultural background, one's experiences may be coloured by attitudes from the majority community, reflecting not only values but also biases that have influenced one's psychological processes.

Knowing that psychological processes are determined to a great degree by culture, counsellors need to identify how cultural experiences limit counselling competencies. Most minority clients, particularly visible minorities, have experienced racism; thus, they recognize that differences between themselves and majority society exist. The counsellor therefore needs to be comfortable with acknowledging and discussing cultural, ethnic and racial differences. The corollary to this point is that there may exist significant differences in terms of beliefs between the counsellor and the clients (e.g., collective versus individual orientations).

Knowledge

Among the many characteristics that counsellors must have in order to be competent, three attributes top the list:

1. Counsellors must have specific knowledge about their own racial and cultural heritage and recognize how this background may affect their personal and professional definitions and biases of normality–abnormality and the process of counselling.
2. Counsellors must have knowledge about and understanding of how oppression, racism, discrimination and stereotyping affect them personally and professionally.
3. Counsellors must be able to acknowledge their own racist attitudes, beliefs and feelings. This point applies to all counsellors, but for whites it may require a better understanding of the concept of "white privilege."

Counsellors should also be aware of their social impact on others. This means knowing how their communication style may clash with or facilitate the counselling process with minority clients. Part of this knowledge involves being able to anticipate how one's communication style impacts others.

Skills

One fundamental commitment from counsellors must be an understanding of themselves as racial and cultural beings and the constant pursuit of an actively non-racist identity. This commitment means that counsellors should recognize the limits of their competencies and seek consultation, training and references from more qualified individuals and/or resources when needed. They should seek out educational, consultative and training experiences to enhance their understanding and effectiveness in working with culturally different populations. Duran and Duran (1995) go further and emphasize that the counsellor should not only learn appropriate strategies but also "believe and practice these beliefs in his/her personal life if the intervention is to benefit the client" (p. 87).

Personal encounters with racism are not part of most counsellors' experiences; therefore, most counsellors do not know how debilitating racism can be to one's view of personality and the world. There is considerable documentation of the negative effects racism may have on one's health and psychological well-being. Therefore, counsellors need to be aware of the negative emotional reactions caused by prejudice and stereotyping. This awareness means knowing the political and social aspects of a specific situation and how they relate to visible minority groups. One attitude that enhances not only multicultural competency but also communication is openness to other ideas, cultures and experiences. Such openness requires taking a non-judgemental position.

Counsellor Awareness of Client's World View

Attitudes and Beliefs

According to Samovar, Rorter and Jain (1981), world view "refers to the outlook or image . . . concerning the nature of the universe, the nature of humankind, the relationship between humanity and the universe, and other philosophical or orientations that help us define the cosmos and our place in it" (p. 21). World view is an aspect of cultural value preferences that frame one's outlook. Therefore, culturally competent counsellors need to acquire specific knowledge of their clients' world view, style and cultural identity development levels. Some clients may have had horrific experiences in regards to poverty and racism, which might have reinforced a sense of powerlessness. Counsellors should be aware of how their own preconceived notions about certain cultural groups influence the client–helper interaction in different ways.

Knowledge

It is fundamental that counsellors possess knowledge about the people they work with and familiarize themselves with some of the historical, social and cultural background of their clients. Additionally, counsellors should be aware of how ethnicity, culture and tradition influence decision-making processes, vocational choices, specific behaviours (e.g., bullying at school) and integration. Recognizing how negative experiences affect client development is imperative in the counselling process. According to Aboud and Rabiau (2002), "the relevance and impacts of racial/ethnic discrimination . . . may affect individuals' health" (p. 304).

Skills

Counsellors should become involved with activities and functions outside of the counselling setting. They can act as advocates and advisors in order to gain a different perspective and see the client in his/her "natural" setting. Participating in community events, social gatherings, traditional celebrations and other relevant happenings could assist counsellors in broadening and fostering their knowledge, understanding and use of cross-cultural skills. One effective way to maintain and enhance good counselling skills is to read professional journals and keep abreast of the latest research and theoretical findings on cross-cultural work. An important aspect of understanding changes in one's profession as a helper involves seeking the appropriate professional development that will ensure that one's competencies are maintained.

Culturally Appropriate Approaches

Because clients bring with them different religious and spiritual beliefs, they may have values that will affect counselling outcomes. In fact, these differences may even affect how they express emotional distress. Clients may see emotions as not being separate from the body or spirit. Because of these differences, counsellors can increase their effectiveness by incorporating indigenous helping practices and the natural helping networks in the minority community.

Another important variable in counselling is the relationship between culture and language. Therefore, the counsellor needs to see that bilingualism is an asset and not a liability.

By and large, counselling training has followed the Eurocentric tradition of counselling theory and practice. This tradition may conflict with the cultural values of other traditions (e.g., the reliance of self-disclosure in the client-centred approach may go against allegiance to the family). While most counsellors are aware that assessment instruments and techniques may be culturally biased, they need to be aware that in most cases institutional barriers have been created based on assessment instruments. Diagnostic techniques fit majority culture but do not necessarily reflect cultural minorities' values. Traditional counselling methods have emphasized the importance of helping the individual, thus going against the influence of family and community structures. Knowing when and how to integrate the family and community into counselling practice will empower culturally different clients and help them seek a collective solution rather than an individual one.

Counsellors need to understand that racism and oppression may be part of the minority experience; thus, goals need to reflect the reality of combatting and dealing with racism and oppression. However, helpers need to understand that racism is very complex and dynamic, and people of colour have developed the strategies of buffering and code switching to deal with it (Cross, Smith & Payne, 2002). Buffering is the process of developing "thick skin," letting hurtful things "bounce off" while accomplishing an immediate task or goal (e.g., learning a skill from a racist teacher). Code switching, which in the black community refers to switching from informal vernacular to more formal communication styles, is an alternative manner of interaction in order to get by (e.g., when dealing with an aggressive white police officer).

A Culturally Sensitive Perspective

When counsellors work with minority clients, trust is a major issue that needs to be resolved, particularly since those with power have often been instruments of oppression in minority cultures. The most effective way of building trust is to ensure that verbal and non-verbal messages are not only congruent but also accurate and appropriate. Minority clients have problems that are external in origin but that may have roots in biases and racism. Therefore, counsellors need to take on an advocacy role to help clients with these external factors by using institutional interventions.

In addition, counsellors should have a working knowledge of the traditional healers and spiritual leaders in their areas and how they work. The key is knowing when it is culturally appropriate to bring these helpers into the process. Part of this awareness will involve recognizing one's own linguistic and assisting limitations.

The culturally competent counsellor also needs to be involved in educational intervention and combatting oppression in the community. Not only should addressing racism be the number-one priority, but the idea of "white privilege" also needs to be addressed.

Similarly, the ethical lines established by organizations like the Canadian Counselling Association or the Canadian Psychology Association must be examined from a cultural perspective. Dealing with multiculturalism is such a new issue that these organizations need reform so that they do not perpetuate racism. As it exists now, counselling, in a post-colonial context, operates in a racist and Eurocentric manner.

The role of counsellors today is empowering clients, and empowerment may mean educating clients about their personal and legal rights. It may also mean challenging the status quo and professional counselling associations to deal with their institutional racism.

Establishing Cultural Empathy

Chung and Bemak (2002) explored empathy and its importance in counselling people from other cultures. Empathy, as a core skill in counselling, is a reflection of the client-centred approach (thus a Eurocentric counselling practice) but is considered in a multicultural context to be of value in certain situations and circumstances. It is a useful skill that needs to reflect the cultural context. A number of guidelines have been established in using empathy to reflect the cultural situation of the clients. The following six guidelines compiled by Chung and Bemak (2002) are considered fundamental:

1. Many cultures are collective in nature; therefore, counsellors need to accept and understand the client's family and the community context.
2. Indigenous healing practices reflect beliefs and values that can easily be incorporated into the counselling environment by working cooperatively with healers.
3. Many clients come to counselling experiencing trans-generational trauma. Counsellors need to be knowledgeable about clients' historical and socio-political backgrounds.
4. Counsellors need to be aware of and knowledgeable about psychosocial develop-

ment and its effect on clients who move from one environment to another, whether it is from a rural area to an urban area or from one country to another.

5. People of colour often experience oppression, discrimination and racism daily. As a result, counsellors need to accept and be aware of how racism negatively affects their clients' well-being.

6. Counsellors need to provide support, resources and practices that can empower clients, including the promotion of social justice.

Conclusion

Many Western therapies are merely methods of colonizing the lifeworld of the . . . client. The end result of many Western therapies is the ongoing cultural hegemony of the client seeking help. Even though the efficacy of the therapeutic arena seems doubtful when the analysis places it in a colonialist paradigm, there are some integrated approaches that have been found to be effective. (Duran & Duran, 1995, p. 87)

Gaining multicultural counselling competencies can ensure that counsellors are actively involved in combatting racism that robs people of their self-respect and sense of dignity. It is a means of ensuring a more peaceful and prosperous society in which all people are equal. The kind of prejudice experienced by ethnic and racial minorities, intentionally or unintentionally, is the essence of the challenge of an open society.

Culture is a human necessity, a way of life. It is the way people establish and maintain a relationship with their environment. As people of understanding interact with those who are culturally different, they must explore the socialization forces that affect behaviour, values and language. Therefore, it is good ethical practice to be multiculturally competent. Arrendondo and D'Andrea (2003) suggest that culturally skilled counsellors need to do the following:

- Recognize the sources of discomfort and differences that exist between themselves and clients in terms of race, ethnicity, culture and religion;
- Identify at least five specific features of culture of origin and explain how those features affect the relationship with culturally different clients;
- Provide a reasonably specific definition of racism, prejudice and discrimination and how they adversely affect individuals identified with "terrorist" groups;
- Be aware of their negative and positive emotional reactions toward other racial and ethnic groups that may prove detrimental to the counselling relationship;
- Recognize the heterogeneity within all ethnic, religious and cultural groups;
- Explain the relationship between culture and power;

- Recognize among a variety of religious and spiritual communities the identified forms of leadership and how these may differ from one's experience;
- Value bilingualism;
- Be aware of discriminatory practices at the social and community level that may affect the psychological welfare of individuals who are identified with terrorist groups;
- Be aware of the effects of family separation on children with parents in the military;
- Recognize that fear, anxiety and vulnerability may be masked with silence or other ways of coping;
- Recognize that differing world views require perspective-taking rather than immediate judgement; and
- Recognize the limits of their multicultural competency.

The transformation from ignorance to multicultural competence is neither simple nor easy. The challenges require that we develop a more open approach to communication with others from different cultural groups, possess a willingness to understand, develop empathy toward foreign and alien cultures and be tolerant of views that differ from our own. The willingness to reach out, risk, learn and experience others is a challenge for everyone.

References

Aboud, F., & Rabiau, M. (2002). Health psychology in multiethnic perspectives. In P. Pedersen, J. Draguns, W. Lonner & J. Trimble (Eds.), *Counseling across cultures* (5th ed.) (pp. 297-318). Thousand Oaks, CA: Sage.

Arrendondo, P., & D'Andrea, M. (2003, April). The cultural universality of anxiety, vulnerability and fears. *Counselling Today*, 26–28.

Chung, R.C.-Y., & Bemak, F. (2002). The relationship between culture and empathy in cross-cultural counseling. In P. Pedersen, J. Draguns, W. Lonner & J. Trimble (Eds.), *Counseling across cultures* (5th ed.) (pp. 154–159). Thousand Oaks, CA: Sage.

Cross, W., Smith, L., & Payne, Y. (2002). Black identity: A repertoire of daily enactments. In P. Pedersen, J. Draguns, W. Lonner & J. Trimble (Eds.), *Counseling across cultures* (5th ed.) (pp. 93–108). Thousand Oaks, CA: Sage.

Das, S. (2000, August 28). Our new 'two solitudes.' *Victoria Times-Colonist*, p. A6.

Duran, E., & Duran, B. (1995). *Native American postcolonial psychology.* Albany, NY: State University of New York Press.

Fleras, A., & Elliott, J.L. (1992). *The challenge of diversity: Multiculturalism in Canada.* Scarborough, ON: Nelson Canada.

Helms, J.E., & Cook, D. (1999). *Using race and culture in counseling and psychotherapy: Theory and practice.* Boston, MA: Allyn & Bacon.

Samovar, L., Rorter, R., & Jain, N. (1981). *Understanding intercultural communication.* Belmont, CA: Wadsworth Publishing Company.

Statistics Canada (2011). *Population by visible minority population in Canada 2006.* Retrieved from www.statcan.ca/start.html

Sue, D.W., Arrendondo, P., & McDavis, R.J. (1992). Multicultural competencies and standards: A call to the profession. *Journal of Counselling and Development, 70,* 477–486.

Vinson, T.S., & Neimeyer, G.J. (2000). The relationship between racial identity development and multicultural counselling competency. *Journal of Multicultural Counselling and Development, 28*(3), 177–192.

Walden, S.L., Herlihy, B., & Ashton, L. (2003). The evolution of ethics: Personal perspectives of ACA ethnics committee chairs. *Journal of Counselling & Development, 81,* 106–110.

Part II

Counselling Procedures

THE FOCUS OF THE CHAPTERS IN PART II of this book is on counselling practices and procedures from a variety of cultural, religious and sexual orientations. We believe that traditional theories of counselling primarily used in counsellor training may do more harm than good in working with culturally different clients. We need to be more culturally centred and accept the perspective of the clients we work with by recognizing that in a post-colonial world, counselling needs to free itself from its colonial past. We have included a number of examples of how a culturally sensitive and knowledgeable counsellor can be more effective. In part, we need to recognize that our Eurocentric education has often failed to meet the academic, social and emotional needs of culturally different clients.

Once people understand cultural differences, such as some of the traditional Asian values, we as a multicultural society can better understand ourselves. Counsellors need to realize the importance of environmental and social influences on behaviour, as well as the implications of counselling in terms of attitude, beliefs, knowledge and skills. An important part of effective counselling is an awareness of a client's perception of mental health and the therapeutic relationship. Since families often play a large part in influencing the therapeutic process of minority clients, counsellors must select approaches that respect this phenomenon. With many people coming from abroad, we need to understand how situations that influence the helping process — such as war, political unrest and human rights violations — affect counselling practice.

One intriguing aspect of a multicultural society is the growth of people of colour and of mixed-race individuals. Consequently there has been an increased focus on counselling research involving biracial identity development. There are a number of models of identity development for biracial individuals as well as differing cultural groups. Research findings show that growing up in two cultural milieus brings challenges that result in difficulty in trying to integrate two cultures (e.g., inside and outside the home). Also, with more and more immigrants moving to Canada, there is increasing intergenerational conflict between the first and second generations. Consequently, we need to be aware of possible stressors faced by young people as well as their parents with regards to value conflicts. From a multicultural perspective, we need to move beyond the therapeutic role of a counsellor and become advocates for our clients.

Most counsellors from mainstream culture have had little experience with what it is like to live as a minority. For example, what are the philosophical foundations of blackness? How does struggling daily with racism affect identity development? Theories that describe the relationship between personality and racism, such as Cross's Nigrescence Theory, provide examples of the frameworks for helping culturally diverse clients. To empower them, we also need to develop counselling strategies that encourage our clients to cope with being different. Anything we as counsellors can do to build a positive and helpful relationship with clients is important if our work is to be successful.

Another aspect of diversity involves being able to understand differing perspectives in regards to religious beliefs. Counselling has often tried to become value free and has sometimes been dismissive of the spiritual aspects of humanness. Those who have taken the time to become familiar with the part religion plays in people's lives — particularly in Muslim clients' lives — know that much can be done to empower clients to use their religious beliefs for their well-being. A basic understanding of how religion shapes behaviour is increasingly important as the number of Muslims in Canada increases. This increase has occurred through immigration and through conversion. Multicultural counsellors require an understanding of the Islamic world view and religious teachings of Muslim clients. As counsellors, we also need to understand our country's history: how the First Nations of Canada were treated by the early settlers and how that struggle affected people on both sides of the conflict.

We believe that in a truly diverse society, issues associated with sexual orientation become an important aspect of counselling. Similarly, our treatment of people with disabilities sometimes reflects an overcompensation that disempowers the very people we want to help. The traditional support structures that exist within our society often fail visible and invisible minority clients, leaving many of them to face abuse, isolation, rejection and violence. As a starting point, we need to be concerned about their particular stressors, and then to promote awareness and provide support. In addition, we need to adopt specific counsellor interventions aimed at addressing all of the needs of our clients, regardless of their differences.

In a truly multicultural society, we must recognize that even within the "white" population people vary in their cultural practices, values, languages and religions. Therefore, we need to identify and value what makes all people distinct and how these differences affect our clients.

4

Counselling in the Indigenous Community

M. Honoré France, María del Carmen Rodríguez,
& Rod McCormick

By keeping the children at school ten months of the year for 12 years, the residential school system succeeded in separating the children from the Nlakapamux adults and the enculturation process which would teach them to be Nlakapamux. This is separation from the cultural self, from parental love and care, from all that is cherished and valued by a hunting and gathering people." — Shirley Sterling (1997, p. 11)

The issues that face Indigenous people in Canada are unique compared with any other ethnic or racial group, personally, politically or socially. All aspects of well-being are fused with these intricate aspects, making effective counselling a challenge. Counselling training as it stands now does not have a solid foundation that would make counsellors effective with the majority of Indigenous clients, who are not only in need of effective counselling but are also demanding culturally competent counsellors both within and outside the Indigenous community. All minorities face the prospect of dealing with a Eurocentric counselling paradigm that starts with a world view and knowledge base that stands as a barrier to effective counselling services. According to Duran and Duran (1995), "a post-colonial paradigm would accept knowledge from differing cosmologies as valid in their own right, without their having to adhere to a separate cultural body for legitimacy"(p. 6).

The population numbers of Indigenous people in Canada presently stand between 3 per cent and 6 per cent, depending on how they self-identify: status versus non-status. However, the birth rate for Indigenous people is one of the highest in Canada and will continue to grow in the coming years. Statistics Canada reports that

The Aboriginal population has grown faster than the non-Aboriginal population. Between 1996 and 2006, it increased 45%, nearly six times faster than the 8% rate of growth for the non-Aboriginal population over the same period. (208)

With the increasing number of Aboriginal people, there is the real possibility that they will become either the majority or close to it in large areas of Canada, such as the North (Dyer, 2001). The phenomenal growth rate can be attributed to more self-identification and a higher birth rate; for example, between 1996 and 2006, the Indigenous population grew by 45 per cent, compared with 8 per cent for the non-Indigenous population. The latest census figure for Indigenous people, including First Nations, Métis and Inuit, was 1,172,790, with a breakdown of 50,485 Inuit, 389,785 Métis and 698,025 First Nations people (Statistics Canada, 2008). Research on counselling effectiveness with Indigenous clients continues to grow. Counselling success has not been present for many minorities, particularly Indigenous people, probably because

counselors may lack basic knowledge about the client's ethnic and historical backgrounds; the client may be driven away by the professional's counseling style; the client may sense that his or her world view is not valued; the client may feel uncomfortable talking openly with a stranger; or the ethnic backgrounds of the counselor may create client apprehension. (Trimble & Thurman, 2002, p. 61)

While many aspects of the counselling process may be blocked due to differing world views, there are some approaches and strategies that can enhance trust and promote a healthy relationship between counsellors, regardless of ethnic background, and Indigenous clients. There are no definitive strategies, but we believe that counsellors can take proactive steps that will help them be more successful. We agree with Duran and Duran (1995), who stress that the difficulty "is not so much with traditional practitioners in the Native American community as with the Western practitioners" (p. 9). The lack of understanding of the historical, political and social aspects of oppression and how they disrupt counselling practice has been one reason that counselling has not been as effective as it could be. We hope that, with a basic understanding of the Indian Act, counsellors will better understand why Indigenous people often feel alienated from Canadian institutions. It is also crucial to acquire some knowledge of the issues, such as the fallout from the residential school system, that affect Indigenous Nations clients.

In this chapter, we have used the term Aboriginal *Nations* and *Indigenous* interchangeably, although we personally like the term Indigenous because it is becoming the standard term in use. We will describe the diversity of Indigenous people and cultures (including urban Indigenous Métis and Inuit), as well as common elements that make us unique.

We will provide a description and discussion of our counselling approach, including the importance of working with elders, rituals, nature, art and culturally friendly strategies. Finally, we will share some important elements of studies on helping strategies and specific tasks that non-Indigenous counsellors can adopt to improve their counselling with Indigenous clients.

Who Are Indigenous People?

The Government of Canada recognizes three main groups of Indigenous people: First Nations, Inuit and Métis. Until Europeans came to the western hemisphere, the people who inhabited the lands were a variety of nations with different languages, customs and beliefs. Like people anywhere else in the world, they were simply the people from this or that place; these were the original people who were mistaken by European explorers for inhabitants of India. The Assembly of First Nations, one of the major organizational bodies of Native people in Canada, adopted the name *First Nations* rather than *Indian*. The significance of the name First Nations is that it proposes that the people came from the earth. (Interestingly, this belief is universal among all the original inhabitants of the western hemisphere.) There are a number of organizations that represent Métis people of Canada in the provinces of Ontario, Manitoba, Saskatchewan, Alberta and British Columbia. The Métis National Council was established in 1983 as the official voice of Métis people. Despite the long history of Métis people in Canada, it was not until 1982 that the Métis and Inuit were recognized as Indigenous people (i.e., in section 35 of the Constitution Act). Recognition of rights for Métis and Inuit people differs from that for First Nations people. In Canada, most First Nations people have sovereign rights under the Constitution; these rights have allowed them to seek redress from oppressive legislation and practices.

Within Indigenous groups, there are many nations and many traditions with a variety of languages and customs, yet there are also some commonalities, such as the relationship between people and the land, wholeness, spirituality and a sense of collectivity or a greater value on the group than on the individual. Indigenous beliefs emphasize that humankind is interdependent and there must be balance not only in thoughts, feelings and actions but also in the spiritual connection between the self and all creation. Since everything is interrelated, well-being is based on ensuring that one is in harmony with one's surroundings. In counselling, the tribal and extended family is of utmost importance. Communication is often circular or non-linear. Spiritualism, as a way of knowing the world and as "good medicine," provides guidance and protection through observation, teaching and healing.

Urban Indigenous People

It is not surprising that there has been a movement over the years in which Indigenous people have migrated to urban areas of Canada. The migration has been generated because jobs tend to be concentrated in the urban areas; thus, more than one-half of Indigenous people live in urban centres. Many reserves are in rural, isolated areas with high unemployment, reduced opportunities for educational advancement and poor infrastructure. Still, according to Silver (2008), Indigenous people in cities "face a host of difficulties — inadequate housing, shortage of work, unsafe neighborhoods, racism in various forms . . . higher rates of unemployment, a higher incidence of poverty and lower levels of income, on the average, than do non-Indigenous people" (p. 11). If we explore the literature on the urban Indigenous experience from the 1960s and 1970s, the overall theme emerges of urban Indigenousness as a problem because Indigenous people had not yet adjusted to urban life; this really means they did not assimilate. However, while living conditions are different, one does not have to give up culture, tradition or even language to fit in successfully when moving from reserve to urban area. One's cultural identity is an asset, not something to be assimilated. Native Friendship Centres, which exist in most urban settings, have been able to provide a place where Indigenous identity can be reinforced and offer a supportive community. Silver (2008) quotes the Royal Commission on Indigenous People, which says "the central issue facing urban Indigenous peoples is one of cultural identity and it argues for measures to enhance the cultural identity of Indigenous peoples living in urban centres" (p. 30).

What are the implications of the urban Indigenous experience for counselling? Our sense is that, along with the challenges of living in a place where one is a minority — and thus exposed to discrimination — and all the problems that exist in the city (such as lack of support and exposure to dangers such as alcohol and drugs), issues around identity become paramount. Counsellors need to understand that there may be pressures around assimilating or abandoning one's cultural identity in favour of the dominate culture. Thus, strategies that reinforce the ego, a sense of collectivism and participation in one's band (such as voting on leadership and other issues) should be encouraged.

Working in the Métis Community

The historical roots of the Métis people of Canada are rich and unique among people of the world, and the Métis impact on the historical development of Canada is immeasurable. As Europeans came to North America, they immediately began to intermingle with the Indigenous people they met, creating what in French were called "metissage," or mixed-blood children. Men who worked for early trading companies such as the Hudson's Bay Company and North West Company routinely married and raised families who lived in both the Indigenous and the European world. Both sides gained some benefits. For Europeans, marriage and children could cement a relationship with a tribe and mitigate the loneliness of an isolated life; for Indigenous people, strategic alliances with European traders and companies made sense. While this practice decreased once women from Europe began to arrive, it did not cease. As people who spoke the European and Indigenous tongues, the Métis were in high demand as translators, negotiators, trappers and traders. According to Dunn (in Cottell, 2004) in

> some communities, Métis people developed a language referred to as Michif, which is a blend of Cree, French and English. The Métis sash also became a unique cultural dress, along with the development of the Métis jig and a unique style of beadwork. The Métis flag, still an important symbol for Métis people today, bears a horizontal figure-eight, or infinity symbol, and represents the creation of a new people who have roots in both Indigenous and European cultures and traditions. (p. 3)

As people of mixed blood, the Métis often faced discrimination because of the racist bias against Indigenous people. However, intermarriage continued. Some Métis were absorbed into the Indigenous community and some into the Euro-Canadian community. As Europeans spread across the continent, different ideas about the Métis identity developed, but it was the events around the Red River Rebellion that significantly developed the Métis identity.

The French-versus-English struggle to control North America had a significant impact on Métis people in that while many Métis did speak English, many more spoke French. The largest and best-known community of Métis (who spoke mostly French) lived in the Red River valley in what became the province of Manitoba. One of the leaders of this community was Louis Riel, who in 1869 opposed the appointed English governor's plan to organize the community along the lines of the lands that the English controlled in Ontario. In addition, French-speaking Métis people were concerned about preserving the French language, Catholic schools and the unique nature of the Métis. Thus they blocked the new governor from entering the area and declared the community in control. Riel then began to negotiate directly with the new government in Ottawa to establish a bilingual province to be called Assiniboia. The government did not want to negotiate, sent troops to capture Louis Riel and sentenced him to death, but Riel escaped across the US border and subsequently returned to Canada in 1885 as a member of the North-West Uprising; he was later hanged. Riel's demands were, however, eventually incorporated into the Manitoba Act of 1870, when the province of Manitoba entered Confederation.

As people living "in-between" cultures and races, the Métis were often plagued by many of the same issues that Indigenous people face, such as oppression and economic and social deprivation, along with all of the issues associated with those challenges. Many Métis people hid their backgrounds as a way to survive; or they integrated, if they could, into communities where there was strength in numbers. Once the Métis were recognized in 1982 as Indigenous people, a movement began to preserve their culture and work together with First Nations groups for a common purpose of gaining the same economic advantages that the majority population had come to accept. According to Cottell (2004), "in particular, developing a strong sense of a Métis self is critical for the creation of the psychological homeland necessary for Métis people's well-being" (p. 75). Cottell postulates that narrative therapy may be the most effective counselling strategy in working with Métis people because they can share their stories – narratives – and thereby explore the historical and social background of their families and relationships as Indigenous people. This sharing is especially important because today's Métis people may lack a physical connection with the land; hence, the connection has to be psychological. Cottell says the narrative approach

addresses the impact of family, community and the sociopolitical climate on how one stories his or her identity, allowing for an increasingly holistic perspective from which to view Métis identity development. In addition, the concept of multiple authenticities central to the narrative approach to therapy perceives individuals as having multiple distinct identity claims. (p. 77)

White and Epston (1990) emphasize that by exploring the effects of challenges in a person's life, rather than the problem, there is a greater chance that distance will be created. In other words, if the client externalizes the problem, the problem becomes easier to focus on as an object. The person can then in effect "re-author" his/her life, refocus his/her strengths and use these skills as a new, invigorated ego, gaining greater control over his/her life. In a sense, the identity-development models used with biracial people can dovetail with those of Indigenous people, creating a greater sense of self. As an illustration of this idea, Cottell (2004) shared some ways in which counsellors can be most effective; in exploring her Métis identity, she said that

my own identity went through a re-authoring process as I investigated family stories that had previously been silenced and began to speak about my life experiences that could not be explained solely through acknowledging my Euro-Canadian heritage. While exploring these subjugated family narratives, it is important to acknowledge emotions that surface as the client begins to speak of stories that have been a family secret for generations. Though this process, the counsellor is encouraged to show respect for the client's ancestors and family member through acknowledging and respecting the choice to bury their Indigenous heritages as a powerful survival strategy when living in a culture that did not allow them to live free of prejudices as Métis people. (pp. 78-79)

Working in the Inuit Community

The Inuit people of northern Canada have a unique culture and traditions that reflect their close relationship with the land. Northern Canada, which encompasses the Arctic and Subarctic, is not only vast, but the climate can be harsh and unforgiving; thus, this relationship of survival, which for some would be forbidding, has allowed the Inuit people to develop a unique lifestyle. The name *Inuit* comes from the word *iñuk*, which means "person," and the Inuit live not only in Canada but also in Alaska, Russia and Greenland, where there are different groups with different names. The former name *Eskimo* is also sometimes still used by the Inuit. Geographically, the Inuit people live in an area known collectively as *Inuit Nunaat*. In Canada, they may live in the territory of Nunavut, which translates roughly to "our land"; in the northern third of Quebec, which is called Nunavuk or "a place to live"; and in areas of Labrador, the Northwest Territories and Yukon Territory.

The Inuit speak a language that is classified as Eskimo-Aleut. Historically the Inuit were nomadic people who built their homes where the hunting was good and moved on to other places where fishing was good or the caribou were plentiful. Like other Indigenous people of North America, the Inuit population was devastated by early contact with Europeans, with large numbers of people dying from diseases that Europeans brought to their communities.

Culturally, as tribal people who lived close to the land and depended on the migration of animals, the Inuit have developed unique tools, skills and practices that help them not only to survive but also to flourish. With European contact, changes in lifestyle have had an impact on people and the way they live their lives. They share similarities with First Nations people of southern Canada, not only in culture but also in social challenges (e.g., abuse, alcoholism, high mortality rates, suicide and illness due to the change in diets, to name just a few). Some differences are that most Inuit still speak their languages and practise their cultural traditions. While the same political and social policies that were applied to First Nations communities in the south were present, these pressures came later and thus affected the Inuit people to a lesser degree. The Inuit also have an advantage in that they already control the political structures in the traditional territories. Interestingly, they control 20 per cent to 30 per cent of the civil services jobs in Nunavut and hold the top political positions, including the premiership, which, at the time of writing, is held by Paul Okalik.

As a collectivist people living close to the land, the Inuit have a close relationship with all living creatures, and although they have moved away from using the harpoon and other traditional tools, they have adapted to the snowmobile and continue to hunt and live in a harmonious way. They believe in the Creator who made all things, and they practise an oral tradition in which beliefs, morality and culture are passed down from generation to generation. In a letter to others grieving in Red Lake, Catherine Swan Reimer, an Inuit psychologist, said:

> When my son died a year ago, last February, I was visited by a symbol in my dream that became the catalyst for healing and hastened up my healing and lessened the grief. The symbol was that of a salamander. My friend asked me, "Do you know what it means?" I did not know. She said, it means, can endure fire. This became so powerful to me that I drew the salamander with fire coming from it. I knew this was my son, and that his death was not the end, but he was being transformed from his earthly state and could endure the fire. (Some family members wanted him cremated.) When I became overwhelmed by grief I looked at the symbol and was elevated to a higher state of grace, to walk in hope and love. (2005, www.swancircle.com)

The process of transformation is a common theme in Inuit culture, based on traditions passed down through the stories of elders. Cultural traditions are believed to be the best medicine to help people bridge contemporary problems. The way one thinks and acts has an effect on the environment and ultimately on the community where one lives; such effects are epitomized by acts of compassion, generosity and sharing. Through listening to the stories from the past, and strategies and ways of living through a healthy lifestyle, a unique form of helping and healing has been established. Like many Indigenous people who have one foot in Western culture and one in Inuit culture, an approach that blends and complements the two is most useful. Reimer (1999) says,

> From the elders' perspective, good parenting and community support guide children to form a positive view of the self and their relationship to the community. The elders share this rich information to help counselors implement some of the age old strategies that helped create healthy families and lifestyles. The Inupiat share positive activities that have helped them build well-being and activities that distract from it through the use of traditional stories and experiences. (p. 3)

Important Issues in Indigenous Communities

According to the Council for Yukon Indians (1993), "Teaching First Nations children is really nothing different from good basic teaching with feeling, concern and understanding!" (p. 1). Counselling practice with Indigenous clients always starts with competent, effective and sensitive counselling strategies. However, because of the diversity of Native people in Canada and their history with non-Native people, there are a number of issues that counsellors need to be aware of. That is not to say that these issues will necessarily affect clients, but the literature does reflect these areas of concern:

- alienation
- anger toward majority and reservation politics
- discrimination
- political & social oppression (including unresolved land claims)
- residential school experience
- sexual and substance abuse
- crisis of the spirit
- loss of culture
- suicide.

The Implications of the Indian Act on the Counselling Relationship

An important implication for counselling work with Indigenous clients can be seen in the historical and political relationship of Natives and non-Natives as expressed in the Indian Act, which is why we believe that every counsellor should be aware of the major tenets of the law. The legislation was passed by Parliament in 1876; its aim, as articulated by Canada's first prime minister, Sir John A. Macdonald, was "to wean them [First Nations] by slow degrees, from their nomadic habits, which have become almost an instinct, and by slow degrees absorb them on the land" (Beltrame, 2003, p. 37). Not only did this law regulate how Canada would deal politically with the native inhabitants, but it also profoundly affected the social, spiritual and emotional psyche of generations of people — even to this day. Because of the Indian Act and the ensuing relationship that resulted from the law, First Nations clients have by and large developed a sense of mistrust of the intentions of political institutions and non-Native people in general.

Why does this law have so much impact on people today? Here are the major aspects of the Indian Act:

> **It defined who is an Indian**: The Act identified status and non-status Indians. Status Indians are registered; non-Status Indians are not registered.

It dictated control of the land: The Act forbade the selling or leasing of any reserve land unless it was first surrendered or leased to the Crown.

It dictated control of government: This control extends to the election of First Nations chiefs. These chiefs essentially functioned as agents of the federal government, under federal supervision (through an Indian Agent).

It dictated control of the people: An 1880 amendment declared that any First Nations person obtaining a university degree would lose status as a First Nations person and member of his/her community. In addition, people could not leave the reserve without a special pass. Finally, First Nations children were taken away to residential schools to be assimilated.

There have been a number of changes over the years, most notably the loosening of some of the more restrictive aspects, such as the extension of citizenship to everyone, the dismantling of the residential school system, the freedom to move off the reserves and the extension of educational rights. In addition, Bill C-31 changed the definition of who is an Indigenous person. Originally, this definition followed the father's ethnic identity, so if a Native woman married a non-Native man, she lost her rights as a Native. Bill C-31 changed that by bringing about greater gender equality.

In terms of day-to-day living, the Indian Act had the effect of controlling even small aspects of First Nations life. According to one person living on reserve, "If I want to paint a room in my house on reserve, I have to get permission from the band, who has to get permission from Ottawa! It is so bureaucratic that I just don't want to bother with it…" (Personal communication, 2009).

Recently the Government of Canada has introduced the new First Nations Governance Act, which is presently being considered by Parliament. This act would supersede the original Indian Act in several ways:

- by adopting codes of transparent administration and accountability that would govern elections of chiefs and councils through secret ballot;
- by establishing rules for regulating the making of laws and stipulating requirements for annual, audited budgets;
- by establishing impartial bodies to allow band members to lodge complaints against chiefs and councils;
- by having a companion legislation, which would make it easier for band councils to raise money for economic development through borrowing and internal taxation.

One might ask why are Natives against these changes, and the answer is surprising, given the recommendations of various royal commissions. Essentially, the new Act (C-7) is a top-down process rather than a cooperative and consultative process. As a result, the federal government will end up paying the price because they have left out the very people who might benefit. Like many other actions of the government, the Act reveals the government's paternalistic attitude because the values underlying the legislation do not take into account the values of the people. For example, how do these changes work with hereditary chiefs? According to the former chief of the Assembly of First Nations, Mathew Coon Come, if the government followed what the Royal Commission recommended — that an ombudsperson and auditor general be a part of the new legislation — then there might be some room for accommodation. Chief Coon Come emphatically states that the new law, just like the old law, goes against the spirit of self-government rights as stated by the Constitution. What upsets the Assembly of First Nations is the assumption behind the Act: that poverty stems from poor management by the chiefs and councils rather than a lack resources and an inadequate land base (Beltrame, 2003).

The Importance of Building Trust and a Positive Working Relationship

While Canada never had the many Indian wars that characterized the founding of the United States, there has been considerable conflict between First Nations people and the Europeans who settled in Canada. Most Canadians, having developed their historical attitudes about "Indians" from American television, see First Nations primarily as a "conquered people" (Newman, 1989). As such, many whites expected "Indians" to accept European culture as dominant and therefore superior. If the "Indians" would only adapt to the white man's way, then everything would be all right.

In fact, the "Indians" never fought extensive battles nor were they ever defeated in Canada. They made treaties with the British and French Crowns that, at the time, seemed advantageous to all parties. Yet the view of a "conquered" people and "conquered" land persists. This is not to say that Indigenous people do not feel dispossessed, because their way of life, their custodianship of the land and so much of Indigenous tradition were taken away, sometimes by force but more often by the use of laws. Duran (2006) calls this loss a soul wound, a term that describes the deep inter/trans-generational sorrow that Indigenous communities experience as a result of the historical injustice, conquest and destruction that was — and is — perpetrated upon them. The suffering experienced by Indigenous communities is, at its core, spiritual because it involved a violation of the most meaningful aspects of their culture: family, language, traditions and connections to spirit, nature and each other.

For Indigenous people, humankind has custodianship of the environment. For European settlers in North America, the land was something to conquer and subdue. The land is part of each person. This idea of the connectedness with the land is eloquently expressed by Carl Jung (Smoley, 1992), who said, "Children born there [in a foreign land] would inherit the wrong ancestor spirits who dwell in the trees, the rocks, and the water of that country. . . . that would mean the spirit of the Indian gets at the [person] from within and without" (p. 85).

The road to technology, strongly associated with European civilization, has led society to pollution and a "scorched Earth" policy. While the road to spirituality is less scientific, it reflects traditional Native belief: that the environment reflects the way people relate to a Higher Being. While there is one Supreme Being, the Great Spirit, there are also spirits of locality, spirits of natural forces and animal spirits. All have distinct powers. For some Indigenous people, the animal powers are greater than the Great Spirit. In fact, the Great Spirit is rarely invoked, while the spirits under the Great Spirit are routinely involved. Among the Salish people, for instance, "almost every action in life is centered around the Spirit Power" (Ashwell, 1989, p. 68). One spirit is not greater than another; rather, spirits are omnipresent: in Mother Earth, Father Sky and the four directions. Spirits are everywhere. The spirit is in the trees, in the universe, everywhere in life.

Duran's Post-Colonial Psychology and Counselling with Indigenous People

One of the most difficult challenges for non-Indigenous counsellors is understanding the effects of colonialism, oppression and racism on Indigenous people. Often these experiences produce shame and guilt, an important outcome to recognize; but it is vital to let these self-doubts go and to recognize that oppression occurred in the past. One does not have to be a part of it. Duran and Duran (1997) emphasize that to work successfully with Indigenous people, one has to accept the legitimacy of Indigenous ways of knowing and understand the cosmology and metaphors in order to deal with specific issues such as drug and alcohol abuse, suicide and spousal abuse. Duran (2006) goes on to describe how to use strategies to heal the "soul wound," intergenerational trauma and historical trauma. It is our belief that to be successful, the counsellor must use and work within the client's belief system. In addition, the two critical concepts — internalized oppression and liberation discourse — must be understood from the beginning of therapy, and the counsellor must be wary of over-pathologizing the client's situation.

Duran notes that a Western psychotherapeutic model "loses relevance when imposed on people of color because its orientation is basically micro-social, concentrating itself almost entirely on personal characteristics of the individual actors in social processes rather than on socio-historical factors" (p. 8). Duran suggests, for example, that by helping the client see the alcohol as a spirit, a living entity that one fights as a warrior would, the counsellor can help with alcohol abuse. One needs to change people's thinking in terms of how they see things; it is common for clients to see themselves as defective as opposed to being infected by a bad influence (e.g., alcohol). The metaphor of the vampire, which the colonialists used when they came to Turtle Island (in the Americas), is not that difficult to understand once we see history from an Indigenous perspective. Indigenous people were infected with internalized oppression, which then becomes a collective ailment. The result was intergenerational trauma that produces self-hatred, domestic violence and institutional violence. An Indigenous perspective deconstructs Western psychotherapy to help the counsellor understand that there are culturally based strategies for dealing with some of the major issues facing Indigenous people.

As Indigenous people, we strongly support what Duran says and believe that not only must it be said but also that issues around historical trauma need to be part of counselling philosophy and practice. Duran believes that the mental health profession has been instrumental in fostering the colonial ideation of Native peoples. One needs to look at counselling from a non-Western perspective and adopt practices that have a closer relationship with natural processes. One of the methods Duran describes is his "dreamtime groups," which he uses because intra-psychic material from the dream can be a good tool for clients to use later in their recovery, after they have left counselling. Duran uses the metaphor of Coyote, who uses tricky language to deceive the ego that would censor the dream. Since the dream often seems strange or full of symbols, the ego is tricked into letting it through. Dreaming is also the way that the Creator speaks to humankind, so whatever is present in dreams is very important. Duran goes on to describe step by step his method of using dreams. His approach is clear, and he uses excellent examples to demonstrate his approach. Consider the work of Clements (as cited in Duran, 2006), an anthropologist who chronicled traditional healing as categorized into the following:

- object intrusion
- loss of soul
- spirit intrusion
- breach of taboo
- sorcery.

Must one be Indigenous to work successfully with Indigenous people? Duran (2006) emphatically states that it is less important to be Indigenous than it is to have "a high level of training within the Western paradigm, as well as an excellent cultural understanding, to utilize these methods effectively" (p. 6). To understand the Indigenous client, counsellors must shift from psychologizing to spiritualizing; in other words, counsellors need to go back to the original meaning of psychology – the study of healing the soul – by being true therapists or soul healers. Western science has left us with the legacy of the Cartesian split, which caused people to become estranged from their soul-spirit. Duran says that to be successful with Indigenous clients, the counsellor must deal with his/her own history; otherwise the counsellor may unconsciously project onto the client: "If we inflict a system that is based only on cognitions, as the logocentric Euro-American tradition, we are committing hegemony (imposing a different world view on someone) on the patient who believes otherwise" (p. 20). We believe counsellors need to understand from a post-colonial perspective that they must explore their own history and privilege before they can work effectively with Indigenous clients. Duran states that it might even be a good idea for the therapist to apologize for his or her role in the soul-wounding process. Interestingly, Duran feels that all people in North America — even those from African, Asian and European backgrounds, as well as those with Indigenous backgrounds — have been colonized by what he calls the collective consumer process. The colonization process affects people's souls at a deep level.

In explaining what a counsellor can do, Duran (2006) uses his own experiences to explain how to start a new narrative. For example, when working with different forms of violence, he says that his method of searching for answers is to pose simple questions such as, Where did you learn to do this? His rationale is that this question will encourage the client to explore and eventually understand historical trauma. It also de-pathologizes the problem and takes away the blame of the client being somehow defective. Duran says that clients will often respond to his question by answering, From my family, or From my parents. This response is followed by the next question: Where did they learn it from? This question allows the client to see the historical element objectively, apart from his or her problem. In a sense, the question leads to the journey of "formulating a counter hegemonic narrative to replace the colonial oppressing ideology" (p. 27). It is interesting to note that the use of narratives can be helpful in understanding the client's perspective and in helping the client release his/her tension around a problem. According to Cottell (2004), in discussing her work within the Métis community, "narrative therapy values and focuses on the way people story their experiences and their problems, seeing identity as a process of meaning creation within a personal, relational, and cultural context" (p. 77). This follows some traditional Indigenous beliefs in which the client, in telling the story, allows the counsellor to help the client name the problem as a sickness so the client can begin to see the relationship with the energy of the sickness. Illness, including emotional illness, is not seen as being inherently bad, nor is it necessarily something to be wiped out. Once a relationship is established with the illness, the client can discover the purpose for the illness and then work at harmonizing his or her life.

One Therapeutic Example: Counselling Residential School Survivors

Residential schooling was one of the more odious strategies used by the Canadian government to assimilate First Nations people. The consequences of this strategy are still haunting the government and Indigenous people today. This failed tactic discontinued only after the Supreme Court stepped in and unanimously condemned residential schools as being disgraceful and even criminal. As a result, the government and the churches, who operated the schools, are paying the price of lawsuits for their despicable behaviour. In developing a treatment program for residential school survivors, we used a therapeutic strategy that was culturally oriented and followed strict traditional guidelines. When putting together our counselling approach with the groups we worked with at a healing lodge, we wanted not only to use a culturally sensitive approach but also to adopt important elements of the cultures of the West Coast. Our theme, as expressed by Couture (1991), is that

> Being in relationships is the manifest spiritual ground of Native being. In traditional perception, nothing exits in isolation, everything is relative to every other being or thing. In the same vein, we also believe that deconstructing the myth of Canada as a "happy place" that accepts all people and uncovering the realities of colonialism and its effects in engendering internalized oppression is a must for our clients. This misconstruction of the realities of racism, colonialism, and all the consequences of policies such as the Indian Act have been detrimental to our people as a people. As [First Nations people] we are wont to exclaim: And all my relations. . . . (p. 59)

As counsellors we believe it is important to explain to everyone in our groups that to make mistakes is a human condition and it is a constant struggle to be on the Red Road. By this we mean that as human beings we want to embrace our culture and bring back the true spirit of the "village life," knowing that we live in an industrialized country in a modern world. As one of our elders always reminded us, "we do not live in a village anymore, but we can recreate the village in our hearts" (Personal communication, 2002). Our approach to healing and helping is holistic, focussing as follows:

- cognitive processes: e.g., "How are you thinking about yourself vis-à-vis the problem and environment?"
- affective processes: e.g., "How do you feel about the problem, people concerned and your relationship to them?"
- social or action processes: e.g., "How is your behaviour blocking problem resolution in the group?"
- spiritual processes: e.g., "How can you fulfill spiritual yearning?

An important element of counselling when using a cultural approach is to incorporate elders as co-facilitators/counsellors in the therapeutic process. Our experience is that healthy elders provide the traditional well of knowledge and can share their own healing journeys. Because they are active in the therapeutic process, they provide valuable support, cultural reinforcement and positive models of behaviour. According to Ross (1992), elders can also provide an alternative way of sharing that is unique to them: "Elders favour the use of instructive parables over direct criticism. Criticism focuses almost entirely upon the past and upon failures in the past, while enlightening parables instead serve to coax people forward towards better ways of doing things in the future" (p. 173).

We also incorporated a number of rituals that reinforced the cultural–spiritual connections. In each group session we sit in a circle, starting our work with a prayer offered by the elders, which is followed by an invitation for anyone to join us on a powwow drum with a traditional song. These songs were given to us to sing and are songs of joy and challenge. The large powwow drum is a powerful symbol of the work we hope to accomplish in our groups. The drum can be played by up to ten participants, and the drumming creates a focus for energizing the group and reminding everyone that they are united in healing. There is also an element of the sound that reminds us of our heartbeat and the way we strive to reunite with the spirit of Mother Earth. We used an eagle feather as a means to allow everyone in the circle to share their thoughts for the day; often it gave us a clue to the emotional state of a participant to know whether someone was ready to enter the circle and work on an issue. We believe that any therapeutic work should happen within the circle so that the participants may not only learn from one another's healing but also support whoever needs it. Black Elk (1961) expressed that all that is holy happens in a circle. Sitting in a circle not only reinforced our belief in the power of the circle but also corresponded therapeutically with the healing we are trying to accomplish. Our belief is that everyone needs to be heard and needs to say it in their own words. In a sense, the circle is sacred and follows the belief that thoughts and ideas are

> passed from generation to generation through ceremonies, lodges, and storytelling. Sacred Circle symbolism is enacted in meetings, sun dances, sweat lodges, sweet grass ceremonies, pipe ceremonies, and feasts where participants confer, celebrate, and pray. This symbol represents unity, interdependence, and harmony among all beings in the universe, and time as the continual recurrence of natural patterns. (Regnier in Hart, 2002, p. 62)

Emotional expression or cleansing is an important component of the healing process. Emoting, particularly anger or hurt, is important because these emotions were either suppressed or inappropriately expressed (e.g., towards a loved one rather than towards perpetrators of sexual abuse or racism). Therefore, participants go through the process of learning how to vent, express and channel their emotions. The final part of the daily work emphasizes resolution and living more constructively. We often "brushed off" a participant with cedar, a sacred plant for people of the Northwest, or with an eagle feather. Sometimes we used role-playing, in which a participant rehearsed a constructive method of dealing with an issue in everyday life. It was not uncommon for participants to face their village elders or those they felt they had "wronged" in simulation, so that they would know how it feels to tell others of their pain and sorrow for any mistakes they have made in dealing with family or community members. Importantly, we want our participants to understand that absolution goes with atonement. Not surprisingly, at the end of these simulations, a great deal of respect is shown by the other participants. Finally, we end our groups with a talking circle (check out of the circle), with insights and verbally supportive statements from the participants, followed by advice and comments from the elders and a prayer.

Traditionally, First Nations people have practised informal helping in their communities by reaching out to their families, friends and neighbours in time of stress. Accordingly, we try to create a sense of family or community within the circle. In the literature, this is referred to network therapy. This therapeutic approach stresses that all the social forces that affect someone are related to one another. Thus, family, relatives and friends are used when someone is experiencing emotional distress. Red Horse (1980), a Sioux, developed a network therapy program called *Wido-Ako-Date-Win*, which brings everyone who wants to be supportive into the helping process. Red Horse stressed that one could not help someone without including those important people in his or her social network. This idea reflects the notion that the best way to help is to regard everyone in the First Nations community as a family. In fact, many traditional First Nations people stress that mental well-being cannot be separated from the context of the community. In other words, in order to heal someone's emotional problem, the community must be involved in the process. To emphasize this further, consider that studies involving help-seeking attitudes of First Nations university students indicate they "would typically seek help from family members before seeking psychological services" (LaFromboise, Trimble & Mohatt, 1990, p. 152).

For specific counselling strategies, we borrow from art therapy, particularly with the carving that is part of our work. With carving, participants project their ideas and thus have a ready "canvas" of thought and vision that can be used for helping. Nuu-chah-nulth carver and elder Harold Lucas told us, "What is in the heart flows through the hands" (Personal communication, 2002). We also use nature in our therapeutic approach by ensuring that participants experience the outdoors as a daily ritual. In our groups, we take everyone outside for a walk, but we do not just walk and enjoy nature; instead, we show them that nature is a medicine cabinet of well-being. There are plants with traditional qualities that can be used for different purposes; healers who know these qualities show everyone in the group. We demonstrate how to prepare four-bark medicine and as a group we invite everyone to experience it. The main function of this exercise is to reconnect us all to the natural world. The implication for counselling is that therapy must go beyond the boundaries of the training and ensure that clients feel a greater connection between themselves and their culture; clients begin to develop a solid identity, ensure their learning can work in a variety of cultural situations and reclaim themselves as First Nations people. Finally, whenever it was necessary or requested, we would "lay hands on" and pray for someone's comfort, thereby reinforcing the power of spirit to one's well-being.

Facilitation of Healing with First Nations Clients

Research undertaken by McCormick (1995) focussed on what traditional First Nations people feel facilitates healing. The significance of this study is that First Nations people, from traditional healers to clients, shared what worked successfully with their clients and within themselves. The following conditions and actions were the themes identified as facilitators of the healing process.

> **Anchoring oneself in tradition and participation in ceremonies**: This theme consists of being involved and taking an active interest in cultural activities such as powwows and ceremonies and gaining traditional knowledge. There is a close relationship between knowing one's culture and being healthy because building a foundation of connectedness, both with those in the community and with culture, leads to a healthier lifestyle.
>
> **Setting goals and pursuing challenging activities**: Having a clear sense of purpose and balance in all dimensions of life, as exemplified by the medicine wheel, not only brings about a feeling that life is meaningful but provides goals to work toward for the future. Pursuing activities that relate to completing a difficult project, going back to school or preparing for more a challenging job was found to help people feel better about themselves and their abilities.
>
> **Expressing oneself**: The ability to express emotions, including anger, love, frustration and other feelings, helps to alleviate stress and allows the client to communicate feelings in a healthy manner. The means to express one's emotions range from the physical (e.g. screaming in the forest, carving, singing) to the psychological (e.g., reflecting, journal writing, counselling) to the spiritual (e.g., smudging, sweats).
>
> **Support from others**: Social support not only involves feeling connected by blood to others in the community, but it also entails taking more specific actions towards

others in the form of acceptance, encouragement, reassurance and validation. There is strength in the collective.

Spiritual connection: Developing a sense of spirituality not only gives one a sense of connectedness but also helps develop a sense of morality, constructive living, humility and transcendence. Participating in sacred ceremonies and rituals brings a sense of closeness and interaction that is distinct from the relationships one has with other people. Spirituality is represented in different ways in everyday situations such as brushing oneself with cedar, praying, singing sacred songs and so forth.

Role models: Good role models, such as elders, relatives and successful people in the community, provide inspiration and guidance to alternative ways for problem solving, decision making, constructive living or conducting oneself in a healthy manner. Among First Nations people stories, myths and legends are elements for teaching about morality, good behaviour, the consequences of one's actions and life in general.

Natural connection: A feeling of being part of the land and therefore of something greater than oneself provides opportunities for people to reflect on and analyze life situations through metaphoric relationships (e.g., one could use a nature walk to reflect on one's life, obstacles, wisdom along the way and so forth). Nature also offers curative effects such as calming and relaxation. Additionally, roots and plants are often used to make medicine and to complement meals.

The implication of these themse for practice is that they could easily be incorporated into the interventions that counsellors use with their clients: "A counsellor with more knowledge might make a more concrete suggestion such as encouraging the client to watch a river flow for a few hours or attend a Pow-Wow" (McCormick, 1995, pp. 142–143). Clearly, these themes could fit a variety of intervention modalities, and human resources, such as elders, could be incorporated into the counselling.

Guidelines for Working with Indigenous Clients

For a counsellor from the majority community, there are many challenges to confront, including his/her own identity development, his/her therapeutic competency, the ability to work within a differing world view and being culturally sensitive. According to Hart (2002) and Duran (2006), being centred as a counsellor is extremely relevant for majority counsellors of First Nations people. This is focal with any ethnic group, but because of the historical context of First Nations people in dealing with the churches, government and other institutions, genuineness, trust and congruence are important factors for credibility. Establishing a trusting relationship might begin by being aware of the different ways of understanding Indigenous identity. This point is exemplified in an anecdote narrated by Harold Lucas, one of the elders with whom we work. Lucas said that a non-Native counsellor had come to their village once and wanted to get to work with people right away. The elder asked the young counsellor one question: "Where do you come from?" The counsellor replied: "I am from Manitoba." The elder repeated the question: "No, where do you come from?" The counsellor's answer was still the same: "I am from Manitoba." The elder replied: "But who are your people? **Where do you come from?**" (emphasis added). The elder then thought: "How can I trust this person if s/he does not know where s/he comes from?" (H. Lucas, personal communication, January 12, 2012)

There is no question that mistrust exists; thus, counsellors need to ensure that they come to the counselling process with a strong sense of self and the ability to project sincerity. Recently, there is more and more research in the area of what First Nations people want in helpers, whether Native or non-Native. In a study with Alaskan Inupiat people, Reimer (in Trimble & Thurman, 2002) found that the desirable characteristics in helpers and healers include the following:

(a) virtuous, kind, respectful, trustworthy, friendly, gentle, loving, clean, giving, helpful, not a gossip, and not one who wallows in self-pity; (b) strong physically, mentally, spiritually, personally, socially, and emotionally; (c) one who works well with others by becoming familiar with people in the community; (d) one who has good communication skills, achieved by taking time to talk, visit, and listen; (e) respected because of his or her knowledge, disciplined in thought and action, wise and understanding, and willing to share knowledge by teaching and serving as an inspiration; (f) substance-free; (g) one who knows and follows the culture; and (h) one who has faith and a strong relationship with the Creator. (p. 67)

With the help of 36 First Nations participants from various Coast Salish communities, Bruce (1999) explored what non-Native counsellors could do to establish a positive working relationship. The results of the study provide non-First Nations counsellors with guidelines for building a positive therapeutic bond. The protocol is organized into five themes: personal counselling skills and personal and therapeutic qualities that enhance counselling; community relations; cultural matters; historical components; and general issues.

1. Important counselling skills, personal qualities and therapeutic qualities that enhance counselling include the following:
   Core skills: Being genuine, respectful, willing to listen; using effective questioning; giving positive reinforcement. Although some of these qualities are used with both Indigenous and non-Indigenous people, the counsellor's approach to

questioning, for example, might be different as well as the construct of respect, which might entail involving some members of the extended family to demonstrate that they too are part of the process.

Personal qualities: Clients always have certain expectations of themselves while in a helping relationship, but they also have expectations of the counsellor as an individual and guide. Qualities that clients look for in a counsellor include being personally healthy, open, patient, non-judgemental, supportive, flexible, compassionate, humble, reliable and willing to explain who she/he is and what she/he wants to do. For some First Nations clients, this is vital information as they establish new relationships of trust and confidence. For those who are dealing with issues of mistrust (e.g., residential schools, being a battered spouse and so forth) and betrayal, self-disclosure from the counsellor could prove to be an additional benefit to the work that is being done.

Therapeutic qualities: Besides the personal qualities that clients need from a counsellor, Bruce's study demonstrates that professionalism, expertise and competence are desired qualities. People also look for counsellors who use culturally appropriate methods, have a willingness to know and understand the culture and language, have and can set clear boundaries, demonstrate informality, confidentiality and rapport, are able to self-disclose and are personable.

2. For counsellors entering a First Nations community, Bruce suggests the following protocol:

   Contact the liaison person from the community: Most communities have a designated person who acts as a liaison between her/his own people and those who do not belong to the community. Establishing such a connection ensures not only that protocol is followed but also that people in the community start becoming familiarized with the counsellor(s).

   Meet with the chief and counsellors: To follow the appropriate protocol to enter the community, the helper should meet with the chief and other council members to demonstrate respect, and should follow their suggestions and working approaches.

   Be cautious and respectful of protocol: Some non-First Nations counsellors enter a community with little or no knowledge of how to proceed and interact within the culture. The best tactic is to wait to be invited to work with the people. Sometimes being overly enthusiastic might send the wrong message. Be visible but cautious and learn to become part of the community, including attending funerals and other cultural events.

   Be open to explaining the counsellor's role: It is important that the counsellor explains and describes how she/he intends to work with the community and what approaches she/he will use, and always to let people know her/his openness and willingness to learn. Self-disclosure is an asset when doing this.

Establish a relationship with other professionals already there: Since First Nations people work from a collective perspective, wherein others are involved in different processes and tasks at different times, the counsellor should find ways to establish contact with other professionals already working in the community. This tactic not only represents a willingness to use team work and a collective approach but also denotes professionalism.

3. Culturally sensitive counsellors must do the following:

Be aware of the culture: It is always important to educate oneself about general cultural principles and specific cultural components of the community, including history, beliefs and traditions, stories and legends. The counsellor should know that there are cultural elements that belong to everyone in the community but there may also be elements that belong only to those who have permission to use them (e.g., songs, healing practices, medicine, etc.).

Be knowledgeable about cultural and spiritual practices: Although many Indigenous groups share cultural components and elements (e.g., all of them have their own stories, ceremonies, symbols, rituals and so forth), it is important to know that methods, practices and approaches to teaching, healing and organizing are varied. Recognize the diversity within the culture.

Know about the extended family: Counsellors must remember that extended family members are part of the helping relationship. It is not only polite to invite the family into the helping process but also valuable to ask for their input and advice, especially if there are elders in the family.

Work with healthy elders: Elders are respected members of the community as they offer insight, knowledge and advice that is considered part of the transmission necessary to keep the culture alive. Work with them either as supporters or as collaborators. Unfortunately, some elders may not have good health due to issues that might be endemic to the community (i.e., unavailable clinics, substance abuse and so forth).

4. Understanding the effect of history on people is vital to learning how to work within an Indigenous community. Counsellors benefit if they understand the following:

The cultural and political history of the community: Part of the understanding and knowledge that a counsellor must possess before or while getting involved with a community involves recognizing how socio-political aspects of history influence the way in which people live and relate to others, shaping their world view.

The importance of loss: After contact with Europeans, First Nations people lost most of their culture as the result of assimilation. This included children being sent to residential schools where their language was taken from their daily life; land being seized by the government; and laws being created that damaged communities' ways of life.

The impact of the Indian Act: It is important that helpers have at least basic knowledge of relevant documents such as the Indian Act, in order to have a clearer understanding of the laws and actions that affect First Nations communities in several ways (e.g., education, land ownership, health services, housing rights) and the relationship between government and the people (e.g., the ministry of social services).

5. Indigenous communities face some general challenges. It is an asset when counsellors are aware of such issues and educate themselves about the causes, consider alternative ways to reach people and implement preventive actions that are respectful of individuals and their community.

Residential schools: In the history of First Nations people, residential schools and their devastating consequences have brought a plethora of unhealthy issues that have been difficult to overcome. Being physically, emotionally, culturally and spiritually abused has affected not only those who were directly involved but also subsequent generations. Relationships among family members have been destroyed due to substance misuse, abusive situations where physical force is used (which may result in sexual abuse) and the impact of acculturation, suicide, discrimination and racism.

Inconsistency of services: Social services are often inadequate to serve First Nations communities that are isolated and lack the essential health services. While recently children and youth have been the focus of diverse social service agencies, the truth is that as programs and budgets change, so do the types of available services for First Nations people. Counsellors must therefore know that people in the communities might be mistrustful about the services being provided to them.

The notion of time: It is vital that helpers working with First Nations understand and value the notion of time in a way that is different from a non-First Nations' view. People in communities realize that appointments and schedules are related to the moment when people are ready to work. In group work, for example, people can agree on a time to gather for a meeting during the day, but it is important to remember that the meeting will begin when everyone gets there and is ready to start. It is respectful on the counsellor's part to wait for everyone to be ready. Furthermore, counsellors will benefit from knowing that family and community affairs are regarded as more important than working with a counsellor.

Conclusion

> What we must understand is that this struggle to retrieve and restore the traditional value of respect for all creation is central to the Elders' concerns about the loss of Native culture. . . . All the outlawed and denigrated facets of traditional culture — the spirit dances, the sweat-lodge and the pip ceremonies, the regular ritual offering of tobacco as a symbol of gratitude — must be seen for what they really were: tools to maintain and deepen a belief in the inter-connectedness of all things. (Ross, 1992, p. 183)

As Black Elk stated so long ago, people of all cultures are united "under one tree," working for the good of our children and way of life; but it is vital to continue strengthening our rituals and values. It is fascinating to see all the shared beliefs that we have as First Nations people, regardless of our geographic location or tribal affiliation. As Ani-yun-wiya, Kikapoo and Mohawk helpers, we have been really fortunate and blessed to have had the opportunity to live and work with different Indigenous people in Canada, Mexico and the United States. We know that as we reflect on our experiences and what we have learned from various researchers on Indigenous issues and convey our vision for counselling in a post-colonial atmosphere, we need to broaden a sense of community among Indigenous people. This means going beyond the roles of what is commonly accepted in counselling by engaging in a variety of roles from advisors and facilitators to community advocates. We believe that community is more than just a group of people (family, neighbours, colleagues); community has a larger connotation in that communion is necessary to engage with one another. We understand communion in a spiritual sense where together we are able to respond to the guiding principles of the Indigenous world view: respect for all creation, balance in relationships, reverence towards the Higher Power and connection to nature. These four principles are in themselves a communion, and we would like to see them lived and represented in everything we do together, from culturally appropriate counselling to supporting community self-reliance, ensuring that families have all of the assistance necessary and ensuring the end of institutional actions that limit First Nations development. We believe that acceptance of other world views will free counselling from its colonial past and ensure that respect is the foundation of counselling practice. Sometimes words like *respect* are overused and their meaning is reduced. Our understanding of respect is related to the many small particles that form it: in the same way in which the sky is made up of millions of stars, planets, asteroids and other life forms we have yet to discover, respect is made of many small elements, some of which we are unable to perceive. Acting with respect towards others is embodied in the way we listen, how we respond, how we engage, how we commit, how we achieve, how we love. Our elders always remind us that respect is the simplest form of love.

The literature and our experience tell us that uniqueness in Indigenous people should be respected. That is, family is important, and the extended family is usually involved in everyday life. In the first encounter, being respectful, being genuine, listening fully and observing how a person shares his or her experience is vitally important and thus is the foundation of successful counselling. Since trust is a vital key, it has to be built on genuine interest in the culture and life of the clients. Duran (2006) suggests that in order to be an effective counsellor, one needs to know where one's centre is, which "is the process . . . [of] being in constant awareness of his own soul's healing process" (p. 46). Duran goes on to paraphrase the words of Black Elk, who said that the centre of the universe was everywhere, although not everyone realizes that. Thus Duran advises non-Indigenous counsellors to find out where they come from and what their creation story is. While active listening is important, the research also demonstrates that being directive in regards to a recovery plan is equally important. Trimble and Thurman (2002) go on to say that

> the directive style seems more effective because many Indian clients, especially more culturally traditional ones, are likely to be reticent and taciturn during the early stages of counseling, if not throughout the entire course of treatment . . . tradition oriented Indian clients are very reluctant to seek conventional counseling because they perceive the experience as intolerable and inconsistent with their understanding of a helping relationship. (p. 75)

All counsellors need to remember that Indigenous people are as diverse and unique a group as any of the nations in the world. They all have differing traditions and practices, but as First Nations people move around the country, we are seeing people from many more different groups. So while we acknowledge that differences exist, we should remember that there are many more similarities, which are much stronger than the many differences we might perceive. If one had to put the idea of similarities in a few words, one might say that what unites First Nations people is the desire to give voice to our ancestors. What this means is that we look at the world in a holistic way, which recognizes and acknowledges all aspects of our existence (mind, body, spirit and feelings). We do not value one part of ourselves over another part since they all are equally valuable and important to make us who we are. In part, one might say that the aim of the helping process is to heal and reconcile these different parts of ourselves to empower and strengthen our identity. From a therapeutic view, all counsellors, regardless of background, need to remember that:

The idea of self-determination must be allowed to flourish throughout all facets of life including the therapeutic, research and training areas. Self-determination is the sine qua non of having a relevant psychology and is the beginning of the process of absolution for the profession of psychology. (Duran & Duran, 1995, p. 198)

References

Ashwell, R. (1989). *Coast Salish: Their art, culture and legends.* Vancouver, BC: Hancock House.

Beltrame, J. (2003, June 16). First Nations: Time of reckoning. *Maclean's*, pp. 37–38.

Black Elk (1961). *Black Elk speaks: As told through John Neilhardt.* Lincoln, NE: University of Nebraska Press.

Bruce, S. (1999). *First Nations protocol: Ensuring strong counselling relationships with First Nations clients.* Unpublished doctoral dissertation, University of Victoria.

Cottell, S. (2004). *My people will sleep for one hundred years: Story of a Métis self.* Unpublished doctoral dissertation, University of Victoria.

Council for Yukon Indians. (1993). *Cross-Cultural strategies*, Whitehorse, YK: Curriculum Development Program.

Couture, J. (1991). Explorations in Native knowing. In J. Freisen (Ed.), *The Cultural Maze: Complex Questions on Native Destiny in Western Canada.* Calgary, AB: Detselig Enterprises, Ltd. pp. 53–76.

Duran, E., & Duran, B. (1995). *Native American postcolonial psychology.* Albany, NY: State University of New York Press.

Duran, E. (2006). *Healing the soul wound.* New York, NY: Columbia University Press.

Dyer, G. (2001). The new majority. *Canadian Geographic,* January-February, Retrieved from http://www.canadiangeographic.ca/magazine/jf01/multicultural_canada.asp

Hart, M.A. (2002). *Seeking Mino-Pimatisiwin: An Indigenous approach to helping.* Halifax, NS: Fernwood Press.

LaFramboise, T., Trimble, J.E., & Mohatt, G. (1990). Counseling intervention and American Indian tradition: An integrative approach. *Counseling Psychologist*, 18, 628–654.

McCormick, R. (1995). Facilitation of healing of First Nations people in British Columbia. *Journal of Native Education*, 21(2), 251–322.

Newman, D. (1989). Bold and cautious, *Maclean's*, July 12, pp. 24–25.

Reimer, C.S. (1999). *Counseling the Inupiat Eskimo.* NY: Praeger Press.

Smoley, R. (1992). First Nations spirituality. *Yoga Journal* (January), 104–108.

Statistics Canada. (2008). Retrieved from http://www12.statcan.ca/census-recensement/2006/rt-td/appa-eng.cfm

Sterling, S. (1997). Skaloola the Owl: Healing power in Salishan mythology. *Guidance & Counselling,* 12(2), 9–12.

Red Horse, J.G. (1982). American Indian elders: Unifiers of Indian families. *Social Casework*, 61, 80–89.

Ross, R. (1992). *Dancing with a ghost: Exploring Indian reality.* Markham, ON: Octopus Publishing Group.

Rimer, C.S. (2012). http://www.swancircle.com.

Trimble, J.E., & Thurman, P. (2002). Ethnocultural considerations and strategies for providing counseling services to native American Indians. In P. Pedersen, J. Draguns, W. Lonner & J. Trimble (Eds.), *Counseling across cultures* (5th ed., pp. 53–91). Thousand Oaks, CA: Sage.

White, M., & Epson, D. (1990). *Narrative Means to Therapeutic Ends*. NY: Norton.

5

Counselling Issues within
the Asian Community

DAVID SUE

Mr. S. is a second-generation Canadian whose parents immigrated from India. The guidance counsellor has requested an appointment with him because his 15-year-old son is being harassed by classmates calling him "Paki," and his grades have suffered. Mr. S. is apologetic and extremely embarrassed explaining that "Canada is a good country," and his son has been taught never to cause problems. (Christensen, 1989, p. 277)

THE OPENING CASE ILLUSTRATES some of the issues that I will address in the discussion of problems faced by Asian Canadian youth and their parents. Although Canada has prided itself as a multicultural society, certain groups have had difficulty with feeling fully accepted. In one study, over one-quarter of Southeast Asian refugees living in Canada reported experiencing racial discrimination (Noh et al., 1999). Some of the other problems experienced are more subtle, such as the use of Western standards in evaluating the behaviour of various cultural groups.

In this chapter, I describe some of the traditional Asian values and contrast them with mainstream Canadian culture, discuss the importance of environmental and social influences on behaviour, present the implications of counselling in terms of attitudes/beliefs, knowledge and skills, and offer suggestions for intervention strategies in working with Asian Canadian youth and their families. Before I begin, I must point out that Asian Canadians are a highly heterogeneous group comprised of individuals who immigrated or originated from countries such as China, India, Korea, Pakistan and Vietnam, to name only a few. In addition, some are refugees who have faced trauma and a variety of stress-ors while fleeing their countries. Others may have been living in Canada for generations. Asian individuals can also differ in their degree of acculturation and identification with the host society. Asians are becoming an increasingly visible population as evidenced by the election of Ujjal Dosanjh as premier of British Columbia (Connelly, 2000) or the more than 300,000 Chinese Canadians residing in the lower British Columbia mainland (Jani-gan, 1997). In fact, over half of the children attending Vancouver schools are non-white and most are Asian (Turner, 1997). Clearly, school counsellors are increasingly likely to encounter counselling issues faced by Asian Canadian youth and their families.

Culturally Skilled Counselling

In discussions of appropriate and ethical interventions with Asian populations, minority mental health specialists have identified characteristics of a culturally skilled counsellor within three broad areas:

Beliefs/Attitudes: The counsellor is aware of his/her own set of values and assump-tions and how they may influence the counsellor's perceptions of members of other cultural groups. What is considered appropriate or inappropriate is a function of our own set of values and beliefs. The Western perspective dominates in the Ameri-cas. It is associated with individualism, egalitarianism, self-expression and inde-pendence. A "good" student is seen as a child who can voice his/her opinion in the classroom, can express differences in views to teachers and develops self-oriented goals. In contrast, in the Asian community, a "good" student listens to the teacher, carefully writes down the teacher's views and does not challenge ideas presented. In working with Asian children, a counsellor must be careful not to evaluate a cultur-ally accepted form of behaviour as "deficient."

Knowledge: The counsellor is aware of the socio-political history of the cultural group and has information about the group's values and characteristics. It is im-portant to acknowledge, assess and address environmental factors. Both the DSM IV (American Psychiatric Association, 2000) and American Psychological Associa-tion (1993) *Guidelines for Providers of Psychological Services to Ethnic, Linguistic, and Culturally Diverse Populations* indicate the importance of a) determining the impact of social stressors (language problems, discrimination, unfamiliar role ex-pectations and conflicting value systems); b) assessing the individual's degree of cultural identity; and c) determining whether the problem lies primarily within the individual or the environment. In the case of the Asian boy who was being racially harassed by his classmates, a counsellor would help the victim develop strategies for dealing with the situation and also evaluate the necessity to change the school environment. If the harassment is not an isolated incident, interventions may include examining the culture of the school regarding the ways in which differences are accepted and whether it promotes respect for other cultures. This examination may need to include an evaluation of staff attitudes and beliefs, teaching styles and strategies, and instructional materials and the learning style of the school (Banks & Banks, 1993). In counselling the father about the harassment his son is facing, the counsellor could agree that Canada is a "good" country but might mention that societal problems still exist and openly discuss issues of racism and discrimination. In this case, the counsellor would point out that neither the response of the son nor his parenting was responsible for the harassment. Different means of dealing with the problem could be discussed and developed with the aid of the father.

Skills: A culturally competent counsellor should have a wide set of intervention strategies and means of communicating effectively with culturally different clients. In the case above, intervention may necessitate a system-wide approach to promote greater acceptance of cultural differences and pro-social attitudes. Counselling strategies and techniques such as empathy need to be changed from a primarily individual focus to one that also includes family and environmental variables.

I will now discuss some of the values and characteristics of Asian populations. Remember that these are generalizations, and the counsellor must assess the degree to which a particular child or family adheres to these values. After presenting some of the traditional Asian values, I will discuss the implications they have for a culturally competent counsellor.

Traditional Asian Values and Family Characteristics

As I mentioned above, there are substantial differences among the groups subsumed under the heading "Asian Canadians." In addition, there are also within-group differences in terms of generation status, ethnic identity and degree of acculturation. Differences between Asian and mainstream Canadian values and characteristics are noted in Table 1. The information that follows involves generalizations. The counsellor is left to assess characteristics and values and determine how they apply to a particular child and family.

Collectivism

Unlike the individualistic orientation of Western cultures, Asian groups tend to be collectivist — that is, their "self" definition involves relationships with others. The individual is less important than the goals and harmony of the family and group. Because of this orientation, Asians are more attuned to the social environment and the way others are responding to them. They are relatively high self-monitors compared to North Americans. In a sample of Asian American college students, avoiding shame was a strong motivational factor, and 40 per cent conformed to "white society" in order not to be seen as different (Yeh & Hwang, 1996). In countries where aggression is discouraged and qualities such as deference and respect are important to ensure group cohesion, childhood problems tend to be for "overcontrolled" behaviours such as fearfulness and somatization. In Western countries, where independence and competitiveness are emphasized, "undercontrolled behaviors (disobedience, fighting, arguing) are more likely to be reported" (Tharp, 1991).

Table 1

VALUES AND CHARACTERISTICS OF ASIAN AND EURO-CANADIAN GROUPS

Asian	Euro-Canadian
Collectivism; family-group focus	Individual or self focus
Interdependence of the family; behaviour reflects individual achievement	Assent of children is obtained
Patriarchal family relationships	Egalitarian family relationships
Restraint of emotions is a sign of maturity	Expression of emotions is healthy
Role of children is to be obedient	Children can challenge parents

Characteristics of Asian Families

> When she does something wrong . . . I will sit down first, think about how to solve this problem. If I have difficulty, I will consult an expert . . . . (Kass, 1998, p. 3)

This statement was made by a father, Hou-Lin Li, after he and his wife were required to complete a parent training course after being accused of slapping their daughter for lying and forging their signatures on a note to the teacher. The process probably made the parents feel even more inadequate and increased tension with the daughter. If you were the counsellor in this situation, how would you work with the parents?

A strength of Asian families is their interdependency and social ties that can help buffer youth from environmental stressors. A strong family minimizes the potential destructiveness of minority status. Within this context, the family needs to nurture adaptive life skills among its members (Yee, DeBaryshe, Yuen, Su Yeong & Yess, 2006). In Asian families, there is less display of emotion to older children, and care is shown by addressing the physical needs of the members. Shame and guilt are used to control children. In general, Asian parents consider discipline to be necessary to prevent delinquency or other behaviours from their children that would bring shame to the family. Overindulging a child is more likely to be considered "child abuse" than disciplining a child (Wu, 1981).

Compared to their Euro-American counterparts, Asian male and female undergraduates (85 per cent ethnically Chinese) described their parents' style as more authoritarian and involving both physical and emotional practices (Meston, Heiman, Trapnell & Carlin, 1999). In Asian families, family structure is hierarchical, with higher status accorded to males and those of the older generation. Sons are responsible for carrying on the family name while daughters are less valued since they will leave the family. Even when married, sons are expected to give their primary allegiance to their family of origin. Children are expected to be obedient and are not allowed to argue with their parents. For example, in one study, Japanese American parents rated "behaves well" as the most important attribute in a child's social competence; in contrast, Euro-American parents rated "self directed" most important (O'Reilly, Tokuno & Ebata, 1986).

Counsellors working with the Hou-Lin Li family might consider their own reactions or attitudes regarding hierarchical family structures where obedience of children is required. Gray and Cosgrove (1985) studied the normative child-rearing practices of different ethnic minority groups and concluded that some of them would likely be considered abusive by child protective services. Other cultures may regard Western child-rearing patterns as leading to selfishness and increased violence. A counsellor might help the family identify different cultural methods of disciplining and explore the possibility that the daughter's misbehaviours stem from conflicting expectations between the family and the school. Acculturation conflicts for both the daughter and the parents could be discussed. In this way, the problem would not be seen as poor parenting but as a struggle being experienced by the family in their attempt to maintain traditional cultural values in a society with different expectations.

A teenage Asian student with acting-out problems in school was recommended to take family counselling. During the family session, the father seemed uncomfortable and non-communicative. The counsellor asked the son and the mother about their perspectives on the problems. The boy criticized the father, complaining about unfair rules and restrictions. The family did not return for counselling. (Sue, 1990)

In the case above, what possible cultural and value conflicts exist? According to your own upbringing and values, what constitutes a well-functioning family? How might you modify your thinking when working with a traditional Asian family? If you were the counsellor involved, what would be your goals, course of action and rational for your approach?

In Western societies, parenting is egalitarian and is based on helping children become self-reliant. A child's view is taken into consideration and decisions are either explained to or developed in negotiation with the child. In the family situation above, it is unclear what led to the termination. In working with the family, the counsellor might have been best to work hard to involve the father. Again, reframing the problem as involving difficulties with acculturation conflicts could take the stress off the sense of having a "bad" family. It might also be helpful for the counsellor to modify statements from the son in a way that would show more respect to the mother and father. The counsellor could serve as the mediator and ask for suggestions from the father for ways of resolving the problem.

Ethnic Identity and Acculturation Issues

Asians living in Canada are regularly exposed to mainstream standards and norms. Many begin to adopt Western standards and may denigrate their own background and physical appearance. Among Asian American children and adolescents, scores are lower on measures of physical self-esteem compared with their Euro-American counterparts (Lee & Eng, 1989; Pang et al., 1985). South Asian–American university women scored lower on a measure of body satisfaction than did Euro-American co-eds. They also indicated dissatisfaction with their skin colour (Sahey & Piran, 1997). For many minority children, exposure to the majority culture produces confusion and conflict. They must straddle their own set of cultural values and those of the larger society. Expectations may be different between home and the larger society. At school, characteristics such as assertiveness and independence are stressed while at home obedience is expected. On personality measures, Chinese American students scored lower than their Euro-American counterparts on assertiveness, need for variety and imaginative fantasy (McCone et al., 1998), a finding that probably reflects Asian values for practicality and emotional restraint. Attempts to resolve conflicts from competing cultural values may lead to identity issues and questions such as "Who am I?" and "Where do I belong?"

Asian youth may compare their parents' style to those they are exposed to in books and mass media. In Asian families, displays of affection are generally less overt, especially from the father. Korean novelist Chang-Rae Lee noted the lack of emotional display and writes of his father, "I wasn't sure he had the capacity to love" (1995, p. 58). The evaluation of parents from the majority perspective can result in estrangement. Lorenzo et al. (1995) found that the majority of Euro-American adolescents picked their parents as adult role models; only 18 per cent of Asian American adolescents made the same choice. It is important for counsellors to remain aware that issues over conflicting cultural values may have a powerful impact on the parent–child relationships of ethnic minorities.

Parents are also aware of conflicts between traditional and mainstream values. They may worry that they are losing their children. Immigrant parents may have lower English proficiency than their children and require their help in translating during interactions with the larger society; this dependency can result in a loss of status for the parents. One daughter returned to India with her parents and discovered that their version of Indian values and norms was much more restrictive than those in contemporary India. She described her parents' standards as a "museumization of practices" (Das Gupta, 1997). However, exposure to the dominant culture can also lead to acceptance of mainstream values in raising children (Jain & Belsky, 1997; Lee & Zahn, 1998), and immigrant parents may begin to feel inadequate (Salvador, Omizo & Kim, 1997). Some parents respond to the situation by becoming more rigid and restrictive.

For Asian youth, culture conflict can result in processes that have been described in different racial and cultural identity development models (Sue & Sue, 2007). These models attempt to indicate the development of racial identity among minority group individuals when exposed to the majority culture. Lee (1994) found four major types of reactions to ethnic identity among Asian American students in high school.

1. "The Korean Students": The Koreans in this group identified themselves solely as Korean and rarely socialized with other Asians. Their parents instructed them to learn American ways, although they were expected to maintain their Korean identity at home. The youth were encouraged to have a bicultural focus with an accommodation to the larger societal values while maintaining traditional values at home. They were encouraged to succeed academically because it was seen as important for upward mobility; the students were expected to work hard in school.

2. "The Asians": Individuals in this group adhered to traditional Asian values and included immigrants, American-born Chinese and Southeast Asians. This group most closely resembled the quiet, studious and polite stereotype of the model minority. Students in this group stressed the importance of studying in getting ahead, although they acknowledged that discrimination would limit their opportunities. As with the Korean students, they were motivated to study from a feeling of obligation to their parents' sacrifices. Low achievers in this group expressed feelings of shame and the fear that academic failure would cause their family to lose face.

3. "New Wavers": Students in this group identified completely with the majority culture. This group attempted to escape from the stereotypes of Asians by dress-

ing in unorthodox ways and socializing instead of studying. Their primary role was to party and get by in their classes with a minimum of effort. They regarded tradition-oriented Asians as "nerds." Acceptance by non-Asian students was a primary goal. Teachers viewed members of this group as Asians "gone wrong."

4. "Asian Americans": Individuals in this group had a pan-ethnic identity. They studied and worked hard in school. However, they were also outspoken about racism and wanted to use their education to give them tools to fight against racism.

Lee's observations indicate some of the ways Asian students dealt with their minority status. With the exception of the "new wavers," students felt pressure to succeed academically. Low-achieving Asian students reported feeling ashamed, depressed and unwilling to seek academic help because of the embarrassment such a request would bring to the family.

Lee's observations indicate that Asian adolescents can respond to their ethnicity, cultural background and interaction with the larger society in different ways. The issues found in the different Asian orientations can be quite varied from one another. For example, the "new wavers" would probably not be open to a discussion of acculturation problems. Their attempts to assimilate into white society may cause them to reject their own ethnicity. The "Asian Americans" may be suspicious of counselling staff and consider them to be part of the establishment whose purpose is to make them adjust to a racist society. Those with a traditional Asian orientation may feel intense shame during counselling and present only vocational issues rather than personal ones.

Academic and Vocation Concerns

Among Asian American families there is great emphasis on academic achievement as a means of bringing honour to the family and as a way of ensuring success in society. Japanese, Chinese and Korean parents of sixth- and seventh-grade students had higher educational aspirations for their children than did Euro-American parents (Lee, 1987). In the United States, Asian Americans are under-represented in special-education programs and overrepresented in gifted programs, and have the highest college-completion rates of any ethnic group (Blair & Qian, 1998). The pressure to succeed academically can be extreme, and the achievement of Asian American ninth-graders appears to be motivated by a fear of academic failure: they report low levels of self-efficacy beliefs even when outperforming their Euro-American comparison group (Eaton & Dembo, 1997).

Asian American students have restricted career interests and tend to go primarily into the fields of science and math, or other fields that do not require good communication skills. They are underrepresented in the social fields or other occupations requiring forceful self-expression (Park & Harrison, 1995). This may be due to factors such as a lack of facility with the English language, socialization that fosters self-consciousness or a perceived lack of receptivity of society. Asians may need career counselling to help them broaden their search for educational and employment opportunities. The same is true for academic achievement. Success needs to be redefined more broadly so that low-achieving students and their parents do not feel like failures. Additionally, it may be necessary to reduce the pressure on high-achieving students who are experiencing stress and anxiety related to fears of failure.

General Treatment Strategies

When working with Asian students and their families, counsellors may want to consider the following guidelines:

1. Be aware of your own values and how they might affect the way you perceive the problem.
2. Identify strengths and assets rather than focussing only on the problem.
3. Assess the world view of the individuals involved.
4. Consider the impact of situational, environmental and cultural issues.
5. Consider using culture conflict as the focus of discussions.
6. Determine what the student and family consider to be possible solutions.
7. Be ready to act as the mediator in family counselling.
8. Help family members broaden their definition of what is acceptable and consider alternative solutions and ways of dealing with situations.
9. Be willing to offer ideas and suggestions for consideration.

In working with Asians, the overall goal is to help identify and develop a broad range of skills that are acceptable within their cultural orientation. Often a number of useful techniques and philosophies already exist within the Asian tradition. Opening a dialogue to discover and evaluate different cultural strategies can be useful and increase flexibility in dealing with problems. I agree with the view of Ivey, D'Andrea and Ivey (2011), who define cultural intentionality as a goal for both counsellor and client:

> The ability . . . to generate the thoughts, words, and behaviors necessary to communicate with a variety of diverse groups and individuals . . . to communicate within their own culture and learn the ability to understand other cultures as well . . . to formulate plans, act on many possibilities existing in a culture, and reflect on these actions. (pp. 9–10)

References

American Psychiatric Association. (2000). *Diagnostic and statistical manual of mental disorders* (4th ed.). Washington, D.C.: American Psychiatric Association.

American Psychological Association. (1993). Guidelines for providers of psychological services to ethnic, linguistic and culturally diverse populations. *American Psychologist*, 48, 45–48.

Banks, J.A., & Banks, C.A. (1993). *Multicultural education: Issues and perspectives* (2nd ed.). Boston: Allyn & Bacon.

Blair, S.L., & Qian, Z. (1998). Family and Asian students' educational performance. *Journal of Family Issues*, 19, 355–374.

Christensen, C.P. (1989). Cross-cultural awareness development: A conceptual model. *Counsellor Education and Supervision*, 28, 270–286.

Connelly, J. (2000, Feb 21). B.C. premier breaks racial barrier. Province is first in Canada to elect man of Asian descent to post. *Seattle Post-Intelligencer*, p. A1.

Das Gupta, S.D. (1998). Gender roles and cultural continuity in the Asian immigrant community in the U.S. *Sex Roles*, 38, 953–974.

Eaton, M.J., & Dembo, M.H. (1997). Differences in motivational beliefs of Asian American and non-Asian students. *Journal of Educational Psychology*, 89, 433–440.

Gray, E., & Cosgrove, J. (1985). Ethnocentric perception of childrearing practices in protective services. *Child Abuse and Neglect*, 9, 389–396.

Ivey, A.E., D'Andrea, M., & Ivey, M.B. (2011). *Counselling and psychotherapy: A multicultural perspective* (7th ed.). Boston: Allyn & Bacon.

Jain, A., & Belsky, J. (1997). Fathering and acculturation: Immigrant Indian families with young children. *Journal of Marriage and the Family*, 59, 873–883.

Janigan, M. (1997, May 26). That West Coast difference. *Maclean's*, p. 21.

Kass, J. (1998, May 11). State's attorney needs some sense knocked into him. *Chicago Tribune*, p. 3.

Lee, C-R (1995). *Native speaker*. New York: The Berkeley Publishing Group.

Lee, L.C., & Eng, R. (1989). The world of Chinese immigrant children of New York City. In *Proceedings of the International Conference on Chinese Mental Health*. Taipei, Taiwan.

Lee, L.C., & Zhan, G. (1998). Psychosocial status of children and youths. In L.C. Lee & N.W.S. Zane (Eds.), *Handbook of Asian American psychology* (pp. 137–163). Thousand Oaks, CA.: Sage Publications.

Lee, S.J. (1994). Behind the model-minority stereotype: Voices of high- and low-achieving Asian American students. *Anthropology and Education Quarterly*, 25, 413–429.

Lee, Y. (1987). *Academic success of East Asian Americans: An ethnographic comparative study of East Asian American and Anglo American Academic Achievement*. Seoul, Korea: American Studies Institute, National University Press.

Lorenzo, M.K., Pakiz, B., Reinherz, H.Z., & Frost, A. (1995). Emotional and behavioral problems of Asian American adolescents: A comparative study. *Child and Adolescent Social Work Journal*, 12, 197–212.

Meston, C.M., Heiman, J.R., Trapnell, P.D., & Carlin, A.S. (1999). Ethnicity, desirable responding, and self-reports of abuse: A comparison of European- and Asian-Ancestry undergraduates. *Journal of Consulting and Clinical Psychology*, 67, 139–144.

Noh, S., Beiser, M., Kaspar, V., Hou, F., & Rummens, J. (1999). Perceived racial discrimination, depression, and coping: A study of Southeast Asian refugees in Canada. *Journal of Health and Social Behavior*, 40, 193–207.

O'Reilly, J.P., Tokuno, K.A., & Ebata, A.T. (1986). Cultural differences between American of Japanese and European ancestry in parental valuing of social competence. *Journal of Comparative Family Studies*, 17, 87–97.

Pang, V.O., Mizokawa, D., Morishima, J.K., & Oldstad, R.G. (1985). Self-concepts of Japanese-American children. *Journal of Cross-Cultural Psychology*, 16, 99–109.

Park, S.E., & Harrison, A.A. (1995). Career-related interests and values, perceived control, and acculturation of Asian-American and Caucasian-American college students. *Journal of Applied Social Psychology*, 25, 1184–1203.

Sahay, S., & Piran, N. (1997). Skin-color preferences and body satisfaction among South Asian–American and European-American female university students. *Journal of Social Psychology*, 137, 161–171.

Sue, D. (1990). Culture in transition: Counselling Asian-American men. In D. Moore and F. Leafgren (Eds.), *Men in conflict* (pp. 153–165). Alexandria, VA.: American Counselling Association.

Sue, D.W., & Sue, D. (2007). *Counselling the culturally different* (5th ed.). New York: John Wiley.

Tharp, R.G. (1991). Cultural diversity and treatment of children. *Journal of Consulting and Clinical Psychology*, 59, 799–812.

Turner, C. (1997, November 22). Has American land hit its limit? *Los Angeles Times*, p. A1.

Wu, D.Y.H. (1981). Child abuse in Taiwan. In J. E. Korbin (Ed.), *Child abuse and neglect: Cross-cultural perspectives* (pp. 139–165). Berkeley: University of California Press.

Yee, B.W.K., DeBaryshe,, B., Yuen, S., Su Yeong, K., & Yess, H.M. (2006). Families: Life-span socialization in a cultural context. In F. Leong, A. Inman, A. Ebreo, Y. Hsin & L. Kinoshita (Eds.), *Handbook of Asian American psychology* (2nd ed., pp. 83–135). Thousand Oaks, CA.: Sage Publications.

Yeh, C.J., & Huang, K. (1996). The collectivistic nature of ethnic identity development among Asian-American college students. *Adolescence*, 31, 645–661.

6

Where Are You Really From?

Counselling in the
Asian Canadian Community

Andrea Sum

"So, where are you really from?" is a question that has brought about complex emotions, inspired much self-reflection and pushed me to explore my own divided identity as a Chinese Canadian woman living in Canada in 2012. The question is seemingly harmless to someone who is not from a minority culture and ethnicity. For me, the question has inspired confusion and anger. I have been forced to justify my Canadianness and, when doing so, have felt disloyal to my Chinese roots. I have often had to tackle this apparently simple question on the spot and have felt uncomfortable doing so.

Although I have been on this journey of self-exploration since my earliest memories, I did not think about the subject in the context of culture, common societal views, racism and government policies until I started travelling outside of Canada. In this chapter, I aim to discuss my "in-betweenness" by first exploring my roots: how my family came to Canada. I will talk about my feelings and experiences of being in the middle and how my upbringing affected my experiences, and will discuss literature that supports my experiences. Last, I will discuss the implications for counselling people from a background similar to mine. I acknowledge that everyone's experiences are unique, and mine are no exception. One cannot generalize about how to treat all Chinese Canadians based on my individual story and perceptions.

Coming to Canada

When I discuss the development of my identity, it goes hand in hand with the journey of my ancestors to Canada. Without their story, my story would be incomplete, as my identity is only a small part of a larger picture. On my paternal side, my great-great-grandfather came to Canada with the first batch of railroad workers around 1881. Like many of the Chinese men working abroad, he came alone and sent money back to China to support his family. He fathered two sons. One son immigrated to Peru; my great-great-grandfather sponsored the other son to come to Canada before 1923 (H. Sum, personal communication, August 3, 2009).

My great-grandfather paid the $500 head tax to Canada. Head taxes rose from $50 in 1885 to $500 in 1903; in 1923 the Exclusion Act, which endured until 1947, was instituted (Fernando, 2006). Like many immigrants, my great-grandfather ran a laundry service on Abbott Street in what is now Vancouver's historic Gastown. My great-grandfather too sent money back to his family in China. In China, that money was spent on land. My extended family were therefore considered landowners. This status posed a problem when Mao Zedong started the Communist Party in 1921. The land was taken away, and my great-grandmother was purged, assaulted and tortured for being a landowner's wife and head of the household. This trauma tainted her life and health for her remaining years.

My great-grandfather made two trips back to China, both times fathering a child. One child was my grandfather; the other was my great-aunt who was twenty years younger than her brother. My grandfather was an educator and principal in a school; in the midst of the Cultural Revolution, he joined the Communist Party. When the opportunity to go to Canada was offered, he was obligated to the Communist Party and could not leave. He allowed his oldest son, at six years of age, to take the opportunity, as he thought his son would get a better education overseas. His oldest son was my father. My father left with his grandmother (my great-grandmother) and her daughter, his aunt (my great-aunt, who is six months older than my father), on an epic journey. Because my father and his aunt were close in age, he posed as the son of his grandmother. My father and his aunt had to change their ages as their close age difference would raise suspicion with Canadian officials. My father's age on paper was therefore younger than his true age. This age change became relevant later when he faced schooling and socializing in Canada, as he was developmentally older than many of his classmates. Unbeknownst to my father, he would not see his mother, father, sisters and brothers for another twenty years.

The first stop on the way to Canada was Hong Kong. As landowners, my family went there first to escape the Communists for two years. From there, my great-grandmother, my father and my great aunt took a long and arduous boat trip to Vancouver, British Columbia. My great-grandmother was reunited with her bachelor-husband, and they all lived in his small two-room bungalow at the back of the laundry on Abbott Street. My father was eight years old when he came to Canada. At that age, children were sent to the fields on Southwest Marine Drive in Burnaby to pick strawberries to earn a little extra cash for their families. When my father was older, he started to work in grocery stores. He expressed to me that he had tried to get jobs in department stores like Woodward's, but he felt he was not hired because he was Chinese. When my father graduated from university in the early 1970s, he sponsored the rest of his family to come to Canada. Because they did not have either the language or the education, they started restaurants that served their own village-style food. Around this time, my father married my mother.

On my maternal side, my great-grandfather came to Canada in his late teens and worked as a houseboy. He worked for wealthy British families doing menial work (S. Sum, personal communication, July 27, 2009). They taught him how to read and write in English. He would visit China every three years; there he married his wife and had four daughters, one son and an adopted son. His third daughter was my grandmother. My grandmother and grandfather had three daughters and two sons. My mother was third in line. In 1952, in the early years of the Communist regime, my grandfather decided to leave China and make a life in Canada. He came to Canada posing as his father-in-law's son. Since my great-grandfather's actual son had decided to move to Texas, his papers were left unused, and my grandfather took advantage of this opportunity. While the rest of my grandfather's family (including my mother) stayed in Hong Kong for the next seven years, my grandfather thought he would search for gold in what many believed to be the Gold Mountains of British Columbia. Unfortunately, he did not find an ounce of gold, so he worked as a cook at a Chinese restaurant and saved enough money to bring his family over to Canada in 1959.

Because my grandfather had used his brother-in-law's papers, his age on paper was ten years younger than his actual age. This change also meant that my mother and her siblings had to adjust their ages. My mother had to pose as ten months younger than she actually was. Her sisters had to pose as two and four years younger than their actual ages. As well, their last names were changed from Wong to Yee. The implications of these changes affected their self-esteem and sense of identity. In 1967, there was a period of amnesty. The Canadian government allowed the "paper people" to change their names and ages back to their original names and ages without penalty. My mother recounts how surprising it was when one day her classmates came to school with different identities.

When my mother arrived in Vancouver, the whole family moved to my grandfather's rooming house on Powell Street, in the heart of what is now Vancouver's notorious Downtown Eastside. King Rooms is a working rooming house to this day. There my mother helped her family run the rooming house and picked strawberries like my dad. My mother attended Lord Strathcona Elementary School, where she and my dad were in the same class. This was their first meeting; little did they know they would marry nearly 20 years later. As a teenager, my mother worked at a cannery peeling shrimp, and as a university student, she worked in clothing stores. My grandfather was then able to afford to buy a house and move his family out of skid row. My parents reunited once again in university. They were bonded with an intrinsic understanding of common struggles, poverty and cultural values. Their parallel outlook on the universe allowed them to steer their way through the world with similar goals and needs.

My Experience

The experiences of my parents (and extended family) affected the way in which they interacted with their world and thus how they raised my sisters and me. The sentiment surrounding some of the first Chinese immigrants entering Canada has trickled down through the generations and affects me. Chinese immigrants to Canada have often been unwelcome: "The Chinese were considered useful to the development of western Canada but were not desirable citizens" (Li, 1998, p. 17). My paternal great-great-grandfather entered Canada on the premise that he was a temporary solution to the shortage of white workers. He was paid much less than his white counterparts and was not trusted as a social equal. Social evils such as epidemics, overcrowding, prostitution, opium-smoking and corruption were blamed on the Chinese. Among the many unfair assumptions about Chinese culture was the accusation that the Chinese were unable to assimilate and took their savings out of the country, with no intention of settling in Canada (Royal Commission, 1885, as cited in Li, 1998). Although this statement is true in the case of my great-great-grandfather, many Chinese immigrants settled in Canada and never left. For the Chinese who did leave, I can hardly blame them for feeling that they did not belong in Canada. Ideas of a "white" race and even the term "race" itself is a fairly recent definition, since according to Mensah,

> there are indications that the term was first used in the English language in 1508 in a poem by the Scottish poet William Dunbar (1460–1520) to refer to a line of kings…however, the French physician Francois Bernier is believed to be the first to use "race" to categorize humans primarily on the basis of facial characteristics and skin colour in 1684. (2010, p. 13).

Van den Berghe suggests that "race has no intrinsic significance, except to a racist" (1967, p. 21). Ash reinforces the notion that people of non-European origin were viewed as "merely guest[s] in someone's home who were expected to accept the way things [were] done and stay in their place" (2004, pp. 407–408). People of Asian descent came to Canada's coast to work in a variety of activities, including mining and railroad construction. There was a "head tax" imposed on people from China coming into Canada that finally morphed into the Chinese Immigration Act of 1923. This act excluded all people of Chinese heritage until 1947, when it was repealed during a reform of Canada's immigration policy (Asian Canadian Web Site, 2012).

The combination of shame and guilt inherent in the Chinese culture and the discrimination of the dominant society contributed to a perpetuating cycle of feeling separate and not fighting for equal rights within Canadian society. I can imagine that one would not feel entitled to fight for a place one would never call home. My great-great-grandfather worked hard for his family and returned to China to die on his home soil.

Newspaper reports often described Chinese people as docile, patient and hard working (Roy, 1989, as cited in Li, 1998). The notions that the harder one works, the more one will achieve and that achievement equates with success resonate with me. In Chinese culture, hard work correlates directly with achievement; if you do not achieve, you try harder. Whether this is a cultural value, an individual experience or a combination of the two, I am uncertain. My mother expressed that when she was a child, the pressure to assimilate was an unspoken expectation. Sometimes that expectation meant pushing one's native culture, language and customs to the wayside. Both my parents lost much of their native language and did not speak it to each other. Therefore, my sisters and I did not grow up immersed in the Cantonese language. My mother dealt with acceptance in Canada by working hard in school. Her parents worked long hours to support the family and were rarely home. My mother derived worth from school, where she earned praise for her academic achievement. The same is true for my father. Both my parents worked hard to make their parents' decision to move to Canada worthwhile. Ultimately, success in school and beyond merited approval, and approval is the Chinese culture's expression of love (Wang, 1995).

My parents did not receive the affection that we often see in Western cultures: "Aside from expressing emotions in words, the Chinese tend to show concern for and take actual care of one another's physical needs" (Tseng & Hsu, 1970, as cited in Tian, 1999). The fact that my grandparents worked long hours is evidence that caring and affection was not expressed in "being with" someone. (Consider my father, whose own parents remained in China.) Instead, "doing for" someone is valued as caring. I see this in my own relationship with my parents in the present. My mother tends to show her affection for us by cooking wonderful meals and keeping her house immaculately. My father tends to the yard and handles our financial affairs.

When I was a child, my parents rarely praised us overtly. To go to university, to get good grades, to do the right thing — this was expected of us and warranted no action out of the ordinary from them. All we knew is that if we did not live up to their expectations, there would be disappointment. Disappointment in a sense was the loss of approval from my parents. According to Nancy Wang, compliments or acknowledgment of a positive trait disrupts the collective by singling out the individual (Wang, 1995). Presently, when it comes to choosing a partner, a school, a job or even a material item, I feel the need for my parents' approval. It is somewhat jarring and annoying to come to this conclusion when I have fought my entire life to achieve distance from many of their values. My friends, my previous partners and even my younger sisters have not understood this need on my part. They have asked me why it matters and why I care about what my parents think. I am, after all, an adult and have the ability to live my own life, right? I cannot answer these questions simply. My existence has been a juxtaposition of a radical departure from my parents' reign with a desperate need for their approval.

The tug of war occurs in part because I have been raised in the dominant culture where praise is offered freely. At school, I was praised but at home, I was rarely praised. The only way that I knew my parents truly approved of what I did was if I heard them tell their friends about it or if through subtle body language I could sense when I gave them good news. The messages from dominant culture contradicted my experiences at home. I often believed that no matter how much I tried, it would not be good enough. I internalized my parents' casual comments about their friends' children and would make mental notes not to do the same thing, or at least not let my parents know I was doing something they disapproved of.

This underlying need for approval has followed me wherever I have travelled. I realized years ago that geographical distance did not remove me from living my life as if my parents were watching or judging me on the merits of my behaviour. This mentality has affected me in my personal and professional life. I have been trained to be hypersensitive to verbal and non-verbal viewpoints of others. I watch social cues to determine my own actions. I do not want to be confrontational for fear that I will lose respect, friendship or collegiality. I often catch myself falling into this passive role and overcompensate by taking the opposite route; then I feel that I come off as being opinionated or domineering. Whether I succumb to my upbringing or battle against it, I revolve around the unwavering axis of the need for approval.

Shame and guilt are common themes in my life. They dictate and discipline my actions. I question how things I do or say come off and what people may think of me. I believe this mentality stems from the Chinese collectivist mentality that what affects one affects the entire family: "In the Confucian idea of the self, even the concept of self-development is viewed as inherently communal" (Tian, 1999, p. 60). I cannot count how many times my parents told me not to talk about an incident, a comment or an opinion to other people. A few years ago, when my sister moved in with her boyfriend, my mother was distraught, ashamed and angry. She expressed the importance of not disclosing my sister's action to anyone. She cried for days because she thought she had failed as a mother and could not bear the thought that her friends may find out about this grand downfall. Their living together outside of marriage would discredit her parenting skills and dishonour our family. This mentality seeps into the dealings I have in my daily life. I find myself often pre-empting a comment or disclosure with, "This is between me and you" or "I'd appreciate it if you didn't tell anyone about what I said." This need for secrecy is ingrained into my being. I disguise it by telling myself that it is my need for privacy that drives me. Secrecy breeds guilt and shame as guilt and shame motivate secrecy. It is a vicious cycle that only pauses with conscious awareness and intention.

As generations pass, Chinese cultural values become diluted. If parents do not make a conscious effort to educate and instill knowledge of the Chinese culture and language, we operate from a mostly dominant culture point of view. We are saturated by popular culture, media and education. Yet we look Chinese. A constant negotiation and justification of our Chineseness or our Canadianness emerges. Since the days of my great-great-grandfather, "kinship is no longer the primary principle of social interaction; instead, individual-centered social relationships between . . . cultural groups . . . have become more important" (Lai et al., 1988, as cited in Tian, 1999, p. 82).

I live somewhere in the middle of two cultures: on one side of the scale, individualistic; on the other side of the scale, collectivist. At times, I am assertive and direct. At other times, I am accommodating and non-confrontational. These identities are not *either/or*. Rather, they intersect and meld into one. I believe that, for the most part, I can make sense of this within myself. The struggle arrives when I feel the perceptions of others being imposed on me. People have made statements like, "You're really not *that* Chinese," "You're Chinese; you should be good at math" and "I love Asian women; they're so exotic." Many people come with preconceived notions of what Chinese is and is not. I too used to think I had a concrete definition of what Chinese was.

Nancy Wang discusses a concept called double-blind racism. It is an agreement between others and oneself to commit racist attitudes and behaviours against ourselves. This agreement binds us in our own cycle of self-hatred (Wang, 1995). At one point, I was proud of the fact that I was not "*that* Chinese." I have come to realize that being Chinese is not a single thing: Chineseness is a sliding scale. I fall somewhere in a grey area on this scale. Where I fall changes and shifts with experiences, exploration, acceptance and denial of ideas constantly brought forth to me. In fact, labelling someone as "Chinese" or "Canadian" comes loaded with a myriad of assumptions. I prefer to position myself between different sets of values. If I squeeze a drop of food colouring into a pitcher of water, the colouring dilutes and becomes its own shade. I take from and reject both sets of values, and this makes me who I am.

Implications for Counselling

In working with Chinese Canadians, it is important to remember factors around accul-turation, because according to Li (1983) "traditional Chinese familism has little to do with the development of the Chinese-Canadian family" (p. 87). Thus, I cannot speak for every Chinese Canadian woman who seeks counselling. I can, however, give an individ-ual perspective of how I, as a person who inhabits the "in-betweenness" of Chinese and dominant culture, feel comfortable in a therapeutic setting.

When I told my extended family that I was doing a master's degree in counselling, they nodded with polite acknowledgment. In traditional Chinese culture, formal counselling is non-existent. You keep your problems hidden, behind closed doors and within the confines of your own family: this is how one saves face. Seeking counselling is sometimes seen as a last resort and carries a taboo. You do not share your problems with a stranger. A counsellor needs to be aware of this frame of reference. He/she needs to be non-judge-mental and accepting in order to minimize the shame the client may feel about seeking outside help. Because the North American concept of counselling is absent in Asia, thera-pists in Canada may need to take on a more structured form of therapy (Sue & Sue, 2007).

It is important that the counsellor not only goes through the usual informed con-sent session but actually explicitly discusses what counselling means. Even for someone brought up immersed in the dominant culture, it is sometimes unclear what counselling entails. For someone who has not grown up with counselling being valued or discussed, education about counselling in itself is an important process for establishing safety. Dur-ing informed consent, the counsellor should also demonstrate sensitivity and restraint when collecting information, being aware of the cultural tendency towards modesty. Therapy should be as brief as possible and focus on the present or immediate future (Sue & Sue, 2007).

When approaching a client, the counsellor should deal with the concrete issues before addressing the emotions underlying the issues. Focussing on the concrete issue brought to the session and developing goals towards resolution will reduce the likelihood of the therapist's world view being imposed on the client (Sue & Sue, 2007). For example, I will not reveal my inner emotions until I trust someone, until I am assured I am not being judged. I have been trained to be acutely aware of subtle nuances in gestures and affect. I sense immediately when someone is being insincere. If a counsellor is merely a present, understanding, accepting statue who does not utter a word, that is better than someone who pretends to understand by offering senseless dialogue or superficial paraphrases to fill in space. I do not necessarily need a counsellor who is just like me. In fact, I prefer a counsellor who is outside of my culture because I associate judgement and shame with someone from my culture. Yet the benefit of having a counsellor from a similar background is an innate cultural understanding. At the moment, this is not enough of a factor to outweigh the perceived judgement I would feel from a stranger of the same culture as me. Whoever the counsellor is, it takes time to trust, and once I trust, the loyalty I feel toward the counsellor is binding.

In my eyes, an effective counsellor is not just someone with a broad knowledge of how to counsel Chinese people or even people from a collectivist culture. It is useful and proactive to have this knowledge but limiting if the counsellor pigeonholes a client or makes assumptions based on that broad knowledge. A truly effective counsellor sees me as a whole person and is curious to find out what makes me who I am. We are all different; making generalizations based on a perceived cultural background is judgemental. Although many people treat Chinese people as a collective group, just as many differences occur among sub-groups of Chinese people as between two distinct ethnicities (Tian, 1999). The same is true when making similar judgements towards someone raised in the dominant culture. However, counsellors need to keep in mind the wide variety of people in Canada from Asian decent with different cultural traditions. Delivering counselling to Chinese-Canadians, and other Asian-Canadians

> is a goal still in process, with professionals demonstrating a growing appreciation for the dynamics involved in ethnic matching of professionals and clients as well as some of the possible outcomes of such matching. . . . Assimilation and ethnic identity remain as important processes related to ethnicity and culture. (Maki & Kitano, 2002, p. 126)

Conclusion

The question "Where are you really from?" penetrates and puzzles me. I am from Canada geographically. My values are from a mixture of two or more cultures. I internalize the experiences of my ancestors and the ideas of the Western society I live in. To ignore any one of these elements is to deny myself, and to deny a part is to deny the wholeness of who I am. I believe that to live in a truly multicultural society, we need to understand that no one's identity can be summed up in a one-sentence response. We are each a collage of values, experiences and beliefs, layered, textured and painted into the individuals we are. No two paintings are the same.

Where I'm Really From
Andrea Sum

I am from the subtle scent of Nabob coffee in the morning
I am from tasty egg tarts, chasuy bow and coconut buns from Maxim's Bakery
I am from "practise the piano!" and "do your homework!"
I am from the feeling of warmth when my dad tickled my chin
I am from the places I've travelled and the people I've met
I am from ripped jeans and plaid shirts
I am from hairspray and platform shoes
I am from Nirvana and Fresh Prince
I am from guitars, hacky sacks and diablos
I am from cherry pits and grass stains
I am from cleaning windowsills with Q-tips
I am from beneath the sea and high above the mountains
I am from bourgeoisie and following the rules to the tee
I am from cardboard boxes and sofa cushion forts
I am from the fights and rivalry between my sisters
I am from heart-wrenching sadness and pain
I am from ecstatic joy and elation
I am from my mother's insight
I am from Communism and Democracy
I am from searching for crayfish and wading through creeks
I am from airplanes, automobiles, buses, boats, tuk-tuks, trains, trucks and trolleys
I am from grand skyscrapers and rich rust-coloured soil
I am from oceans and cliffs
I am from playing the djembe in NYC subways
I am from the teachable moments
I am from *yela! allons-y!* and *chevre!*
I am from judgement and discrimination
I am from loyal friends and endless conversations
I am from red wine sangria on a sunny patio
I am from failures and achievements
I am from here, there and everywhere.

References

Ash, M.C. (2004). But where are you really from? In Camille Nelson & Charmaine Nelson, *Racism, eh? A critical interdisciplinary anthology of race and racism in Canada* (pp. 398-409). Concord, ON: Captus Press.

Asian Canadian Web Site (2012). History of Asians in Canada. Retrieved from http://www.asian.ca.

Fernando, S. (2006). *Race and the city*. Vancouver, BC: UBC Press.

Li, P.S. (1998). *Chinese in Canada*. Toronto, ON: Oxford University Press Canada.

Li, P.S. (1983). The Chinese Canadian family. In P.S. Li & B.S. Bolacia (Eds.), *Racial minorities in multicultural Canada* (pp. 86-96). Toronto: Garamond Press.

Maki, M. & Kitano, H. (2002), Counseling Asian Americans. In P. Pedersen, J. Draguns, W. Lonner, & J. Trimble (Eds.), *Counseling across cultures* (pp. 109–132). Thousand Oaks, CA: Sage Publications.

Mensah, J. (2010). *Black Canadians: History, experience, social conditions* (2nd ed.). Halifax, NS: Fernwood Publishing.

Sue, D.W. & Sue, D. (2007). *Counselling the culturally different* (5th ed.). New York: John Wiley.

Tian, G. (1999). *Chinese-Canadians, Canadian-Chinese*. Wales, UK: The Edwin Mellen Press.

Van der Burge, P. (1967). *Race and racism: A comparative perspective*. New York: John Wiley.

Wang, N. (1995). Born Chinese and a woman in America. In J. Adleman, G.M. Enquidanos & G.M. Enquidamos-Clark (Eds.), *Racism in the lives of women* (pp. 97–110). Binghamton, NY: Haworth Press.

7

Counselling in the Indo-Canadian Community

Challenges and Promises

RUBY RANA & SUKKIE SIHOTA

FULL INDIAN, HALF INDIAN, PART INDIAN, not Indian at all: these are all points along a metaphorical spectrum of Indo-Canadian cultural identity. Growing up as an Indo-Canadian typically refers to being born in Canada to immigrants from India; or more generally, being born in Canada into an ancestral lineage originating in India. Because of early migration from India, globalization and biracial marriages, being "Indo-Canadian" is, like many bicultural identities, increasingly difficult to define in linear terms. Cultural context, social groups and personal journeys through the processes of identity development (Guzder & Krishna, 2005; Sue & Sue, 2007) determine how people negotiate their cultural sense of belonging (Benet-Martinez, Lee & Leu, 2006; Benet-Martinez, Leu, Lee & Morris, 2002; Tadmor & Tetlock, 2006). Negotiating the boundaries of cultural exclusion and inclusion is a complex issue; while people may say that they have a strong footing in both the Indian and Canadian cultures, at times they may also say they feel completely Canadian or on other occasions assert their "Indianness" fully. Finding a way to integrate two very different cultures — the individualistic Canadian culture and the collectivist Indian culture — does not often happen without a struggle. That would be too easy.

It is ironic that even if, as an Indo-Canadian, one may look the part, or have citizenship to legitimate membership in the "appropriate" cultural or national groups, one's identity is still questioned. The realization of this irony comes from situations where one encounters racism with taunts from strangers as Indo-Canadians are called "curry," "hindu" or "paki" alongside hurtful comments such as, "You need to go back to your own country." Canada is *our* country! This not only hurts, but draws into question whether we, as second-, third- or fourth-generation Indo-Canadians, will ever be accepted. To be abundantly clear, "curry" is a very general name, mostly used outside of India, describing Indian vegetarian and non-vegetarian dishes. It is not an adjective. Although our ancestors are from India, we don't eat Indian food every day — though there are definite favourites in the Indian cuisine. A "hindu" is a person who follows Hinduism, one of the dominant faiths in India. If a person took the time to notice the kara on our right hand, and knew what it is, he/she might be accurate in calling us a Sikh. The word "paki" refers to people from originating from Pakistan. If that is how we are addressing people these days, then should a Canadian be called a "cana" and an American an "amer"?

Expectations can also pose challenges in finding ways to belong in an Indo-Canadian bicultural context. These are a few of the challenges of living between cultures (Abouguendia & Noels, 2001; Sodhi, 2008; Ying & Lee, 1999). It is experiences and challenges like these that remind us of how proud we are to be Indo-Canadian – whether on our own terms or on our families' terms; and how useful it is to have knowledge about one's own cultural, familial and religious history. In terms of cultural belonging, Indo-Canadians have two identities to claim, assert and protect; and no matter how many ignorant, angry people we encounter, they cannot take that away from us.

What does it mean to be Indo-Canadian? We have been challenging and struggling with this question for much of our lives. When we occasionally dress up in our saris to attend an Indian function, we feel completely Indian. More often, however, we dress in our Canadian clothing, not only because it is more comfortable for us but because it is a part of our identity. While our external appearance may signify an aspect of our identity, how we dress or the colour of our skin has not been in the forefront of our struggle. Instead, the conflict lies in our internal sense of self. Are my values and beliefs obtained from my Sikh parents, or do they come from the Canadian culture that we are exposed to and part of on a daily basis? What roles, rules and expectations we are adhering to? These are some of the questions we began exploring in our adolescent years and continue to explore as adults.

Many second-generation Indo-Canadian young people are faced with the same struggles and questions about their identity and sense of belonging. Are they Indian, Canadian or Indo-Canadian? They may feel they have two cultures that do not blend together easily. Ghuman (1994) noted that recent South Asian immigrants to Canada are acculturated firmly rooted in their religion and culture and sure of their personal identities. Their sense of belonging is not jeopardized because they are certain of their identity as Sikhs.

However, the children of these immigrants are less sure of their personal and social identities. Second-generation Indo-Canadians are more likely to question values and beliefs. They more commonly struggle with their sense of self and may suffer from culture clash. For many Indo-Canadian students, the values and beliefs at school contradict those at home. Therefore, Ghuman believes the focus should lie on bridging the gap between the culture of the home and the school.

Diversity among Indo-Canadian Population

Members of the Indo-Canadian population have also been called East Indian or South Asian. To be called "East Indian" or "South Asian" does not reflect the significance of our Canadian identity. We are products of two cultures, Indian and Canadian, and it is important to honour this dualism. The term South Asian is used only to refer to individuals who have spent the majority of their lives in India and are not Canadian citizens. It is also important to note the diversity among the Indo-Canadian population in terms of religion, culture, language and food. In fact, India's constitution recognizes 15 official languages, and a recent Indian census tabulated more than 500 mother tongues spoken within the nation's boundaries (Mogelonsky, 1995). So, although the Indo-Canadian population may share the original mother country of India, they do not necessarily share the same cultural backgrounds or personal experiences.

Our main focus in this chapter is on the Sikh Indo-Canadian population, although there are some generalities that can apply to anyone who traces his/her culture to South Asia. Religion does matter, but it is our experience that it plays a secondary role to culture. Sikhs make up the largest Indo-Canadian group in Canada, particularly in British Columbia. The Sikh religion combines Hinduism, Buddhism and Islam, so if we can generalize to all Indo-Canadians, regardless of background, this would be a good place to provide the best perspective.

A Historical Background of Sikhism

There are many wonderful explanations on the theory of Sikhism, but we feel most qualified to share our own personal perspective and sense of identity as young Canadian women born into Sikh families. As children we grew up with fairly regular visits to the gurudwara (Sikh temple). As university students, we studied Indian religions, contemporary issues in India, Indian history, psycho-linguistics of the Punjabi language (which is the language generally associated with Sikhs) and intercultural dynamics. As people we have an interest in exploring the experiences of the Indian Diaspora, and as individuals we have shaped our academic careers around intercultural dynamics of India, Canada and the Diaspora. It is with this background that we share our understandings with you.

The first wave of immigration to Canada came in the nineteenth century and settled in British Columbia. The majority of Indo-Canadians are from the state of Punjab, India, and the majority of Punjabis in BC are Sikhs. Therefore, it is common for the Sikh faith and the Punjabi culture in BC to be closely related. While you keep these cultural and religious demographics in mind, it is important to understand the implications of counselling with Sikh Canadians. However, you must first understand Sikh Canadians and what it means to be Sikh.

Sikhism was founded by a young individual named Nanak, who later became known as Shri Guru Nanak Dev Ji, the first of the ten gurus, or teachers, of the Sikh faith. During this time there was disharmony between two of the dominant religions in India, Hinduism and Islam. Guru Nanak Dev Ji founded Sikhism on a number of principles, some of which were social equality, honest living, community service and sharing. Sikhism stressed equality to mediate the caste system in India, and community service to get everyone actively giving back to their community and looking out for the concerns of others. Sikhism and its teachings were further strengthened to reflect the social needs of the time. The nine following gurus recognized what those needs were and clarified them within the Sikh scripture, *Sri Guru Granth Sahib*.

Around the time that Sikhism was founded, India was frequently invaded by neighbouring countries. Many of the invasions took place through the Khyber Pass, which meant travelling through the state of Punjab, a state that later became associated the Sikhs (Rai, 2011). As a result, many violent attempts were made to convert Sikhs to different faiths. In order to survive, Sikhs needed to learn how to protect themselves, as well as their country. The value of protection, strength and defense became an ingrained part of the Sikh identity (Rai, 2011). If one follows the pattern of change in the teachings of the ten Sikh gurus, it becomes apparent how the peaceful society in Guru Nanak's time developed into a more defence-oriented one as it was marked by the torturous experiences the later gurus faced. By the tenth guru, Gobind Singh Ji, the Sikh brother- and sisterhood were born: the Khalsa. Men and women both became baptized Sikhs, wore their religion courageously and visibly, abolished any caste or class indicator and settled on equal ground with all the men using Singh (meaning "lion") and all the women using Kaur (meaning "princess") as a last name. Guru Gobind Singh Ji emphasized the importance in standing up for oneself and one's beliefs. Many of the approaches to creating social order in the beginning stages of Sikhism were passive, due to the social times. As a result, many violent acts were committed against Sikhs, and Sikhs endured these injustices until Guru Gobind Singh Ji infused the warrior spirit into Sikhism, a spirit to defend oneself and those who are defenceless irrespective of their caste, creed and religion (Dorn & Gucciardi, 2011; Rai, 2011).

Violence was not, and is not, part of the Sikh religious way of life. Yes, Guru Gobind

Singh Ji was a warrior. Yes, there is a long history of Sikh warriors that is a proud part of many people's sense of Sikh identity. However, by no means does this suggest Sikhs as a group are violent people. Curious to learn, peaceful, gentle-hearted, strong, courageous, just, protective of others and equal — these are some attributes that have been born from our Sikh experiences as well as those of our peers. As Indo-Canadians, we have background knowledge of the historical facts that led to and followed the creation of the Sikh Empire in 1801, secular in nature, and ruled by Maharaja Ranjit Singh as the Emperor of Punjab.

The Golden Temple is the holiest place for Sikhism (i.e., the equivalent of the Vatican for Roman Catholics), but it is also viewed as a religious sanctuary. This point better illustrates the impact of a brutal attack on this gurudwara in 1984, an attack called Operation Blue Star, led by the Indian government. This operation was intended to extract the leader of the Sikh separatists, Jarnail Singh Bhindranwale (Rai, 2011). This political mission of the government of India infringed on the peace of the holiest Sikh shrine, and subsequently led to major bloodshed that was documented in the Golden Temple museum. Not only have Sikhs had to fight to maintain their cultural identity in India; anti-Sikh sentiments are still felt in everyday life in India. Sikhs remain a marginalized group. One of many reasons Sikhs came to Canada was so they could practice their religion and have a sense of safety. Many Punjabi-Sikhs in BC have formed opinions and values on the basis of key religious and/or cultural traumas that took place in the history of India and the state of Punjab (Rai, 2011; Shani, 2005). Still, we must underscore the point about violence in the Sikh faith: Sikhs are not taught to be violent. The reason we emphasize this idea is that we have heard comments linking violence and Sikhs, through a misinterpretation of the importance placed on defending oneself and others.

Ethnic Identity

Achieving a sense of identity is an important psychological task for an adolescent. This undertaking includes the ability to know and understand oneself as an individual, as well as recognizing one's particular place in society. The influence of one's ethnic identity is most pertinent in societies that have diverse ethnic backgrounds among the dominant social group. Ethnic identity can be defined as "one's sense of belonging to an ethnic group and the part of one's thinking, perception, feelings and behaviour that is due to ethnic group membership" (Rotheram & Phinney, 1987, p. 13). According to Rosenthal (1987), ethnic identity can be conceptualized by two parts: objective and subjective. Objectively, one can relate to one's ethnic group in terms of ascribed or external characteristics. These characteristics may include geographical birthplaces, language, religion, racial or physical attributes, history and customs. These external characteristics may not necessarily meet one's subjective affiliation with the ethnic group. Subjective affiliation is defined as one's sense of identity and feelings of belonging with the ethnic group. The subjective identification with an ethnic group leads to the development of a social identity based on ethnic-group membership.

What does it mean to have a bicultural identity? Can second-generation Indo-Canadian youth be identified as bicultural? Phinney and Rotheram (1987) state that "bicultural identity refers to an identification of oneself with two ethnic groups" (p. 39). From our personal perspective and experience, it is evident that second-generation Indo-Canadian youth indeed have bicultural identities. Given their exposure to both cultures on a daily basis, second generation Indo-Canadian youth tend to relate to and identify with both the Indian culture and the Canadian culture.

Racial/Cultural Identity Development Model

Sue and Sue's (2007) Racial/Cultural Identity Development Model describes the conflicts an individual encounters while trying to find his/her identity in relation to his/her own culture, the dominant culture and the oppressive relationship between the two inherently different cultures. The model is made up of five stages: the Conformity Stage, the Dissonance Stage, the Resistance and Immersion Stage, the Introspection Stage and the Integrative Stage.

According to Sue and Sue (2007), in the conformity stage, "minority persons are distinguished by their unequivocal preference for dominant cultural values over their own" (p. 99) and so an individual in this stage strives for identification with the dominant culture. Changing appearance, such as dress and hair, in order to be more like the dominant culture is typical in this stage. In the Dissonance Stage, the individual is in conflict between appreciating the minority heritage and looking at it as an inhibitor. In the Resistance and Immersion Stage, the minority person resists conforming to the dominant culture and instead strongly values and appreciates the minority ethnic heritage. The individual in this stage may accept the dominant culture as oppressive and consequently may have strong reactions against it. The Introspection Stage involves the individual's deliberation about the cost and benefits of having negative feelings toward the dominant culture. At this stage, "the individual begins to discover that this level of intensity of feelings (anger directed toward the White society) is psychologically draining and does not permit one to really devote more crucial energies to understanding themselves or to their own racial-cultural group" (Sue & Sue, 2008, p. 104). Lastly, the Integrative Stage involves the individual's acceptance of both his/her own ethnic identity and the culture of the dominant society. At this point, the individual is able to accept and reject the values and beliefs from each culture that he or she does not find advantageous or appealing.

Cultural Conflicts

Sikh people take great pride in their religion and culture. Many of them have overcome great obstacles in order to reside in Canada, a country that is quite different from their homeland. Although the values, beliefs and overall culture in Canada often clash with the norms that Indian immigrants are accustomed to, they have nevertheless managed to make themselves comfortable and call the Western world their home. So, what does this mean for the immigrants' children, who are born and raised in Canada? They seem to be caught in the middle of two distinctly different cultures.

As we mentioned above, Indo-Canadian youth may start to question their identity and wonder what cultural background they actually belong to. Parents often try to preserve their Indian culture by pushing traditional values on their children. At the same time, these youth are challenged daily to adhere to the norms of Canadian society. Not surprisingly, conflict between parents and children arises because of differences between Indian culture and Canadian culture. Although there may be many areas of internal self-conflicts for Indo-Canadian adolescents, as well as many areas of discord between them and their first-generation parents, the most prevalent themes that have affected youth identity are discussed below.

Racial Discrimination

Ghuman's (1994) study, which had an Indo-Canadian sample and a British Asian sample, showed a significant difference from our research in terms of racial comments directed at youth. Although Ghuman noted that the British Asian participants reflected on their personal experience of racism, not one member of his Indo-Canadian sample admitted to having met any overt racial prejudice. This was contradictory to our research, which concluded that the majority of Indo-Canadian participants had personally experienced racism from white people. Mann-Kahalma's (1997) study reflected the same conclusion. The Indo-Canadian women within her study also spoke of their direct experiences with racism.

In our study, the racism that participants encountered led them to question their ethnic background and their sense of identity. The majority of respondents reported that in childhood and adolescence they tended to back away from Indo-Canadian culture and adopt Western views because of overt racism. This response is congruent with Sue and Sue's (2008) Conformity Stage, when the individual strives for identification with the dominant culture. The young women showed signs of this stage as they tended not to make friends with Indo-Canadians, refused to speak their native language and spoke of feelings of shame when they were forced to interpret for their parents. Although the women could not change their Indo-Canadian appearance on the outside, they attempted to convince themselves and others they were purely Canadian on the inside. The participants felt there was no easy compromise between the two cultures, and therefore they moved in a direction to fit in with the majority culture.

Family Structure

The Punjabi culture, like many collectivist cultures, is all about the family, and decisions are typically made in consideration of the collective family benefit rather than individual advantage. This is not to say that the family-centred approach exists only within Punjabi families; however, it seems that even the most personal decisions, like dating (if it is allowed), marriage, education and career goals are set with family norms and allowances in mind. In the case of many Punjabi-Sikh youth growing up in Canada, these family restrictions and expectations add pressure to the everyday decisions of how and where they express themselves as individuals and as members of a larger cultural community. We use the following descriptions to illustrate the ideals of many, but not necessarily all, Punjabi-Sikh families as experienced in BC.

- Family is number one.
- One sacrifices personal happiness for family expectations and traditions.
- The opinion of society matters; behave accordingly.
- The household speaks Punjabi.
- Indian food is often eaten in the home for breakfast, lunch and dinner.
- A disconnect exists between the home culture and the dominant Western culture outside of the home.
- Immigrant parents attempt to raise their children with the cultural values instilled in them when they themselves were young.
- On occasions of remembrance, celebration and thanks, family and friends gather together to read from the *Guru Granth Sahib*, remember God with their words and sing religious hymns called *shabads*.
- Religious faith is present in the house (e.g., a designated prayer area with the *Guru Granth Sahib*; pictures of the Sikh gurus around the house; shabads playing on the music system; listening to or watching broadcasts from Shri Harmandir Sahib Gurudwara).

A major social factor that determines the family culture of Punjabis in BC is the rural/ urban division. This division speaks to some of the cultural differences found in family structures of immigrants coming from rural lifestyles in Punjab and immigrants coming from city lifestyles in Punjab. We have seen this split most often in new immigrant and second-generation families. Another social factor influencing family dynamics is the length of time families have been in Canada, specifically focussing on multiple generations being born and raised in Canada. Cultural norms and values, as we have seen among local social circles, of those who are third-, fourth- or fifth-generation Punjabi-Sikh have a layered, complex dynamic. Here, rural or city lifestyles may play a role, though perhaps less formative in this context than in first- or second-generation families. Of course, the factor of social experiences and personal values also comes into play. Trends that we have observed in our own cultural communities are noted here, though there is some presence of individual difference even in this collectivist culture.

We are also inclined to mention that there are families who belong to the category of Sikh/Indo-Canadian/Punjabi and who define themselves outside of many of the characteristics we have listed. It is important to remember that while there are some striking commonalities among family life in the Punjabi Indo-Canadian community, we cannot say that there are universal truths among Punjabi families.

Having listed several characteristics, we believe it is clear that family life, religion and culture are closely related in this specific Punjabi-Sikh context. Some families choose religion to justify any or all of their actions in ways that religion serves to excuse any or all of their behaviours. We have seen this, and at times feel this use of religion leads to negative perspectives on religion. Some people chose to act at whim, and when questioned about their actions, they fall back on a religious excuse in attempt to make an action less offensive. On the other hand, some families sincerely believe the Sikh values they have learned and live their lives in accordance with these principles. In our experiences, it is the people who hold the religion close to their hearts, and those who are inspired by their faith to act in genuine ways, from whom we have a true sense of what it is to be a Sikh in Canada. Our experiences with those of other religious backgrounds are similar.

Being a minority has its challenges and the cultural dynamics that have followed our ancestors from Punjab, India, to Canada definitely pose challenges. To provide insight into the immigrant experience, we offer the following typical story.

After speaking to Mom a few days ago and discussing what it was like for her coming on her own to Canada when she was 19, I was surprised at what she had to say. Surprised not at the fact that she had challenges and cultural adjustments to deal with when she first arrived, but surprised that after more than three decades, she was still experiencing some cultural adjustment. Is it possible that because I was born and raised here in British Columbia, it is easier for me to overlook the significance of this cultural adjustment? When I had time to process what Mom had told me, indeed, it made a lot of sense and was also very noticeable. I suppose there is something to be said for the comment that you can see only what you are trying to look for, and that there is more than meets the eye!

Mom was born and raised in northern India and belongs to a Sikh-Punjabi family. Her parents and grandmother attended the gurudwara on a daily to weekly basis; but as mom was a young and active teenager, she was involved in a number of activities and did not attend the gurudwara as often as her elders. Mom has told me on a number of occasions of her trips to various gurudwaras with her grandmother. While Mom has said that she is not extremely religious, it seems, from her stories of her grandmother, that going to gurudwaras, listening to *katha* (the oral tradition of sharing Sikh stories and history) and participating in religious activities was a means through which she connected with people who were close to her. Mom completed post-graduate education and, in combination with her people skills and business savvy, continued into a successful career with tourism and hotel management. She was working in an environment bustling with tourists and celebrities — a Westernized Indian approach to hospitality — and intra- and intercultural exposure. Mom has the personality of a go-getter. She is an independent thinker who handles challenges with success and finesse, and embraces spontaneity and adventure when she can. She was that little girl in Ambala who had dreams to have a small house and a small and close-knit family. Material possessions were not where her interests lay; connections, of the genuine and sincere variety, were and are what her dreams are about.

Dad was born in north India and also belonged to a Sikh family. He came to Canada 40 years ago, when he was in his early twenties. He came as a graduate student on scholarship, the first in his family and extended family to come to Canada. Needless to say, it was a big deal. When I talked to Dad about his experience here in his early years, it sounded like there was a certain amount of pressure. It sounded like he had no other choice but to make it work in Canada. He needed to make school work; he needed to make sure he had a way to earn money; he needed to make sure he could pay off his loan for his air ticket, for which the mortgage on his uncle's house was collateral.

Dad was from a modest Sikh family and was born in the city of Patiala, in Punjab. During the partition of India in 1947, both Dad's parents and Mom's parents migrated from present-day Pakistan to present-day India, leaving all that they had known up to that point in their lives (their village, home, friends and relations, jobs, etc.). During the partition, certain states bore the brunt of the change. The northwestern state of Punjab was one. Both Mom's and Dad's families were uprooted from present-day Pakistan and were forced to make new homes for themselves in what was newly defined as India. Family connectedness is typically of high importance in Indian families, and being uprooted in such a way had its implications on family dynamics for many families.

Dad had one older sister; he was the eldest son out of four siblings and had a certain level of responsibility added to this role of being the eldest son. My grandfather spent a lot of one-on-one time with Dad to ensure Dad's academic success. Generally Dad's family was quite religiously inclined. The norm in his family was not to socialize with drinks and gala affairs; instead, they socialized during religious celebrations and prayer gatherings. After successfully completing his bachelor's and master's degrees in India, in his early twenties Dad left to pursue further studies in mathematics in Canada. Dad mentioned that this new change made for some very stressful times. As he went on to explain some challenges, his approach to the difficulties seemed to be driven by a sense of familial encouragement and responsibility. Although it was his first time away from his home in India and things felt strange, giving up was never an option. Dad's family believed in him; they were proud of him and made grandiose gestures to rally his success as a graduate student in Canada (i.e., a close uncle mortgaged his house as collateral for dad's air ticket to Canada, and other family provided moral support and encouragement because they knew frequent communications between Dad in Canada and relatives in India would be difficult). An investment of trust, responsibility and a once-in-a-lifetime opportunity was placed on Dad as he made his way over to Ontario to the University of Toronto to continue his studies.

Dad met the challenges that arose from a new life in Canada. Coming from a fairly sheltered daily routine in Chandigarh to a big city on the other side of the world surely had a few difficulties. Dad did not cook, did not speak English well (though he could read and write in English with greater ease), had not lived away from home, did not know anyone and was a turban-wearing Sikh male. Dad had very limited contact with his family, the ideal support network, as communication was expensive and written communication could take a very long time. It sounds like a lonely time, and Dad confirmed this. He had one support system that he could take wherever he went, no matter how far away he was from his family: regardless of the fact that tough times would be upon him, he had his Sikh faith.

The Sikh faith was a large part of Dad's life growing up. His family quite often held prayer ceremonies, which they called *path* (pronounced *paaaw-T)*. He described himself as being quite religious when he arrived for the first time in Toronto. While he was studying at U of T, the troubles and great stressors of adjusting to life in Canada and being so isolated posed problems. After some time at U of T, he applied to several other universities and got accepted to many based on his academic standing. The extra study time his father spent with him as a young boy paid off, and because of Dad's academic success, he was accepted to Wharton School (University of Pennsylvania), University of Alberta and a few other good universities in North America. Dad decided to go to U of A, as they offered him funding, which he needed in order to study.

As Dad was in the process of switching universities, he was without funding. This posed a problem because he was on a student visa, which restricted his employment options. His option was to get back into another university quickly so he could continue to collect funding and work on campus. Dad's early life in Canada, for the most part, was centred around university life. He supported himself through academic scholarships, advanced in his academic career by completing three graduate degrees and was employed on campus as well. After completing his studies and various jobs on and off campus, he went to India to get married. In 1975, my parents were married in India. Mom was married in her late teens, and Dad was in his mid-twenties. He had been a graduate student in many universities across Canada for some years when they got married. It was an arranged marriage, as were many of the marriages at that time. A short while after the wedding, Dad went back to Canada to get things set for Mom's arrival. Dad was situated in Edmonton at this time. He had finished graduate school with three graduate degrees. He looked for a secure job to start his married life. He had applied for many but was repeatedly told that he was "over-qualified" or that he didn't have "Canadian experience" — thin excuses for not getting a job that one was qualified for; but something better came along. Dad applied for a job with a provincial regulatory agency. He was hesitant to apply, anticipating another rejection and waste of time. But he got the job and was soon off to Vancouver to work.

Mom said that she was very happy to get away from India. A change was due and going to live in Canada provided that opportunity for her. It was June 1975 when she arrived in the Vancouver International Airport for the first time. As she was telling about her arrival to Canada, she was remembering that they lived in a beautiful one-bedroom apartment on Granville, with 24-hour security. She remembers it fondly. However, life in Vancouver was something she was living, though not enjoying. "Everything was so different," she said to me many times while describing that time in her life. She applied for many jobs and, though she had a very good command of English, found it difficult to get a job. "People wouldn't give me a job because I was young; they would tell me that I didn't have Canadian experience." Although Mom was happy to be away from life in India, she was feeling homesick in Vancouver: "The devil you know is better than the devil you don't. I'd step outside and notice the lack of people. I really missed the food I'd eaten in India. I didn't know how to cook at that time. Not having friends, not knowing people, not knowing the system made things very difficult." From what Mom was saying, it sounded like times in India were challenging but irrespective of that, at least when she was there she could function in the culture she knew well and live in familiar settings. "In India it's not lonely. People are all around; you can make contacts whenever and wherever you go out." She describes her life in Canada as lonely. Though years have passed and she has had a multitude of experiences that have deepened her understanding, feelings, learning and love, it is lonely for her here. She describes living in Canada like living in a bubble, or like "living in your own world." Mom goes on to say, "It's like you are living in your own little India within Canada." Mom says there is a disconnection between the two worlds of India and Canada; they do not blend into one another: "There is this disconnect with one exception; the one thing that permeates the bubble is the necessity to work and pay taxes."

Things started to change for the better. Mom found particular new foods that she could enjoy a little (i.e., KFC), and while she still missed Indian food, this delicious spiced chicken was a treat. And thanks to the gurudwara, she was making social connections. At this early point in my parents' lives, this was the only social connection present. The gurudwara not only served as a place of religion and worship but also as a place to connect with others and make friends. Mom, though not strictly religious, was attending the gurudwara as a way to connect with others. This was, and is, a common function of the gurudwara for many Sikh community members. Mom also mentioned how fellow Sikhs would approach them while they were out and about, because of Dad's easy-to-identify Sikh turban, which he still wears. The recognition of one of the five Ks of the Sikh religion, the *kase* (turban) that dad wore also happened to lead to social connection in addition to a religious/spiritual way of life.

Although many of us are familiar with certain religious or cultural stereotypes, it is important to note that while the family characteristics I've listed above are common, there are many Sikh families that are more culturally or interculturally blended. The blending I'm speaking of is of a physical–ethnic nature, or of a social–cultural one. These families' lives can look quite different from "typical." There are many Indo-Canadians who enjoy the challenge of living "atypically": to have the courage to oppose ingrained norms if these norms don't work for them. This takes strength, guts, confidence and a strong sense of self. To embrace cultural challenges takes a strong individual and a supportive family. Thanks to the unconditional love and support of parents, the wisdom of their experiences and the first-hand knowledge of one's own, one can understand that family life is what one makes it. Indo-Canadian family life in various integrated forms is based in balancing both the individual focus and the family focus (Berry, 1997; Berry, 2005; Berry, Phinney, Sam & Vedder, 2006; Rumbaut, 2005; Tadmor & Tetlock, 2006).

Implications of Gender

Studies conclusively show that issues surrounding dating have not changed over the years and continue to be a source of conflict in the family home. Mann-Kahalma's (1997) research found that young women were still expected to adhere to the "good girl" phenomenon, which includes being passive, obedient and virginal. The same rules do not apply to their male counterparts because males do not hold the responsibility of the family honour. This distinction often leaves females resentful and angry.

The issue of dating is something parents are reluctant to change their views on, especially where their daughters were concerned. According to Wakil, Siddique and Wakil (1981), this is more of a "core belief" rather than of "pragmatic value." The changes in parents tended to be on issues that are more pragmatic in nature rather than the core beliefs of the family. Daughters are considered the repository of the family honour. Consequently, parents put more restrictions on their daughters in order to prevent the family honour from being tarnished.

Arranged Marriages

It is clear that the idea of arranged marriages is evolving to meet the considerations of second-generation Indo-Canadians. Parents are lifting their rigid standards around arranged marriages in hopes of finding a common ground that will not eliminate the notion altogether. Instead of being the sole determiners of their children's marital future, parents are proceeding only with approval from their children. Overall, the second generation appears ambivalent to the idea of an arranged marriage for themselves and strongly believe they should be a part of the process. Young women still fantasize about finding an ideal match on their own. Wakil et al. (1981) found Canadian-born children were generally unwilling to buy the traditional idea that love comes after marriage; instead, young women tended to adopt the Canadian culture's emphasis on romantic love.

Although some parents have modified the tradition of arranged marriage to accommodate the wishes of their Canadian born children, they still believe that the decision should not be left solely to the children. The change in the traditional marriage is summarized by Vidynathan and Naidoon (1991) as follows: greater flexibility in parental authority in the host country as compared to the ancestral country and an increase in the independence and decision-making powers of the second generation.

Studies on Indo-Canadians clearly show that they exhibit adoptive behaviour after discovering that an attitude of compromise and balance is required for optimal functioning in the host country (Vidynathan & Naidoon, 1991).

Growing up as a Sikh Male versus Growing up as a Sikh Female

After speaking to a handful of people, both male and female, who belong to Punjabi-Sikh families in Canada, we would say there is a difference between the treatment of males and females in the Sikh community. While we can say with certainty that the differences vary from family to family, and not all differences in treatment are negative, they do exist. When we asked why there is a difference, we came up with the following reasons.

Punjabi culture is patriarchal, and in Punjabi families, girls are thought to be a temporary presence in their families of origin. The girl child has been viewed as someone to marry to a suitable partner, after which she leaves her family house to live with her husband and then formally "belongs" to her husband's family. An example of this detachment of the daughter from her family is seen in the ceremony following the Sikh wedding, a ceremony called the *doli*. At the doli, the bride's family wishes her farewell; this is the time when everyone is expected to cry. The rationale is that the bride should be terribly sad to leave her family home, as the symbolic ceremony emphasizes detaching from her family and adopting a new one. It is common for brides and their families to cry with the same intensity whether she is moving 10 minutes away from her house, across the country or across the world. In the Sikh-Punjabi tradition, daughters are expected to leave their families of origin after marriage; sons are expected to stay close to and/or live with their parents, before and after they are married. This is especially true for the eldest son. One of the views I have heard explaining the difference between girl children and boy children is that boy children are a better investment for the future as they are expected to stay near their families and financially support and care for their parents in old age.

Individual Stories from Indo-Canadians

Four informal interviews were done with three Punjabi-Sikh Indo-Canadian males and one Punjabi-Sikh Indo-Canadian female. Lived experiences and thoughts about the differences between girl children and boy children in Punjabi Indo-Canadian families were discussed and analyzed. Aside from the gender focus, conversations were not structured. The goal of these interviews was to listen to and understand what interviewees were communicating about their experiences and understanding. Interviewees selected were previously known to the interviewer.

H.S.P.'s Story

H.S.P. is a 20-something male university student. Once turban-wearing, he proudly wears his Punjabi-Sikh identity and shares it with friends. Speaking with him reinforced the ideas about marriage and its relation to male and female differences in a Sikh-Punjabi family. One point came up repeatedly in this conversation. H.S.P. felt that the treatment of girls versus boys and the general Sikh family structure differed depending on whether the family traditions originated from Punjabi rural village life or from city life in India. He notes that the majority of BC's Sikh population is based in traditions of village life, so gender differences are typically more noticeable.

According to H.S.P., boys are viewed as the ones who will pass on family name, tradition and honour. They are expected to provide for the family. On the other hand, girls are considered to be guests in their own home. Once they marry, they leave the family and become part of their husband's family. Male family members, especially the father and eldest son, are seen as the representatives of the family. In our understanding, this is the patriarchal family structure at work. A holiday, called *Rakhri*, to celebrate brothers takes place in August and is marked by sisters tying a colourful piece of string on their brother's wrist while the brother promises to protect her always. The male role can thus be understood as a protective role in the structure of a Sikh family.

Girls are seen as the keepers of family honour, respect and purity. In society at large, not just in Sikh-Punjabi society in BC, these qualities are thought of as virtues to be protected. In this family structure, girls may have limited freedom in their social interactions in order to maintain virtues that in turn maintain their social desirability as a bride. A boy will likely be raised with the values of marrying, having children, managing the house and earning enough to support his wife, children and parents. A girl will likely be raised with values of maintaining her suitability as a desirable prospect for marriage: adding to her skills, getting an education, keeping up personal appearance and trying to maintain fair skin (the ideal Punjabi beauty is fair skinned). Parents generally place strong emphasis on getting married; traditionally, after a girl's parents get her married off, their main responsibility as parents is done. H.S.P. made a point of mentioning in our conversation that "parents just want the best for their children." This is an important point that prompts further thoughts. How parents define "the best" can depend on many factors. In this case we are talking about Punjabi cultural values and Sikh religious influences in relation to life in Canada.

R.R.'s Story

R.R. is a 30-something male. He is a turban-wearing young health professional from a Sikh family. He emphasized that he has noticed that Punjabi families tend to be more protective of girls and more lenient with boys. Girls are expected to act within "guidelines" and show restraint. R.R. illustrated this protectiveness of girls in the relationship between parents and girl children and between an older brother and younger sister. Another interesting point he mentioned was the social competition between Punjabi families in relation to how they raise their children. A competition often exists to see who can raise the most socially and culturally acceptable children. How one's children grow up is kept under a watchful eye of not only the family but the Punjabi-Sikh community at large. If the youngsters turn out to be stand-up citizens, socializing in a "good" crowd, working toward developing their future and generally having good heads on their shoulders, then that is best. In this case, it is not only the family who treats boys and girls differently but the community itself that constructs genders differences. If a girl deviates from favourable social standards, her reputation in the community is harmed more than if she were male. There seems to be a stricter eye watching the girls than the boys. When asked why people were so protective of girls, R.R. thought "maybe it was passed down through generations."

A.R.'s Story

A.R. is a 20-something male. He is a turban-wearing elementary school teacher with views on individual happiness. He discussed the difference in expectations for young adult males versus young adult females. For males, he says, the expectation is to settle down. Once a man has a secure job or career, he is expected to settle down and get married: "There is an expectation to provide for a wife and family. With guys, once they are educated and have a job the emphasis is on the ability to provide financial support." For females, the expectation is to settle down and have children. Having an education is sufficient qualification for settling down. A.R. finds that parents tend to worry about the person when it comes to daughters, versus worrying about the behaviour when it comes to sons. Referring to the current state of differential treatment, A.R. says, "It's a little more open now, a little more equal."

S.C.'s Story

S.C. is a 50-something, professionally employed mother of three and grandmother of two. Born in Kamloops to Punjabi-Sikh parents who had settled in BC before the partition of India in 1947, S.C. was the youngest of five: the first two children were boys and the next three were girls. Both parents worked; her dad worked at the nearby sawmill, like many Punjabi immigrants in BC at that time. S.C. mentioned that when she and her siblings were growing up, the boys always got more food and were allowed to go out more often. A passing comment she made about her parents' view of her brothers, in relation to her and her sisters, was simple and significant: "They were boys, they were special, but that is not to say we weren't valued." S.C.'s eldest brother (the first born), second brother (the second born) and eldest sister (the third born) carried the most responsibility in the house. Even as a grade four student her eldest brother was well aware of his role as caretaker of the family. He would rush home after school to be present to greet the rest of the family as they returned home and make sure his siblings made it home safely; he took it upon himself to keep them out of trouble. Her eldest sister also held the role of caretaker; she was in charge of making food for the family and caring for all her siblings, both older and younger. During her childhood, S.C. remembers that there were few Indians living in Kamloops. Her parents were able to find a sense of community and connection at the gurudwara, a finding that reinforces that the social and cultural role of the Sikh temple extended beyond its religious function.

Implications for Counsellors

Dating is not the only realm where males are granted more freedom; rather, they may enjoy the whole social sphere. Although young women are encouraged to pursue their educational and career aspirations, they are restricted in terms of their social freedom. Ghuman's (1994) Indo-Canadian sample did not find girls and males were treated any differently, but interestingly, a very high percentage of his British sample agreed with the fact that boys and girls had differential treatment. Ghuman was surprised by and skeptical of his findings and attributed the difference to the possibility that the Indo-Canadian sample tended to respond with the "desired" response. Ghuman's skepticism arose after speaking to teachers and counsellors who indicated these females were resentful of the differential treatment at home.

Drury's (1991) study in Britain supports the conclusions in our chapter regarding the resentment women felt toward the freedom males were given. However, Drury noted the majority of these women did not rebel from their parents' wishes. Only a small percentage noted they rebelled secretly in order to avoid confrontation with their parents. In our own work, responses were different; participants noted there was a great deal of secrecy in the lives of young Indo-Canadian women. As one participant reported, "Everyone does it; nobody talks about it." Thus, it was possible to conclude from our work that secret lives were a way for some young Indo-Canadian women to cope with the demands of having two distinct cultures. These women found secrecy a workable condition that allowed them to maintain family honour and respectability as well as to fulfill their own needs in the Western world.

Religion and Its Influence on Identity

Conclusions from our work indicate that most participants went to gurudwaras only when there were special religious ceremonies or weddings. The majority of participants reported that they did not believe in the teachings of Sikhism. Out of the five respondents, only one participant revealed her hope in gaining more knowledge about the Sikh gurus and the history of Sikhism. Wakil et al. (1981) found the same results, as parents' enthusiasm for their children to learn the religion did not match that of the young people themselves. Ghuman (1994), however, was left with a different impression in his study of second-generation Indo-Canadians. Ghuman found that although second-generation Indo-Canadians did not know much about their religion, they had a desire to learn more about it.

Evidently the women in our study did not have positive experiences with the Sikh religion. In fact, some women stated the teachings of Sikhism are not reflected in the actions of its followers. As a result of this perceived contradiction, the majority of respondents felt Sikhism was not a faith they wanted to follow. It is interesting to note that the term *Kaur* ("princess") is used to name women and thus reflects a relationship between gender and religion; for men, the term *Singh* ("lion") is used. What these terms define is a sense of gender roles, not necessarily the same or even equal, but rather what it means to be a man or woman.

Acceptance of Being Indo-Canadian

As we noted earlier, our participants felt they had come to accept their ethnicity as being Indo-Canadian, whereas in the past they attempted to resist the Indian culture by assimilating into Canadian culture. The comments made by young Indo-Canadians around the issue of their identities were particularly positive in Ghuman's (1994) study as well. Ghuman was encouraged to see the official Canadian policy of multiculturalism having a positive effect on Indo-Canadian youth. He concluded that the policy helped to foster a sense of pride and security in the youths' bicultural identities.

According to Sue and Sue's (2008) model, these young women are in the Integrative Stage of the Racial/Cultural Identity Development Model. Hence, instead of trying to avoid their ethnic heritage, they have learned to accept it and integrate it into Canadian culture. They have come to embrace both their ethnic identity and the culture of the dominant Canadian society. One participant made an inspiring comment that, "By accepting it [ethnicity], I am accepting myself."

Practical Application of Ethnicity in Counselling

We have a great level of respect for counselling in the way that it can help people realize their own potential and their ability to help themselves. Being students of intercultural communication and psychology, with training in listening and supporting, and experiences as a client, we have various perspectives when it comes to counselling Indo-

Canadians. Here a few points to focus on:

- As a counsellor, you must understand your own biases toward Indo-Canadians.
- Counselling is focussed on the individual, whereas for more collectively oriented people, the individual is only one member of a larger group (i.e., family and community).
- Learn about the cultural values of Indo-Canadian clients. As a client, it is nice to have the counsellor be able to relate to you.
- If you don't know how to relate, do not fake it.

Things to be aware of when a client is coming to see you:

- The client may be seeking counselling secretly.
- In general, there is a stigma associated with counselling. The community may wonder why the "troubled" person cannot seek advice from his/her own family or extended family and why anyone would take concerns to a stranger.
- Clients may face the "what-will-people-say-if-they-find-out" dilemma, where some Indo-Canadians may have difficulties opening up in fear of telling too much.

An important message for counsellors to receive from this chapter is that each Indo-Canadian person is different. That is to say, there are many differences among our Indo-Canadian peers. We encourage you to inform yourself of the social patterns of this cultural community; but remember, the information presented here is just generalization. You will not be able to understand all the Indo-Canadians you meet after just reading this chapter. The chapter is starting place on which counsellors and the general public can build their client–counsellor or Punjabi–non-Punjabi interactions.

So, what does this mean for counsellors? In a country where biculturalism is no longer uncommon and an emphasis is placed on greater multiculturalism, it is essential that counsellors be aware of and integrate skills that reflect the changing needs. Counsellors need to be open, sensitive and receptive to new ways of helping, which may be different from the conventional methods they are accustomed to. If counsellors choose to remain unaware of Indo-Canadian cultural values and if they feel the Western way of life is superior to the Indian way, then their attitudes will likely lead to conflict with and alienation from their Indo-Canadian clients. On the other hand, if counsellors are empathetic and non-judgemental and cultivate a positive outlook toward their client's ethnic culture, it is more likely that counselling will be a positive experience for the client (Pederson, Draguns, Lonner & Trimble, 2007).

It may be rare for an Indo-Canadian family to come into counselling for conflicts arising at home or school. Typically, the family relies on relatives or friends to help with conflicts and difficulties they are encountering. Assanand, Dias, Richardson and Waxler-Morrison (1990) state,

> There is little experience with social service agencies and sometimes distrust of all government servants. . . . South Asian families are likely to use social service agencies only as a last resort, after seeking help from family, friends, the temple, or a physician. (p. 179)

Likewise, Segal (1991) says, "Even when counselling is sought voluntarily, they often feel they have been reduced to a level beneath their dignity and pride" (p. 239).

Awareness of Values

It may be impossible for counsellors to know all the values and traditions of the Indo-Canadian community, and thus, they may need to rely on their ethnic clients to educate them on the issues they bring into counselling. Sodowsky, Kwan and Pannu (1995) identify some of the values inherent to Asian Americans, which seemingly apply to the Indo-Canadian population as well. The values and characteristics that may come forth in counselling sessions are as follows:

- Silence, non-confrontation, moderation in behaviour, self-control, patience, humility, modesty and simplicity are seen as virtues.
- Respect for older persons and the elderly is expected.
- Less value is placed on individualism, and higher value is placed on family. The family and society exist to maximize the individual.
- Social harmony is achieved through structured family relationships that have clearly defined codes of behaviour, including language use and hierarchical roles.
- There is high respect for parents, and filial piety is assumed. Individual family members seek the honour and good name of the family and protect it from shame. Family duties and obligations take precedence over individual desires. Social control is achieved through family demands for obedience and fulfillment of obligations. There is a strong sense of duty toward family.
- There is a high regard for learning.
- Sexuality and sexual relationships are supposed to be treated with modesty and a degree of formality. Heterosexual affection is generally not demonstrative.
- When an individual is ready for marriage, the family participates in finding a suitable match, so there is less need for dating.

- Importance is attached to preserving the culture and the original religion. Marrying within the ethnic group is expected; marriage outside the ethnic group may be troubling.

Educational Model

Many Indo-Canadians are faced with the challenges of living in two distinct cultures. As counsellors we need to be aware of what it means to "live in two worlds." Indo-Canadian views and ideas are influenced both by their ethnic culture and by the majority culture. Some of the stressors that may come up in counselling include issues around identity, assimilation, intergenerational conflicts, gender-role conflicts and concerns about interracial conflicts.

In order to deal with some of these issues, Segal (1991) proposed an education model. Because Indo-Canadians are disinclined to come to counselling, a lecture-style presentation, which would include group discussion, may be an indirect alternative to counselling. Segal recommends starting with a clarification of mutual values. Ibrahiam, Ohnishis and Sandhu (1997) explain that this relational style allows counsellor and clients to explore both value systems, thereby increasing the trust level as the clients get to know that the counsellor is objective about his/her assumptions and recognizes the boundaries of his/her cultural identity. Segal then states that it is important for clients to understand the myths regarding the Canadian culture and lifestyle. Counsellors should review adolescent psychology and peer-group pressures within the group setting. Fourth, Maydas and Elliot (as cited in Segal) state there should be a discussion about cultural conflicts that occur when accommodating, adapting, assimilating and integrating into a new culture. Finally, various implications and the inevitable changes of immigration should be addressed.

In dealing with specific bicultural issues, an intervention goal for parents is to broaden their intellectual understanding of the struggles facing the youth who are torn between two cultures. For first-generation Indo-Canadians, this education model helps them gain emotional acceptance of the unavoidable changes inherent in their decision to settle in a culture that is often contrary to their own Indian lifestyle (Segal, 1991). For second-generation adolescents who are struggling with their bicultural identities, one goal is to bridge the communication gap between themselves and their parents. There has often been a breakdown in communication due to turmoil in the home. A facilitation that opens the gates to communication benefits both generations. Another goal is to imbue a sense of pride in adolescents' bicultural background by exploring the benefits of being bicultural and bilingual. Another option to the conventional counselling style may be group therapy, in which adolescents or parents can share their experiences with one another and develop support networks (Segal, 1991).

Specific Interventions

Given that the alternative methods proposed by Segal (1991) are not effective, Indo-Canadians may choose to use family or individual counselling. Supplementary guidelines are proposed for counsellors by Ibrhaim et al. (1997):

- The client will need the respect of his/her person, cultural identity and world view. Clients will need a mutually respectful relationship and a sense of autonomy. They will be less inclined to follow through on interventions that they feel they have not come up with on their own.
- Understand the client's level of acculturation and identity status before planning an intervention.
- Clarify the client's spiritual identity before deciding on goals and outcomes. An ideal counselling strategy would incorporate the ideas of both spiritual and identity development because a major source of anxiety involves keeping a balance in both these areas.
- Multi-dimensional intervention is helpful, using the client's cognitive, behaviour, ecological, spiritual and other relevant domains. Use models of counselling that support both individualism and relational aspects.
- Recognize the importance of the life stage and age of the client. Within age and life stage, also evaluate the impact of gender.
- Never assume that the client does not or cannot understand your attitudes and non-verbal attitudes. This culture carries high non-verbal content.
- Recognize the role of humility in the client's cultural identity and do not assume the client has a poor self-concept.
- Respect the integrity and individualism of the clients. Indo-Canadians are individualistic within the familial context.
- Allow the client to educate the counsellor regarding the client's specific identification level between his/her ethnic subculture, religion, values and world view and the larger society.

Conclusion

The studies completed on Indo-Canadian populations have not been conclusive. In particular, the study done by Ghuman (1994) seemed to be contradictory on several issues. Specifically, his study concluded that the Indo-Canadians did not encounter any racial discrimination, females were not treated differently than males and the second generation had a desire to learn about their Sikh religion. Other studies, including the research we have presented in this chapter, indicate the opposite. At the same time, Ghuman did note his skepticism and believed the respondents reported a "desired" response. All studies agree that arranged marriages are evolving to meet the demands of second-generation Indo-Canadians and that parents' stance on dating has not changed in regards to their daughters.

Although Indo-Canadians may not readily seek out counselling, it is important for counsellors to be aware of the group's values and stressors if clients do choose to use counselling services. In order to assist Indo-Canadians through their challenges, counsellors must know how to help, rather than hinder, the counselling process.

References

Abouguendia, M., & Noels, K.A. (2001). General and acculturation-related daily hassles and psychological adjustment in first- and second-generation South Asian immigrants to Canada. *International Journal of Psychology*, 36, 163–173. doi: 10.1080/00207590042000137

Assanand, S., Dias, M., Richardson, E., & Waxter-Morrison, N. (1990). The South Asians. In N. Waxler-Morrison, J. Anderson & E. Richardson (Eds.), *Cross-cultural caring: A handbook for health professionals in western Canada*. Vancouver, BC: University of British Columbia Press.

Benet-Martinez, V., Lee, F., & Leu, J. (2006). Biculturalism and cognitive complexity: Expertise in cultural representations. *Journal of Cross-Cultural Psychology*, 37, 386–407. doi: 10.1177/0022022106288476

Benet-Martinez, V., Leu, J., Lee, F., & Morris, M. (2002). Negotiating biculturalism: Cultural frame switching in biculturals with oppositional versus compatible cultural identities. *Journal of Cross-cultural Psychology*, 33, 492–516. doi: 10.1177/0022022102033005005

Berry, J.W. (1997). Immigration, acculturation, and adaptation. *Applied Psychology: An International Review*, 46, 5–68. doi: 10:1111/j.1464-0597.1997.tb01087

Berry, J.W. (2005). Acculturation: Living successfully in two cultures. *International Journal of Intercultural Relations*, 29, 697–712.

Berry, J.W., Phinney, J.S., Sam, D.L., & Vedder, P. (2006). Immigrant youth: Acculturation, identity, and adaptation. *Applied Psychology: An International Review*, 55, 303–332.

Dorn, A.W., & Gucciardi, S. (2011). The sword and the turban: Armed force in Sikh thought. *Journal of Military Ethics*, 10, 52–70. Routledge. doi: 10.1080/15027570.2011.562026

Drury, B. (1991). Sikh girls and the maintenance of an ethic culture. *New Community*, 17(3), 387–400.

Ghuman, P.A.S. (1994). *Coping with two cultures: British Asian and Indo-Canadian adolescents*. Clevedon: Multilingual Matters Ltd.

Guzder, J., & Krishna, M. (2005). Mind the gap: Diaspora issues of Indian origin women in psychotherapy. *Psychology and Developing Societies*, 17, 121–138. doi: 10.1177/097133360501700203

Ibrahim, F., Ohnishi, H., & Sandhu, D. (1997). Asian American identity development: A culture specific model for South Asian Americans. *Journal of Multicultural Counselling and Development*, 25, 34–50.

Kondapalli, R. (2011). Revealed: The golden temple. *Discovery Channel*. Retrieved from http://www.youtube.com/watch?feature=player_embedded&v=Oeo4BDViHcM

Mann-Kahalma, P. (1995). *Intergenerational conflict and strategies of resistance: A study of young Punjabi Sikh women in the Canadian context*. Unpublished master's thesis, University of Victoria, Victoria, British Columbia, Canada.

Mogelonsky, M. (1995). Asian Indians. *American Demographics*, 17, 32–39.

Pedersen, P., Draguns, J., Lonner, W., & Trimble, J. (Eds.). (2007). *Counselling across cultures*. Newbury Park, CA: Sage Publications.

Rai, J. (2011). Khalistan is dead! Long live Khalistan! *Sikh Formations: Religion, Culture, Theory* (pp. 1–41). Middlesex, UK: Routledge. doi: 10.1080/17448727.2011.561607

Rosenthal, D. (1997). Ethnic identity development in adolescents. In J.S. Phinney and M. Rotheram (Eds.), *Children's ethnic socialization: Pluralism and development*. Newbury Park, CA: Sage Publications.

Rotheram, M., & Phinney, J.S. (1997). Introduction: Definition and perspectives in the study of children's ethnic socialization. In J.S. Phinney and M. Rotheram (Eds.), *Children's ethnic socialization: Pluralism and development*. Newbury Park, CA: Sage Publications.

Rumbaut, R.G. (2005). Sites of belonging: Acculturation, discrimination, and ethnic identity among children of immigrants. In T.S. Weiner (Ed.), *Discovering successful ways in children's development: Mixed methods in the study of childhood and family life* (pp. 111–164). Chicago, IL: University of Chicago Press.

Segal, U.A. (1991). Cultural variables in Asian Indian families. *Families in Society: The Journal of Contemporary Human Services*, 72(4), 233–242.

Shani, G. (2005). Beyond Khalistan? Sikh diasporic identity and critical international theory. *Sikh Formations: Religion, Culture, Theory* (pp. 57–74). Middlesex, UK: Routledge. doi: 10.1080/17448720500132565

Sodhi, P. (2008). Bicultural identity formation of second-generation Indo-Canadians. *Canadian Ethnic Studies*, 40, 187–199.

Sodowsky, G.R., Kwan, K.K., & Pannu, R. (1995). Ethnic identity of Asians in the United States. In J.G. Ponterotto, J.M. Casas, L.A. Suzuki & C.M. Alexander (Eds.), *Handbook of multicultural counselling*. Thousand Oaks, CA: Sage.

Sue, W., & Sue, D. (2008). *Counselling the culturally different: Theory and practice* (5th ed.). New York: John Wiley and Sons.

Tadmor, C.T., & Tetlock, P.E. (2006). Biculturalism: A model of the effect of second-culture exposure on acculturation and integrative complexity. *Journal of Cross-Cultural Psychology*, 37, 173–190. doi: 10.1177/0022022105284495

Vaidyanathan, P., & Naidoo, J. (1991). Asian Indians in western countries: Cultural identity and the arranged marriage. In N. Bleichrodt and P.J.D. Drenth (Eds.), *Contemporary issues in cross-cultural psychology*. Amsterdam: Swets and Leitlinger.

Wakil, R.S., Siddique, C.M., & Wakil, F.A. (1981). Between two cultures: A study in socialization of children immigrants. *Journal of Marriage and the Family*, 43, 929–940.

Ying, Y., & Lee, P.A. (1999). The development of ethnic identity in Asian-American adolescents: Status and outcome. *American Journal of Orthopsychiatry*, 69, 194–208.

8

Acculturation and Adaptation

Providing Counselling for
Immigrants and Refugees

Yali Li, M. Honoré France,
& María del Carmen Rodríguez

According to Statistics Canada (2012), Canada takes in more immigrants, relative to its size, than any other country in the world: about twice as many people, in proportion to Canada's population (currently some 34 million), as does the United States and four times as many as does the United Kingdom. Trends indicate that the pattern of migration is from developing countries (such as China and India) to developed countries (such as Canada and the United States). The cause of the pattern is complex, emanating not only from economic and political instability in developing countries but also from the demand for labour and the declining birth rate in developing countries. And the phenomenon is not just a North American issue; according to Remak and Chung (2000), "the immigrant and refugee populations have been steadily increasing, causing migration to be a global issue" (p. 200). To be effective with new Canadians, counsellors must understand the adaptation process and how it affects adjustment.

The experiences of migrants — whether by choice through immigration or by chance as refugees — put them at risk for developing emotional and psychological problems. The government of Canada has encouraged and supported immigrants and refugees to come to this country; in the last ten years thousands of people have been granted asylum, with the Canadian government sometimes airlifting thousands of people directly out of a war zone (e.g., refugees from Kosovo). The process of change for these individuals adds a great deal of individual stress, and it challenges the social service system to implement culturally sensitive practices. In order to help the resettlement process, multicultural counsellors need to be equipped to deal with a variety of people speaking different languages and valuing different traditions.

What part of the world do the migrants come from? The largest group of immigrants is coming from Asia (see Table 1); the vast majority of new migrants currently living in Canada are of non-European origin, implying enormous cultural and racial changes to Canadian society. The question of whether adaptation, assimilation or acculturation is the ideal process of adjusting to a new cultural environment is not easy to answer. However, it needs to be addressed by each migrant because the answer will determine, to some extent, the level of comfort and accomplishment the individual achieves while interacting in a new cultural milieu.

What Is Adaptation?

When encountering a new environment and culture, people instinctively respond in various ways. The process of adaptation generally may involve one of three responses: adjustment, reaction or withdrawal. In the case of adjustment, people make changes to reduce conflict and seek harmony with the environment and among cultural groups. In the case of reaction, people try to change the environment and culture to suit their needs. Withdrawal occurs when migrants either want to reduce the pressure of environmental factors or are excluded by the host culture.

A further distinction has been drawn between psychological and socio-cultural adaptation. *Psychological adaptation* refers to a set of internal psychological outcomes, including a clear sense of personal and cultural identity, good mental health and the achievement of personal satisfaction in the new cultural context. *Socio-cultural adaptation* refers to a set of external outcomes that link individuals to their new context, including their ability to deal with daily problems, particularly in the areas of family life, work and school. Psychological adaptation may best be analyzed in the context of the stress and psychopathology approach, while socio-cultural adaptation is more closely linked to the social skills framework (Walton & Kennedy, 1993a; Berry & Sam, 1997).

What Is Acculturation?

In theory, acculturation refers to mutual changes in both migrants and host society as the result of interaction. It may involve cultural learning or a compromise from one or both groups to find common ground for relating to each other. In practice, most changes occur in the non-dominant group or the group with weak vitality (Berry & Sam, 1997; Nielsen

Table 1

Canada — Permanent residents by source area, 2001-2010

Source area	2001	2002	2003	2004	2005	2006	2007	2008	2009	2010
Africa and the Middle East	48 237	46 340	43 674	49 531	49 279	51 858	48 562	51 313	56 153	66 691
Asia and Pacific	132 945	119 057	113 728	114 571	138 048	126 469	112 654	117 481	117 172	135 004
South and Central America	20 211	19 469	20 349	22 254	24 642	24 304	25 890	26 493	26 776	28 354
United States	5 909	5 294	6 013	7 507	9 263	10 943	10 449	11 216	9 723	9 242
Europe and the United Kingdom	43 294	38 867	37 569	41 902	40 906	37 944	39 071	40 649	42 310	41 318
Source area not stated	41	21	15	59	101	122	127	94	37	65
Category not stated	1	0	1	0	2	2	1	2	1	7
Total	250 638	229 048	221 349	235 824	262 241	251 642	236 754	247 248	252 172	280 681

Source: Immigration Canada, 2012

Wire, 2009). The process of acculturation is characterized by four strategies: assimilation, separation, marginalization and integration.

In assimilation, newcomers voluntarily or involuntarily give up their heritage culture in order to move into the host culture. For the host society, assimilation implies the absorption of the migrant minority into the dominant culture to create a homogeneous society. If the choice is involuntary, assimilation involves a total surrender of migrants' ethnic identity, imposing a sometimes painful sacrifice on them and inevitably bringing acculturation stresses (Berry, 1997, 1990; Bourhis et al., 1998).

In separation, newcomers retain their heritage culture and remain apart from the host culture. When there is separation, newcomers isolate themselves, setting up relationships with other social groups or participating only partially in the host society (ISS, 1993). Separation indicates unwillingness to be accepted by the host society and has the nature of reaction.

In marginalization, or anomie, groups lose or reject both their traditional culture and that of the larger society (Berry & Sam, 1997). This scheme is characterized by little possibility for merging into the dominant culture because of racial discrimination or exclusion. This outcome is often accompanied by feelings of alienation, loss of identity and considerable collective and individual confusion and anxiety.

The ideal outcome of cultural acculturation is integration, a strategy most migrants and some countries (such as Canada and Australia) prefer. Integration reflects migrants' desire to maintain key features of their cultural identity while they actively adopt principles and values of the host society and modify their own (Bourhis et. al., 1997; Citizenship and Immigration Canada, 2010).

A good example of acculturation strategies can be found in both American and Canadian history. In North America, European migrants learned to function in the new continent successfully, although conflict developed with First Nations people over control of the land, resulting in subjection of the original inhabitants. In some cases, however, Indigenous people have also modified their structure in order to interact with Europeans.

Adaptation and acculturation lead immigrants and refugees to experience feelings of personal satisfaction once they are able to relate to the host culture — or feelings of isolation and anxiety if they are unsuccessful in establishing relationships with the host culture. The difference between the processes resides mainly in the way in which individuals view and approach the host culture, the rationale for change and the orientation (outcome) of such change.

Ideologies of Acculturation

From the preceding discussion, two important keywords in acculturation can be identified: contact (interaction) and change. The primary question in acculturation is, Who should change and in what direction? Even though change inevitably happens in every culture as the result of contact, it is important to note that most research discusses the cultural changes of immigrants and refugees. This may be simply because the era in which invasion and colonization were a norm is over, and today, in most cases, people migrate for personal safety, peace or the pursuit of a better life.

Migrants are thought to have an inevitably weak vitality and are supposed to change, no matter how they come to the new land (voluntarily or involuntarily) and no matter which country they migrate to. In contemporary societies, the only realistic alternative is that both refugees and immigrants change in order to operate in the host society (Berry & Sam, 1997; Furnham, Bochner, & Ward, 2001). Although refugees and immigrants can be the agents of cultural change, they possess limited power to choose the direction of change.

Two main factors influence the directions or outcomes of acculturation: the state policies and the acculturation orientation of the host society. It is generally agreed that national immigration and settlement policies can have a decisive impact on the acculturation orientation of both migrants and members of the host society (Berry & Sam, 1997; Bourhis et. al., 1997; Boutang & Papademetriou, 1994; Halli & Driedger, 1999). National immigration and settlement policies are generally shaped within one of four clusters of state ideologies, or philosophies: pluralist, civic, assimilationist and ethnist (Bourhis et. al., 1997; Breton, 1988; Drieger, 1989; Helly, 1994). Each of the ideological clusters is likely to produce specific public policies around the acculturation of immigrant and refugee groups. Within the context of state policies, migrants and members of the host community develop their acculturation orientations.

The pluralist ideology expects that migrants adopt the public values of the host country; however, this ideology also upholds that the state has no mandate to define or regulate the private values of its citizens, whose individual liberties in personal domains must be respected. One premise of this approach is that the host community values migrants who maintain key features of their cultural and linguistic distinctiveness while also adopting the public value of the host majority. Canada is an example of a pluralist society, adopting multiculturalism as a mechanism for tolerance of minority cultures.

The civic ideology shares two important features of pluralist ideology: the expectation that migrants adopt the public values of the host country and the understanding that the state has no right to interfere with the private values of individual citizens. However, this ideology is also characterized by an official state policy of non-intervention in the private values of specific groups, including those of immigrant and ethno-cultural minorities. Great Britain is an example of a country espousing a civic ideology.

The assimilationist ideology also includes the expectation that migrants adopt the public values of the host country. However, it expects migrants to abandon their own cultural and linguistic distinctiveness for the sake of adopting the culture and values of the dominant group. The United States, although slowly shifting from its original assimilationist policies to a civic position, is still widely viewed as an example of a country that has adopted the assimilationist ideology.

The ethnist ideology also shares the notions that migrants must adopt the public values of the host nation and that the state has a right to limit the expression of certain aspects of private values, especially those of immigrant minorities. Unlike the other ideologies, however, the ethnist ideology usually defines nation as being composed of a kernel ancestral ethnic group determined by birth and kinship. Migrants who do not share this kinship may never be accepted as legitimate citizens of the state, legally or socially. Most homogenous countries, such as Germany, Japan and Israel, are seen to adopt this position.

Only pluralist and civic societies allow people of various cultural backgrounds living together to form a multicultural society. It is undeniable that state policies cannot represent the views of every member of society, regardless of whether the country is democratic or authoritarian. Thus, different attitudes of the host culture will greatly influence the experience of immigrant and refugee acculturation. In most cases, the culture of the host society is the mainstream culture for groups of migrants to appreciate, share and live by; the acculturation orientations of the members of mainstream culture will either support or constrain such processes. One important factor that distinguishes the immigrant's experience from that of the refugee is that even though acculturation is conditional, in pluralistic societies immigrants by and large enjoy freedom to decide their acculturation orientations (outcomes) or how to acculturate (strategies). Furthermore, because the reasons for migration are different for immigrants and refugees, the acculturation process for refugees may not reflect freedom to choose the direction of acculturation. For refugees, for example, assimilation might be the immediate strategy for change since almost inevitably, refugees may feel an obligation to fit into the culture that has accepted them. However, for both groups, orientations (outcomes) are generally identified within a framework identified by researchers.

Relational Acculturation Orientations

Acculturation conflicts emerge when the acculturation orientations of the host community are different from those of migrants or when both groups experience partial agreement and partial disagreement as a result of their expectations of acculturation orientations. Bourhis et al. (1997) point out that "exclusionists and segregationists are likely to have very negative stereotypes concerning migrants and to discriminate against them in many domains including employment and housing" (p. 384).

In acculturation, Berry (1997) points out that both migrants and members of the host society have to deal with two issues: culture maintenance and development, and inter-ethnic contact and relationship. Berry's acculturation framework is built on the belief that attitudes toward these two issues lead to different outcomes of acculturation. Migrants' acculturation strategies are based on the responses to these questions:

- Is it of value to maintain cultural identity and characteristics?
- Is it of value to maintain relationships with dominant society and other groups?

When acculturation is carried out seeking positive outcomes for interaction, harmony appears, social stability is maintained and migrants feel less stressed. If, in the contrary, acculturation is achieved through withdrawal or exclusion, migrants experience high degrees of stress and their mental health is greatly affected. Meanwhile, the host society experiences racial conflicts, problematic migrants and chaotic social order.

As an example, while migrants were working towards an integration policy, public consultations by the Department of Citizenship and Immigration in 1994 revealed that Canadians want to see migrants assimilated into Canadian society rather than integrated under the official policy of multiculturalism (Citizenship and Immigration Canada, 2010). These differences in the relational outcomes could trigger communication breakdowns between the groups, foster negative inter-group stereotypes, lead to discriminatory behaviours and cause moderate levels of stress among migrants.

Cultural Factors Associated with Migration Stress

According to Furnham and Bochner (2001) there is a connection between geographic movement and a change in psychological well-being. Even though research has not reached consensus that there is a positive relationship between long-term migration and psychological disturbance, there is often a sense of stress that occurs during acculturation, such as lowered mental health status (especially confusion, anxiety, depression), feelings of marginality and alienation, heightened psychosomatic symptom levels and identity confusion (Berry, 1990; Furnham, Bochner & Ward, 2001). Acculturation stress is a phenomenon that may underlie a reduction in the health status of individuals, including physical, psychological and social aspects (Berry, 1990).

Behaviour

The individualistic nature of Canadian society contrasts with the collectivist nature of many migrants' own cultures. While individuality and independence are strong values among the majority population, they are often manifest in other areas that reflect culture. Sports that are team oriented, such as soccer (the world's most popular sport), stand in marked contrast with sports like hockey, where one player can stand out because of his skating ability. Hockey is oriented toward the strengths of individuals and the way players use personal strength to overcome opponents. It is one of the few sports in which violence is a clear factor, as opposed to cooperative behaviour in the way soccer is played. Baseball is another example where a lone individual with a bat is capable of turning the game around with a home run. The ability of a tall and skilful shooter in basketball changes the makeup of the game. Making oneself stand out, whether it be in sports or any other area of endeavour, can be negatively perceived in some cultures.

In some countries, affiliation is a highly prized behaviour because one may get ahead due to various interlocking relationships (e.g., family, friends or the compadre system). Sharing information or even answers on a test may be seen as acceptable because the society prizes connections. Giving gifts for a favour is not seen as a bribe but as another way of showing respect. According to Jay (in Remak & Chung, 2000), some people come from "a culture in which they relied heavily on connections, on who could do what for whom" (p. 581). In Canada, using connections has a negative connotation, as does the giving of gifts that might imply someone wants something. In other societies, authority is prized more than it is in countries like Canada, where civil disobedience has been seen as a virtue.

In counselling, collectivist cultures emphasize that decisions that impact the family should be made in consultation with or even decided by the group rather than the individual. For example, educational and career decisions that don't reflect an impact on the family are very negatively perceived in many immigrant families from Asia.

Communication

Communication styles are very different from culture to culture. Many cultures see eye-to-eye contact as invasive, while in Canada, it is seen as showing honesty (i.e., "look me in the eye and say that"). Expressing how one feels about something, such as giving an opinion, is not acceptable for people who have come from societies in which it is dangerous to share one's opinion. Framing one's opinion in relationship to the group may seem conforming rather than respectful.

Psycho-Social and Individual Factors

Psychological characteristics of acculturation include both pre-contact qualities and those that appear during the acculturation process. The former refer to experiences that predispose one to function more effectively under acculturation pressures. The latter refer mainly to the results of choosing certain acculturation strategies and the lack of a sense of cognitive control over the acculturation process.

In addition to these characteristics, other factors affect migrants' mental health, such as the cultural characteristics of the home country, departure status, age and gender, adaptation competence, prior expectations and goals. A friendly, supportive political and social environment cannot guarantee a smooth acculturation process because acculturation is in many ways a personal journey. For example, those who enjoyed high social status in the home country may not experience the same status in the host society. When a doctor cannot get a job even as a nurse, or a professor must work as a dishwasher, it is hard for migrants not to experience stress and poor mental health, especially for those who have very high expectations of the host country. But the problem, as Furnham, Bochner and Ward (2001) observe, is that high expectations are the very motivation of the immigration decision: "apart from refugees, few people would voluntary migrate if their expectations were too low" (p. 175). Thus, the personal rationale for migrating, personal expectations, choice of strategies and ultimate outcomes are key to determining the level of integration into a new society. Consequently, social support is recognized by most researchers as the most important social factor related to increased immigrant psychological well-being and to a lower probability of physical and mental illness. At the initial stage of acculturation, social support is usually perceived to come from the ethnic community and friendship network. Even though social support from the ethnic community is seen to reduce stress (Berry, 1990), frequent contact with co-nationals may hinder the acculturation progress (Kim, 1988) because newly arrived migrants may not be in the position to offer support and hence get offered very little, which in turn may render them particularly vulnerable to mental breakdown (Furnham, Bochner & Ward, 2001).

Impact of Migration on the Family

Like any type of drastic change, migration can have detrimental effects on the family, particularly if the family came from an agrarian-based society. This is especially true for people with large extended families, which are often left behind in the country of origin. Migration not only disrupts the extended family system but also negates the natural support system that characterizes it. The larger the family, the more likely that some close family members, such as older and younger brothers and sisters, are left with aunts and uncles and separated from their parents. Because occupational patterns are different in the new country, the father, often the principal breadwinner and head of the family, may have to take a job beneath his educational and occupational training, causing loss of self-esteem. In addition, one or more other family members, such as an older child or the mother, may have to work to provide an adequate income to meet the family's financial needs. School-aged children might not be able to ask their parents for help because language barriers and cultural values put the parents in an awkward position of deferring to their children for simple language help. The parents might not feel comfortable in the dominant language and therefore might not feel comfortable being involved in their children's education. According to Juntune, Atkinson and Tierney (2002):

> School districts undergoing rapid increases in diversity often experience a concurrent drop in parental involvement, with school officials blaming cultural values and changing family structures and parents blaming discrimination and insensitivity by school officials. (p. 153)

Cultures differ in their views about various child-rearing practices, such as the roles of mother and father, the expectations of gender, the hierarchy of school personnel and the emphasis on extracurricular activities. North American schooling may present migrants with challenges to family structures and values. Concerns about child abuse that prohibit corporal punishment may also pose an issue for migrants even though these practices may be traditional and may be combined with high levels of empathy, intimacy and support. According to Fontes (2002), "some Latino parents are incorrectly accused of abusing or neglecting their children because non-Latino professionals are puzzled by their unfamiliar yet harmless practices" (p. 31). The following differences in punishment were noted during the 1980s (Fontes, 2002):

- African-Americans are more likely to use an electrical cord, belt or switch applied to the back or bottom;
- Euro–ethnic groups are more likely to use a paddle or open hand to the bottom;
- Asian–ethnic groups may be more likely to slap the face or pull hair.

Over time, migrant children incorporate values much more quickly than do their parents, thus creating potential for cultural conflict in the family. Peers start to have much greater influence than family. If the family is racially different, the children may experience overt or covert racial discrimination that impacts the overall family structure, and "Whether physical or psychological, racially motivated discrimination can have a devastating effect on student learning" (Juntune, Atkinson & Tierney, 2002, p. 154).

One of the most documented negative effects on migrants is the change of economic expectations. As we discussed earlier, many migrants come to Canada expecting to find better jobs and improved living conditions. The fact that they may have to go into a different occupation or endure many years of "upgrading" their credentials produces a great deal of stress. Some migrants are helped by extended family members in their home country either to send money back to the family or to help them immigrate; this expectation may be difficult if not impossible to fulfill. With two incomes becoming more and more a necessity, childcare expenses are often an added burden to economically distressed families.

Obviously, stress has a very negative effect on the psychological and physical well-being of all family members. Alongside various challenges to cultural traditions and values, the family working as a whole to make ends meet adds to the overall stress level, contributing to family dysfunctionality.

The Immigrant Experience: Two Cases

Immigrants to Canada come mostly for a better life economically and socially. Many realize their goals, but many face not only the challenges of being uprooted from their family and the familiar but the prospect of starting over professionally, because their credentials are not accepted or because of other factors having to do with the occupational structure of Canada. In 2001, a study conducted by the Conference Board of Canada revealed that the country loses between $4.1 and $5.9 billion in income annually due to a lack of recognition of the professional qualifications of 540,000 people, including almost 350,000 immigrants. The cases of Antonio and Marianna are typical:

- Antonio is a 36-year-old physician who has recently migrated to Canada from Mexico looking for a better life for himself and his family. He is fluent in Spanish, English and Japanese and has several years of experience as a medical doctor. However, life in British Columbia has not been easy so far. He aspired to get a job at any of the hospitals in the province but instead has found himself working as a waiter in order to maintain his family.
- Mariana is a 38-year-old Chilean nurse who came to Canada with her husband several weeks after her third child was born. Mariana did not speak English when she arrived and confesses she went into a depressive episode shortly after getting established on Vancouver Island. Although she and her husband had carefully planned their relocation, they had not anticipated the difficulties they have faced, such as financial constraints, the lack of jobs and weak language skills.

The Refugee Experience

Unlike immigrants, refugees arrive at their new country not by choice per se but as a matter of survival. While many factors are similar to the immigrant experience, some characteristics are distinct. First, refugees come because they feel forced to leave their homeland for any place that will provide them safety. Their leaving is often marked by psychological and physical torture, either by experience or observation. Studies have found that

> many refugees have been subjected to the atrocities of war, such as experiencing and witnessing torture.... and being forced to commit atrocities, being incarcerated and placed in re-education camps, [and facing] starvation, rape and sexual abuse, and physical beatings and injury. These events occured during the actual war or conflict, in the subsequent escape, as well as in the refugee camps. (Bemak & Chung, 2008, p. 202)

Experiences that affect refugees in a negative way may not be apparent immediately on their arrival in the host country due to refugees' survival instinct, but may appear much later, even after the settlement process is complete. Within refugee groups, older people are more prone to experience psychological disorder as a result of their experiences. Not only do age and ingrained patterns of behaviour provide more challenges, but language skills are sometimes unobtainable. Single men have a difficult time because they arrive in the new country with few family supports and may never be able to reconnect with their old families. Bemak and Chung (2008) stress that

> PTSD (post traumatic stress syndrome) among the clinical refugee populations . . . is estimated to be 50% or higher, and depressive disorders range from 42% to 89%. Different studies have found depression ranging from 15% to 80% in the refugee community. (p. 2002)

Both immigrants and refugees suffer from cultural shock and often experience racism.

Helping Immigrants and Refugees Adapt

An understanding of migrants' cultural identity can help to enhance interpersonal communication and counselling. The basic assumption of the Immigrant Identity Development Model is that counselling can best be achieved by starting where the migrant is in terms of how he/she sees him/herself. Adaptation to the new culture should be measured not in terms of the number of years in the new society but how the migrant feels about him/herself in relation to the new society. The higher the levels of adaptation, the greater the possibilities that cultural approaches reflecting adaptation will be successful. Consider the following stages of identity.

Stage 1 — Compliance: For immigrants and refugees, this stage is characterized by strong desires to adapt and embrace the dominant culture. There is some self-negating of old beliefs as migrants try to adapt to the dominant culture. Adaptation is seen as the only way to survive and they desperately want to fit in and belong.

Stage 2 — Conflict: For immigrants and refugees, this stage arises once the realities of minority status and the difficulties of blending in economically, psychologically and spiritually are experienced. There is confusion, conflict and changing beliefs and values about the benefits of immigration. Migrants begin to live the positive feelings of the old country and see it as superior.

Stage 3 — Defiance: For immigrants and refugees, this stage is characterized by rejection of the dominant culture, mistrust, anger and endorsement of their life in the "old country." Migrants see the new country as corrupt, dishonest and unaccepting. They decide to go back to their old lives if they can, recreate their old lives in the new country or become conservative and traditional about their culture, rejecting accommodation in the new country.

Stage 4 — Introspection and accommodation: For immigrants and refugees, this stage is characterized by conflict. Now there is questioning of primary loyalty and responsibility to one's own cultural group. Migrants see that adapting themselves to the new way of life does not mean abandoning their old culture. There is still mistrust but also a feeling of accommodation.

Stage 5 — Adaptation and integration: For immigrants and refugees, this stage is characterized by awareness of being different, gaining personal identity in their own cultural milieu, a sense of cultural self-fulfillment as an immigrant, a greater sense of control and flexibility and an objective outlook on the dominant culture. Migrants have in essence accepted the multicultural ideal and begin to see themselves as hyphenated Canadians.

People move from stage to stage until they achieve self-acceptance. Problems occur when migrants get stuck at stages one to three. Understanding the migrants' cultural background and history will also be extremely important in knowing their world view. In addition, a counsellor who is able to pick up the nuances of their language or ways of describing things will also add greater understanding of how migrants see their problems and issues.

Finally, it is important for the counsellor to know whether the problem is internal (psychological, cognitive, spiritual, physical) or external (employment, discrimination, financial, etc.).

Implications for Counselling Practice

It is vital that counsellors develop culturally sensitive practices and increase their awareness about the diverse nature of the migrant population. Cultural sensitivity and awareness is not about "isms"; instead, it is about human relationships, interdependency, differences and points of connection. When practice is culturally oriented, the model of practice becomes cross-cultural. The term *cross-cultural* refers to a place of cultural intersection where professionals encounter the issues of migrants and the approach they use to deal with their problems. A cross-cultural model provides reasons for one to examine one's own culture, values, beliefs and most of all identity, in order to respect and accept the differences one encounters in professional practice.

Although cultures are maps of meaning through which the world is made intelligible, it is migrants' experience — their interpretation and the meaning of such experiences — and the understanding of their culture and its impact on their values, beliefs and choices that should shape counsellors' practice. This is important because culture is the main source of knowledge that has been passed on from generation to generation, and respecting this dynamic enhances professional competency. In addition, it is important that a cross-cultural approach encourages counsellors to understand, be sensitive and be alert when encountering migrants; such an approach expands the counsellor's ability to be effective.

According to Das, Kemp, Driedger and Halli (1997), counsellors must consider some of the following issues in dealing with migrants.

1. Minority status might predispose people to feelings of social isolation and heightened stress.
2. School-age children of immigrants may become the target of negative stereotyping and social rejection.
3. Second-generation immigrants may experience tension between mainstream values and their ethnic cultural values.
4. Second-generation immigrants may find it offensive to be seen as foreigners.
5. In smaller communities, immigrants are likely to feel socially isolated and lonely.
6. Spouses who stay home and have limited social contact with the outside world are at risk for becoming depressed and have no avenues for seeking help in the case of abuse.
7. Second-generation girls who find their social lives unduly restricted by traditional parents may begin to rebel.
8. Formerly successful professionals who find themselves in dead-end jobs because of racial discrimination and without any remedy may begin to engage in self-destruc-

tive behaviour such as drinking heavily or using drugs.

9. New immigrants may fail to establish themselves in the kind of career they had in mind. (p. 33)

The issues described above may prepare professionals in all human services to be mindful, flexible and open practitioners. This is not to imply that professionals are not trained to serve their clients from diverse cultural, ethnic and racial background effectively. What the list suggests is that awareness of the issues associated with diversity and equity, as well as the role of the professional in addressing migrants' challenges, is a necessary ingredient in facilitating opportunities for clients' success.

Conclusion

To be effective as a counsellor with migrants, one must understand concepts such as adaptation and acculturation, the strategies that guide such processes and the factors that affect them, such as the ideologies of state immigration policies. Furthermore, it is important to identify potential acculturation outcomes, the interactive relations in the acculturation process such as cultural and social components, the impact of migration on the family and the strategies migrants develop to cope with their shifting status in a multicultural society.

In this sense, Canada is unique. The challenge will be to help all of the ethnic and racial groups to reach beyond their own cultural boundaries and to enable them to cross cultural borders freely. Under multicultural policy, people are encouraged to maintain their language and cultural practices. Psychologically, this policy means that government services must help professionals be aware of how cultural identity develops. All people want acceptance, yet their cultural roots bind them and this binding affects how others perceive them. Multicultural policy reinforces the idea that each ethnic group has a strong cultural identity, implying that groups have a greater sense of control over their lives than they may have. By examining the effects that cultural identity has on people, professionals will be well prepared to assist newcomers in their adaptation process. Interestingly, according to Dasko (2003), attitudes about Canada's multicultural policy, from its first inception to today, are generally positive, with an approval rating of 74, which is "a very significant finding and shows that Canadians maintain a strong allegiance to this policy" (p. 1).

The process of acculturation is neither a pleasant experience nor a smooth process. It confronts first of all various state immigration and integration policies, then the different attitudes of host members toward the state policies and toward migrants. These two vital factors either encourage or constrain acculturation orientations and outcomes.

Although under integration policies migrants are allowed to maintain their own culture in pluralistic society, their culture is in fact modified to be accepted by the host society and to be lived by migrants in the host society. This guest culture is like Chinese food abroad — it is Chinese for local people but not for Chinese people or for people who have been to China. During cultural modification, migrants keep the parts that are within the tolerance of the host culture but change or give up those parts that cannot be tolerated in the new culture. As they modify these internalized habits, customs, beliefs and concepts, migrants inevitably experience inner conflicts and stress.

For those migrants who believe individual efforts can make a difference, stress turns into challenge and acceptance, and growth together forms the internal dynamics of acculturation. The breaking up of the old internal conditions for these people usually results not in chaos or breakdown but in the creation of a new internal structure that better fits the host environment. For some migrants, acculturation can be a painful process; for others, it represents an opportunity for personal growth and exciting learning. We must remember that, in the end, every case is unique and as a consequence, every migrant experiences a unique acculturation journey.

The different attitudes towards acculturation among migrants and their different coping strategies have important implications for those in helping professions. They suggest the potential of psychological transformation and the need to learn about philosophies and diverse approaches from other cultures. With individuals who have come from different stages of acculturation and different cultures, it is necessary to open our minds wider and understand the different ways in which people cope, interact and adjust to a new culture. Additionally, one must be aware of the strategies that are useful in some cases, the ones that do not work with certain populations and the way personal and societal expectations affect acculturation. A ready example of psychological transformation can be found in the following ancient Chinese story of the blessing or bane.

Near China's northern borders lived a man well versed in the practices of Taoism. His horse, for no reason at all, got into the territory of the northern tribes. Everyone commiserated with him.

"Perhaps this will soon turn out to be a blessing," said his father.

After a few months, his animal came back, leading a fine horse from the north. Everyone congratulated him.

"Perhaps this will soon turn out to be a cause of misfortune," said his father.

Since he was well off and kept good horses, his son became fond of riding and eventually broke his thigh bone falling from a horse. Everyone commiserated with him.

"Perhaps this will soon turn out to be a blessing," said his father.

One year later, the northern tribes started a big invasion of the border regions.

All able-bodied young men took up arms and fought against the invaders, and as a result, around the border nine out of ten men died. This man's son did not join in the fighting because he was crippled, and so both the boy and his father survived.

References

Bemak, F., & Chung, R.C. (2008). Counselling and psychotherapy with refugees, In P. Pedersen, J. Draguns, W. Lonner, & J. Trimble (Eds.), *Counselling across cultures* (6th ed., pp. 209–232). Thousand Oaks, CA: Sage.

Berry, J.W. (1990). Psychology of acculturation: understanding individuals moving between cultures. In R.W. Brislin (Ed.), *Applied cross-cultural psychology.* Newbury Park, CA: Sage.

Berry, J.W., & Kalin, R. (1995). Multicultural and ethnic attitudes in Canada: An overview of the 1991 National Survey. *Canadian Journal of Behavioural Science, 27,* 301–320.

Berry, J.W., & Sam, D.L. (1997). Acculturation and adaptation. In J.W. Berry, & M.H. Segall (Eds.), *Handbook of cross-cultural psychology,* (pp. 291–326). Boston: Allyn & Bacon.

Bourhis, R.Y., Moise, L.C., Perreault, S., & Senecal, S. (1997). Towards an interactive acculturation model: A social psychological approach. *International Union of Psychological Science, 32*(6), 369–386.

Boutang, Y.M., & Papademetriou, D. (1994). Typology, evolution and performance of main migration systems. In *Proceedings of 1994 OECD Conference: Migration and development,* (pp. 21–41). Paris: OECD.

Breton, R. (1988). From ethnic to civic nationalism: English Canada and Quebec. *Ethnic and Racial Studies, 11,* 85–102.

Breton, R., Isajiw, W., Kalbach, W., & Reitz, J. (1990). *Ethnic identity and equality.* Toronto: University of Toronto Press.

Citizenship and Immigration Canada. (2010). *Finding a new direction for newcomer integration.* Retrieved from http://www.cic.gc.ca

Das, A., Kemp, S., Driedger, L., & Halli, S. (1997). Between two worlds: Counselling South Asian Americans. *Journal of Multicultural Counselling and Development, 25*(1), 23–34.

Dasko, D. (2003). Public attitudes towards multiculturalism and bilingualism in Canada. In *Canadian and French Perspectives on Diversity, Conference Proceedings, October 16, 2003.* Toronto, ON.

Dyer, G. (2001). Canada's visible majority. *Canadian Geographic,* January-February, 46–52. Fleras, A., & Elliott, J.L. (1992). *Multiculturalism in Canada.* Toronto: Nelson Canada.

Fontes, A. (2002). Child discipline in immigrant Latino families. *Journal of Counselling and Development, 80*(1), 31–40.

Furnham, A., Bochner, S., & Ward, C. (2001). *The psychology of culture shock.* New York, NY: Routledge.

Helly, D. (1993). The political regulation of cultural plurality: Foundations and principles. *Canadian Ethnic Studies, 25*(2), 15–35.

Hunt, G. (1996, September). Public says no to Asians, Islanders. *National Business Review,* 13–16.

Hunt, G. (1995, October). Xenophobia alive and well in New Zealand. *National Business Review,* 27–16.

Immigration Canada. (2012). Canada facts and figures immigration overview permanent and temporary residents 2010. Retrieved from http://www.cic.gc.ca/english/pdf/research-stats/facts2010.pdf

Immigrant Services Society of British Columbia. (1993). *Settlement in the 1990s: An overview of the needs of new migrants in the Lower Mainland and Fraser Valley.* Vancouver: Immigrant Services Society of BC.

Juntune, C., Atkinson, D., and Tierney, G. (2003). School counselors and school psychologists as school-home-community liaisons in ethnically diverse schools. In P. Pedersen & J. Carey (Eds.), *Multicultural counselling in schools: A practical handbook* (pp. 149–168). Boston, MA: Pearson Education.

Kim, Y. (1988). *Communication and cross-cultural adaptation.* Clevedon, UK: Multilingual Matters.

Neilson Wire (2009). *Below the wire: US Hispanics and acculturation.* Retrieved from http://blog.nielsen.com/nielsenwire/consumer/u-s-hispanics-and-acculturation

Neuwirth, G., Jones, S., & Eyton, J.E. (1989). *Immigration settlement indicators: A feasibility study.* Ottawa: CIC.

Walton, B., & Kennedy, A. (1993). Psychological and sociocultural adjustment during cultural transitions: a comparison of secondary students overseas and at home. *International Journal of Psychology*, 28, 129–147.

Warnica, R., & Geddes, J. (2012). Is the federal immigration system a failure? The Harper government seems to think so, but the stats tell a different story. *Maclean's.* Retrieved from http://www2.macleans.ca/2012/04/18/

9

Considerations for Counsellors Regarding Refugee Trauma Locally and Abroad

Lisa Kurytnik

ONE OUT OF EVERY 206 PEOPLE ON EARTH is "of concern" to the United Nations High Commissioner for Refugees (UNHCR, n.d.). According to figures from 2010, there were 14.7 million internally displaced people (people displaced within their own countries because of safety threats), and an additional 10.5 million refugees in the world, the majority of whom were women and children (UNHCR, n.d.). Refugees have often been subjected to experiences of trauma through organized violence in the form of rape, torture, imprisonment, destruction of property and killing in their homeland. Refugee and displacement camps provide additional challenges to their social, cultural, familial, psychological and physical welfare. Following migration, hardships can continue in the form of inadequate financial, educational and social support, in the midst of often lengthy legal proceedings and the aftermath of trauma. Miller, Kulkarni and Kushner (2006) postulate that Western interventions have disproportionately and unhelpfully focussed on Western mental health diagnoses, particularly post-traumatic stress disorder (PTSD), to the detriment of culturally appropriate mental health interventions. Cultural distinctions in experience, expression and healing are unlikely to be discovered and used when the focus revolves around the symptoms that make up particular Western diagnostic criteria (Miller et al., 2006). Western practices of healing often perpetuate the power imbalances inherent in the original trauma of people termed refugees. An understanding of the concerns regarding the cultural complexity and treatment of trauma related to refugees is necessary in order to identify potential alternatives to standard Western approaches.

Who Are the Refugees?

At the 1951 United Nations convention relating to the status of refugees, a refugee was defined as

> a person who, owing to well-founded fear of being persecuted for reasons of race, religion, nationality, membership of a particular social group or political opinion, is outside the country of his nationality and is unable or, owing to such fear, is unwilling to avail himself of the protection of that country; or who, not having a nationality and being outside the country of his former habitual residence as a result of such events, is unable or, owing to such fear, is unwilling to return to it. (UNHCR, 1951, p. 14)

The United Nations High Commissioner for Refugees (UNHCR) is the United Nations refugee agency and was created in 1950 by the UN General Assembly to assist remaining refugees of World War Two for a three-year term (UNHCR/Arnold, 2008). The need for assistance with refugees was not resolved, however, and has since grown alarmingly (UNHCR/Arnold, 2008). According to the UNHCR, Canada and the United States have the highest number of resettled refugees globally and continue to receive high numbers (UNHCR-Canada, n.d.). Approximately one out of every ten refugees worldwide resettles in Canada (Citizenship and Immigration Canada, 2011). In 2011, Canada received 25 000 refugee claimants (By the Numbers: Refugee Statistics, n.d.).

Miller et al. (2002) describe the distinction between immigrants and refugees under the considerations of "valence of movement" and "urgency of departure." Immigrants are moving toward hopes and dreams of a better future based on thoughtful decision-making processes, whereas refugees are fleeing, or moving away from, situations of violence and peril with little in terms of preparedness and material possessions (Miller et al., 2002). Cariceo (1998) declares that unpreparedness for migration can cause disorientation for refugees in addition to the extensive challenges they already face.

Experiences of Refugee Trauma

Herman (1992) defines psychological trauma as "an affliction of the powerless, where the victim is rendered helpless by overwhelming force" (p. 33). Potential sources of trauma for refugees include the extensive loss of family and friends through death, disappearance or displacement; the witnessing or experiencing of emotional and/or physical torture, rape, bombings or other forms of violence; concentration camp imprisonment; fear for safety; hunger; and loss of property and homelessness (Yakushko et al., 2008). Violence against women increases during wartime, and sexual violence is a common weapon of war (Aube, 2011; Liebling & Kiziri-Mayengo, 2002). During wartime, "Women's bodies become a battlefield where men communicate their rage to other men, because women's bodies have been the implicit political battlefields all along" (Berman, Girón & Marroquín, 2006, p. 37). Also, according to Gorman (2001), the prevalence of torture is increasing. Gorman explains that torture is often intended to terrorize a population, achieving and maintaining power through the destruction of individuals' personality and sense of agency. Exposure to extreme violence has the potential to create a profound crisis of meaning, faith and identity (Miller et al., 2002). In addition, people can lose a sense of personal safety and safety in the world (Cariceo, 1998). Cariceo asserts that lacking a sense of identity inhibits connection, control and meaning. Gorman affirms that it is important to acknowledge the socio-political and contextual dynamics of torture and hence trauma.

War affects not just individuals but every level of society (Miller et al., 2006). Considerations include the effects of rape on women, their families and communities; the reintegration of former child soldiers who perpetuated violence against their own communities; betrayal by neighbours; the large proportion of orphaned, widowed and disabled victims on scarce resources; and the destruction of reliable and trustworthy social systems and institutions often fallen prey to corruption (Miller et al., 2006). Social contexts are intertwined with individual welfare (Miller et al., 2006). The relevant population's own reports of pertinent psychological and psychosocial stressors must also be given consideration, along with definitions of healthy and impaired functioning among the various strata of the population (Miller et al., 2006). A small number of studies assessing the priority of self-reported mental health concerns among survivors of war have revealed the priority of psychosocial issues such as the loss of social networks, grief and bereavement, family conflict and the inability to provide for one's family (Miller et al., 2006). Displaced persons are often focussed on social isolation, the loss of or separation from loved ones, poverty and a lack of basic resources, which is reminiscent of Maslow's hierarchy of needs (physiological, safety, love/belonging and esteem, followed by self-actualization) (Maslow, 1970, p. 159; Miller et al., 2006). It is essential to consider social networks, economic position, family circumstances, gender, class, ethnicity, linguistic status, religious or spiritual involvement and concepts of self and community when working with refugee populations (Bracken, Giller & Summerfield, 1995; Cariceo, 1998). Hussain and Bhushan (2011) indicate that community ideology, values and beliefs have implications on the appraisal of and adaptation to traumatic events. In non-Western cultures, trauma is a social as well as cultural phenomena (Bloem, Kwaak & Waas, 2003).

The Refugee/Displacement Camp Experience

Refugee and displacement camps are temporary harbours of safety. However, challenges with life in camps include isolation from loved ones; lack of basic needs such as electricity, medical supplies, adequate shelter, privacy, sanitation, comfort, adequate food and clean water; and lack of means of education and income production (Bloem et al., 2003; Stepakoff et al., 2006). The sense of powerlessness induced by war and trauma can be exacerbated by the circumstances of the camps themselves (Stepakoff et al., 2006). Stepakoff et al. (2006) noted unfortunate realities of many camps such as corruption and exploitation by fellow refugees, government officers and even humanitarian aid workers. The transient nature of refugee camps and limited funding contracts available only worsen the circumstances. In her study, Kreitzer (2002) found that several people spoke to the belief that self-sufficiency had not been fostered in the foundation of the camp and that dependency on the system had been created, intensifying disempowerment rather than ameliorating it. Apathy can result from the challenges of trauma and lengthy stays in temporary and inadequate living conditions (Kreitzer, 2002).

A number of social problems were found to be significantly greater for women (Jaranson et al., 2004). In rural areas, particularly in Africa, women are often the main breadwinners through agricultural activity; displacement severely limits opportunities for growing and providing food (Brittain, 2003). Kreitzer (2002) describes how women in refugee or displacement camps are often the sole caretakers of their families (women generally receive the food rations) but lack an adequate supply of nutritious and appropriate food, contributing to illness and exhaustion. The role of men as the patriarchs is severely compromised due to a lack of economic and educational opportunities, encouraging lethargy (Pavlish, 2007). Since women are the caregivers in their families and usually have lower social status than their male counterparts, their education is even more severely limited, causing involvement in riskier work such as the sex trade in order to meet survival needs (Bloem et al., 2003).

According to Brittain (2003), it is common for women and girls to become engaged in sexual-violence traps such as sexual slavery, rape, trafficking, prostitution and domestic violence. Pavlish (2007) conducted a qualitative study using a narrative approach with 29 Congolese refugees in a Rwandan refugee camp, and noted that a major problem related to poverty in the camps is the pressure for women to sell sex for food, clothing and/or aesthetic products. At times, sex is performed for goods at the husband's request (Pavlish, 2007). Rape is commonplace and the spread of HIV continues to rise (Pavlish, 2007). As one example, Physicians for Human Rights has released a report revealing that sexual assault has been experienced by 94 per cent of displaced households in Sierra Leone (Brittain, 2003). Shanks and Schull (2000) claim that perpetrators include peacekeepers who offer food in exchange for sexual activity. The UNHCR and Save the Children released a report stating that their own personnel had engaged in the sexual exploitation of women and girls in displacement camps in West Africa (Brittain, 2003); Brittain claims these are not isolated cases. Women and girls seeking safety are further abused by those purporting to provide them with that safety. In requiring assistance and basic survival needs, women barter with the only resource available to them: their bodies.

Refugee women in many countries do not often verbalize their experiences of trauma, presumably because of stigma, shame and humiliation (Liebling & Kiziri-Mayengo, 2002). In societies where rape is stigmatized, women have often kept these experiences secret, causing feelings of alienation and separation from the potentially ameliorating effect of social solidarity (Bracken et al., 1995). For example, following mass rapes in Rwanda, the pressure of social norms and Roman Catholic values caused women to give birth in secret and often abandon their offspring (Berman et al., 2006). In addition, a heartbreaking but not uncommon occurrence in places such as Afghanistan, Cambodia and the Democratic Republic of the Congo is for families to sell one of their children in order to survive (Brittain, 2003). According to Pavlish (2007), feelings of powerlessness combined with a lack of self-respect because of an inability to provide appeared to be highly related to relationship and sexual violence. Healing directed towards social mending was the most important concern expressed for the women of northern Uganda (Bracken et al., 1995).

Few studies describe positive adaptation in refugee or displacement camps. Almedom (2004) cites a notable exception in Eretria, where foreign assistance was permitted only in order to fill the gaps in national resources and capabilities and when it would not undermine or replace local initiatives and capacities. Research conducted in refugee camps in this area demonstrated relatively high functioning due to the maintenance of original social networks, cultural practices and community sustainability through the empowerment of activity geared towards local self-sufficiency and initiative (Almedom, 2004). In summary, aid, although well-meaning, may often serve to disempower people through the creation of dependency, the resulting lack of self-worth and the negative effects on mental health and well-being. Unfortunately, these effects can reinforce previous traumatic experiences, perpetuate power imbalances and reduce protective factors.

The Post-Migration Refugee Experience

Gorman (2001) asserts that regaining a sense of power and control is essential to recovery but is not always supported within the asylum-seeking system. Cariceo (1998) states that extensive trauma is found to be exacerbated by the resettlement process in other countries with their accompanying asylum proceedings, restrictions and threats of deportation. Yakushko et al. (2008) state that fear of the tenuousness of one's legal status can induce long-term stress and debilitation. Refugees commonly present urgent situational, economic, legal, social and/or medical problems (Cariceo, 1998; Gorman, 2001). For example, refugees frequently arrive with health issues related to unsanitary conditions in refugee and displacement camps (Yakushko et al., 2008). Moreover, on reaching a new country, refugees may be further affected by issues of poverty, language, isolation, loss of family and friends, self-esteem and identity (Century, Leavey, & Payne, 2007). Often, rural, traditional or village cultures are replaced by modern, secular and urban settings. Severe stressors include the adjustment to a new and potentially discriminatory culture; loss of professional or economic status and privilege resulting in loss of self-esteem; and the absence of social support, contributing to loneliness and isolation (Yakushko et al., 2008). Fazel, Wheeler and Danesh (2005) conducted a meta-analysis of 20 studies, including a total of 6743 refugees, regarding the prevalence of major depression, PTSD and psychotic illnesses among refugee populations in Western countries. They identified that refugees were ten times more likely to have PTSD than their Western counterparts. Yakushko et al. indicate that depression, anxiety and suicide rates are higher for immigrant and refugee populations and that domestic violence and intergenerational conflict intensify following relocation. Yakushko et al. claim that positive adjustment is associated with language skills, positive expectations, voluntary migration and support available, factors that may be absent in situations of forced relocation due to organized violence.

Miller et al. (2002) found that Bosnian refugees in Chicago regularly cited the following challenges: social isolation and the loss of community, the loss of lifelong endeavours, a lack of environmental mastery (largely due to transportation and language issues, which are intensified by the trauma-related impairments to memory and concentration), the loss of social roles and the corresponding loss of meaningful activity, a lack of sufficient income for adequate housing and other basic necessities (the most common source of distress among the participants) and health problems not previously experienced (both physical and psychological). Stijk et al. (2011) conducted a study of 30 refugees and asylum seekers in the Netherlands regarding social and health needs, and identified the following common concerns: loss, social disadvantage, loneliness, flashbacks and the struggle to acquire basic needs. Social disadvantage was apparent in the new country, and there was an associated uncertainty and lack of sense of belonging. One refugee participant stated: "I feel torn between two worlds, Africa and Europe. I have no place of my own anywhere" (Stijk et al., 2011, p. 51). According to Stijk et al., anger stemmed from injustice experienced in the home country and injustice continuing in the new country. All respondents reported sleep issues, and nightmares were a reoccurring complaint. Stijk et al. found that uniforms were frequently frightening, an issue that, along with fear of flashbacks, inhibited public travel. Finally, faith in people had been damaged, translating into a fear of meeting new people and contributing to loneliness. Gorman (2001) indicates that mental health practitioners around the world are increasingly facing the treatment of refugee populations, for whom traumatic experiences and situational stressors may be intertwined.

Schweitzer, Greenslade and Kagee (2007) studied resiliency factors, which are relatively absent in the literature, among Sudanese refugees in Australia; they identified several coping responses. Family and community support were deemed essential. During the pre-migration phase, this support came primarily from friends and family. Due to loss of loved ones through violence or separation, the larger Sudanese community played this role post-migration. Religion served several functions. A belief in God helped participants regain a sense of control and meaning and provided emotional support as well as community and material support through church connections. Personal qualities were noted by participants as important because they believed that attitude toward challenges made a difference. Finally, and to a lesser extent, comparison with others played a role in the post-migration phase by providing a sense of hope that the participants were better off than those back home (Schweitzer et al., 2007).

Post-Traumatic Stress Disorder

Post-traumatic stress disorder is a Diagnostic and Statistical Manual of Mental Disorders (DSM-IV-TR) diagnostic category containing the following criteria: experiencing or witnessing a traumatic event involving extreme fear, horror or helplessness regarding real or threatened death or serious harm to oneself or others and exhibiting particular symptoms of intrusive recollections, hyper-arousal and avoidance/numbing for a period of more than one month causing significant impairment or distress in an important area of functioning (American Psychiatric Association, 2000). PTSD first entered the DSM in 1980 and was geared towards American soldiers who had experienced combat in the Vietnam War (Breslau, 2004). Kienzler (2008) declares that the inclusion of PTSD in the DSM-III reflects a moral and political climate with respect to Vietnam veterans and legitimacy surrounding disability compensation, victimhood and moral absolution. The PTSD diagnosis subsequently expanded to include survivors of childhood sexual abuse, automobile accidents and natural disasters before moving on to a global application (Breslau, 2004).

Kienzler (2008) argues that PTSD and other biomedical diagnoses and constructs are based on Western conceptions of normal and deviant conditions without acknowledging the contextual milieu and cultural/social embeddedness of human experience. Summerfield (2008) argues that mental health diagnoses such as PTSD would be more universally viable if there was a clear biological cause rather than a description of a constellation of symptoms. Summerfield notes that official psychiatric categories change, are removed or are added based as much on Western cultural and social trends as on medical thinking. For instance, homosexuality was removed from the DSM-III the same year PTSD was added. Summerfield declares, "This is medical imperialism, similar to the marginalisation of indigenous knowledge systems in the colonial era, and is generally to the disadvantage of local populations" (p. 992). Miller et al. (2006) claim that imposing Western cultural definitions of psychological and psychosocial well-being and impairment is misleading, presumptuous and harmful to the populations being served and the research being conducted. Breslau (2004) suggests that the scientific basis of PTSD and its political relevance are being treated as more important than the dimension of clinical treatment.

Zarowsky and Pederson (2000) note that PTSD is an individual diagnosis that ignores collective trauma and the cultural, social and political environment it is extracted from: they deem treatment largely ineffective. Shoeb, Weinstein and Halpern (2007) claim that the diagnosis of PTSD situates trauma within the individual rather than social context and emphasizes pathology rather than cultural and religious dislocation. Diversity in which that trauma is experienced, interpreted and expressed is often disregarded (Miller et al., 2006). For example, Marsella (2010) suggests there is a phenomenon called "Post-traumatic Growth Syndrome" in which an improvement in mental health is experienced, possibly stemming from a belief that crises are also opportunities. Traumatic experiences can lead to an increase in social cohesion, resistance and resiliency (Zarowsky & Pederson, 2000).

One consideration with respect to diagnostic categories such as PTSD is the category fallacy — the false assumption that diagnostic categories established in one culture are applicable to another simply because the same characteristics can be found (Miller et al., 2006). Western categories may be imposed in situations that would not support such material independently. In Uganda, researchers discovered that evidence of PTSD symptoms could be found but often were not the presenting concerns. Current methods of research frequently use questionnaires, which assume the population being researched understands the concepts in the same way the researchers do (Kienzler, 2008). In addition, PTSD surveys do not take into consideration unspecified variables or relevance to the refugees themselves (Gozdziak, 2004). According to Eisenbruch, de Jong and van de Put (2005), Western quantitative research instruments to measure PTSD that are not founded on culturally sensitive qualitative data should be avoided because they may maintain the category fallacy.

Summerfield (2008) claims research on diagnoses of PTSD and other mental health issues may deflect attention from more critical issues such as poverty, violence and injustice (Summerfield, 2008). He suggests that research and interventions conducted with foreign aid often represent outside interests rather than the priorities of those in afflicted areas. Breslau (2004) proposes that the global expansion of PTSD research is opportunistic and intertwined with the political agenda of defining victim versus aggressor, as well as the "legitimacy" of rights to funding and the ensuing distribution of aid based on such diagnoses. Treatment for PTSD is increasingly directed towards drugs distributed by pharmaceutical companies (Breslau, 2004). Criticisms of the staff of humanitarian aid projects often include the assertion of ignorance regarding local politics, economics, history, culture, power dynamics and health care (Kienzler, 2008). Western pathological diagnoses with the accompanying focus on negative symptoms can promote a state of victimhood rather than individual resiliency and coping (Crosby & Grodin, 2007). Despite considerable debate regarding the appropriateness of the PTSD diagnosis and its standardized symptom checklist, PTSD remains, internationally and in North America, the most common framework for treatment in which clinicians work (Shoeb et al., 2007).

Cultural Considerations for Counselling

Vontress (2001) notes that concepts of illness, healers and therapeutic methods — in other words, causes and cures — are culturally bounded. Schultz, Sheppard, Lehr and Shepard (2006) emphasize that the difference in beliefs about attributions of causation for illness range from the biological to the supernatural (p. 117). Cultural differences can include the importance of the role of the larger community or family in decision-making processes and in healing practices (Hunt, 2008). Liebling and Kiziri-Mayengo (2002) indicate there are cultural variations in the expression of emotions and distress. For instance, Indonesian culture discourages sharing emotional or psychological concerns (Bloem et al., 2003). Many Asian cultures lack the language to express psychological distress (Ruwanpura, Mercer, Ager & Duveen, 2006). According to Bloem et al. (2003), Asian people's symptoms frequently include somatization and therefore refugees are usually more comfortable seeking medical treatment than help for mental illness. Ruwanpura et al. (2006) also found that Tibetans often initially presented with somatic complaints before disclosing further difficulties.

The assumption that Western knowledge and healing practices are superior to local ones can cause harm by perpetuating the power imbalance of the original trauma (Duran, 2006). Duran defines epistemic violence as the damage inflicted to a client's "knowledge life-world" by the therapist's imposition of a different world view (p. 9). Marsella (2010) argues that trauma is universal but the behavioural, psychological and social responses and consequences are moulded by ethno-cultural determinants. Bracken et al. (1995) assert that the subjective meaning of traumatic or violent incidents must be taken into consideration, reflecting phenomenological and constructivist perspectives. Similarly, Miller et al. (2006) suggest a social constructivist approach would be most conducive to assisting foreign populations; according to this perspective, universal truths and diagnoses are eschewed in favour of an understanding of unique world views and conceptions of mental health created within social contexts. The centrality of the process of meaning-making and its applicability to how one experiences traumatic events is inherent in the constructivist position (Miller et al., 2006). Marsella's concept of ethno-cultural competence refers to the ability to understand accurately the relevance and importance of cultural considerations in the areas of teaching, research and clinical service.

The intrapsychic orientation of the West is not universal; many cultures place the interpersonal and spiritual forces above intrapersonal ones (Bracken et al., 1995). The loss of familiar and comforting cultural practices for refugees who may have experienced extensive trauma can stymie the healing process (Bracken et al., 1995). Englund (1998) found that the most salient feature of distress for Mozambican refugees in Malawi was the inability to participate in burial rituals and bereavement practices because of displacement. Strong cultural beliefs and practices such as burial rights may stimulate trauma if circumstances do not allow their completion and there are perceived negative consequences to the spirits of one's loved ones for not having done so (Bracken et al., 1995). In their study, Eisenbruch et al. (2005) describe a situation in which an Ethiopian woman who had lost her child while fleeing her country was diagnosed with bronchial asthma and then psychosis until it was understood that she had not been able to grieve properly by performing the purification ritual of her culture. Miller et al. (2006) propose that it is imperative to understand traditional views of health and healing, and the source and manner of that assistance, in order to provide the most effective care. They state that traditional healers or spiritual figures are resources often previously called upon in times of duress and that supplanting comforting and familiar practices with unfamiliar and unknown ones with no correspondence between the two is counterintuitive and ineffective. Furthermore, Miller et al. declare that an understanding of local spiritual and religious beliefs and practices as well as their role in the process of healing may be pivotal.

Insight-based talk therapy is built on the premise that the person is distinct and independent, capable of transformation apart from the social context (Bracken et al., 1995). In non-Western cultures, trauma is typically not an individual experience but a social and cultural one. Consequently, Bloem et al. (2003) advocate the development of a supportive social environment as the most effective therapeutic intervention. Almedom (2004) suggests that research indicates individual "debriefing" is less effective than peer support among those with similar experiences. Bracken et al. (1995) assert that there are social and political factors involved in the culture of trauma and violence that are not addressed in an individually oriented course of therapy. In a study of 1134 East African refugees, less than 1 per cent accepted or requested mental health services despite high scores on psychological impairment (Jaranson et al., 2004). Bracken et al. declare that it is essential for people to reconstruct social, economic and cultural identities as a significant part of their healing process. A meta-analysis looking at 56 published studies of the mental health of 67 294 participants found social conditions after displacement to be the strongest ameliorating factor (Summerfield, 2008). In Africa and other developing countries, healing practices often involve the family and the larger community. Individuals seen in isolation may interrupt the healing process of the community as a whole (Bracken et al., 1995). Frequently, individual and collective trauma coexist; Zarowsky and Pederson (2000) deem therapeutic approaches embracing this interrelationship worthy of consideration.

Stepakoff et al. (2006) designed a program in Guinea to support a locally self-sufficient system through the training of paraprofessionals drawn from the refugee population itself and through the development of more sustainable social networks. Stepakoff et al. used a relationship-based, supportive, group-counselling three-stage model (safety, mourning and reconnection) of trauma recovery with Liberian and Sierra Leonean survivors of war and torture living in refugee camps. A combination of Western and local indigenous healing practices was used; paraprofessionals drawn from the local population promoted culturally competent service. Participants' bereavement practices were explored and modifications made (when necessary) to bring healing and show respect to traditional beliefs and rituals. Social activities were used to expand social networks and increase resiliency. Measures of psychological symptoms, daily functioning and social support were administered at intake and at one, three, six and twelve months post-treatment, consistently indicating significant reductions in symptoms of trauma and increased indications of daily functioning and social cohesion during and after treatment. The diagnosis of PTSD was not used. The Centre for Victims of Torture–Guinea 2004–2005 International Mental Health Team (who conducted the program) received the International Humanitarian Award for its work (Stepakoff et al., 2006).

Conclusion

A significant portion of the worldwide population today is made up of refugees and internally displaced people, many of whom will find asylum in Canada. I have described conditions and concerns related to refugee/displacement camps and the post-migratory experience. Additionally, I have summarized several common experiences of trauma among refugees and presented the debate questioning the appropriateness and helpfulness of the PTSD phenomena with this population, particularly in relation to cultural considerations. It is apparent that trauma related to organized violence involves a sense of powerlessness, which appears to be exacerbated by refugee/displacement camp experiences, post-migratory conditions and, ironically, methods of aid offered by Western clinicians. Crises in meaning, isolation and agency can be addressed through culturally sensitive and relevant counselling practices, addressing both the individual and the community. I have described projects in which Western counselling is combined with indigenous healing practices, beliefs and values, allowing refugees to maintain their own integrity and identity while taking into consideration the social and cultural context. Awareness of these issues will, I hope, translate into counselling practices on a larger scale that honour the diversity of the human race and its ways of being.

References

Almedom, A.M. (2004). Factors that mitigate war-induced anxiety and mental distress. *Journal of Biosocial Science*, 36(4), 445–461.

American Psychiatric Association. (2000). *Diagnostic and statistical manual of mental disorders* (revised 4th ed.). Washington, DC: Author.

Aube, N. (2011). Ethical challenges for psychologists conducting humanitarian work. *Canadian Psychology*, 52(3), 225–229.

Berman, H., Girón, E.R.I., & Marroquín, A.P. (2006). A narrative study of refugee women who have experienced violence in the context of war. *Canadian Journal of Nursing Research*, 38(4), 32–53.

Bloem, M., Kwaak, A., & Waas, J. (2003). Psychotrauma in Moluccan refugees in Indonesia. *Disaster Prevention and Management*, 12(4), 328 – 335.

Bracken, P.J., Giller, J.E., & Summerfield, D. (1995). Psychological responses to war and atrocity: The limitations of current concepts. *Social Science and Medicine*, 40(8), 1073–1082.

Breslau, J. (2004). Cultures of trauma: Anthropological views of post-traumatic stress disorder in international health. *Culture, Medicine, and Psychiatry*, 28(2), 113–126.

Brittain, V. (2003). The impact of war on women. *Race Class*, 44(4), 41–51.

By the Numbers: Refugee Statistics. (n.d.). Retrieved April 8, 2011 from www.cdp-hrc.uottawa.ca/projects/refugee-forum/projects/Statistics.php

Cariceo, C.M. (1998). Challenges in cross-cultural assessment: Counselling refugee survivors of torture and trauma. *Australian Social Work*, 51(2), 49–53.

Century, G., Leavey, G., & Payne, H. (2007). The experiences of working with refugees: Counsellors in primary care. *British Journal of Guidance and Counselling*, 35(1), 23–40.

Citizenship and Immigration Canada (2011). *The refugee system in Canada*. Retrieved April 8, 2011 from http://www.cic.gc.ca/english/refugees/canada.asp

Crosby, S.S., & Grodin, M.A. (2007). Ethical considerations in crisis and humanitarian interventions: The view from home. *Ethics and Behavior*, 17(2), 203–205.

Duran, E. (2006). *Healing the soul wound: Counseling with American Indians and other native peoples*. New York, NY: Teacher College Press.

Eisenbruch, M., de Jong, J.T.V.M., & van de Put, W. (2005). Bringing order out of chaos: A culturally competent approach to managing the problems of refugees and victims of organized violence. *Journal of Traumatic Stress*, 17(2), 123–131.

Englund, H. (1998). Death, trauma and ritual: Mozambican refugees in Malawi. *Social Science and Medicine*, 46(1), 1165–1174.

Fazel, M., Wheeler, J., & Danesh, J. (2005). Prevalence of serious mental disorder in 7000 refugees resettled in western countries: A systematic review. *Lancet*, 365(1), 1309–1314.

Gorman, W. (2001). Refugee survivors of torture: Trauma and treatment. *Professional Psychology: Research and Practice*, 32(5), 443–451.

Gozdziak, E.M. (2004). Training refugee mental health providers: Ethnography as a bridge to multicultural practice. *Human Organization*, 63(2), 203–210.

Herman, J.L. (1992). *Trauma and Recovery*. New York: Basic Books.

Hussain, D., & Bhushan, B. (2011). Cultural factors promoting coping among Tibetan refugees: A qualitative investigation. *Mental Health, Religion and Culture*, 14(6), 575–587.

Jaranson, J.M., et al. (2004). Somali and Oromo refugees: Correlates of torture and trauma history. *American Journal of Public Health*, 94(4), 591–598.

Kienzler, H. (2008). Debating war-trauma and post-traumatic stress disorder (PTSD) in an interdisciplinary arena. *Social Science and Medicine*, 67, 218–227.

Kreitzer, L. (2002). Liberian refugee women: A qualitative study of their participation in planning camp programmes. *International Social Work*, 45(1), 45–58.

Liebling, H., & Kiziri-Mayengo, R. (2002). The psychological effects of gender-based violence following armed conflict in Luwero District, Uganda. *Feminism and Psychology*, 12(4), 553–560.

Marsella, A.J. (2010). Ethnocultural aspects of PTSD: An overview of concepts, issues, and treatments. *Traumatology*, 16(4), 17–26.

Maslow, A.H. (1970). *Motivation and personality* (2nd ed.). New York: Harper and Row.

Miller, K.E., Kulkarni, M., & Kushner, H. (2006). Beyond trauma-focused psychiatric epidemiology: Bridging research and practice with war-affected populations. *American Journal of Orthopsychiatry*, 76(4), 409–422.

Miller, K.E., Worthington, G.J., Muzurovic, J., Tipping, S., & Goldman, A. (2002). Bosnian refugees and the stressors of exile: A narrative study. *American Journal of Orthopsychiatry*, 72(3), 341–354.

Pavlish, C. (2007). Narrative inquiry into life experiences of refugee women and men. *International Nursing Review*, 54(1), 28–34.

Ruwanpura, E., Mercer, S.W., Ager, A., & Duveen, G. (2006). Cultural and spiritual constructions of mental distress and associated coping mechanisms of Tibetans in exile: Implications for western interventions. *Journal of Refugee Studies*, 19(2), 187–202.

Schultz, W.E., Sheppard, G.W., Lehr, R., & Shepard, B. (2006). *Counselling ethics: Issues and cases*. Ottawa, ON: Canadian Counselling Association.

Schweitzer, R., Greenslade, J., & Kagee, A. (2007). Coping and resilience in refugees from the Sudan: A narrative account. *Australian and New Zealand Journal of Psychiatry*, 41(3), 282–288.

Shanks, L., & Schull, M.J. (2000). Rape in war: The humanitarian response. *Canadian Medical Association Journal*, 163(9), 1152–1156.

Shoeb, M., Weinstein, H.M., & Halpern, J. (2007). Living in religious time and space: Iraqi refugees in Dearborn, Michigan. *Journal of Refugee Studies*, 20(3), 441–460.

Stepakoff, S., Hubbard, J., Katoh, M., Falk, E., Mikulu, J.B., Nkhoma, P., & Omagwa, Y. (2006). Trauma healing in refugee camps in Guinea: A psychosocial program for Liberian and Sierra Leonean survivors of torture and war. *American Psychologist*, 61(8), 921–932.

Strijk, P.J.M., van Meijel, B., & Gamel, C.J. (2011). Health and social needs of traumatized refugees and asylum seekers: An exploratory study. *Perspectives in Psychiatric Care*, 47(1), 48–55.

Summerfield, D. (2008). How scientifically valid is the knowledge base of global mental health? *British Medical Journal*, 336(7651), 992–994.

UNHCR. (n.d.). *UNHCR statistical online population database*. Retrieved December 17, 2011, from http://www.unhcr.org/statistics/populationdatabase

UNHCR. (1951). *Convention and protocol relating to the status of refugees*. Geneva, Switzerland: UNHCR Communications and Public Information Service.

UNHCR, Arnold, R. (2008). *Protecting Refugees and the Role of UNHCR*. Retrieved April 8, 2011, from http://www.unhcr.ie/images/uploads/pictures/pdf/4034b6a34.pdf

Vontress, C.E. (2001). Cross-cultural counseling in the 21st century. *International Journal for the Advancement of Counselling*, 23(2), 83–97.

Yakushko, O., Watson, M., & Thompson, S. (2008). Stress and coping in the lives of recent immigrants and refugees: Considerations for counselling. *International Journal for the Advancement of Counselling*, 30(1), 167–178.

Zarowsky, C., & Pederson, D. (2000). Rethinking trauma in a transnational world. *Transcultural Psychiatry*, 37(3), 291–293.

10

The "Hardest Burden"?

Helping and Working with People with Disabilities

ABEBE ABAY TEKLU

"A nation's greatness is measured by how it treats its weakest members."
— Mahatma Gandhi

AN ETHIOPIAN PROVERB SAYS, "When one hand is ill, the other hand will suffer. We cannot clap with one hand." This proverb illustrates the belief that a society cannot enjoy prosperity when some social groups are neglected. Almost all studies of disability have a "grand theory" underpinning the "personal tragedy" theory of disability (Oliver, 1996, p. 1). People with disabilities, like me, have taken up the challenge of questioning the personal-tragedy theory, which assumes that there will be an inevitable dependency on society. Research is often based on critical philosophies that uncover power dynamics and structural oppression.

The research literature is scarce regarding coping, employment issues or social experiences of people with various impairments, especially those with visual impairment. As a person with a visual impairment, I have examined the issues of personal strengths and social support that help blind youth obtain education and employment. Despite cultural and economic differences, disability experiences, support and challenges in diverse nations can be compared. Socio-cultural environments may differ, but one common factor remains: "disability" is a construction, often one with negative results. Therefore, there is value in considering global differences in the lives of people with disabilities.

In this chapter, I discuss the research literature on coping strategies, strengths and successes, rather than tragedies, and reveal environmental challenges that must be overcome. In addition, I want to share what counsellors can do to support, empower and help those with disabilities use their full potential. The notion of disabilities, like racism, limits counsellors' thinking of what a person with disabilities can do, so counsellors need to examine their biases around the disabled and see not a person with a personal tragedy but a person with limitless possibilities.

Personal Strengths, Social Supports and Challenges for Persons with Disabilities

Teferra (1998) set out to determine personal resilience qualities, coping strategies and social protective factors for persons with disabilities. He was seeing strengths in individuals and the environment. Participants included people with visual impairment and people with motor and hearing impairment. All were "high achievers" who were employed and deemed successful. As students, they had been able to enter a variety of fields of study; however, limitations to access certain fields were based on attitudes of policy makers and university officials, the nature of the learning and teaching process and the type or degree of impairment. Challenges included "being undermined and ridiculed by teachers and non-disabled students, lack of disability specific educational support and inaccessibility of instructional materials and other school facilities" (p. 70). Teferra says that challenges in school and the workplace include misrepresentation of people with disabilities with a variety of stereotypes. Interestingly, over 94 per cent of the participants in the study reported positive self-efficacy, and 94.7 per cent believed they had the potential for learning and taking care of themselves. The findings of high self-efficacy imply that high self-efficacy occurs along with success, which supports Bandura's (1982) research. Teferra also found that personal strengths included "strong desire and devotion to learn and work and (having) patience; spiritual strength, special ability to communicate with people; accepting oneself and one's limitations and working hard to compensate; exerting effort not to be a burden to others" (pp. 76–77). What all of the participants had in common was social support from family and community, affiliation with a peer group and advice from successful people with disabilities. Regarding attaining education and employment, participants coped by "accepting one's disability; being patient; exerting effort to learn and develop one's potential; acquiring knowledge and skills through education/training; demonstrating one's potential to gain acceptance and recognition; steadily seeking to establish close relationship or friendship with others, and efficient utilization of time" (pp. 77–78).

Burke, Hagan-Burke, Kwok and Parker's (2009) study of children with disabilities in an inclusive classroom found that there were no differences in achievement compared to those without disabilities. What is startling about this study is that many students with disabilities fall short of their potential because they lack access to the general curriculum and could be helped if they had help from teachers with expertise in the content area. What is apparent is that schools often fail students with disabilities because of lack of resources and because of teachers who do not understand how best to help disabled students. Teferra (1999) found the quality of early family psychosocial support for children with disabilities plays a critical role in subsequent achievement: "the greater the environmental resources, the less the individual's disability is likely to result in a handicap" (p. 195). Sometimes a label defines a person, thus making labels something counsellors need to avoid. "Disability" can mean a physical condition such as visual impairment, but "handicap" means that a person with a disability cannot do something or cannot do it to the level of achievement of an able-bodied person. The more social resources there are, the less a person's disability results in a handicap.

Wasting Human Potential: Cultural Ableism

If we examine policies in the Western world, such as in Australia, Canada and the United States, it is easy to see people's attitudes in what I call the construction of disability. Despite protective social policies in these countries, a disability is usually associated with poverty (Clear, 1999). The Human Resources Development Canada (HRDC) reports that Canadians aged 15 to 64 with a disability are almost twice as likely to experience lower incomes as are able-bodied persons, and employment rates are substantially lower (2003). Among adults aged 25 to 54, the Participation and Action Limitation Survey (PALS) study reported by HRDC disclosed that 42.7 per cent of people with a disability are not in the labour force. In the 25-to-54 age group, 27.9 per cent experience low income, almost triple the rate for able-bodied persons (HRDC, 2003). According to Clear (1999), the discouraging impoverishment of persons with disabilities, even in wealthy countries such as Canada, Australia and the US,

> flows from the way we organize our production systems, distribute resources. . . . In a just and equal society, there would be no reason why any particular form of difference should result in systematic disadvantage, injustice and discrimination. . . . society disables people who have an impairment. (p. 7)

Clearly there is a bias in the way that disabled people are treated; cultural "ableism" appears in attitudes, stereotypes and cultural representation of disability and assumes that disability inevitably involves dependency, helplessness and tragedy. The effect is that this type of exclusion leads to economic and social disadvantage, not to mention the psychological effect on the "disabled." Historically, injustice to people with disabilities has been explained away by looking at individual pathology. We neglect to examine and challenge the social foundations of disability. Ableism is similar to racism because entrenched structures of economic and cultural power reproduce themselves, and create alienation, oppression and an unjust and significantly "ableist" world.

Clear (1999) emphasizes that the experience of disability is political. "Disability" is more than a physical limitation: it is a social construction. Disadvantage from impairment is not natural or inevitable, he states, as have others (e.g., Teferra, 1998, p. 195; Beaty, 1994; Oliver, 1990; Mcreath, 2011). What the research states is that the ableist construction of disability causes cultural and economic oppression, and its effects constitute a human rights violation. Weeber (1999) defines ableism as a "form of prejudice and bigotry that marks us as less than those who are non-disabled. . . . that being 'non-disabled' makes a person superior; and, everyone who is disabled wishes they could be non-disabled — at any cost" (p. 23). It is an attempt to convince people with a disability that there is something fundamentally wrong with them, that they are "defective" and not acceptable the way they are. Thus, ableist attitudes hurt both the disabled and the non-disabled. Before working with the disabled, counsellors need to examine their biases around the ableist construction of disability.

Gender and Disabilities: Voices of Women

Hawley (2003), working with women with disabilities, found they are more than twice as likely to be divorced and/or to be single parents and are the group most vulnerable to abuse, including sexual assault. Fawcett (1996, 2000) and HRDC (2003) also found that women with disabilities are the most employment-challenged and have the highest rate of poverty of any social or ethnic group, with over 60 per cent depending or partially depending on the welfare system to meet basic daily needs. HRDC (2003) analyzed earnings for people with disabilities and found huge disparities. From age 25 to 54, men with a disability earn on average $34,536 annually while able-bodied men earn $44,312. In the same age group, women with a disability earned an average of $23,302 while able-bodied women earned $28,697. In regard to employment status, HRDC (2003) found huge gaps: 55.5 per cent of men aged 25 to 54 with a disability are employed, compared to 88.9 per cent of able-bodied males. Of women who have a disability, 48.4 per cent are employed, compared to 78.2 per cent of able-bodied women.

According to Williams (2002), in countries like Canada, employers lack knowledge about assistive technology and about the abilities and productivity potential of people with a disability. Such a lack of awareness leads to high unemployment rates for people who ought to be in the labour force; without employment, they cannot obtain full citizenship.

General Advice about Working with Impairment

Oliver (1996) developed the social model of disabilities, which describes the manner in which the dominant society reacts to people who are impaired; it may be compared to the medical model of disability, in which the body is viewed as a machine to be fixed. In the medical model of disability, anyone who has an impairment needs to be healed to conform to the norm of society. The social model of disabilities focusses on the attitudes society holds about people who appear imperfect and identifies the barriers, negative attitudes and exclusions from society. The idea is that a person, whether hearing- or seeing-impaired or having to use a wheelchair, needs to be accepted; instead the environment can be fixed to conform to any special needs. If society does not change the environment, then it contributes to disabling people from fulfilling their full potential.

What You Need to Know When You Help Clients Who Have an Impairment

As a man with a visual impairment, I often sense that some people are not sure what I can or cannot do. I sense their discomfort and sometimes am aware that they overcompensate because of their discomfort. I realize that they lack knowledge about disabilities and have little training about how to treat people. Ward (cited by Beecher, Rabe & Wilder, 2004) suggests the following interaction guidelines, sometimes called the "Ten Commandments of Communicating with People with Disabilities" or impairments.

1. Speak directly rather than through a companion or sign language interpreter who may be present.
2. Offer to shake hands when introduced. People with limited hand use or an artificial limb can usually shake hands, and offering the left hand is an acceptable greeting.
3. Always identify yourself and others who may be with you when meeting someone with a visual disability. When conversing in a group, remember to identify the person to whom you are speaking. When dining with a friend who has a visual disability, ask whether you can describe what is on his/her plate.
4. If you offer assistance, wait until the offer is accepted. Then listen or ask for instructions.
5. Treat adults as adults. Address people with disabilities by their first names only when extending that same familiarity to all others. Never patronize people in wheelchairs by patting them on the head or shoulder.
6. Do not lean against or hang on someone's wheelchair. Bear in mind that people with disabilities treat their chairs as extension of their bodies. So do people with guide dogs and help dogs. Never distract a working animal without the owner's permission.

7. Listen attentively when talking with people who have difficulties speaking, and wait for them to finish. If necessary, ask short questions that require short answers or a nod of the head. Never pretend to understand; instead, repeat what you have understood and allow the person to respond.

8. Place yourself at eye level when speaking with someone in a wheelchair or on crutches.

9. Tap a person who has a hearing disability on the shoulder or wave your hand to get his/her attention. Look directly at the person and speak clearly, slowly and expressively to establish whether the person can read your lips. If so, try to face the light source and keep hands, cigarettes and food away from your mouth when speaking. If a person is wearing a hearing aid, don't assume that he or she has the ability to discriminate your speaking voice. Never shout to a person. Just speak in a normal tone of voice.

10. Relax. Don't be embarrassed if you happen to use a common expression (such as "See you later" or "Did you hear about this?") that seems to relate to a person's disability (pp. 85–86).

Organizations and people who deal with visually impaired people, including myself, have developed general tips on working with visually impaired people to augment the "Ten Commandments of Communicating with People with Disabilities." The most important issue for building a relationship is never to assume what a person can or cannot do. While I cannot see, I am just like anyone else and there are many things that I can do, which is why I went to university and became a professor. The following are tips that you may find helpful.

- Identify yourself when you approach the person, and speak directly to her/him.
- Never touch the person without asking permission, unless it's an emergency.
- If you offer assistance, wait until you receive permission.
- Offer your arm (the elbow) to guide the person and then walk slowly.
- If you're giving directions or verbal information, be precise and clear. For example, if you're approaching a door or an obstacle, say so.
- Don't just assume the person can't see you.
- Don't leave the person in the middle of a room. Show her/him to a chair, or guide her/him to a comfortable location.
- Identify landmarks or other details to orient the person to the environment around her/him.
- Don't walk away without saying goodbye. Similarly, let the visually impaired person know if you are stepping out of the room for a moment and will return.
- Be patient. Things may take a little longer.

In relationships, I value honesty and I value people with the following behaviours, which I believe are good human qualities that all counsellors need to possess in building a relationship with an impaired person:

Demonstrate genuineness: Be yourself (open, transparent) in the relationship; do not hide behind a mask of professionalism. This concept is also known as congruence, realness or authenticity.

Show unconditional positive regard: Accept the client without judgement or conditions attached. This concept is also referred to as caring, valuing, prizing or respect.

Convey a deep level of empathic understanding: Strive for the ability to step into the client's world, as if you are in his/her shoes and without losing the "as if" quality.

Understand the qualities of acceptance: These are caring, concern, compassion, consistency, courtesy, firmness, interest, listening, prizing, respect, valuing and warmth.

I should also mention that there are things I experience in my life that become obstacles to acceptance. One major stumbling block is stereotyping. Stereotyping is also described as labelling, classifying, typecasting, pigeonholing, categorizing, putting someone in a mould, pre-judging or making assumptions. Stereotyping comes from our beliefs about people or groups of people. Stereotyping allows no room for individuality and is generally negative. It stems from our deeply embedded and often conditioned convictions about others and may be caused by fear or a lack of understanding about people who are different from ourselves. My hope is that everyone, especially counsellors, who works with people with disabilities will first examine their biases and understand that some beliefs about people with impairment are socially constructed, block basic human interactions and keep people in a subjective state. Once you are aware that you have these beliefs and realize that they will block you from working effectively with those with impairment, then you can educate yourself and others.

Counselling Implications for Working with the "Disabled"

From my perspective, as a person who is visually impaired, I would advise counsellors to make themselves fully aware of the social barriers clients with impairment face, whether the clients are in counselling with regard to finding employment or with regard to depression or family issues. Counsellors need to be aware that negative stereotypes are still deeply rooted in Canadian society. They might consider taking an activist role themselves in some way to help raise public awareness about the issues and harmful stereotypes that challenge visually impaired people every day — that is, counsellors can become advocates.

I also believe that for most people with an impairment, lack of sight is not a barrier but simply a characteristic of who the person is. I am a man who comes from Ethiopia, Africa, and who just happens to be visually impaired. I am also a father and a husband with a deep conviction that I can make a difference in the world in regards to social justice. I am also a human being with challenges, and sometimes I need to work on those things that keep me down; so if I come to see you, I am looking for answers, and my lack of sight has nothing to do with any of these challenges. Visual impairment is just a physical characteristic that I have and not a barrier for me to overcome.

Consider the following themes that might improve your counselling practice when working with people with impairment (Beecher, Rabe & Wilder, 2004).

Therapeutic alliances: This practice allows counsellors to talk about how the impairment might block counselling; by talking about this idea, counsellors can work within the contours of the disability, so it does not block the purpose of counselling, which is to empower.

Learned helplessness: Many clients who have challenges, even if these challenges are not obvious, develop a sense of helplessness, which is defined as a learned response of being unwilling to attempt a task after repeated failures or control by others. Counsellors may have to work with this phenomenon knowing that illness or other aspects of life cannot be controlled.

Lack of consistency: With so many barriers in life for some people with impairment, including illness, transportation and so on, some aspects of life cannot be predictable. People with impairment have come to accept this as a fact of life. Understanding on the part of counsellors and working with clients by planning interruptions that allow for inconsistency can be empowering.

Lack of validation: With society only recently becoming more knowledgeable about the social barriers that keep those with impairment down, stigmatization and discrimination still exist and sometimes keep those with impairment socially isolated. This lack of validation is stressful, particularly if the disability is not apparent. Beecher, Rabe and Wilder (2004) state that "helping individuals understand that they are having normal reactions to abnormal conditions may assist them in understanding their frustrations" (p. 88).

Lack of accountability: In my experience, most people with disabilities are very accountable and accepting of their responsibilities; their concerns are more about social barriers. However, with those who have become dependent or have accepted a label on themselves as being unable to do something, counsellors will have to help the person with an impairment develop a strategy with those that they work with to recognize the person might need some accommodation in terms of time. Interestingly for me, with the development of technology I have begun to rely less on accommodations from others because I know I can do the job with the tools that I have.

Unrealistic goals and the inability to compensate as before: Some clients with impairment who have recently become disabled are still adjusting to life in a wheelchair or with a guide animal. Thus counsellors may have to help clients learn alternative strategies to help them accomplish a given task.

Lack of resources: One of the great issues for many people — even those without impairment — involves knowing where to go to get the information or materials they need. Sometimes they lack awareness of where to go, because there are organizations, such as the Canadian National Institution for the Blind (CNIB), which McCrath (2011) calls an organization that reinforces helplessness. Counsellors are in a good position to find information or become advocates for their clients who are impaired. Counsellors need to make themselves aware and be knowledgeable about resources that can help their clients.

Conclusion

Teferra's research has shown that people with a disability can achieve education, fulfilling careers and independence with persistence, and if social conditions and policies are supportive. Teferra (1999), Beaty (1994), Clear (1999), Weeber (1999) and McCrath (2011) stress that we must change the social construction of disability. Today, ableism creates an unjust situation in many nations. We are capable of creating better living conditions and employment opportunities for people with disabilities than exist today. The current situation for people with disabilities is a social, cultural and economic tragedy (Williams, 2002; Teklu, 2007). It rests on us all to change the social conditions that present barriers to employment, fulfilment and thus full citizenship for people with disabilities, in Canada and around the world. I will close with the following poem, which brings to life the situation for visually impaired people. Let us not allow tragedy to be the end of the story.

When a Blind wakes up in the morning
Abebe Teklu

When a Blind wakes up in the morning, he hates the day.
Even though there is beautiful weather, he doesn't see it that way.

It's a new day, what am I going to do?
I wish I was getting ready for work, like you.

I believe I'm capable of working, like you,
They barred the door to me and never knew.

Just for being a Blind, nothing else could they see.
I wonder who was really blind; them, or me?

When boredom drives me out of the house, I start to walk.
My cane or my dog is the only one to talk.

Even walking miles and miles, I still have the blues,
I have gotten tired and worn out my shoes.

As I walk along, "Hmmmm!", I breathe the fresh air.
The sun is shining, the wind is touching my ear.

I can smell the odours, I can hear the traffic noise.
I hear the beautiful voices of girls and boys.

I listen to music from doorways and from cars passing by
And in the park, the birds sing and fly.

But so what? I cannot see it. I never will.
I cannot visualize it. It cannot lift my soul.

And I know I am talented. Gifts were given to us all.
I can't use my skills because I hit that wall.

What is life, if you cannot work, earn money, and go home
To look back on the day's work that you have done?

As a blind father, I have children and a wife,
And I want to support them with a fulfilling life.

I am sitting at home, with no production.
Music and talk shows don't bring satisfaction.

They keep me in the dark, in something of a dream,
It isn't reality. A dead end, it seems.

The family is stressed. They know I'm angry or crying;
I cannot find employment despite all my trying.

I'm an "unfortunate creature" in some people's sight.
They bar me from working — is that justice? Is that right?

Is that humanity? I've struggled on my long trek,
Instead of a job, I get that bloody welfare cheque!

The night is here again . . . and I prefer the dark.
Everyone is home from their day of work.

So I am like the rest, when the dark is here.
I pretend to forget the sadness and fears.

The children are sleeping, quiet once again.
Their love is the only thing that heals my pain.

If I can get myself tired, I might sleep, anyway.
But at least I am hiding; dark is better than the day.

References

Bandura, A. (1982). Self-efficacy mechanism in human agency. *American Psychology*, 37(2), 122–147.

Beaty, L. (1994). Psychological factors and academic success of visually impaired college students. *RE:view*, 26(3), 131–139.

Beecher, M., Rabe, R., & Wilder, L. (2004). Practical guidelines for counseling students with disabilities. *Journal of College Counseling*, 7 (Spring), 83–89.

Burke, M.D., Hagan-Burke, S., Kwok, O., & Parker, R. (2009). Path analysis of early literacy indicators from middle of kindergarten to end of second grade. *Journal of Special Education*, 42, 209–226

Clear, M. (1999). Disability and the political perspective. *Social Alternatives*, 18(1), 6–11.

Council of Canadians with Disabilities. (2001). Immigration challenge. *Equality Matters*. Retrieved March 5, 2005, from http://www.ccdonline.ca/publications/equality-matters/index.htm

Fawcett, G. (1996). *Living with disability in Canada: An economic portrait*. Hull, QC: Office of Disability Issues, Human Resources Development Canada.

Fawcett, G. (2000). *Bringing down the barriers: The labour market and women with disabilities in Ontario*. Ottawa: Canadian Council on Social Development.

Hawley, J.P. (2003). *From the margins: Voices of women with disabilities*. Dissertation Abstracts International. DAI-A 63/12, p. 4502. AAT 3074707.

Human Resources Development Canada (2003). *Disability in Canada: A 2001 profile*. Retrieved December 1, 2004, from http://www.hrdc-drgc.gc.ca/bcoh.odi

Human Resources and Skills Development Canada (2004). *Defining disability: A complex issue. Part II: Disability definitions in federal laws and programs*. Retrieved March 5, 2005, from http://www/hrsdc. gc.ca/asp/gateway.asp?hr=/en/hip/odi/documents/Definitions/Definitions005.shtml&hs=hze

McCreath, G. (2011). *The politics of blindness: From charity to parity*. Vancouver: Granville Island Publishing.

Oliver, M. (1996). *Understanding disability, from theory to practice*. London: Macmillan.

Statistics Canada (2002). *A profile of disability in Canada, 2001*. Catalogue No. 89–577–XIE. Ottawa: Author. Retrieved December 1, 2004, from http://www.statcan.ca/english/freepub/89-577-XIE/

Teferra, T. (1998). Self-esteem, coping styles and social dimensions of persons with disabilities of high achievements in Ethiopia. *Ethiopian Journal of Development Research*, 20(2), 65–91.

Teferra, T. (1999). Retrospective study of early childhood experience among persons with disabilities of high achievement and resilient personality qualities. *Ethiopian Journal of Health Development*, 13(3), 196–204.

Teklu, A. (2007). *The voices of Ethiopian blind immigrants and their families: Facing the challenges of life in Canada*. Unpublished doctoral dissertation, University of Victoria, Victoria, Canada.

Weeber, J. (1999). What could I know of racism? *Journal of Counseling and Development*, 77(1), 20–24.

Williams, J. (2002). *They have the ability, so why aren't more working?* Washington: National Organization on Disability, March 30, 2002. Retrieved January 14, 2005, from http://www.nod.org/index. cfm?fuseaction=page.viewPage&PageID=661&C:\CFusionMX7\verity\Data\dummy.txt

11

Counselling in the Latino(a) Community

Jorge Garcia
& María del Carmen Rodríguez

CULTURE IS A HUMAN NECESSITY and a way of life. It is the core of internal ways in which human beings develop their sense of self, including values, beliefs, thought patterns, perceptions and world view. All these qualities help determine and shape the aspects of one's external culture that inform the way(s) in which one establishes and maintains relationships through implicit norms, language, traditions, rituals and loyalties that influence attitudes, behaviours and customs (Gushue, 1993).

Since the origin of humanity, mobility has been a way to experience and explore new ways of life, ways of knowing and ways of survival, exposing people to beliefs, values, customs, behaviours and artifacts that members of a particular society share in order to cope with daily life and that are transferred from generation to generation (Koslow & Salett, 1989). These encounters can often cause culture shock, dissatisfaction and a judgemental attitude toward the new culture. Adapting, coping, assimilating and resisting such values are ways in which newcomers choose to relate to the new context. When interactions become difficult or become a barrier that prevents people from interacting with and in their environment, counsellors or other helping professionals can suggest ways to alleviate such challenges and break down the barriers.

This chapter explores the nature of cultural clashes, family dynamics and gender roles as important values for Latino(a) immigrants in North America and how these values may at times clash with those of North American society. It also discusses perspectives and approaches on how individuals can learn to adjust to the new culture.

Historical and Demographic Considerations

It was not a coincidence that Christopher Columbus and his crew reached the American continent the same year that the Spaniards destroyed the last Moorish stronghold in Spain (Skidmore & Smith, 2005). The Spanish reconquest down the Iberian Peninsula saw the warring Christian nobles acquiring land and the Crown strengthening its control. The outcome of the 1492 event was that the nobility and would-be nobility were eager for more conquests, and the Crown was ready to send explorers overseas (Skidmore & Smith, 2005). Thus, the Spaniards reached the New World imbued with the spirit of conquest. The encounter of the European and American civilizations was part of the remarkable European expansion of the fifteenth century. The Europeans came to know the rest of the world as its navigators and explorers pushed back the frontiers of their previously limited knowledge. By the early 1600s, they had woven a network of communications all the way around the globe and had established the economic dominance that would shape the modern world (Skidmore & Smith, 2005).

Historically, some Latino/Latina families are native to the land that today we call the United States of America and Canada. According to Berdichewsky (2007), the presence of Spanish-speaking populations in Canada dates back to the end of the 1700s in the form of the settlers who arrived prior to Cook's exploration, leaving their legacy in some areas of British Columbia with names such as Quadra, Galiano, Valdes, and Malspina, among many others. Since then, Canada has experienced waves of Latino/Hispanic immigrants who have made North America their home following a dream of opportunities and freedom or escaping political and civil unrest. Most Latin American Canadians are immigrants who arrived in the late twentieth century from Mexico, Central America and South America as well as from the Dominican Republic and Cuba.

Who Are Hispanics and Latino(a)s?

Within the United States and Canada, designations are given to groups of people whose origins share language, geography and other defining characteristics. It is no different for Hispanics and Latino(a)s who, according to Statistics Canada (2006), share a language (Spanish) but who come from different places. Hispanics are people who are originally from Spain and speak Spanish; Latino(a)s are people from Latin America (including Brazilians even though the language is not a shared characteristic). Other terms that describe this population are Latino Canadians or Latin Canadians. For purposes of this chapter, however, we will use the words Hispanic Canadian and Latin American Canadian interchangeably.

In 2006 the total Latin American population in Canada was 520 000, concentrated in metropolitan cities like Toronto, Vancouver, Calgary, Ottawa and Montreal (Statistics

Canada). Despite the report from Statistics Canada (2006) that most Latino immigrants declared feeling a sense of belonging, adapting to a new culture can present challenges for immigrants. Those who claim entrance as refugees are reported to have more difficult experiences with learning the language, learning about their rights and responsibilities, finding a job and integrating into a community they can call their own. Immigrants have come to Canada at different times for diverse reasons; some have arrived escaping political and civil unrest in their countries of origin, while others have come looking for a better future and employment opportunities. According to Rubio (2004), however, 30 per cent of Latin American refugees live below the poverty level. Overcoming poverty and other barriers, such as not knowing how to access services and lacking adequate skills to function in a different culture, puts refugees at a disadvantage. Further, racism and discrimination, coupled with a lack of language skills, limit people's possibilities to access information about their civic rights and responsibilities as well as to be informed about employment opportunities. Some immigrants are able to overcome challenges using their own life skills, the information and help they can gather and their lived experience. Some are able to create a safe network of connections within a community of Spanish speakers or with other communities such as schools, church or religious offices and so forth.

Each person's journey is filled with varying feelings of isolation, discrimination, loneliness, socio-economic challenges, discrimination and, ideally, eventual cultural adjustment. For these reasons, and for the benefit of the growing Latino/Latina population across North America, it is important to disseminate knowledge about this community. This chapter hopes to contribute to that goal, because understanding the belief system of the population, its traditions, culture, values and behaviours, can give the mental health establishment essential parameters to contribute to the development of this segment of the Canadian population.

Family Dynamics and Cultural Values

The traditional Latino(a) family tends to be an extended one, where members beyond the nuclear component, such as grandparents, aunts, uncles and cousins, are integral to the unit. This cultural norm is reinforced by the tradition of *familismo* (familism), which means the habit of extending kinship relationships beyond nuclear-family boundaries and emphasizing interdependence over dependence, affiliation over confrontation and cooperation over competition (Koslow & Salett, 1989). Latino(a) families are further extended by including non-blood-relations such as close family friends, who are often called "aunt" or "uncle" and treated like blood family (Koslow & Salett, 1989). Interdependence is a Latino(a) cultural value that prevails among many families and reinforces the value of collectivism. Likewise, activities surrounding family developmental milestones assume a high priority, and all family members are expected to participate. Families come together for events such as weddings, baptisms, anniversaries and funerals as well as for holiday celebrations. Participation in such family rituals reinforces the sense of belonging to the group.

There are large cross-cultural differences in the patterns of reciprocal relationships between the values of individualism among Caucasians in North America and the values of collectivism among the Latino(a)s. This convention resonates through most of the social arrangements that regulate daily life because it constitutes an implicit contract defining the balance between the freedom of the person, on the one hand, and restrictions on that person to achieve common goals, on the other. The structure of the family, the political system, industrial relations and the delivery of health, education and criminal justice services are only some examples of the institutions affected by this equation (Bochner, Furnham & Ward, 2001). Bochner and Furnham (1986) point out that migration involves a great number of potentially stressful changes and that the development of psychological or physical illnesses may be directly attributable to such changes. On the scale that predicts culture shock, the greater the score, the greater the shock.

Another cultural value ingrained in the traditional Latino(a) family is *respeto* (respect). This concept governs all positive reciprocal interpersonal relationships, dictating appropriate deferential behaviour toward others on the basis of age, socio-economic position, gender and authority (Koslow & Salett, 1989). Thus, for example, older people expect demonstrations of respect from the young, parents from offspring and employers from employees. On the other hand, when Latino(a) migrants living in the US or Canada perceive they are being treated without respect by people who have different manners or who are unaware of the importance of polite address — using Mister, Miss or Madam, for example — it comes as a shock.

Gender Roles

Another important Latino(a) immigrant value that may be challenged by differing values (causing cultural shock) is the role of the "king of the castle." In traditional Latino(a) culture, gender roles are rigidly defined; nevertheless, female/male relationships may often be complex and paradoxical. Boys and girls are taught different codes of gender behaviour. Latino men are expected to be cool, intellectual, rational, profound, strong, authoritarian, independent and brave, whereas Latina women are raised to be submissive, dependent, sentimental, gentle, intuitive and docile (Crow & Gotell, 2000). Traditional sex roles of immigrant Latino(a)s are changing, however, through contact with new cultures; some values erode, and others disappear. Cultural transition itself encourages sex-role reversal for Latino men and women. The pressures of economic survival in the new context, as well as the need for marketable skills, may result in a reversal of roles among many low-income Latino immigrants, since it is often easier for the women to obtain work (Rubio, 2004).

Prejudice and Discrimination

At present, prejudice against ethnic minorities and immigrants seems to have reached its maximum level around the world. Even though prejudice is almost universal and is not limited to one particular group, it tends to manifest itself differently from one person to another or from one group to another (Al-Issa, 1997). As a result of mass immigration from developing to developed countries during the second half of the twentieth century, prejudice toward ethnic minorities and immigrants has become a socio-political problem in almost every developed nation. Moreover, prejudice and discrimination are the foundation of many ethnic and religious conflicts around the world (Al-Issa, 1997).

Latino(a) Adolescents between Two Universes

Latino(a) immigrants, and even second-generation Latino(a)s, must learn to live in two different realities, because they must cope with two different cultures, languages and sets of values and world views (Falicov, 1998). Consequently, anxiety, depression and confusion are endemic. Latino families are historically assailed by experiences of discrimination, cultural alienation and poverty (Falicov, 1998). Moreover, adolescent Latino(a)s may face social and ethnic discrimination. Falicov (1998) points out that this marginalization may affect self-esteem: such institutionalized racism often results in feelings of helplessness as society's low expectations are internalized. The collision between two social realities may detonate in anti-social behaviours (Falicov, 1998), especially during the teenage period when the dominant culture is no longer safely outside the family as it seemed to be when children were small. Conflict and confusion enter the family's inner sanctum and, like an imperious guest, clamour for attention. Falicov (1998) suggests that there are differing views of connectedness and separation, collectivism and individualism, as well as different conceptions of age and gender hierarchies, which can no longer be ignored.

Falicov (1998) also mentions that the complexity of resolving these issues may bring Latino(a) families to counselling. While the premise of respect and obedience to one's parents is universal, cultural norms about transgression and its consequences vary. For example, for some Latino families, talking back to one's parents or evading one's responsibility to society or to one's family is not considered to be the parents' fault but is simply the bad luck of having an ungrateful son or daughter (Falicov, 1998). However, for the majority culture, having children who deviate from society's norms is a reflection on the parents' ability to raise good citizens. On the other hand, the Latino(a) adolescent is often the guilty one, shamed by his or her parents for breaking the rules and not exhibiting an appropriate demeanor. Cultural norms and practices inhabit the core of our humanity and help us develop our sense of self, including values, beliefs, thought patterns, perceptions and world view. All these qualities help determine and shape one's external culture — that is, the way(s) in which one establishes and maintains a relationship with the environment and others through implicit norms, language, traditions, rituals, and loyalties that influence attitudes, behaviours and customs (Gushue, 1993).

Social Stress and Psychological Distress

Some of the resources for Latino(a) adolescents' counselling can help families navigate through adolescence by finding culturally consonant ways for parents to understand and accept their adolescent's growth while keeping the parents-child bond intact. A counsellor usually acts as a family liaison, clarifying expectations, justifying conflicts, translating family members' cultural behaviours and encouraging compromise and negotiation between parents and adolescents. Misunderstandings can occur when the developmental time frame for dating, curfews and other freedoms is out of sync between parents and teenagers (Falicov, 1998).

Counselling with Latinas and Latinos

Vasquez (1994) suggests that an awareness of factors specific to Latino(a) culture and a sensitivity to variations among people are both necessary in order to understand the conditions that affect Latino(a)s' mental health. Counsellors must be well informed and respectful of significant environmental and socio-cultural influences in order to provide competent, ethical and responsible therapy. Vasquez (1994) also mentions that mental health practitioners often ignore cultural values, attitudes, behaviours and experiences that differ from their own. This lack of knowledge results in a tendency to rely on their own world view and to make assumptions about their clients in an erroneous and possibly destructive manner.

Conversely, therapists should avoid making simplistic, unfounded assumptions solely on the basis of their own or their client's ethnicity and gender. Many therapists — sometimes even well-intentioned ones — apply ethnic stereotyping instead of carefully assessing, for example, a particular person from Latin America. It is important to have some knowledge of cultural and socio-economic contexts: such knowledge is best used as a basis for informed inquiry, rather than as a blanket opinion with which to stereotype the client (Vasquez, 1994). McGoldrick, Giordano and Pearce (1996) suggest that, in therapy, eliciting, listening to and validating stories about how clients' lives are affected by living in a new context will help families to see themselves beyond their problems and not be restricted by them.

Koslow and Salett (1989) note that no single method or approach can be considered best for treating Latino(a)s: some individuals respond better to one approach and some to another, depending on their complaints. A variety of treatment modalities have been used with Latino(a)s. Some counsellors tend to invoke cultural values such as familismo in family therapy. Other treatments have included behavioural and dynamically oriented approaches. Culturally relevant treatment interventions, such as *cuento* therapy (the use of folktales in treatment), have also been developed (Comas-Diaz & Green, 1994).

Regardless of the approach used with Latino(a)s, counsellors need to address their clients' complex set of treatment expectations, involving a multiplicity of physical, psychological and environmental dimensions. Counsellors should probably give due attention to the socio-cultural context (Kostow & Salett, 1989).

Therapeutic Intervention for the Latina American Population

Given the often rigid expectations with regard to sex roles within family and community, it is suggested that the helper use both feminist and multicultural types of treatment when working with Latinas. Vasquez (1994) points out that both therapeutic approaches are based on philosophies asserting that external factors be examined as causative in Latina women's problems. The therapeutic process endorses the importance of empowering the client to engage in change, if that is what she wants, instead of pathologizing or blaming her. Vasquez (1994) recommends emphasizing the client's strengths instead of her weaknesses. Vasquez (1994) also suggests that counsellors must guard against a tendency to apply psychotherapy in a way that encourages clients to adapt to an unhealthy environment rather than empowering them to change such an environment. Cultural sensitivity is important in services for Latina women because they tend to assume blame and responsibility for failures and painful experiences. Thus, the role of the counsellor is to help the client to realize the importance of compassion toward herself, to take care of her body and her feelings and to learn to expect respect from those who are important to her (Vasquez, 1994).

Reducing Prejudice

Al-Issa (1997) points out that, by taking the opportunity to get to know members of other groups and to interact with them as individuals, people can minimize discrimination and prejudice in society. He also notes that differentiation of an out-group and discovering the exclusivity of its individual members may maximize positive responses towards them. Another important element in minimizing prejudice is to accept that contact between people should be based on an egalitarian structure. Moreover, the interaction among members of a normal group usually behaves as if the status characteristics such as race, colour, age and ethnicity were relevant to the skills involved in the task.

Al-Issa (1997) says it is important to remember that, in the West, the history of colonization and slavery has resulted in a domination relationship between whites of European origin and other races and nations. In order to support whites' belief in their own superiority, as well the inferiority of other cultures, they may invoke science and the Christian religion. As a result, the influence of the historical background or Western ethnocentrism has been passed down from one generation to the next, by social learning through their families, peers, friends, the mass media, school and other institutions (Al-Issa, 1997). Comas-Diaz and Green (1994) suggest that in order to improve Latina clients' mental health, direct advocacy activities may be required, for instance, learning to write a letter (with appropriate releases) for a student to re-enter school. Furthermore, advocacy may also include efforts to improve policies, laws and judicial decisions.

Some organizations or institutions like universities habitually provide counselling facilities for those who struggle in a new culture or who experience challenges related to diversity in its broad sense and understanding. Corey (2007) points out a series of approaches that have contributed to multicultural counselling, like solution-focussed therapy, which is very well suited to people with adjustment disorders and problems of anxiety and depression. Narrative therapy has been used for a broad range of human predicaments including relationships concerns, eating disorders, family distress and depression. These approaches can be of use in working with people of all ages: children, adolescents, adults, couples, families and the community in a wide variety of settings. In addition, narrative and solution-focused therapy lend themselves to group counselling. Because these postmodern approaches focus on the social and cultural context of behaviour, stories that have been explained in the therapy office need to be anchored in the real world, where Latinas/Latinos live.

A counsellor does not make assumptions about individuals who come to counseling; rather, he or she honours each individual's story and cultural background. Moreover, the counsellor takes an active role in challenging cultural and social injustice that lead to oppression of any group. Therapy thus becomes a process of liberation from oppressive cultural values and enables individuals in counselling to become active agents of their own destinies.

Corey (2007) mentions Adlerian therapy, stating that it focusses on social interest, helping other people, collectivism, pursuing meaning in life, the importance of family and goal orientation — points that are congruent with the values of Latino(a)s and other cultures. Focussing on the person-in-environment allows cultural elements to be explored. Another approach that is very useful for the Latino/Latina community is cognitive–behaviour therapy, because it takes a collaborative approach, allowing individuals to express their areas of concern. This therapeutic approach has a psycho-educational component, which is useful in exploring cultural conflicts and suggesting new behaviours. Despite the fact that this approach emphasizes thinking rather than identifying and expressing feelings, it can be acceptable for clients. The process of focusing on learning and teaching tends to avoid any stigma of mental illness. The Latina/Latino community may value the directive stance of such a therapist (Corey, 2007).

Family system therapy is another important approach for the Latina/Latino community because it focuses on the family or community system. In addition, many family therapies deal with extended family members and with a support system like the Latina/Latino community. Another important aspect of the family system therapy is the networking, which is congruent with the values of many members of the Latin community. Consequently, there is a good chance for individuals to change if other family members are compassionate. This approach offers ways of working toward the health of the family unit and the welfare of each member of the Latin community (Corey, 2007).

Although these therapies can be beneficial, they also have limitations in multicultural counselling. For instance, some critics argue that these therapies endorse "cheerleading" and an overly positive perspective. There are individuals in the "industry" of counselling who are critical of the stance taken by most postmodern therapists in relationship with assessment and diagnosis and also react negatively to the "not-knowing" position of the counsellor. One limitation of family system therapy includes difficulties in involving all the members of a family in the process, which may result in some of the family members resisting change in the structure of the system. Counsellors' self-knowledge and willingness to work on their own family-of-origin issues are crucial because of the high probability of counter-transference. Therefore, it is important that therapists be well trained, receive quality supervision and be competent in assessing and treating individuals in a family context (Corey, 2007).

The Three-Dimensional Model

Atkinson, Thompson and Grant's (1993) multi-modal approach to counselling describes eight alternative roles that involve the counsellor more actively in the client's life experiences than do conventional approaches. These roles may be used independently or jointly depending on the problems, situation or goals of the client. Although they might overlap at some point due to their nature, each role includes some components that make it unique.

The model consists of three elements or variables (dimensions) that exist in a continuum and need to be considered when working with minorities:

- the goal of the counselling situation (preventive/remedial);

- the etiology of the problem (internal/external);

- the client's level of acculturation (low/high).

According to Padilla (1980), acculturation is a central variable in the delivery of counselling services to Latino(a)s because it encompasses a wide continuum and is affected by socio-economic status, value orientations and language proficiency, preference and use (Elliot, 2000). Acculturation, however, has the potential to become a risk factor when individuals lack a support network. As a result of changing life experiences and cultural clash of values, day-to-day situations become unfamiliar, stressful and conflictive. Individuals struggle to maintain a cultural identity while at the same time trying to adapt to their new one. Some factors related to acculturation among Latino(a)s, include the following:

- status according to generation (related to family history, and educational and occupational opportunities);

- use of English language (corresponding to needs and preferences [at home and at work] and level of proficiency);

- frequency of mobility to the original country (maintenance of culture-specific attitudes and value orientation).

The Roles of the Counsellor

Atkinson et al. (1993) identified eight therapist roles to help clients in different ways depending on the interdependent variables and situations: advisor; advocate; facilitator of indigenous support systems; facilitator of indigenous healing systems; consultant; change agent; counsellor; and/or psychotherapist. The role(s) assumed by the counsellor will shift based on the three dimensions described above. Table 1 illustrates how the role(s) would unfold according to the juxtaposition of the dimensions.

Table 1

Counsellors' Roles

Role	Degree of Acculturation	Type of Problem	Goal
Advisor	Low	External	Preventative
Advocate	Low	External	Remedial
Facilitator of Indigenous Support System	Low	Internal	Preventative
Facilitator of Indigenous Healing Methods	Low	Internal	Remedial
Consultant	High	External	Preventative
Change Agent	High	External	Remedial
Counsellor	High	Internal	Remedial
Therapist	High	Internal	Remedial

1. Advisor: The counsellor acts as an advisor when the client's level of acculturation is low, the problem is external and the goal of the treatment is prevention. The counsellor tries to prevent difficulties from arising by advising the client about the problems he/she or his/her family might encounter. The counsellor initiates discussion of a potential developing problem and advises the client about alternatives or options to prevent it from emerging. This approach is used mostly with new immigrants who may need advice concerning difficulties in the new country. This role of the advisor serves clients who want to know what to do to reduce the impact of newly encountered conditions such as culture shock, adjustment, assimilation and adaptation, among others.

2. Advocate: The counsellor serves as an advocate when the client's level of acculturation is low, the problem is external and the goal of the treatment is remediation. As an advocate, the counsellor speaks on behalf of the client, who may be one individual or a group of people experiencing harsh conditions. In this role, the counsellor represents the individual/group and must be willing to pursue alternative courses with or for the client. As an advocate, the counsellor has the responsibility to ensure that the client benefits from the diverse resources of the majority culture without losing what is unique and valued in the client's own culture. The role of counsellor as advocate has gained strength among ethnically diverse schools. The National Coalition of Advocates for Students (1988) developed a number of recom-

mendations for advocacy on behalf of immigrant students. School counsellors are urged to advocate to school personnel that immigrant children have a legal right to free, appropriate public education and to restructure policies and practices that sort immigrant students into programs that prepare them for inferior futures. School counsellors must also ensure that immigrant students experience a school environment free of victimization, harassment and intergroup conflict, and ensure an equitable allocation of resources to the schools that serve such students.

3. Facilitator of indigenous support system: This role is helpful when the client's level of acculturation is low, the problem is internal and the goal of counselling is preventive. Counselling can be thought of as a social support system to help prevent and remediate problems; because support systems are more acceptable to many cultures than professional counselling or therapy, it is likely that clients will trust the counsellor who assumes the role of facilitator of indigenous support. Some of these support systems include ethnic churches, community centres, family networks and the like. The counsellor is invited to acknowledge strongly the importance of the support systems and encourage diverse ethnic or governmental organizations to provide the services needed by the individual or the community. Additionally, counsellors might facilitate the use of indigenous support systems by referring clients and encouraging them to use the available services.

4. Facilitator of indigenous healing methods: If the client's level of acculturation is low, the problem is internal and the goal of the therapy is remediation, the counsellor assumes this role. It is the counsellor's duty to acknowledge, honour and respect the client's belief system. Every culture has different effective means to deal with and solve problems once they develop; the effectiveness of such means lies mostly in the members' positive beliefs about the methods. Thus, individuals who believe in certain healing procedures are likely to comply with them. By undertaking this role, the counsellor accepts that healing methods from the client's culture are more likely to be effective than conventional dominant treatments or strategies. When dominant approaches are advised for the client, the result might be a divergence between the need and the help provided, loss of credibility in the counsellor and finally the client's disengagement from counselling.

5. Consultant: Hansen, Himes and Meier (1990) have defined consultation as an association that involves a collegial relationship between the consultant and the client, who work together to affect the behaviour of a third party. In this role, the counsellor tries to prevent problems from developing; counsellors can help minorities to learn skills needed to interact successfully with the dominant society. Because values and the potential to respond in assertive ways differ from one culture to another, minority groups such as Latino(a)s might struggle with the inability to perform

skills valued by the dominant culture; such struggles place them at a disadvantage for coping with the majority culture. Thus, counsellors are encouraged to be able to teach basic coping and social skills to minority group clients. One way to do this, according to LaFramboise and Rowe (1993), is by modelling in small groups, since this procedure involves a different way of transmitting knowledge that — though indirect — is effective.

6. Change agent: Egan (1985) describes a change agent as "anyone who plays an important part in designing, redesigning, running, renewing, or improving any system, subsystem, or program" (p. 12). In this role, the counsellor attempts to change, modify or adjust the social environment that afflicts racial/ethnic minorities. The counsellor helps the client identify the external sources of his/her problem as well as methods of resolving the problem. Together they develop a strategy for eliminating or reducing the effect of affliction on the client's life. Often, facilitating the formation of racial/ethnic minority political groups accomplishes this. The counsellor serving as a change agent assumes a low profile, often finding it useful to mobilize other influential persons in the stressful institution to bring about change. Lewis and Bradley (2000) identify four ways in which a counsellor can act as a change agent: the counsellor can assess community needs; the counsellor can coordinate activities and resources; the counsellor can provide training in skill-building; and the counsellor can advocate change. Ponterotto (1987) described a multi-modal approach for counselling Mexican-Americans that includes a change-agent component that could apply to other ethnic groups. As described by Ponterotto, this role involves identification of the social, environmental and institutional factors that are oppressing the client but are external to his/her control.

7. Counsellor: The helper follows the conventional counselling role when the client has a high acculturation level, the problem is internal and the goal is the prevention of problems. The main role of the counsellor is to help the client make decisions, taking into consideration the client's history, beliefs, attitudes, values and background. Each alternative considers goals and consequences, probability for the outcome to occur, decision-making processes and decision-making skills. Since the client has high acculturation (which means that he or she has developed adaptation skills), it is important that the counsellor be aware of his/her own biases that might influence the client's decision for choosing a specific alternative or option.

8. Psychotherapist: The facilitator serves as a psychotherapist when the client's level of acculturation is high, the problem is internal and the client wants to resolve the situation. Two important elements the counsellor must consider when taking on this role are to maintain credibility as a counsellor and to offer clients a benefit from therapy as soon as possible. Sue and Zane (1987) suggest that three factors are sig-

nificantly related to maintaining the counsellor's credibility: the conceptualization of a client's problem must be congruent with the client's belief system; the counsellor's required responses from and suggestions to the client must be culturally compatible and acceptable; the definition of goals must be the same for counsellor and client. By giving, the counsellor reinforces his/her credibility. Giving could be described as a meaningful gain in therapy; it includes (giving) reassurance, hope, faith, skills acquisition, a coping perspective and anxiety reduction alternatives among others.

General Considerations When Counselling Latino(a)s

Some professional and personal attitudes and beliefs affect the process of counselling minorities negatively. Cultural history and experiences of oppression cause changes in behaviour, which might have different meanings for counsellor and client. To avoid stereotypes and biases, the counsellor must seek specific information regarding the client, such as demographic information (historical and cultural background), professional expertise (what kinds of job experience has the client had) and personal experiences (racism/exclusion/acceptance).

In order to assist Latino(a) clients, the counsellor must consider several factors such as language maintenance, social relationships, family structure and history, and religious affiliation. Since the vitality of a language indicates how well a group is maintaining itself in society, it should be considered within the broader framework of social, political and ideological factors; language operates as one of the most important practices within our society wherein cultural production and reproduction take place (Corson, 1998; Darder, 1991). Despite the many similarities that Latino(a)s share as a group bound mostly by language, spiritual beliefs and values, counsellors must understand that differences in world view are important. In Canada, the reality for Latino(a)s is different from that in the United States, given their history and place of origin. As a result of stereotyping and biases, Latino(a)s in particular have been diagnosed more often with problems, yet, interestingly, have received less time with helpers than have any other group. The notion of what is considered "normal" by various health organizations should be challenged when dealing with non-mainstream individuals. What is considered to be "normal" must be evaluated and understood according to the situation, personal history and background, as well as the circumstances under which a particular event occurred.

The counsellor's interpretation or discernment of a situation would benefit from having an awareness of the following:

- Being aware that the counsellor might be perceived as an authority figure who deserves respect and whose advice is to be followed. In patriarchal societies, people expect to be guided and even told what to do and how to proceed in a variety of situations.
- Knowing that the notion of "self," as understood in individualistic North American societies, operates collectively with Latino(a) clients. Counsellors must understand the value of connecting, supporting and relying on extended family.
- Being careful not to fall into stereotyping, especially when it comes to anticipating results within the therapy or helping process. Stereotyping uses the racial or ethnic background of an individual as a simplistic, straightforward predictor of beliefs or behaviours.
- Recognizing that Latino(a) people embrace alternative therapies, such as massage therapists, healers and herbal remedies.

What Clients Might Experience

Among Latino(a) clients, history of oppression, personal experiences and specific cultural background cause different reactions and behaviours. What is taken for granted by a counsellor (often based in stereotypes) might be a different and unique reality for the client. As a result, clients frequently are not understood and treated according to their own experiences. Therefore, it is necessary that counsellors seek statistical and empirical information that will provide them more ample opportunities to help Latino(a)s adequately. From such a foundation, say Diaz, Vasquez and Ruiz de Esparza (2002), "[counsellors] can expand their ability to distinguish between stereotype and truth, bias and health, and effective counselling and cultural oppression" (p. 146). Some general perceptions from the Latino(a) client's perspective include the following:

- Interdependence is viewed as healthy and necessary.
- Family plays an important role in the client's life in regards to encouragement, educational expectations, critical life events, vicarious learning and work identity (Fisher & Padmawidjaja, 1999).
- Due to the history of poor job opportunities, social relations, oppression, discrimination, access to education and the way Western cultures perceive them, some Latino(a)s experience low self-esteem that could be reflected in aggressive behaviour, isolation and so forth (McNeill, Prieto, Pizarro, Vera & Gomez, 2001)
- Some clients may believe that counsellors should go a step further by helping clients change the environment and not merely adjust or adapt to it.
- Disclosing intimate problems may be difficult since it may negatively affect the

family. Being verbally open and direct is not the norm among Latino(a)s. This point should be understood as a value of the culture and not as a deterring aspect of the counselling process.

- Instant familiarity, especially when meeting a new person (e.g., at the time of the initial office visit), is not advisable. Formality with people the counsellor does not know well is a sign of respect and deference.
- The history of the client's past is important and can affect his/her immediate feelings and actions.
- Thinking can be linear (cause–effect) or circular (events are viewed as independent of consequent events). It is possible that situations may be attributed to God's will, good luck or forces beyond the client's control.

Alternative Approaches

According to Casas, Vasquez and Ruiz de Esparza (2002), the counselling process should focus on the client's expectations, preferences, values and attitudes; they suggest taking into consideration the following approaches:

Use of existential philosophy: This approach enhances and honours cultural differences and organizes experiences that reflect universal concerns of humankind.
Cultural empathy: The counsellor must generate thoughts, words and behaviour to communicate effectively with diverse cultural groups.
Use of a multi-modal approach: A multi-modal approach provides the flexibility to be adaptable to the intracultural diversity of Latino(a)s; it enhances the probability of behaviour change and attends to behaviour, images, cognitive processes, sensations and interpersonal relationships.
Procure a degree of commitment: The counsellor could participate actively in some of the activities that the Latino(a) community offers and be actively involved. This is a form of social responsibility that should be embraced.

Conclusions

According to Vanier (1998), "love and respect, like fear and prejudice, are legacies passed on from one person to another. The movement from seeking approval to taking responsibility, to being open to those who are different, implies a shift of consciousness" (pp. 81–82). The shift for counsellors involves viewing cultural identity as a major element of a person's behaviour; thus, being sensitive to and understanding the cultural background of clients is imperative. As a cultural group that is racially diverse yet shares a common language, Latino(a)s are in a unique situation.

Latino(a) is one the fastest growing populations in North America, particularly in the US but also in Canada. We argue that cultures are not static: they are always changing, just as humans do. Our understanding is that the socio-economical situation in Latin America is worse then ever: levels of poverty are high, and the unemployment rate has reached the skies. Consequently, the need to migrate to the "North" became urgent for some of our citizens in order realize their dreams. During the last two decades, the Latino(a) population has grown rapidly. When Latino(a)s come to the US, they are dismayed by the attitude of non-Latino(a)s toward them. Their language, colour and culture — all that is essential to their being — seem a cause for oppression. I do not doubt that the diversity of knowledge and culture that exists among Latin American immigrants creates great opportunities for their new country; one hears only negative impressions of our communities, however. We cannot deny that some Latino(a)s' views may be old-fashioned; but the US needs to correct its exploitation of new immigrants and change its narrow views regarding Latin American countries. Americans tend to see Latin American immigrants as being all the same; however, they are individuals as well, each with his/her own life experience and world view. When Latino(a) immigrants arrive in the United States, they have often left behind family, friends, spouses, relatives and precious traditions; in the United States, almost everything is different. The infrastructure and many components of the superstructure, like laws, rules and regulations, are new to immigrants. Consequently, the probabilities of culture shock are high and can cause depression in Latino(a) immigrants.

It is important to be aware of how clients' cultural backgrounds contribute to their perception of their tribulations. Although it is imprudent to stereotype Latino(a)s who come to counselling, it is important to assess to what extent the cultural context has a bearing on their concerns. There are many approaches in psychotherapy, some of which may be contraindicated because of the client's socialization; thus, the client's responsiveness (or lack of it) to certain techniques is an important measure in judging the effectiveness of a given technique. The research on cross-cultural counselling is extensive and suggests diverse modes and models for counselling minorities. Atkinson, Thompson and Grant's (1993) three-dimensional model for counselling racial/ethnic minorities is one of the most useful paradigms for counsellors working with Latino(a) clients. However, it is the helper's judgement and responsibility to choose the procedure(s) that will bring forth the most benefit and positive outcomes for the client. It is in our willingness to be accepting of others that we as helpers begin to understand other people's needs and hopes without forgetting that respect, openness and common sense will always be crucial components of what constitutes a good counselling practice.

Effective counselling for the Latino(a) community involves proficiency in a mixture of cognitive, behavioural and affective techniques. Such a combination is important to help Latino/Latina people analyze their beliefs and assumptions, to experience on a feeling level their conflicts and struggles and to translate their insights into action programs by learning to behave in new ways in their day-to-day living.

References

Al-Issa, I., & Tousignment, M. (1997). *Ethnicity, immigration, and psychology*. New York: Plenum Press.

Atkinson, D.R., Thompson, C.E., & Grant, S.K. (1993). A three-dimensional model for counselling racial/ethnic minorities. *Counselling Psychologist*, 21, 257–277.

Bochner, S., & Furnham, A. (1986). *Culture shock*. New York and London: Methuen.

Bochner, S., Furnham, A., & Ward, G. (2001). *The psychology of culture shock*. New York and London: Routledge.

Berdichewsky, B. (2007). *Latin Americans' integration into Canadian society in B.C.* Vancouver: BC. Retrieved from http://www.lulu.com/shop/bernardo-berdichewsky/latin-americans-integration-into-canadian-society-in-bc/ebook/product-17482201.html

Casas, J.M., & Vasquez, M.J.T. (1989). Counseling the Hispanic client: A theoretical and applied perspective. In P.B. Pedersen, J.G. Draguns, W.J. Lonner & J.E. Trimble (Eds.), *Counseling across cultures* (3rd ed., pp. 153–175). Thousand Oaks, CA: Sage Publications.

Comas-Diaz, L., & Beverly, G. (1994). *Women of color: Integrating ethnic and gender identities in psychotherapy*. New York: The Guilford Press.

Corey, G. (2007). *Theory and practice of counseling and psychotherapy*. Belmont, CA: Thompson.

Corson, D. (1998). *Changing education for diversity*. Bristol, PA: Open University Press.

Darder, A. (1991). *Culture and power in the classroom: A critical foundation for bicultural education*. Toronto, ON: OISE Press.

Egan, G. (1985). *Change agent skills in helping and human serving settings*. Monterey, CA: Brooks/Cole.

Elliot, K.A.G. (2001). *The relationship between acculturation, family functioning, and school performance of Mexican-American adolescents*. Unpublished doctoral thesis, University of California, Santa Barbara.

Falicov, C.J. (1998). *Latino families in therapy: A guide to multicultural practice*. New York, NY: The Guilford Press.

Fisher, T., & Padmawidjaja, I. (1999). Parental influences on career development perceived by African American and Mexican American college students. *Journal of Multicultural Counselling and Development*, 27, 136–152.

Gushue, G.V. (1993). Cultural-identity development and family assessment: An interaction model. *The Counselling Psychologist*, 21, 487–513.

Koslow, D. & Salett, E.P. (1989) *Crossing cultures in mental health*. Washington DC: SIETAR.

McGoldrick, M., Giordano, J., & Garcia-Preto, N. (2005). *Ethnicity and family therapy*. New York, NY: The Guilford Press.

McNeill, B.W., Prieto, L.R., Pizarro, M., Vera, E.M., & Gomez, S.P. (2001). Current directions in Chicano psychology, *Counseling Psychology*, 29, 5–17.

LaFramboise, T., & Rowe, W. (1983). Skills training for bicultural competence: Rationale and application. *Journal of Counselling Psychology*, 30, 589–595.

Lewis, J., & Bradley, L. (Eds.). (2000). *Advocacy in counseling: Counselors, clients, and community*. Greensboro, NC: ERIC-CASS.

Moursund, J. (1995). *The process of counseling and therapy*. Portland, OR: Prentice Hall.

Padilla, A.M. (1980). *Acculturation: Theory, models and some new findings*. Boulder, CO: Westview Press.

Ponterotto, J.G. (1987). Counselling Mexican-Americans: A multi-modal approach. *Journal of Counselling and Development*, 65, 308–312.

Rubio, F. (2004). *Social inclusion: The basis of and possible effects of social inclusion and exclusion on the Hispanic community in Toronto.* Unpublished paper. Toronto, ON: Hispanic Development Council.

Skimore, T. & Smith, P. (2005). *Modern Latin America.* New York, NY: Oxford University Press.

Statistics Canada (2006). The Latin American Community in Canada. Retrieved from http://www.statcan.gc.ca/pub/89-621-x/89-621-x2007008-eng.htm

Sue, S., & Zane, N. (1987). The role of culture and cultural techniques in psychotherapy: A critique and reformulation. *American Psychologist, 42,* 37–45.

Vasquez, M. J.T. (1994). Latinas. In D. Comas-Diaz & B. Greene (Eds.), *Women of color: Integrating ethnic and gender identities in psychotherapy* (pp. 114–135). New York, NY: The Guilford Press.

Vanier, J. (1998). *Becoming human.* Toronto, ON: House of Anansi Press.

12

Counselling Black Canadians

Elias Cheboud & M. Honoré France

My family's history in Canada is one of the many untold stories buried in the margins. My parents migrated to Montreal in the 1940s from areas in Nova Scotia that were economically depressed. They came seeking a better life for themselves and their children but soon discovered that, for black people, life anywhere in Canada was one of racial discrimination and lack of opportunities. Life in Nova Scotia had been a daily struggle for survival — unemployment, segregation, lack of education, alcoholism and a general condition of despair had engulfed many of the Nova Scotian Black communities. I saw the toll it took on successive generations in my family. It left a bitterness that would haunt many of my relative for the rest of their lives, and many sought to escape the disillusionment and hardships of life through the "demon" bottle that finally destroyed them. (Ruggles, 1996, p. 5)

THE ISSUE OF RACISM that Ruggles describes persists at every level of Canadian society from the overt to the covert; yet despite this, Canadians of African descent continue to contribute to Canadian society. Most people are familiar with the overt forms of racism embodied by laws that are reminiscent of apartheid in South Africa. The subtler forms, covert and sometimes unintentional, are more difficult to recognize. According to Mensah (2010), systematic racism "is the common practice, until quite recently, of requiring prospective transit drivers or police offers to be of a certain weight or height . . . [but] invariably goes against some ethnoracial groups" (p. 17). Mensah (2010) goes on to say it is "ironic that the Charter of Rights and Freedoms — which seeks to protect ethnoracial minorities — has ended up giving legal ammunition to extremists to advocate racial surrealism in the name of freedom of speech" (p. 17). To us, the form of racism in the education curriculum is an absence of systematic exposure of students to issues of diversity. In recent years educational institutions, at all levels, have taken steps to ensure that diversity has a greater priority and importance on campus; however, there are still attitudes and practices that need to be revised. What needs to be emphasized in counsellor training is the crucial and complex role that culture plays in becoming competent — that everyone in intercultural training is in process and bound to make mistakes. The call is to be patient and helpful to each other. The purpose of a cross-cultural counselling and teaching course is to enlighten, inform, sensitize and teach curriculum approaches, theories of helping and strategies that can be used to help others. All people of every culture in Canadian society are "brothers and sisters"; embracing each other and ridding society of racism is the only way of building a just society. Let go, in order to allow everyone to grow cross-culturally. We need to teach each other to be more sensitive. The idea of respecting others is a difficult task filled with stumbling and mistakes. It requires sensitivity to others at a degree that reflects what Ridley and Lingle (1996) identify as *cultural empathy*. Cultural empathy is a

> learned ability of counsellors to accurately gain an understanding of the self — experienced of clients from other cultures — an understanding informed by counselors' interpretation of cultural data. Cultural empathy also involves the ability of counsellors to communicate this understanding effectively with an attitude of concern for culturally different clients. (p. 32)

Cultural empathy can also be called multicultural empathy. While helpful, multicultural empathy can supersede factors such as cultural similarity between counsellors and clients. People of dissimilar cultural backgrounds can learn to decode cultural cues. This process is not dependent on neutralizing one's cultural values, because not being in touch with one's cultural identity is an insecure personal foundation. And, like any other skill, cultural empathy can be learned. The process involves first learning how to empathize and then decode meaning(s) embedded in culture. This step is followed by being able to respond in a culturally appropriate manner, including the affective, cognitive and spiritual dimensions of human nature. Ridley and Lingle (1993) indicate that in order to be competent in cultural empathy, the counsellor must be able to differentiate between self and other from a cultural perspective. Cultural sensitivity requires the ability to understand cultural information from the client accurately and includes the following processes: perspective taking ("walking in the other's shoes"), vicarious experience (how the client feels things), and responding expressively to client issues.

Who Are Black Canadians?

People of African descent have been living in Canada as long as Europeans have, although in comparison to the United States, their numbers nationwide are relatively small. According to Statistics Canada (2011), out of a population of approximately 34 million, 274 630 people identified themselves as having origins from the Caribbean or Africa (1 per cent of the Canadian population compared to 12 per cent in the US). While the term *African-American* is widely accepted in the United States, many people who descended from people who came to Canada from the Caribbean prefer the name *Caribbean Canadian* or *black Canadian* to reflect their Caribbean ancestry. Rinaldo Walcott, who is of black and African Canadian descent, says, "I use the archaic and ancient term *black* as a way of framing the political discourse that I am structuring" (1997, p. 2). He feels that the use of *black* becomes political and thus goes beyond the narrow sense of identity of someone whose ancestors originally came from Africa. On the other hand, American political activist Jessie Jackson considers the use of *black* outdated in multicultural America. He has said, when criticized by others, that there is no such place as "black" but there is a place called Africa with a long history and culture. Many who first criticized Jackson have begun to use the term African-American. We have chosen to use *black Canadian* and *African Canadian* interchangeably in this chapter, because of the use of both terms in the literature. With few exceptions, in Canada *black* is much more widely cited than "black and African-Canadians." Notwithstanding events in the United States, the terms *black* and *African Canadian* include not only "black" Loyalists but more recent immigrants and their children from the Caribbean, Fiji and the many countries of Africa.

In the last thirty years, the number of people immigrating or coming as refugees from Africa has increased. The largest group of sub-Saharan immigrants has come from Kenya, Ethiopia, Somalia, South Africa and Tanzania, with numbers expected to increase; the overall numbers are small, however, in comparison to the number of immigrants from Asia. There are 32 000 more black women than black men in Canada. Interestingly, about 30 per cent of black Canadians have Jamaican heritage and have come to Canada as immigrants; an additional 32 per cent have heritage elsewhere in the Caribbean or Bermuda. Sixty percent of black Canadians live in the province of Ontario, although 90 per cent of Canadians of Haitian origin live in Quebec. Sixty percent of black Canadians are under the age of 35, and 97 per cent of black Canadians live in urban areas.

Historical Background of Black and African Canadians

According to Walker (1976), for Canadians "to overlook black history is not only to ignore an important cultural heritage; it is to misunderstand the direction of Canadian history in its entirety" (p. 51). Mainstream Canadian history texts have clearly overlooked the place and role of those of African descent. From the very beginning of European immigration to Canada, people of African descent lived and worked in this country. Before slavery was outlawed in the British Empire in 1834, most blacks were brought to Canada either as slaves or as indentured servants. However, there were many exceptions, including more than 5 000 who came at the end of the American revolution as Loyalists. African Canadians' history of racism and segregation has been overshadowed by the widely documented experience of African-Americans' struggles against discrimination. The fact is that the government and people of Canada have a long history of discrimination and racism against people because of the colour of their skin. While many thousands of blacks escaped from slavery in the United States, finding freedom in Canada, they were still segregated. Even as late as World War One, there were separate battalions for people of colour in the Canadian army. Segregation officially ended in Nova Scotia schools in 1954, but the struggle for equality still persists all over Canada, with gradual gains in acceptance and recognition.

Consider that British Columbia's first governor, Sir James Douglas, was a person of mixed British and African blood. His mother, born in the Caribbean, was the daughter of a freeman who was brought from Africa originally as a slave. Interestingly, Douglas was also instrumental in inviting the first blacks to the British Colony of Vancouver Island in the spring of 1858. Many settled on Salt Spring Island and in the Central Saanich area. The colony's first police force was the all-black African Rifles, organized by Douglas in the summer of 1858. One of the more visible successes in BC was the 1972 election of Rosemary Brown, the first black woman elected to a provincial legislature in Canada. While African Canadians have become an integral part of British Columbia's society, there is still a persistence of racism among people in Canada. Moreover, black people's participation and deeds receive little recognition or have gone unrecorded in the history books. Blacks remain the invisible and yet visible minority. One has to remember that culture is evolutionary and influenced by the historical and social forces around it. However, the influence of the black and African Canadian community on cultural evolution is often omitted or forgotten outright. To fail to acknowledge the contribution is to deny the existence of the contributor.

The Role of Racism and Its Psychological Impact

> Why the hell do I want to go to a place like Mombasa [Kenya]? . . . I'm sort of scared about going there . . . I just see myself in a pot of boiling water with all these natives dancing around me. (ABC News, June 26, 2001)

Former Toronto mayor Mel Lastman denied being a racist despite what he said during a tour of Africa in support of his city's drive to be awarded the Olympic bid in 2008. However, his statement not only embarrassed the city and Canada but reinforced many minorities' perceptions that many Canadians just do not understand how racism destabilizes the community and individually humiliates and hurts African Canadians. Consider the case of Quebec high school teacher William Kafe, who complained to the Human Rights Tribunal in 1993 about his treatment at his school. At the trial,

> Kafe testified that over the years students had brought excrement to throw at him; twice the students set fire to his classroom and shouted "we're going to burn down the nigger"; they flooded his classroom and shouted, "We're going to drown the nigger." They kicked him and held him down by his tie, pulling him around like a dog. They told him he was dirty and brought soap and a face cloth to "wash the dirty nigger." They did mocked African dances, chanting "Zulu, go back to Africa." (Ruggles 1996, p. 94)

Kafe reported he was so anxious and depressed with the racial taunts he received from his students that he was unable to continue teaching. Two days before the judgement was heard, Kafe was arrested for a letter he sent to his local mayor, in which he complained about racism and made a "shooting rampage" reference. The tribunal agreed that Kafe had been racially harassed and awarded him $10 000. At his trial for writing a threatening letter, Kafe was found guilty but was released on his own recognizance if he underwent counselling. What the evidence suggests is that the pressure on Kafe was so intense that he suffered from a mental illness, even though his perception about the abuse he was receiving was concrete. The case may be extreme, but then again, it may not be. What it does illustrate is that racial taunts alienate people and make them feel desperate.

Ruggles (1996) describes the following situation to demonstrate how perceived or real incidents of racism affect people individually by putting them in the position of analyzing situations in regards to racism:

> After an exhausting day of sightseeing, I sat down at an outdoor restaurant in a well-to-do [area]. Instead of being approached by an eager waiter anxious to rattle off the specials of the day, I was rudely warned that unless I planned to order something, I was not to sit down. On what basis did he decide that I was not going to eat? As soon as my wife and children appeared from the washroom, his attitude changed dramatically. I wondered, is a black man with a family less suspect? (p. 90)

In 2007, the winner of the Commonwealth Writers' Prize for Best Overall Book was Lawrence Hill, who wrote the highly regarded novel *The Book of Negros*. Many in the literary field touted Hill's contribution to contemporary Canadian fiction as outstanding, saying it brings to light the human story of the struggles of Canadians of African descent.

To get a feel for what it was like for black Canadians who escaped from slavery in the United States, consider this quotation from one of the characters in the novel: "'Slaves and free Negros together in Nova Scotia?' he said, sucking his teeth. 'Some promised land.'" (p. 294). It was true that people could find freedom, but they did not find acceptance.

The internal tension creates anxiety, self-doubt and isolation so deep that many racial minorities desperately look for solace in separation or ways of anaesthetizing themselves. When listening to these types of stories or situations, a counsellor might remember that the perception of how something feels is far more important than whether it is imagined or real. The key to being effective is to sensitize oneself to how it feels to be belittled. Racism can often be very subtle, but the results are just as damaging as overt racism. Consider the following research results: the costs of racism are immense for minorities. In a study of racial awareness preference with whites and African American children in 1947 (cited in Sue & Sue 2007), researchers found African-American children preferred playing "with a White doll over a Black one, the Black doll was perceived as being 'bad,' and approximately one-third, when asked to pick the doll that looked like them, picked the White one" (p. 99). In 1987, a group of researchers reported at the American Psychological Association that their results were similar to the 1947 study.

> The path to a more perfect union means acknowledging that what ails the African-American community does not just exist in the minds of black people; that the legacy of discrimination — and current incidents of discrimination, while less overt than in the past — are real and must be addressed. (Barack Obama in Henfield, 2011, p. 141)

What this quotation emphasizes is that the discourse on racism has shifted from overt acts to more subtle acts, described as micro-aggressions, which in many ways are more hurtful than overt actions. Sue and Sue (2007) describe micro-aggressions as "brief and commonplace daily, verbal, behavioural, and environmental indignities, whether intentional or unintentional, that communicate hostile, derogatory, or negative racial slights and insults to the target person or group" (p. 273). Micro-aggressive acts invalidate people while at the same time assaulting them in insidious ways that reinforce racial stereotypes or attitudes (e.g., intellectual inferiority) that are a carry-over from the period of more overt racial discrimination. In a revealing study of black male adolescents in a traditionally white middle school, Henfield (2011) found that young people are aware of different types of micro-aggressions.

African Philosophy: The Basis of the African Canadian World View

Much has been written about world views of different peoples living in North America and how misunderstandings take place when people do not know how others view the world. World view is based on philosophical perspectives; greater understanding can occur if we are familiar with African philosophy. Why would African philosophy be so important many years after the original ancestors of black and African Canadians came to North America? According to Nobles (1972),

> Its unique status is derived not from the negative aspects of being black in white [North America], but rather from the positive features of basic African philosophy which dictate the values, customs, attitudes, and behaviour of Africans in Africa and the New World. (p. 18)

The following dimensions of African philosophy provide one with a sense of how people act, speak and think in their everyday lives. It is a collective unconsciousness that provides a framework for how people will behave in a systematic and natural manner. Behaviours are derived from all of these aspects of being "black." While there are ethnic and tribal differences among the peoples of Africa, as anywhere, there is also a communal quality that binds people because of their location (Cheboud, 2001).

Beliefs and religion: One's humanness is based on being part of the whole, including one's community and the universe. Beliefs and acts are one and the same; thus, to live is to be involved in a natural cycle of birth, death and revival (belief in life after death is found in all African societies).

Unity: While God is the centre of the universe, every living thing, including animals and humans, is bound together. Each individual contains the universe within him/herself in a kind of collective force.

Time: The present and the past are always bound together, with the direction of the life system from the present to the past. Time always contains these two elements of past and present.

Death and immortality: Life does not begin with birth but in naming, puberty, initiation and marriage/procreation. Immortality is present as long as the person is remembered; thus, one lives as long as one is recognized. Procreation ensures one of being remembered.

Relationships: Survival of the family, clan or tribe, which is dictated by kinship with others, is basic to all African peoples. Kinship is not just vertical (grandparents, parents, child) but horizontal (aunts, uncles, cousins and everyone in the tribe). The individual is secondary to the family, clan and tribe.

Nigrescence Theory: Identity Development

According to Rowles and Duan (2012), "despite the proven negative effects of racism and the fact that racism and discrimination are still very much alive, [blacks] . . . have continued to improve their positions in society exponentially and succeed in all walks of life" (p. 11). In essence, they moved from "adaptive inferiority," in which they presented a demeanour of humility and emulated whites, to "black pride" and "black power." The development of African ethnic identity has its roots in the theory of *nigrescence*, described by William Cross, Jr., in 1971 and revised in 1991 with the publication of his book *Shades of Black: Diversity in African American Identity*. Nigrescence is a French word that means the process of becoming black in a cultural–psychological sense. The theory is intended to reveal the nuances of identity development that are unique to the experiences of people of African descent. The stages of nigrescence have provided the foundation for thinking about Asian-American identity development, feminist identity development and gay/lesbian identity development. Nigrescence theory has been revised to capture "real-world" identity conflicts and ideological splits found among contemporary black leaders (Vandiver, 2001). For example, rather than suggest commonalties in the identity dynamics of all persons who reach the internalization stage, the revised model allows for the existence of ideological "splits" at that stage, or Afro-centric world view versus a bicultural frame of reference.

One of the most influential theorists on identity development was Erikson (1968), who has influenced generations of psychologists and counsellors. Later, other theorists such as Phinney (1989) modified Erikson's original theory, which is still relevant in terms of understanding identity development of those from European ethnic backgrounds, while Cross's nigrescence model is considered appropriate for blacks, African-Canadians and others. While widely used in counselling, the nigrescence theory is not the only theory of identity development for those of African ethnic ancestry. Other theories include Baldwin's African self-consciousness, which is sometimes called a Black Nationalist perspective (Worrell, Cross & Vandiver, 2001). The model presents four stages of development: pre-encounter, encounter, immersion–emersion and internalization.

1. Pre-encounter: Some black persons at this stage place low salience on Africanness or blackness. This stage originally indicated a pro-white and anti-black stance; however, the revised view is that this stage is characterized by assimilation or self-hatred. In assimilation there is "a low salience for race but a strong reference group orientation centered on being an American" (Vandiver et al., 2001, p. 176). Self-hatred or possessing a negative self-image as an African Canadian was dropped from the definition, although this feature may be present. Positive psychological

functioning or self-esteem issues are variables that are not necessarily a part of nigrescence. Vandiver et al. (2001) describe that those in the pre-encounter stage may have achieved a self-image grounded in "mis-education" created by a racist school curriculum. It is possible that some will show signs of having internalized racist notions about black people as a result of mis-education. As a result, they may display low self-esteem and weak ego development. Both types may undergo nigrescence once there is an increase of the salience of race in their lives (other than as a corrective to racial self-negativity).

2. Encounter: This refers to the event or events that led a person to conclude that he/she needs to change in the direction of greater cultural awareness. This is a stage when lack of acceptance, self-examination or experiences of racism lead people to question who they are. It may also occur as one becomes introspective and looks for meaning in life.

3. Immersion–emersion: This is the transition stage during which the old and emergent identities struggle for dominance (e.g., pro-black and anti-white). There are two aspects. One involves intense black involvement characterized by "the excessive embracing of everything Black . . . [as] . . . the first step on the journey toward an internalized Black identity" (Vandiver et al., 2001, p. 177). There is positiveness about African heritage and great enthusiasm for all things African. On the other side, however, Vandiver et al. (2001) stress that there is a price, which is "rage, anxiety, and guilt, emotions that are potentially destructive when uncontrolled" (p. 177). Sometimes this rage is turned towards others in the pre-encounter stage. Vandiver et al. say that "anti-white attitudes are an inevitable consequence of immersing oneself in Blackness and becoming fully enamoured with Black people, culture and history" (p. 178).

4. Internalization: Persons at this stage show high salience for race and culture; however, they cluster into divergent ideological camps. Persons in the internalization stage can be expected to have higher self-esteem and healthier ego-identity development than persons at the pre-encounter stage, who show signs of internalized racism. However, no differences can be expected with persons at the pre-encounter stage who exhibit low race salience but little evidence of internalized racism. The primary shift in this stage is one of identification with reference groups and the development of one of three independent ideological orientations: black nationalism (e.g., Black Empowerment, economic independence and heightened awareness of black history and culture), biculturalism (identifying as equally black and Canadian) and multiculturalism (acceptance of being black but identifying with at least two other characteristics in equal fashion). There is a range in the way individuals internalize themselves in relation with members of other ethnic groups. In addition, there is an uncoupling of self-acceptance and mental health. In other words, healthy psychological function does not hinge on acceptance of blackness.

The key factors influencing nigrescence are individual differences (such as social identity, education level, occupation, sexual orientation, religious affiliation, etc.) and situational factors that define a person's context (such as family structure, socio-economic status, neighbourhood quality and dynamics). In some contexts, affiliation with blackness may be appropriate for optimal psychological functioning. The context in which a person finds him/herself seems to be the explanatory or moderating variable.

Counselling Implications

According to Thomas, for those of African ethnic descent, "the transmission of values occurs through racial socialization within the family" (p. 7). Family not only helps socialize children but also provides them with a strong sense of self in a hostile racial climate. Thus the family should be used as a resource in counselling. Also, since the church has not only provided a sense of community but also is an institution that has protected and advocated for African Canadians, it too is a valuable resource for the counsellor (Wilmore, 1978).

To be effective and culturally competent, counsellors need to keep the following in mind when counselling African Canadians:

- Avoid presumptions about level of adjustment being tied to one's identity being centred on race;
- Be aware of how context can affect healthy black adjustment;
- Attempt to understand the client's frames of reference;
- Base social and other interventions on multi-dimensional models of black psychological functioning.

Counselling Black and African Canadians: Barriers and Challenges

For counsellors to be successful, they need to consider a set of four factors that mediate a presenting problem for black and African Canadians. These factors include the following:

- reactions to racial oppression;
- influence of majority culture;
- influence of Afro-American culture;
- personal experiences and endowments.

For counsellors, particularly those who are not from the black or African Canadian community, accepting that racism is part of the client's experience is crucial. While the client may not have experienced racism first-hand, he or she is aware of the history of slavery and other violent acts that others experienced. The feeling of oppression manifests it-self as a sense of powerlessness, the loss of dignity and the deprivation of human rights; psychologically, it brings about a sense of helplessness, depression, anxiety and a host of other behaviours that disempower a person. Atkinson, Morten and Sue (1993) describe the following examples of types of oppression that many minorities experience: "under-representation in the 1990 census, sub-minimum wages paid to undocumented workers, the racial/ethnic slurs that permeate written and oral communication, and physical at-tacks upon individuals by racist perpetrators" (p. 12). In addition, the unquestioning ac-ceptance of "black consciousness" reinforces the counsellor's understanding of the strug-gles that have been made. Recognizing the reality of the situation is important, because pretending to be "colour blind" or using a paternalistic approach in regards to racial back-ground verges on racism. This idea is reinforced eloquently in Shanee Livingston's poem:

> Stuggle for equality
> Racial unrest.
> They're trying to kill an idea . . .
> Black consciousness. (Miller, Steinlage & Prinz, 1994, p. 47)

Black and African Canadians have had to develop a protective mechanism to help them survive in a climate of racial discrimination. These mechanisms include being guarded, "sizing up" and challenging. These and other mechanisms help keep those who experi-ence racism in a state of defensive balance that maintains sanity. Not becoming defensive or being put off by these mechanisms not only helps the counsellor build a bridge for communication but also demonstrates that these mechanisms are positive qualities. Once the bridge is built, the defences are no longer necessary. Qualities that can help counsel-lors overcome these mechanisms include being patient, natural and straightforward. Ob-viously, spending time creating a climate of trust is paramount. Building trust includes not only taking a risk in giving and sharing but also being accepting, cooperative, open, non-judgemental and supportive with others: in essence, being human.

The pressures of racism are enormous and affect psychological levels of functioning; however, black Canadians, just like anyone else in society, face all the human problems that bring about issues in well-being. Racism is a fact of life, but living in society also brings about the same problems of relationship, family, self-esteem and so on. It is our belief that we need to develop proactive strategies so that counsellors, particularly non-black counsellors, can make themselves more sensitive and more effective:

1. Become aware of the historical and current experiences of being black.
2. Consider value and cultural differences between blacks and other ethnic groups

and how your own personal values influence the way you conduct therapy.

3. Consider the way your personal values influence the way you view both the presenting problem and the goals for therapy.

4. Include the value system of the client in the goal-setting process.

5. Be sensitive to variations in black family norms due to normal adaptations to stress, and be flexible enough to accept these variations.

6. Be aware of how ineffective verbal and non-verbal communication due to cultural variation in communication can lead to premature termination of therapy. Become familiar with non-standard or Black English, and accept its use by clients.

7. Consider the client's problem in the large context. Include the extended family, other significant individuals and larger systems in your thinking, if not in the therapy session.

8. Be aware of your client's racial identification, and do not feel threatened by your client's cultural identification with his or her own race.

9. Learn to acknowledge and be comfortable with your client's cultural differences.

10. Consider the appropriateness of specific therapeutic models or interventions to specific black families. Do not apply interventions without considering unique aspects of each family.

11. Consider each black family and each black family member you treat as unique. Do not generalize the findings of any study or group of studies on black families to all black clients. Use the studies to help you find your way, not to categorize individuals.

Conclusion

According to Walcott (1997), the African Canadian identity is "syncretic, always in revision and in a process of becoming [because] it is constituted from multiple histories of uprootedness, migration, exchanges and political acts of defiance and self-(re)definition" (pp. 120-121). In other words, the ending of segregation laws and the implementation of multicultural policies do not necessarily change people's attitudes about race. Much has been made of the changes one sees in the media, with athletes, actors and other personalities in very visible places. Yet according to Castle (2000),

> Racism against African-Americans continues. Distinctions between whites and blacks in income, occupational status, unemployment rates, social conditions and education are still extreme. Racial violence and harassment remain serious problems . . . the increasing complexity of inter-ethnic relations is leading to new types of conflict and to a politicization of issues of culture and ethnicity. The Los Angeles riots of 1992 were indicative of such trends. (pp. 178-179)

Perhaps racism is part of the human condition? However that may be, counsellors will be faced with those traumatized by racism as they try to bridge the "colour" gap. The research on whether clients are affected by the race or ethnic background of the counsellor is mixed. Many researchers feel that those of European ethnic backgrounds cannot counsel those of African ethnic background; in fact, research indicates that African-Americans prefer someone who is similar to them (Pederson et al., 1996). Where one is situated on racial identity stages of development affects one's ability to be sensitive to others. Yet counsellor competency and style remain important variables in counselling across cultures. To match client and counsellor background is a form of stereotyping, and some minority clients resent it. Even in the best of circumstances, those of African descent drop out of counselling more often than those of European heritage (Jenkins, 1982; Pederson et al., 1996; Aponte & Wohl, 2000).

One of the keys to successfully counselling African Canadians is a thorough understanding of identity and how individuals identify themselves. Identity remains a complex and situational phenomenon that needs more research. The interpretation of "self," or one's identity in general, seems to depend on the degree to which an individual feels connected, the degree he or she relates, feels balanced and is able to transcend racism. These components help the person to acknowledge the process where one is involved and to design, construct and finally claim a positive sense of identity. Therefore, the development or the transformation of self within the process leads to a broader and specific definition of one's identity. This activity in fact is a process of knowing and restructuring. At the same time, the process helps evaluate the individual's relationship between self and others, self and society, and self and the world. It is important to realize that the notion of identity avoids two extreme theoretical positions. First, it does not presuppose that one steps into the world a full-blown personal self and only then starts choosing an identity as if from a supermarket shelf. Nor does it presuppose that identity is simply bestowed by fate, and that one can merely respond by being either faithful or unfaithful to that destined identity.

According to Young (1993), "the ability to confront the unadulterated truth with resolve and fortitude, together with spirituality, humanness, and love of life, has been part of the unique heritage of African [Canadians]" (p. 86). The ability of people to withstand generations of genocidal actions on the North American continent attests to the strength of people of African heritage. The segment of society that has been the most influential with and supportive of African Canadians is the community church. The church has been not only a place where people could come together as a spiritual community but a source for political and social action. It was the leaders of the church who led the civil rights movement in Canada and the United States — people such as Martin Luther King, Jr. (cited in Siccone, 1998), who said, "It really boils down to this: that all life is interrelated.

We are all caught in an inescapable network of mutuality, tied into a single garment of destiny. Whatever affects one directly, affects all indirectly" (p. 91).

References

ABC News, June 26, 2001, http://abcnews.go.com/International/story? id=80865 &page=1#.UBrTrqPdf0p

Atkinson, D., Morten, G., & Sue, D.W. (1993). *Counseling American minorities: A cross-cultural perspective* (4th ed.). Madison, WI: Brown & Benchmark.

Aponte, J., & Wohl, J. (2000). *Psychological intervention and cultural diversity*. Boston, MA: Allyn & Bacon.

Cheboud, E. (2001). *A heuristic study of Ethiopian immigrants in Canada*. Unpublished doctoral dissertation, University of Victoria, Canada.

Erikson, E. (1968). *Identity: Youth in crisis*. New York: Norton.

Henfield, M. (2001). Black male adolescents navigating micro-aggressions in a traditionally white middle school: A qualitative study. *Journal of Multicultural Counseling and Development*, 39(3), 130–140.

Hill, L. (2007). *The book of negros*. Harper-Collins: Toronto, ON.

Jenkins, A. (1982). *The psychology of the Afro-American: A humanistic approach*. New York: Pergamon General.

Mensah, J. (2010). *Black Canadians: History, experiences, social conditions, 2nd Edition*, Halifax, NS: Fernwood Publishing.

Miller, L., Steinlage, T., & Prinz, M. (1994). *Cultural cobblestones: Teaching cultural diversity*. London: Scarecrow Press.

Nobles, W. (1972). African philosophy: Foundations for Black psychology. In R. Jones (Ed.), *Black psychology*. New York: Harper & Row, pp. 18–32.

Phinney, J. (1989). Stages of ethnic identity in minority group adolescents. *Journal of Early Adolescence*, 9, 34–49.

Ridley, C. & Lingle, D. (1996). Cultural empathy in multicultural counselling: A multidimensional process model. In P. Pederson, J. Draguns, W. Lonner & J. Trible (Eds.), *Counseling across cultures* (4th ed.) (pp. 21–46). Thousand Oaks, CA: Sage.

Rowles, J. & Duan, C. (2012). Perceived racism and encouragement among African American adults, *Journal of Multicultural Counseling and Development*, 40(1), pp. 11–23. 13.

Ruggles, C. (1996). Outsider blues: Voices from of the shadows. Halifax, NS: Fernwood Publishing.

Siccone, F. (1998). *Celebrating diversity*, Boston, MA: Allyn and Bacon.

Sue, D.W., & Sue, D. (2007), Counseling the culturally different (5th ed.). New York, NY: John Wiley.

Statistics Canada. (1996). *Population by visible minority*. Ottawa: Canada: Government of Canada.

Thomas, A.J. (1998). Understanding culture and world view in family systems: The use of the multicultural genogram. *Family Journal*, 6(1), 1–19.

Thompson, C. & Issac, K. (2003), African Americans: Treatment issues and recommendations, In D. Atkinson, (Ed.), *Counseling American minorities: A cross-cultural perspective* (4th ed.). Madison, WI: Brown & Benchmark. pp. 116–130.

Vandiver, B. (2001) Psychological nigrescence revisted: Introduction and overview. *Journal of Multicultural Counseling and Development*, 29(3), 165–173.

Vandiver, B., Fhagen-Smith, P., Cokley, K., Cross, W., & Worrell, F. (2001). Cross's nigrescence model: From theory to schale to theory, *Journal of Multicultural Counseling and Development*, 29(3), 174–199.

Walcott, R. (1997). *Black like who?* Toronto, Canada: Insomniac Press.

Wilmore, G. (1978). The gifts and tasks of the black church, In V. D'Oyley (Ed.), *Black presence in multiethnic Canada*. Toronto, ON: Canada: UBC & OISE.

13

Islamic Identity

Counselling Muslim Canadians

ABDULLAHI BARISE & M. HONORÉ FRANCE

PEOPLE WHO CALL THEMSELVES MUSLIMS are not just people originally from Arab countries but also from more than 60 different ethnic groups including African-Americans, Europeans, Hispanics, South Asians, African immigrants and even Aboriginal people. Muslims in Canada have originally come from a variety of countries including Algeria, Bosnia, China, Egypt, Iran, India, Pakistan, Lebanon, Syria, Somalia and Turkey; but there are also Muslim people from France, Germany and the UK, to name just a few. The list is endless, but it is not only people who have immigrated to Canada who are Muslims; many native-born people from a variety of ethnic groups represent a "rainbow coalition" of Islamic peoples. The 9/11 terrorist attacks have put renewed light on Muslims in the world and particularly in North America, where some regard them as potential terrorists or people who are so different that there is no possibility that the Islamic faith can be reconciled with the Canadian mosaic. Some publications have suggested that being a Muslim makes one a terrorist suspect (Kingston, 2012). When people in Tunisia revolted against their government, followed by the uprisings in Egypt, Yemen and Libya in what we know as the Arab Spring, attitudes around the world toward Muslims began to change. This modern, progressive movement, largely led by young people, has shown that there is a moderate side to Islam. Yet the idea that the Islamic world has replaced the old Soviet Empire as the new enemy of the West persists.

Who are Muslims? What do they believe and value? Is there a difference across immigrant groups? Islam is not just a religious belief or path but also a framework of morality and righteous behaviour that is shared with Judaism and Christianity.

Despite recent political events and increased immigration from Muslim countries,

Islam is one of the fastest-growing religions of native-born peoples of North America. Thus, Islam is not only the fastest-growing religion in the world but also quite profoundly one of the most multicultural religious groups in Canada. According to Sayyid Syeed, the secretary general of the Islamic Society of North America (an umbrella organization for Islamic groups throughout the US and Canada), the variety of people of Muslim faith is challenged by the political consequence of governmental policy:

> At a time when Muslims constitute one of Canada's fastest growing immigrant communities and Islam the fastest-growing religion, Canadians will find much to reassure them, but also much to ponder, in a new study of Muslim public opinion in Canada. (Macdonald-Laurier, 2011, p. 1)

According to Dawood Hassan Hamdani, an Ottawa economist who has analyzed Muslim immigration and birth rates, the number of Muslims in Canada has more than doubled, from 293 000 in 1991 to more than 650 000 today. Toronto alone has at least 16 Muslim schools. In short, Muslims are a significant factor in Canadian society.

Islamic World View

The word *Islam* comes from the Arabic *salaam,* which means peace; yet a subtle projection of the word also means submission. When one examines Islam as a religion, this second meaning, submission, becomes quite powerful. To become a good Muslim, one must submit to the will of God; thus, religion shapes how one views the world and lives one's life. Farid Esack's book *On Being a Muslim* is revealing on this point in terms of the role religion plays in life as a South African Muslim living in Germany. Esack (1999) wrote that

> a number of factors made me carry my "Islam," my submission to Allah's will, in my hand just about every day, factors which regularly threatened to have it fall to the ground, melting into nothingness like snowflakes . . . . we are inexorably tied to each other from the day known as *yawmi alast*; the day when our souls faced our Lord and we were asked: "*Alastu bi rabbikum*" (Am I not your Lord)? We said: "*Bala*" (Indeed)! . . . I cannot smother it . . . I know that my humanness and my Islam depend on how hard I try to discern its message and to live alongside it. (p. 59)

The Muslim consciously submits to the will of God and subsequently gains internal and external harmony, synchronicity and peace. Internal peace refers to one's psychological well-being due to a lack of conflict within the self, while external peace stems from a harmonious and loving relationship with God and the environment.

In Islamic cosmology, all creatures exist in compliance with God's will. All creatures, from tiny atoms to mighty galaxies, worship God and thus coexist harmoniously according to God's will. When one accepts Islam, one becomes part of this harmonious coexistence willingly. Being a Muslim thus necessitates revolving around God on an assigned course (just like electrons and celestial bodies do) without transgressing boundaries or infringing on the rights of the self, the environment and God. Through this pious life the Muslim strives for an all-encompassing peace, which is a fundamental concept in Islam. The term *Muslim* means peaceful in Arabic. One of God's names is *Assalaam*, which also means peace. Both Muslims' greetings and the concluding words of Muslims' daily prayers are *Assalaamu aleikum*, which means "Peace be upon you." Heaven in Islam is called *Darussalaam*, which means "the abode of peace" (Barise, in Turner, Cheboud, Elvira & Barise, 2002).

There is no separation of religion and politics in Islam as is customary in Canada and the West. It does not seem strange that imams (religious leaders) would be involved in politics or run a government (such as in Iran) or the educational system (as the Wadis do in Saudi Arabia). All schools following the Islamic tradition see the study of the Koran as essential not only to being a good person but also to being educated. Consider that in Egypt, the largest university, "Al Azhar, has 350,000 students, 100,000, women, and all can recite the Koran [with 114 chapters & 666 verses]" (*National Post*, 2002, p. A12). Reciting and reflecting on the Koran is a basis not only for knowing about God but also for learning good judgement and moral development. In fact, at least one-third of the verses of the Koran encourage learning or thinking in one way or another (Barise, 1999).

According to Rashid (in Altareb, 1996), there are seven elements that form the Islamic world view. It should be understood that because the roots of Islam are bound up in the Arabic language and the holy places are in Arabic lands, it is difficult to separate Arabic culture from the practice of Islam — in much the same way that it is difficult to separate the historical foundations of the Christian faith from the life of Jesus. Understanding the enormous part that Islam plays in the identity of believers goes a long way in working successfully with clients who are shaped by the Islamic world view. The Islamic world view consists of the following seven elements:

- Humankind are innately good;
- Morality is absolute;
- God (in Arabic, *Allah*) is unitary;
- One lives in a community of the faithful;
- Women are the source of civilization;
- Allah is the centre of the world, and thus of human life and thought;
- All wisdom comes from Allah, and peace can be achieved only by submission to Allah.

As the central force in life, the spiritual focus of Muslims dominates actions, including what one thinks and feels and how life is conducted. With Islam as the centre of life, all actions have the aim of fostering God-consciousness, or *taqwa*, and becoming closer to Allah. Thus every action, including dress, dietary habits, the rearing of children and home life, revolves around the teachings of Islam. There are five pillars that regulate how one lives. These five pillars help the Muslim to become spiritually whole and to develop a good and moral existence.

1. Declaration of faith (*shahadah*): This is the belief that must be avowed, "that there is no god but Allah and Mohammed is the prophet of Allah."
2. Prayers (*salat*): The ritual of prayer is to be performed five times a day facing the Holy Ka-abah in Makkah (Mecca);
3. Charity (*zakat*): All Muslims are required to pay a fixed amount of their possessions for the welfare of the whole community and in particular the poor;
4. Fasting (*siyam*): During Ramadhan, the ninth month of the Islamic calendar, all Muslims must abstain from all food, drink and sexual activity from dawn to sunset;
5. Pilgrimage to Mecca (*hajj*): At least once in life, all Muslims must make a journey to Makkah (birthplace of the Prophet) during the closing month of the Islamic year, Dhul Hijah.

Islamic Beliefs that Transcend Culture

"Since Sept. 11, Muslims feel that in the minds of the West, devoutness and regular attendance at the mosque implies fundamentalism and a penchant for violence" (*National Post*, 2002, p. B6). There is no relationship between being religious and being extremist. A religious person, by obvious intent, is a person of the Book, whether the Book is the Koran, the Bible or the Torah. This is not to say that there are intolerant people in all religions, but because of politics, beliefs or attitudes about people are hard to erase. Because of what they have experienced, Muslims in Canada, regardless of where they are from, will probably experience some of the following (Abudabbeh & Nydell, 1997):

Stress: Either stemming from cultural shock or experiences or from events associated with the Arab–Israeli conflict.
Family: The sense that the family is the foundation of the individual and thus needs to be at the centre of counselling.
Dependence: Regardless of children's age, they are always dependent on their parents, and thus counsellors need to adjust their procedures to incorporate this cultural value.

Values: Some values — such as those concerning roles of women, divulging one's private life and the way parents and children are to behave — are very different from those in mainstream Canadian society, and even Muslims born in Canada may adopt Islamic values.

Islamic ideas of behaviour can be incorporated into counselling objectives, thus ensuring that clients do not have to reject their cultural ways of thinking and being.

A Muslim is required to believe in and revere all prophets of God, from Adam to Mohammed, without discrimination. Noah, Abraham, Moses, Jesus and Mohammed are revered by Muslims as the greatest prophets of God. In describing his position in relation to this chain of prophets that God sent at different times in history, Mohammed says,

> My similitude in comparison with the other prophets before me, is that of a man who has built a house nicely and beautifully, except for a place of one brick in a corner. The people go about it and wonder at its beauty, but say: "Would that brick be put in its place!" So I am that brick, and I am the last of the Prophets. (from *The Authentic Book of Bukhari*)

Muslims also believe in all the revealed scriptures. They believe in the original Torah given to Moses to guide the Jews; Muslims also believe in the original New Testament that God revealed to Jesus. Islam is a continuation of the pure teachings of these great prophets. However, it was Mohammed, in the seventh century, who received the last message of God: the Koran that guides all Muslims today. Muslims believe that God revealed the Koran to the prophet Mohammed; the Koran is not a text by many different men, as is the case with the present-day Torah and the Bible.

Norms and Values of Muslims

In many ways the values of Muslims are similar to others in Canada, but some values predominate. Consider this quotation: "I watched Oprah the other day. She was talking to pregnant 13-year old girls who were unmarried. I am glad I don't have those complications in my life" (*Time*, p. 53). With strict views about chastity and remaining pure, Muslims can come into conflict with Western ways of life. Alcohol and other intoxicants are forbidden in the Koran. In many traditional Islamic societies, such as in Kuwait and Saudi Arabia, the sale of alcohol is strictly forbidden, while in other Muslim countries, only foreigners and non-Muslims can buy alcohol with a special permit. Here are some other Islamic values that exist in many Muslim traditions around the world:

- Children and marriage are essential for happiness.
- The man is considered head of the family, with the authority to direct and protect the family. (The man's authority is conditional on following Islamic principles such as *adl*, or fairness, and *shura*, or mutual consultation.)
- Mothers are three times more deserving of their children's good treatment than are fathers.
- Respect is given to older generations and siblings. Thus, everyone in the extended family is valued.
- Children should not only take care of older members of the family but also show respect to everyone in the extended family. Widowhood is an especially important state.
- Women have a greater responsibility to the family and their behaviour can easily damage the family; thus their honourable behaviour is important.
- The family has more importance than the individual, including the career aspirations of individual members.
- The belief in Islam is valued above all other ideas.

The Family, Gender, and Marriage

The role of woman is at the heart of any culture. Apart from stealing Arab oil, the wars in Iraq and Afghanistan are about stripping Muslims of their religion and culture, exchanging the burka for a bikini. I am not an expert on the condition of Muslim women and I love feminine beauty too much to advocate the burka here. But I am defending some of the values that the burka represents for me. For me, the burka represents a woman's consecration to her husband and family. Only they see her. It affirms the privacy, exclusivity and importance of the domestic sphere. The Muslim woman's focus is her home, the "nest" where her children are born and reared. She is the "home" maker, the taproot that sustains the spiritual life of the family, nurturing and training her children, providing refuge and support to her husband. In contrast, the bikinied American beauty queen struts practically naked in front of millions on TV. A feminist, she belongs to herself. In practice, paradoxically, she is public property. She belongs to no one and everyone. She shops her body to the highest bidder. She is auctioning herself all of the time.

In America, the cultural measure of a woman's value is her sex appeal. (As this asset depreciates quickly, she is neurotically obsessed with appearance and plagued by weight problems.) (Makow, 2009)

There is much debate in the West about how women are regarded in Islam and Muslim countries. Sometimes the reality gets lost in the cultural maze of traditions and values. It is clear that for many Muslims, the West is morally corrupt; drugs, teenage pregnancy, incest, alcoholism and the family breakup are rampant. For many in Islamic countries, the relationship between the genders in the West seems to have not only undermined the family but also contributed to the decline of social moral values. The debate as to whether separating God from the schools or the state leads to moral corruption cannot be resolved. Muslim societies are presently in a state of transition, wherein modern influences, traditional values and Islamic values are competing for supremacy. Islamic teachings encourage dynamic interactions and mutual learning between nations. According to many historians of science and philosophy, when correctly interpreted and implemented, Islam has an in-built great power in not only absorbing every form of human progress but also spearheading it (Hitti, 1970). The Western Renaissance was greatly influenced by Islamic scholars, who not only assimilated the positive aspects of Greek and Persian civilizations but also formed their own distinctive thinking in science and philosophy. Many talk about the Judeo–Christian–Islamic heritage of the West. However, Menocal argues "Westerners — Europeans — have great difficulty in considering the possibility that they are in some way seriously indebted to the Arab [Islamic] world, or that the Arabs [Muslims] were central to the making of medieval Europe" (1987, p. xiii).

At present, most Islamic societies exist in the developing world, where high illiteracy still persists. There are secular Muslim states, such as Turkey, that claim to have created a gender-egalitarian society. However, many believe that Turkey falls short of both Islamic principles and Western democratic principles when it comes to respecting women's basic human rights. For example, a Turkish woman wearing a headscarf is not allowed to attend a university or hold a government office. (Surprisingly, debate in France about whether to ban women wearing headscarves from French schools is ongoing.) Some Muslim countries have separate but equal schools for men and women; yet, just as in the West, gender inequity is an issue. What is clear for counsellors is that for many people with an Islamic identity, the teachings of the Koran, as they see it, affects their belief about the primacy of the family and how gender relations inside and outside of marriage are practised.

The Koran is very clear that women have all the rights that men do: "And women shall have rights similar to the rights against them, according to what is equitable" (2, 228). However, just as happened historically in the West, women have been treated differently. In most Muslim countries, women have the same rights in law that men do, but here is where the controversy lies. The idea is not that men and women are the same, but that they are different because of their sex and are thus treated differently. Yet, they are still equal in the sight of God. According to Safaa El Meneza, Islam does not make women suffer: "It's true that in some Muslim countries the cultural traditional is for men to try to control and dominate their wives, but that has nothing to do with Islam. Islam actually preserves women's rights" (*National Post*, 2002, p. 12).

Not all women in Islamic societies agree that they are equal to men. Javed (1994) suggests that in some Islamic societies, "the concept of hijab (a dress that is from head to toe covering) is used as one of the strategies for coercing women to live an imposed identity rooted in misogynistic assumptions" (p. 58). However, the use of the hijab or even the burka (completely covering the body, including the face and hands) makes some Muslim women feel more free. These women believe that the hijab makes the people they interact with focus on their intelligence rather than on their bodies. Here is another explanation of why a woman has chosen to wear the hijab:

> because that was how the West had made me feel. I was put on the defensive by the assumptions of the Western media that we were the guilty parties and I wanted to show that I was proud of Islam. (*Time*, p. 36)

Clearly, Islam teaches that men and especially women should dress and act modestly. It is evident in the Koran that Islam freed women from the former practice of female infanticide, gave them inheritance rights long before Christian women had them and brought about financial and social supports. On the other hand, growing extremism at times reinforces cultural mandates in regards to gender (e.g., the Taliban in Afghanistan). Interestingly, Javed (1994) emphasizes that women's roles have not always been subservient; for example, Muslim women need to remember that there have been three female heads of state in Muslim countries in recent years (Bangladesh, Pakistan, and Turkey). She advocates that the women's movement to retrieve gender egalitarianism can come from increasing levels of literacy in which women become aware of narratives that "celebrate women's power and accomplishments in the public domain [in Muslim countries]" (p. 67).

Counselling Muslims

Only recently have people with Islamic backgrounds been given consideration as distinct and different. In part, this change has arisen because of recent political events such as the Gulf War, the terrorist attack in New York City, the Israeli–Palestinian conflict and the American–Iraqi war. People with Islamic backgrounds have been grouped according to culture or country of origin or as international students. The fact is that counsellors need to have a greater awareness of how Islam, as the fastest-growing religion in Canada, influences the identities of individuals living in Canada.

Mental Health Issues

According to Abudabbeh (1992) and our own investigation, the most frequent issues concerning Muslims involve the following:

- people blaming all Muslims for the events of 9/11 or the breakdown in the Israeli–Palestinian dispute;
- discrimination and racism for being Muslim;
- differences between generational values (first and second generations);
- differing parenting styles between strict religious and secular values;
- physical abuse;
- cultural gender differences such as assertiveness or agoraphobia (especially among women unaccustomed to going out alone);
- identity confusion;
- differing social and economic status among immigrants;
- loss of extended network of family support.

Communication Style

A counsellor with competent multicultural therapy skills must be sensitive to cultural differences and must have a strong personal identity. The work of Abudabbeh and Nydell (1996) focusses on questions that counsellors need to address in counselling Arab-Americans, but it also has relevance for all those of Islamic background. Consider the following issues.

Distinguishing between direct and indirect communication: A counsellor needs to know that feelings on certain issues related to the family may not be shared directly but rather with subtle clues in an indirect fashion.

Becoming sensitive to non-verbal cues: Various gestures, such as eye contact, may suggest that what is being said in the session is difficult; thus the eyes may be averted.

Distinguishing Islamic cultural and linguistic groups: People of Arab extraction generally speak directly or even aggressively on an issue, while Bangladeshis, for instance, speak more softly and indirectly about a concern.

Understanding basic Islamic values and their effect on counselling: Islam is not just a religion, but also as a way of life. The family is of central importance, and elders are held in high esteem not only for their age and experience but also because they are sources of wisdom.

Recognizing the immediate context: Social and political events affect and per-petuate stereotypes that Canadians hold about Muslims. Events in the news, par-ticularly around the 9/11 attacks, make Muslim people vulnerable to racism and discrimination and create a sense of personal mistrust and self-doubt.

Recognizing personal biases about Islam and Muslims: Different ways of think-ing and believing may evoke misunderstanding. A strong belief in Islam does not equate with anti-Western feelings.

Interacting with various people of Islamic backgrounds can be perceived by some as chal-lenging, yet people of Arab or Somali ethnic groups, just to name two ethnic groups in Canada, are very open and welcoming to all people regardless of ethnic or religious back-grounds. The demonstration of friendliness is inherent in the culture and religion. For example, a frenzied handshake becomes very important, for it is not only a greeting but also a way of allowing "guilt to slip away through the hands, for any hostile or revengeful feelings evaporates when you greet people in that way" (Post, 2002, p. 23). Many people with Islamic backgrounds, such as Arabs, tend to use euphemisms when sharing feelings or even facts about their family in regards to illness, death or any bad event. Abudabbeh and Nydell (1997) provide the following example:

> They often say that someone is tired when the person is sick ("He's in the hospital because he's a little tired"), hesitate to state that someone is growing worse or dying and hesitate to predict or even discuss bad events. Such events can be discussed more comfortably, however, with appropriate benedictions such as "May he/she soon be better" or "God willing, may this never happen." (pp. 274–275)

Implications for Counselling

Counsellors need to know that, although mutual help is a central value in Islam, many Muslims are unfamiliar with professional counselling as practised in Canada. From the Islamic point of view, God is the ultimate source of help, although this help may come through the environment, including humans. Reliance on God and on oneself is expected in Islam. However, if there is a need, seeking help from others is encouraged to the ex-tent that the seeker would see helpers as means only and God as the ultimate provider. Practising Muslims pray to God, "We worship You and we seek help from You" at least 17 times every day.

The challenges for counsellors working with Muslim clients are very complex because the diversity within the Islamic society is so great. In addition, many factors within these differences can shape intervention. For counsellors to be successful with Muslim clients,

they first need to be aware of their personal stereotypes about Islam. With all of the turmoil in the Middle East, and the growth of worldwide terrorism, openness to diversity is
of primary importance. Interestingly there is little information on issues around working
with Islamic identity, even in the multicultural counselling literature, despite the Islamic
presence in North America going back to the growth of Islam among African-Americans
and the rise of immigration to Canada from the Islamic world. Unsurprisingly, the average Canadian is not only unfamiliar with Islam but may have a negative view of the Muslim world. Research on prejudicial relations found that values

> especially those favouring both openness to change and self-transcendence . . . im-
> prove the willingness of persons who hold these values to be open to inter-group con-
> tacts of the sort that might reduce prejudicial relations. In contrast, those who favor
> values of conservation are less interested in having these contacts with differences.
> (Sampson, 1998, pp. 102–103)

Along with the diversity that exists within Muslim clients, counsellors need to address the
different circumstances of those who immigrated versus those born in Canada. For immigrants, levels of acculturation need to be ascertained along with levels of religiousness,
including the particular sect that clients belong to. The process of acculturation brings
clients more in line with values consistent with those of the Canadian majority. The less
acculturation, the greater the differences; thus, clients who recently immigrated reflect
traditions and values of their home countries. Because of the central place religion holds
for Muslim clients, the degree of religiosity will affect not only what clients want to focus
on but also how counsellors can prescribe treatment. Obviously, accepting and working with Islamic religious values will help counsellors' work be more effective. For the
multicultural counsellor this point cannot be overemphasized. Using religious values to
solve problems will greatly enhance counsellors' ability to work for solutions. That means
becoming acquainted with the Islamic viewpoint on issues of importance. Many in the
Canadian Islamic community live in a double bind: while they support Arab and other
Islamic causes, which may not be popular in the larger society, they also feel love for the
Canadian state. In a world in which people are often forced to take sides, being a devoted
Muslim is very difficult.

One area that counsellors might explore is the way religion and culture shape how Muslims see the world. Dwairy (2006), for example, suggests that the "Arab/Muslim adult does
not have an independent personality, but rather has a personality that is enmeshed in the
collective identity" (p. 57). The nature of the family and religion requires every member to
submit to the collective good of the family and creates an alliance with all members. Islam
itself means "submission"; therefore, a healthy-thinking Muslim or Arab does not differ-

entiate self from group or family. Consider a Muslim from a Turkish background where, "Turkish culture is located at the authoritarian-relatedness (or collective) end of the continuum, while the prototypical Western culture falls closer to the horizontal-separateness (or liberal-individualistic) end" (Dwairy, 2006, p. 61). With this sense of culture and family, counsellors need to find a place within the collective framework of the family. For example, if a client were angry at the family for blocking some feelings or thoughts, rather than have the client express anger towards the family, the counsellor should do the opposite and reframe the situation by having the client join the power structure to take care of the family.

Three of the most important issues facing Muslims are discrimination, racism and lack of acceptance of Islamic ideas and views. There is also is the perennial problem of bias against visible minorities. The turmoil in the Middle East exacerbates these problems. In addition, clients may be under stress because of what is happening to their families in their country of origin. Traumatic events, particularly for refugees, such as those from Kosovo, contribute to a sense of alienation and isolation. Therefore, it may be helpful to incorporate or consult with imams, Muslim organizations and Muslim individuals during the counselling process. Religious and community leaders are greatly respected in the Islamic community, and their help and support can go a long way not only in assisting clients to solve their problems but also in bringing extended support after clients leave counselling. Imams can enlighten counsellors on basic Islamic world views and values. Traditionally, the mosque has been open to outsiders, regardless of religious background (Lago, 2011).

Finally, it is vital that counsellors be able to separate cultural issues from spiritual or Islamic issues. Sometimes these seem so intertwined that it is a challenge to separate one from the other. For example, Altareb (1996) provides the example of a Muslim woman client who is "struggling with the desire to work outside the home . . . because such a practice was not supported within their native culture" (p. 36). The Koran does not prohibit such a practice, but religious issues are sometimes cultural in origin. The challenge is to help reconcile the reality of Canadian society with the cultural norms of the client's previous way of life. Issues of gender equality are often misunderstood as being religious rather than culturally derived. One way of reconciling this issue can be through the stories of early historical Muslim women. Altareb (1996) suggests to counsellors working with Muslim women who are raising their children alone that "what they do for their children or families can be considered acts of worship" (p. 36). Counsellors should also broaden their perspectives in regards to Eurocentric counselling practices. For example, there are a number of Sufi meditation strategies derived from Islamic traditions such as

1. *zekr*, a contemplation on the 99 names or attributes of God;

2. *takhliya*, a meditation aimed at obviating one's moral weaknesses;

3. *tahliya*, a meditation designed to strengthen one's virtues so that vices become weak and ultimately die. (Sheikh, Kunzendorf & Sheikh, 1989, p. 477)

Conclusion

The collapse of the Soviet Union and the demise of the Cold War have led some analysts to debate whether the next arena of global confrontation will be between Islam and the West. This argument, however, is profoundly flawed as Islam itself is deeply divided (Samad, 1996, p. 90).

All of the literature that discusses working with Muslims shares some general themes. First, a distinction needs to be made between religious and non-religious Muslims, between Muslim Canadians who have immigrated and those who are native born and the level of the client's acculturation in Canada. Cultures vary widely (e.g., Saudi Arabia versus Bosnia) as does religious affiliation (e.g., Sunni versus Shia). However, the Islamic faith has general principles and customs that transcend cultures and religious affiliations. According to Abed al Jabri (1994),

No matter what framework is being considered, be it religious, nationalistic, liberal or leftist, each one possesses a "known" *(shahid)* over which it will trace an "unknown" *(gha'ib)*. The unknown is the case of the future as it is conceived or dreamed of by the adherents to these schools. The known is the first part to the double question that they all ask (e.g., for the fundamentalist movement) . . . . (p. 17)

Working within the Islamic identity does not mean that counselling methods used with other multicultural groups will not work. Any counselling strategy that brings about a solution and reinforces clients' Islamic values will be helpful in solving personal issues. The strength of the Islamic identity lies in the way the values inherent in the Koran guide everyday interaction, but that strength does not imply the person will have no problems. Problems coming from within, such as depression or low self-esteem, and external problems, such as marital discord, discrimination and unemployment, need to be addressed with solutions and strategies that will help bring resolution. Counsellors who work with a multicultural flavour are much more likely to succeed within the Islamic framework than outside it. Javed (1994) emphasizes that woman's empowerment lies in

Literacy modes that facilitate a desire for rearming [and] must include storytelling as a major technique. Storytelling can be done in several ways including popular theatre. The content of the stories, however, must be drawn from Islam, past and contemporary role models and women's lived experiences. (p. 68)

Canada's Muslims, whatever their ethnic backgrounds, need to be understood in terms of Islamic identity first rather than cultural aspects. That is, counsellors need to understand Islam as a way of life, not just as a religion. Islam is a set of values that guide Muslim people; thus, to counsel Muslims adequately, one must understand their values. Finally, regardless of ethnic backgrounds, Canadians need to realize that Islam is growing not only among those from Muslim countries but also among the general population. In fact, Muslims are doing "well in adapting and involving themselves in practically all spheres of the country's economic, educational, and cultural activities" (*National Post*, 2002, p. 13). The events of the Arab Spring demonstrate that people in the Arab world will make adjustments and demand change, because cultures are dynamic and capable of change when conditions change. Islam adapted to a variety of cultural settings over the years, and there is no reason that it cannot be at home in Canada, Europe and other countries of the world:

Reason is a beacon that we must not only light in the middle of darkness but also learn to carry around well into broad daylight. (Abed al-Jabri, 1999, p. 6)

References

Abed al Jabri, M. (1994). *Arab Islamic philosophy: A contemporary critique*. Austin, TX: Center for Islamic Studies.

Abudabbeh, N., & Nydell, M. (1999). Transcultural counselling and Arab Americans. In J. McFadden (Ed.), *Transcultural counseling: Bilateral and international perspectives*. Alexander, VA: American Counseling Association, pp. 261–284.

Altareb, B.Y. (1996). Islamic spirituality in America: A middle path to unity. *Counselling and Values*, 41, 29–36.

The Authentic Book of Bukhari. Retrieved from http://www.allaboutworld view.org/islamic-theology-and-revelation-faq.htm

Barise, A. (1999). *Thinking and Learning in the Qur'an*. Unpublished manuscript.

Dwairy, M. (2006). *Counseling and psychotherapy with Arabs and Muslims*. New York: Teachers College Press.

Esack, F. (1999). *On being a Muslim: finding a religious path in the world today*. Oxford, UK: One World Publications.

Hitti, K.P. (1970). *History of the Arabs*. New York: St. Martins Press.

Javed, N. (1994). Gender identity and Muslim women: Tool of oppression turned into empowerment. *Convergence*, 27(2/3), 58–68.

Lago, C. (2011). *The handbook of transcultural counselling and psychotherapy*. London, UK: Open University Press.

Makow, H. (2009, September 24). Bikini vs. burka: The debauchery of women. 2009. Retrieved from http://www.savethemales.ca/180902.html

McDound-Laurier Institute (2011). *Much good news and some worrying results in new study of Muslim public opinion in Canada*. Ottawa, ON.

Kingston, A. (2012, January 17). Veils: Who are we to judge? *Maclean's*. Retrieved from http://www2.macleans.ca/2012/01/17/who-are-we-to-judge/

Menocal, M.R. (1987). *The Arabic role in medieval literary history: A forgotten heritage*. Philadelphia. PA: University of Pennsylvania Press.

Sampson, E. (1998). *Dealing with differences: An introduction to the social psychology of prejudice*. Orlando, FL: Harcourt College Publishers.

Samad, Y. (1996). The politics of Islamic identity among Bangladeshis and Pakistanis in Britain, In T. Ranger, Y. Samad & O. Stuart (Eds.), *Culture, identity and politics*. Aldershot, UK: Avebury.

Sheikh, A., Kunzendorf, R., & Sheikh, K. (1989). Healing images: From ancient wisdom to modern science, In A. Sheikh & K. Sheikh (Eds.), *Eastern & Western approaches to healing* (pp. 470–515). New York, NY: Wiley-Interscience.

Turner, D., Cheboud, E., Elvira, R., & Barise, A. (2002). *Challenges for human rights advocacy and conflict resolution: The case of racism and racial conflict*. Paper presented at the Conference of International Schools of Social Work, Montpellier, France, July 15–18, 2002.

14

My Multiracial Identity

Examining the Biracial/Multiracial Dynamic

NATASHA CAVERLEY

Identity is a simple word yet it raises many complex issues and causes introspection. We grapple not only with ourselves, men and other women, but also with broader influences of history, society, cultural heritage, and traditional structures. (in Featherston, 1994, p. 7)

AS CHILDREN DEVELOP AN APPRECIATION of their inner mental world, they begin to think more intently about themselves. During early childhood, they start to construct a self-concept, "the sum total of attributes, abilities, attitudes and values that individuals believe define who they are" (Berk, 1997, p. 428). Over time, children organize these internal states and behaviours into dispositions that they are aware of and can verbalize to others. The knowledge that we exist as individuals, separate from everyone else, emerges by the age of 18 months (Stipek, Gralinski & Kopp, 1990). As children get older, they soon develop a sense of themselves as separate individuals, ultimately forming a self-concept. For some multiracial individuals, development of their ethnic identity between two or more racial backgrounds can cause cultural conflicts and a struggle in defining who they are. Some multiracial individuals may feel lost between two or more worlds. The purpose of this chapter is to explore and gain insight into the family life and social development of multiracial individuals as these aspects relate to their self-concept and racial identity. It is important to examine the implications of these aspects in the area of cross-cultural counselling and teaching.

Personal Perspective

In this chapter, I have chosen to use the inclusive term *multiracial* to acknowledge individuals who identify as being of two or more races, including biracial people. The reasons for this specific focus are first to examine the dynamics that occur when an individual has parents who are from two or more different socially designated racial groups. Second, as a person from a multiracial background [Caucasian (Irish), West Indian (Jamaican) and Aboriginal (Algonquin)] myself, I feel my own reflections and experiences will be more accurately expressed from this perspective.

Forming One's Racial Identity

Self-concept refers the set of beliefs about one's own characteristics. One's self-concept makes up one's sense of identity, the set of beliefs we hold about what we are like as individuals (Breakwell, Hattie & Stevens, 1992). The development of one's self-concept leads to the formation of self-esteem, or the judgements one makes about one's own worth (Baumeister, 1993; Brown, 1995). An individual's self-concept affects identity formation, reflecting a combination of one's social identity, the roles or group membership categories to which one belongs, and one's personal identity, the traits and behaviours that people find descriptive of themselves (Brown, 1995; Tajfel & Turner, 1986).

According to Erik Erickson (1956), personality develops through a series of eight stages. He examined the integration of the biological, psychological and social aspects of development. His theory of development holds that at each stage of life, we face the task of establishing equilibrium between ourselves and our social world (Erickson, 1956). For some multiracial individuals, an implication of this theory involves the fifth stage, which revolves around identity versus role confusion.

The fifth stage of development occurs from age 13 through 19. At this stage, the adolescent experiments with different roles while trying to integrate identities from previous stages. Self-examination occurs as many adolescents examine their roles in their family, school and peer groups. At the same time, adolescents are trying to figure out who they are and who they want to become within their larger society (Erickson, 1956). It is during this time when some multiracial adolescents struggle with the uncertainty of their racial and ethnic identity. The conflict and confusion that some multiracial adolescents may be going through could be an example of Erickson's identity crisis. This refers to individuals who are struggling to find out who they are (Erickson, 1956). Youths who have not adequately resolved their conflicts may develop a negative identity, in which they act in scornful and hostile ways toward roles considered proper and desirable by the community. Lacking a clear sense of identity, some multiracial individuals may exhibit a range of negative emotional states, including shame, anger, personal confusion and feelings of helplessness (Fukuyama, 1999). Key parts of multiracial individuals' identities rest on the support they receive from their society and family and on their internalization of the ideals of their race and culture. Braun Williams (1999) and Hall (2005) believe that racial identity for multiracial individuals is a fluid, seamless part of who they are. Racial identity, especially for multiracial people, tends to be centred in the person, not in societal constructions. There is no one correct identification for multiracial people: it is the person who gets to name his/her experience. Therefore, some multiracial individuals may choose to align themselves with one or more ethnic groups that complement them in personal characteristics such as birthplace, language, race/physical attributes or customs. I realize that race is not concrete but rather only a label, a term that individuals use to describe how they see themselves in relation to others. The various cultures and racial backgrounds are only elements of who I am as a multiracial individual. I am free to define myself as I see fit. As I stated earlier, it is important to realize and encourage multiracial individuals to value the freedom to choose which aspects of their cultural and racial backgrounds they wish to embrace.

During my teen years, I was approached by various individuals who asked, "So, where are you from?" "I live here in Victoria," I said, but I realized that was not what some of them wanted to hear. "No, what nationality are you?" they would clarify, saying, "What is your ethnicity?", "What colour are you?" or "What is your race?" I was never bothered by these questions as I felt I could do one of two things: feel victimized/threatened by the questions or educate these individuals about what it is like to be multiracial. I chose the latter. By briefly describing my ethnic background to these individuals, I felt I was doing my part in enlightening others about multiculturalism and diversity and thus making them more aware of the unique population of which I am a part. I realized that no one meant harm in asking me to define myself; they were merely curious because I did not look like anyone they had seen before, and perhaps my parents were unlike any other couple they knew.

One of the frustrating things I had to go through during my adolescence was being excluded on certain questionnaires when applying to various universities and for scholarships. The statement concerning race usually directed, "Please fill in one of the following boxes," but my race was never there. As a multiracial individual, I do not easily fit into any racial group. I am not ONLY black, not ONLY Aboriginal and not ONLY white: I am all three races simultaneously! I was bothered by this question on forms, particularly federal and post-secondary forms from the United States, because these institutions appear to be saying, "Listen, you have to pick a portion of your identity and deny the others. Are you Black, Native American or White? You cannot be all three simultaneously." There appeared to be no consideration or understanding on the part of these organizations that some of the population did not view these existing racial categories as valid in terms of their identity or affiliation. Prior to 2000, the U.S. Census Bureau asked individuals to identify with only one race on the census, creating angst for multiracial individuals and evoking feelings similar to those I noted above. Multiracial groups in the US lobbied to have the Census Bureau update this question to ensure a more accurate reflection of the racial makeup in the country; the change occurred during the 2000 census (Gaskins, 1999; Holmes, 1997; Townsend, Markus & Bergsieker, 2009). In Canada, Statistics Canada affords the opportunity for respondents to provide two or more ethnic origins when completing Canadian census forms.

In order to gain a clear sense of identity, an individual needs a sense of continuity of him/herself over time. According to Erickson (1956), a sense of identity requires consistency between that which individuals conceive themselves to be and that which they perceive others to see in them and expect of them. For multiracial individuals, "simultaneity" should be stressed and acknowledged as a means of empowerment and pride in their multiple racial backgrounds (Braun Williams, 1999). For these individuals, one environment where simultaneity should be encouraged is in the home.

Family Life

The family performs important functions for its children. Jackson (1999) recognizes that parents play a critical role in shaping and influencing their child's racial identity development. Parents should ensure they provide children with an adequate foundation for socialization and emotional support. A key element to the family is the promotion of positive family interactions, which in turn will aid in enhancing a child's development (Berk, 1997). During adolescence, young people know they are an integral part of the family, and yet they also have a budding sense of independence and personal efficacy. They are realizing and recognizing their own competence, can take initiative and are able to see a variety of tasks through to completion. Thus, they enter adolescence with a variety of loosely related segments of identity based on experiences in the earlier stages (Conger & Galambos, 1997).

Growing up as a multiracial individual, I embraced all aspects of my cultures equally. I was exposed to my Canadian and Jamaican roots, fascinated by the differences and similarities between these two Commonwealth nations. My parents instilled in me at an early age never to judge people based on their racial/ethnic/cultural backgrounds. Through the years, they have taught me there is more to learn from other nations than to fear. It is through my parents' actions, letting me value all aspects of my racial and cultural backgrounds, that I really felt I was somebody. Another component of my upbringing was the fact that my parents provided emotional support and freedom to explore within my multicultural heritage, from letting me play with my black Barbie dolls to visiting relatives in Ontario who shared their stories of their early years in Canada to reading the *Daily Gleaner* (the national Jamaican newspaper). From my teenage years into my early twenties, I found out more about my Aboriginal ancestry as my late grandfather (on my father's side) was a First Nations member. During this time, my father and I explored our Algonquin cultural heritage and history, especially through the process of genealogical mapping and connecting with distant relatives who are part of the Algonquins of Ontario. From this shared journey and learning experience with my father along with my learnings from my (Jamaican) mother, I incorporated my multiracial experiences into my values and perspectives related to spirituality, family and career endeavours, working in multicultural settings at the provincial and national levels in Canada. I am so appreciative that my family served as a secure base from which I could confidently develop my racial identity, which was enhanced by my many positive life experiences.

Social Development

Identity development also depends on schools and communities that provide young people with rich and varied opportunities for exploration (Tajfel & Turner, 1986). Within society, multiracial individuals transgress racial boundaries and put into question the entire basis of social order, the racial hierarchy entrenched in history. Multiracial individuals have the opportunity to reveal how artificial the colour/race line is within society (Kawash, 1997).

Society differentiates and discriminates on the basis of colour. One's ascribed colour may denote acceptance or non-acceptance in various social circles. Braun Williams (1999) states that, "in a world where socially constructed categories of race are misconstrued as biological, little encouragement is offered to multiracial people like me to claim an identity that falls outside prescribed frameworks" (p. 33). As a result, social groupings tend to be based on physical characteristics tied to skin colour/race. In Western-influenced culture, skin is the greatest signifier. It is the first thing people see and is used to define who one is (Kawash, 1997). The privileges, or lack thereof, attached to different shades of skin colour, textures of hair and eye shape are encoded into the social fabric. For some multiracial individuals, the social pressure can force them to identify with the racial group of one parent as opposed to the other, potentially leading to confusion, guilt and resentment.

The dynamics surrounding white privilege and power express the realities of cultural/ethnic group status and categorization within society. The term *privilege* "confers dominance, gives permission to control, because of one's race or sex" (McIntosh, 1992, p. 77). Power represents an ability to control and shape the behaviour of others. Through historical relationships and perceptions between various cultures, what tends to result is some type of separation between "us" and "them" — resulting in the classification of "other." Groups such as multiracial individuals have been classified as "other" and are believed to be different from the dominant groups in society. The categorization of "other" can become an expectation, based on stereotypes that may have arisen from personal experiences, media and/or social messages used to classify groups within society. It appears that being "other" can stem from any trait that contributes to a group's social identity or emphasizes privilege differences from the dominant group, such as class, sex, colour, ethnicity, nationality, socio-economic status or political status (LeBaron, 2003).

Some biracial individuals may tend to experience something called biracial guilt. This occurs when the biracial individual feels terrible guilt wondering if he/she has the right to call him/herself, for example, African Canadian, even though the individual was not raised in an African cultural environment. Other questions stemming from biracial guilt include, "Can I really say I am black even though my skin colour is white?" and "By saying I am white based on the colour of my skin, am I rejecting the black parent I have come to love?" For biracial individuals who have a Caucasian parent, there may be feelings of guilt as they associate themselves with the oppressive majority that has caused much pain for those individuals of colour.

Fukuyama (1999) described how, as a young adult, she felt a need to fit into the dominant white culture. At one point in her life, she adopted the Anglo-American name of her husband so as to assimilate into the dominant culture as much as possible. Some multiracial individuals may feel the pressure from society to fit into the dominant culture and conform in what is called "passing" or crossing over. Passing/crossing over means that an individual internalizes the values and beliefs of the dominant culture and rejects the other aspects of his/her ethnic and racial heritage (Parrilla de Kokal, 1997). Socially, an individual might ignore, laugh at or join in disparaging remarks made about his/her ethnic group. Some of the reasons that one might deny part of one's racial identity may include such things as racial stereotypes, racial epithets and discrimination one faces personally or observes among family and friends. When some individuals pass/cross over, they truly believe they are making themselves more desirable with the dominant group to obtain the privileges afforded to them, at the expense of recognizing and embracing all aspects of their racial identity (Kawash, 1997).

An interesting twist to passing/crossing over happened once when I went to meet with a human resource management advisor for a potential job interview. The session was going well, and then I asked what kind of support networks were offered at this organization for a visible minority like myself. The human resource management advisor stated, "You are a visible minority?" I replied, "Yes, I am!" The advisor proceeded to tell me that it would be in my best interest not to mention that I was multiracial as, "You have a good thing going with your scholastic achievements and work experience. You do not want to jeopardize your chances by bringing something up like that." That was my definite cue to remove myself from the interview session and look for work elsewhere. Though I have fair skin, I am very much a Caucasian, West Indian and Aboriginal woman who will not let someone else tell me to deny my racial and cultural heritage.

Peer relations play an important role in adolescent development. Peers serve as socialization agents through the use of modelling, reinforcement and direct pressures to conform to social behaviours, whether they are positive or negative (Conger & Galambos, 1997). I think another reason for feeling comfortable living among three races was my parents' decision that I attend an international school for girls. By attending an international school (from kindergarten to Grade 12), I happily embraced all aspects of my racial heritage equally. At this school, Caucasian, Asian, Hispanic and multiracial women were treated as equals who came from diverse backgrounds. It was through my years at this school that I came to solidify my racial identity, realizing that I did not have to choose between being black, Aboriginal and white; I could happily be all three simultaneously. As a result of these experiences and the fostering of multiculturalism, I have found that I have developed a comfort zone in the community and at university with individuals who come from different cultural/ethnic backgrounds. I have been told by these acquaintances that my warm, non-judgemental manner has made them feel very much at ease with me and made it easy for them to approach me. Again, I attribute these abilities to the fact that by being multiracial, I can identify with various needs and concerns of other visible minority groups in the community.

Benefits of Being Multiracial

From a psychological perspective, some multiracial individuals feel empowered to incorporate and accept all aspects of their racial and cultural backgrounds. This empowerment may result from interactions with friends or family members who provide the richness of diverse cultural knowledge and experiences regarding the many facets of the multiracial individual's racial/cultural heritage. Schwartz (1998) brings forward other positive aspects of being multiracial, such as having greater intergroup tolerance, language facility, appreciation of minority group cultures and ties to single-heritage groups than do monoracial people (Thornton, 1996). In addition, some multiracial individuals have the ability to carry multiple perspectives simultaneously and are able to identify diverse aspects of a situation (also known as frame switching or border crossing), thus recognizing and seeing all sides of a conflict seamlessly (Binning et al., 2009; Kerwin et al., 1993; Root, 1996).

Implications for Cross-Cultural Counselling and Teaching: Strategies and Interventions

The role of culture is becoming more recognized in the area of counselling. The growing multicultural factor continues to be present in our lives. In a world where communities have expanded to include individuals from different nationalities and racial backgrounds, the natural by-product of this interaction is multiracial children. According to the 2006 Census of Canada data, 12 921 445 people out of the total Canadian population self-identified that they were of multiple ethnic origins (Statistics Canada, 2006). These statistics indicate that educators and counsellors must expand their knowledge and enhance their cross-cultural competence in working with multiracial students and clients. Cross-cultural counselling and teaching are fundamental tools. The following considerations should be observed when working with multicultural individuals.

Educators

- Use stories, role playing, films, photos and picture books. Show students how people have effectively mixed religions, national heritages, ethnic, racial, political and linguistic differences through marriage (Diller, 1999). For example, access multiracial children's books at www.comeunity.com/adoption/books/0multiracial.html.

- Lead a family tree project in your classroom, allowing students to research as far back as they can with both sides of their family. Note the differences and origins of each child — nation, language, culture and so forth. Use photos and artifacts, and encourage parents, grandparents and other relatives to come to the classroom to talk with the children.

- Encourage and support discussions about individual differences (Diller, 1999; Wardle, 1992). Children are very curious; they are also uncertain and sometimes afraid of the unknown. "Why do you look different from your mommy?" "Why is your daddy white and you're not?" "Can I touch your hair?" "Are you adopted?" Respond to these questions, and use the interest to talk about children getting their physical characteristics from their parents. Use both multiracial and monoracial children to make this point. This activity may naturally lead to a project on different families. Develop a bulletin board or collage showing every variety of family — foster, adoptive, two-parent, single-parent, interracial, extended and minority. Invite as many of these families as possible to visit your classroom.

Counsellors

- It is important to realize that multiracial people have the same concerns and questions about their ethnic and racial origins as any other visible minority group.
- When working with multiracial clients, remember to reinforce the counselling philosophy of non-judgemental thinking in therapy sessions. Do not assume that simply because a client has a certain skin tone, he/she will identify more with the ideals, values and morals of the racial group that reflects his/her skin colour than with another.
- Validate the experiences and identity of multiracial individuals such as the client's feelings (i.e., anger) about racism (Fukuyama, 1999).
- Familiarize yourself with the client's multiple racial and ethnic backgrounds to determine values and characteristics that may be rooted in the person's cultural background as opposed to a general personality trait. In addition, encourage clients to explore their multiracial heritage as part of their racial identity development (Lyles et al., 1985; Sebring, 1985).
- Recognize that traditional developmental, life-span and personality theories are based on monocultural experiences. Failure to recognize the limitations of these traditional theories may cause you to view aspects of the multiracial person's behaviours and perspectives as symptoms (negative) rather than strength-based attributes (positive) (Gibbs, 1989).
- When appropriate, look for multiracial role models for clients as a means of finding someone in the community (e.g., family members or friends) or in society at large (e.g., celebrities) who acknowledges and embraces his/her multicultural heritage (e.g., singers Mariah Carey, Alicia Keys, Drake; actors Halle Barry and Cameron Diaz; elite athletes Jarome Iginla, Derek Jeter and Carmelo Anthony). Multiracial individuals may often feel pressure from society to choose role models who are from one specific ethnic group or another (Braun Williams, 1999). Opportunities of this nature to discuss and share experiences allow those who are uncertain of their self-concept to identify with other members of the multiracial community and thus feel more at ease with their racial heritage.
- "Demonstrate ability to interpret assessment results including implications of dominant cultural values affecting assessment/interpretation, interaction of cultures for those who are biracial and the impact of historical institutional oppression" (Arredondo, 1999, p. 108).
- Be aware of language use during sessions. The power of language and terminology in describing multiracial individuals is another important aspect to note.

Some terms — such as *hybrid, mixed, half breed* and *mulatto* — have been used to describe members of the multiracial community. These terms are derogatory and can lead to one having a negative self-image/self-concept. The term *mulatto*, for instance, is used to refer to individuals who are both Caucasian and black; it has the same negative/politically incorrect connotation as calling a black person a Negro. The word mulatto was initially coined to refer to the sterile mule, the progeny of a mating between two diverse species; the term was used to "prove" that members of the black community and members of the white community were indeed separate and distinct species (Kawash, 1997). The terms *biracial/ bicultural* and *multiracial/multicultural* are now being used to refer to people of multiple racial and ethnic heritage. Word choice/terminology in identifying others is crucial and necessary to ensure a positive image of oneself.

Some key multiracial websites that can be used in the multicultural counselling experience include

- Biracial Portraits (www.pbs.org/wgbh/pages/frontline/shows/secret/portraits);
- Interracial Voice (www.webcom.com/intvoice/);
- Mixed Folks (www.mixedfolks.com);
- Multiracial Sky (www.multiracialsky.com).

As a counsellor working with members of various ethnic groups, you may wish to consider the following ideas.

- Empathy should be a foundation to all counselling. Clients want to be understood and validated by the therapist (Braun Williams, 1999).
- Recognize and realize that counsellors are powerful agents of change in affirming ethnic and racial identity (Fukuyama, 1999).
- Commit to being a lifetime learner of cross-cultural issues, whether through informal or formal training, such as multicultural competency training. Cross-cultural training allows counsellors to recognize their own feelings of defensiveness, resistance, mistrust and vulnerability regarding the subject of race (Robinson, 1999).
- Examine your own cultural heritage as it relates to comfort and positive orientation to cultural differences (Braun Williams, 1999; Torres, Howard-Hamilton & Cooper, 2003).
- Lead from behind by feeling comfortable as a counsellor in exploring racial issues with the client (Braun Williams, 1999).

As counsellors and educators, we should continue to reflect interventions that acknowledge the diverse communities in which we live. One must view these cross-cultural issues not as barriers for clients but as challenges brought before us: challenges for which we are ready.

Conclusion

The development of a multiracial individual reflects many needs that are common to all people. I hope the integration of my first-hand experiences and analysis of existing literature will allow some insight into the struggles and concerns that face those who are multiracial. I should note that my experiences in no way reflect the family life and social development of all multiracial individuals. By gaining first-hand knowledge of the developmental aspects of multiracial individuals, we hope to move away from the social labels and stereotypes associated with multiracial individuals. Through the thoughts expressed in this chapter, I wish to shed some light on how multiracial individuals are influenced by their family and society in the development of their self-concept and racial identity.

References

Arredondo, P. (1999). Multicultural counselling competencies as tools to address oppression and racism. *Journal of Counselling & Development*, 77(1), 102–108.

Baumeister, R. (1998). Self-esteem: The puzzle of low self-regard. In R.S. Feldman (Ed.), *Social psychology* (2nd ed.). Upper Saddle River, NJ: Prentice-Hall.

Berk, L.E. (1997). *Child development* (4th ed.). Needham Height, MA: Allyn and Bacon.

Binning, K.R., Unzueta, M.M., Huo, Y.J., & Molina, L.E. (2009). The interpretation of multiracial status and its relation to social engagement and psychological well-being. *Journal of Social Issues*, 65(1), 35–49.

Braun Williams, C. (1999). Claiming a biracial identity: Resisting social constructions of race and culture. *Journal of Counselling and Development*, 77(1), 32–35.

Breakwell, G.M., Hattie, J., & Stevens, R. (1998). Social psychology of identity and the self-concept. In R.S. Feldman (Ed.), *Social psychology* (2nd ed.). Upper Saddle River, NJ: Prentice-Hall.

Brown, U.M. (1995). Black/white interracial youth adults: Quest for a racial identity. *American Journal of Orthopsychiatry*, 65, 125–130.

Conger, J.J., & Galambos, N.L. (1997). *Adolescence and youth: Psychological development in a changing world* (5th ed.). New York: Addison Wesley Longman.

Diller, J.V. (1999). *Cultural diversity: A primer for the human services*. Boston, MA: Wadsworth.

Erickson, E. (1997). The problem of ego identity. In J.J. Conger, & N.L. Galambos (Ed.), *Adolescence and youth: Psychological development in a changing world* (5th ed.). New York: Addison Wesley Longman.

Featherston, E. (1994). *Skin deep: Women writing on color, culture and identity*. Freedom, CA: Crossing Press.

Fukuyama, M.A. (1999). Personal narrative: Growing up biracial. *Journal of Counselling and Development*, 77(1), 12–14.

Gaskins, P. (1999). *What are you? Voices of mixed-race young people*. New York: Holt & Co.

Gibbs, J.T. (1989). Biracial adolescents. In J.T. Gibb & L.N. Huang (Eds.), *Children of color: Psychological interventions with minority youth*. San Francisco, CA: Jossey-Bass.

Hall, R.E. (2005). Eurocentrism in social work education: From race to identity across the lifespan as biracial alternative. *Journal of Social Work*, 5, 101–114.

Holmes, S.A. (1997, October 30). People can claim more than one race on federal forms. *New York Times*, p. A1.

Jackson, K.F. (2009). Beyond race: Examining the facets of multiracial identity through a life-span developmental lens. *Journal of Ethnic and Cultural Diversity in Social Work*, 18(4), 293–310.

Kawash, S. (1997). *Dislocating the color line: Identity, hybridity, and singularity in African-American literature*. Stanford, CA: Stanford University Press.

Kerwin, C., Ponterotto, J.G., Jackson, B.L., & Harris, A. (1998). Racial identity in biracial children: A qualitative investigation. In Schwartz, W. (Ed.), *The identity development of multiracial youth*. New York: ERIC Clearinghouse on Urban Education.

LeBaron, M. (2003). *Bridging cultural conflicts: A new approach for a changing world*. San Francisco, CA: Jossey-Bass.

Lyles, M.R., Yancey, A., Grace, C., & Carter, J.H. (1985). Racial identity and self-esteem: Problems peculiar to bi-racial children. *Journal of the American Academy of Child Psychiatry*, 24, 150–153.

McIntosh, P. (1992). White privilege and male privilege: A personal account of coming to see correspondence through work in women's studies. In Margaret L. Andersen and Patricia Hill Collins (Eds.), *Race, class and gender, An anthology* (pp. 70–81). Independence, KY: Wadsworth Publishing.

Parrilla de Kokal, M.D. (1999). 'White chocolate': An inquiry into physical and psychological identity. *Journal of Counselling and Development*, 77(1), 27–30.

Robinson, T.L. (1999). The intersections of dominant discourses across race, gender and other identities. *Journal of Counselling and Development*, 77(1), 73–80.

Root, M.P.P. (Ed.) (1996). *The multiracial experience: Racial borders as the new frontier*. Thousand Oaks, CA: Sage.

Schwartz, W. (1998). *The identity development of multiracial youth*. New York: ERIC Clearinghouse on Urban Education.

Sebring, D. (1985). Considerations in counseling interracial children. *Journal of Non-White Concerns in Personnel and Guidance*, 13, 3–9.

Statistics Canada (2006). *Ethnic origin, single and multiple ethnic origin responses for the population of Canada, 2006 census*. Ottawa, ON: Government of Canada.

Stipek, D., Gralinski, J.H., & Kopp, C.B. (1997). Self-concept development in the toddler years. In L.E. Berk (Ed.), *Child development* (4th ed.). Needham Height, MA: Allyn and Bacon.

Tajfel, H., & Turner, J. (1998). The social identity and intergroup relations. In R.S. Feldman (Ed.), *Social psychology* (2nd ed.). Upper Saddle River, NJ: Prentice-Hall.

Thornton, M.C. (1998). Hidden agendas, identity theories, and multiracial people. In Schwartz, W. (Ed.), *The identity development of multiracial youth*. New York: ERIC Clearinghouse on Urban Education.

Torres, V., Howard-Hamilton, M.F., & Cooper, D.L. (2003). *Identity development of diverse populations: Implications for teaching and administration in higher education* (6th ed.). San Francisco, CA: Jossey-Bass.

Townsend, S.S.M., Markus, H.R., & Bergsieker, H.B. (2009). My choice, your categories: The denial of multiracial identities. *Journal of Social Issues*, 65(1), 185–204.

Wardle, F. (1992). Supporting biracial children in the school setting. *Education and Treatment of Children*, 15(2), 163–172.

15

Upon Arrival

Ordeals and Challenges in Working with International Students

María del Carmen Rodríguez

BEING A FOREIGNER DOES NOT ONLY MEAN finding oneself in a different geographical place: it could also mean finding oneself without the familiar cues that tie people to their most cherished belongings: a sense of trust, intimacy, self-confidence, self-worth and empowerment. *Foreign* or *international student* are terms that must go beyond the simple description of someone who studies overseas, since it conveys much more than just living and studying abroad. According to the *New World Dictionary* (2012), *foreign* means "a person belonging to or owing allegiance to a foreign country" (n.p.). However, this definition does not embrace all the processes an individual must undergo to function adequately in an environment that is dissimilar to his or her own. Loneliness, depression, homesickness, academic concerns, language proficiency, discrimination, cultural differences, personal characteristics and financial concerns are just a few of the difficulties experienced by many international students (Surdam & Collins, 1984; Heikinheimo & Shute, 1986). On the other hand, willingness to learn about another culture, establish relationships and share common interests are viewed as stimulators (Heikinheimo & Shute, 1986).

Who Are International Students?

Foreign or international students compose a heterogeneous group with diverse needs and concerns that face relatively common issues and challenges related to the acculturative experience. Although the extensive growth in the international student population has been positive for colleges and universities in North America, it has exceeded the ability of those in helping professions to assess, comprehend and address students' needs. The increasing degree of interest in internationalizing institutions in the form of student mobility programs, policy, partnerships and recruitment efforts has opened possibilities and opportunities for studying abroad.

Between 1992 and 2008, enrolment at Canadian universities doubled, rising from 36 822 in 1992 to 87 798 in 2008, with New Brunswick, Prince Edward Island and Nova Scotia representing the largest proportional growth (Statistics Canada, 2012). Ontario and British Columbia have also witnessed ample growth, the latter experiencing an increase of 9 per cent between 1992 and 2008 (Statistics Canada, 2012). Interestingly, the origin of most international students was similar during the same time period, with Asian students accounting for the largest share of international students, while the largest change has been a significant decrease in the number of international students coming from countries in Africa. With regard to age demographics, in 2008 students were younger and more likely to be enrolled in programs at the bachelor's level than in doctoral programs; there was an increase in female students' registration in the same period, from 39 per cent in 1992 to 45 per cent in 2008 (Statistics Canada, 2012).

However, when it comes to offering a definition for who international students are, we must note that within that frame of reference, there are no subgroups or categories that take care of this group's specific characteristics. Within the group there are intersections. For example, one may find single and married students (with or without a family); those who form part of a co-op program and those who have no job; students who were sent from their country of origin and those who chose to study abroad; students who will return home and those who are planning to make a new home in the new context. Notwithstanding individual struggles for acculturation, the ordeals and adversities international students face are similar. It is due to these characteristics, needs and challenges that academic advisors and counsellors need to be prepared to guide and assist international students in this cultural — and often emotional — transition.

Contrast and Variance: Premises

The most severe culture shock does not result from dealing with external matters but rather from status change and status loss in responding to the new situations (Alexander, Klein, Workneh & Miller, 1981). Despite technological advancements, possibilities to connect through social networks or opportunities to learn about a new context before arrival, coping with loss, and newfound independence when students first arrive in a new culture could be interpreted as a first sign of culture shock. The concept implies that the experience of visiting or living in a new culture is an unpleasant surprise or a trauma, partly because it is unexpected and partly because it may lead to negative evaluations of one's own and/or the other culture (Furnham,

1989). Students are on their own and must ponder and choose from an extensive range of possibilities, from finding a place to live to deciding what to do with all the options that lie ahead. However, sooner or later they understand that culture shock goes beyond dealing with bus routes, money matters and finding buildings or restaurants.

Of Finnish descent but Canadian born, anthropologist Kalervo Oberg (1957) was the first to use the term *culture shock*. He identified four stages and six aspects to this reaction, which has been understood as a normal part of a routine process of adaptation to ethnic/cultural differences and the manifestation of a longing for a more predictable and understandable environment. The stages, according to Oberg (1957), are as follows.

1. Initial euphoria: Most people begin their new responsibility with great expectations about themselves and a positive frame of mind toward the host country. Anything new is intriguing and exciting, but soon disappointment is inevitable.
2. Irritability and hostility: Gradually, the focus shifts from the excitement of being in interesting places with fascinating people to the difficulty of living among them. People seem to focus on the differences (which suddenly seem to be everywhere) and begin to emphasize them.
3. Gradual adjustment: The crisis is over, and people seem to be more open to others and willing to share. Once students are able to interpret some of the subtle cultural clues, which were overlooked earlier, the culture seems more familiar. One becomes more comfortable in it and feels less isolated. Interestingly, a person's sense of humour returns and he/she realizes the situation is not hopeless after all.
4. Adaptation: Full recovery results in an ability to function in two cultures with confidence. Students might even enjoy a great many customs, ways of doing and saying things and personal attitudes to which they have acculturated (to some extent) and which they might even miss when the time comes to pack up and return home.

Oberg (1957) also described six aspects that accompany culture shock:

- Sense of loss and feelings of deprivation (in regard to friends, status, profession and possessions; decrease of social interaction);
- Strain (anxiety as a result of the efforts to make the necessary adaptations);
- Rejection (being rejected by and/or rejecting members of a new culture because of stereotyping);
- Confusion (mixed feelings in role, values, feelings and self-identity);
- Surprise and distress after becoming aware of cultural differences;
- Feelings of being less important or capable (low self-esteem) and perceived inability from not being able to cope with the new environment due to language limitations.

The levels of anxiety, stress and rejection vary from person to person and culture to culture. Everyone experiences culture shock differently, and different variables determine which reaction a person is likely to experience and how long he/she will remain in shock. Culture shock may be more or less intense for some groups (e.g., older/younger students, men/women, more-/less-educated individuals, university/college students or youth, etc.). Nevertheless, culture shock is not always an unpleasant experience. Paradoxically, according to Adler (1975), "the more one is capable of experiencing new and different dimensions of human diversity, the more one learns of oneself" (p. 22).

Students' Ordeals

Oberg's (1957) description of the six aspects that accompany culture shock serves as a starting point in describing some of the ordeals international students face when living and interacting with/in a new culture.

Loss

In moving to another country for the first time, international students experience a unique and profound sense of loss. They lose social support and status, familiar cues, certainty and even self-worth. As a consequence, they often feel less confident and tenser and tend to take less time off; instead, they become preoccupied with academic demands and may even become confused over how to live day to day. Financial restrictions are also part of this sense of loss; these might create tension while the person learns the best ways in which to use money (e.g., grocery shopping, transportation options, recreation and so forth). Such responses can give rise to behavioural dysfunction in new cultural contexts (Heikkinen, 1981). In the increasing number of cross-cultural counselling studies, self-esteem, self-efficacy and social concern have been identified as some of the biggest problems facing international students (Day & Hajj, 1986; Heikinheimo & Shute, 1986; Meloni, 1986; Pedersen, 1991). As an initial reaction, international students lose the shared identity that comes from being with family and peers (Pedersen, 1991; Romero, 1981). According to Puthey (1981), the need to identify and develop skills to function in the host culture, alongside the need to develop new roles and rebuild a support system, intensifies students' levels of anxiety: "To be alone amongst strangers, with whom there is no historical association, can be an alienating and negative experience which threatens identity and self-esteem" (Wheeler & Birtle, 1993, p. 110).

Detriment of Social Interaction

Since each person's ability to achieve success in relationships fluctuates (e.g., family, romance, friendship), individual differences must be considered when we attempt to understand why some students are more likely than others to encounter barriers to potential support. Understanding how these factors interact with one another to create barriers can help counsellors to intervene more effectively. Similarly, appropriate social behaviour is associated with self-esteem and interpersonal control. International students who experience more anxiety in the new and unfamiliar cultural environment might have limited ability to succeed socially. Conversely, students who are confident in their capabilities in dominant domains do not experience much general anxiety (Paulhus & Martin, 1987).

External factors also contribute to feelings of alienation. Host nationals generally recognize that international students have language difficulties and are often insensitive to the international student's need for conversation. When they recognize that the contribution of the partner in conversation plays an important part in adapting, host nationals can be seen as sharing equal responsibility with international students for building cross-cultural friendships.

Stress

International students will relate to others in order to develop active strategies such as learning new skills and talking with others to learn the language, and might even choose direct counselling over indirect methods as a means for socializing (Exum & Lau, 1988; Leong & Sedlacek, 1986). Yet most international students deal with stress in isolation. This is a difficult endeavour because it is an unconscious situation where the helper might not be able to identify the symptoms or the origins of distress and restlessness, in turn making emergence more difficult. As a result, students may estrange themselves from potential sources of social support such as cultural and sports groups. They isolate themselves from others who can help them learn about the new environment and from co-nationals with whom they could discuss similar problems. Consequently, peer counselling becomes an important helping strategy for counsellors and academic advisors.

Research (Leung, 2001) suggests that international students have to deal with stress manifested in various ways such as the loss of their social ties, adjusting to social customs and norms (Carr, Koyama & Thiagarajan, 2003; Leung, 2001), language barriers (Carr, et al., 2003; Toffoli & Allan, 1992) and dealing with cultural shock and acculturation stressors (Constantine, Okazaki & Utsey, 2004; Poyrazli, Kavanaugh, Baker & Al-Timimi, 2004; Winkelman, 1994).

Stereotypes

The particular prejudices that members of the host culture may hold for international students can serve as powerful obstacles to establishing social networks. Given the heightened awareness that international students possess, they are often highly sensitive to the meanings of verbal and non-verbal cues that convey intolerance and discomfort. In addition, different students may encounter prejudice in the form of stereotypes and/or criticisms depending on their own specific stigmatized characteristics. This tendency to think of members of other cultures in terms of stereotypes might be considered as another stumbling block that compounds the problems of culture shock. Interestingly, people who are prone to anxiety might find it comforting to hold on to stereotypes because they may lessen the threat of the unknown by making the world predictable. Once a stereotype is found, a person can behave, think and feel accordingly to what is expected based on such an image. This response leads to predictability, which is exactly what the foreigner needs. However, such predictability might delay the emergence from culture shock. Certain ethnic/cultural groups might be more prone to developing depressive symptoms as a result of perceived prejudice (Rahman & Rollock, 2004). On the other hand, according to Poyrazli and Grahame (2007), indicators of a healthy attitude toward a new culture are personality attributes, good communication skills in the host language, a positive approach to forming social relationships with the host community and the ability to manage prejudice and/or stereotypes.

Self-Esteem and Identity

Pedersen (1991) mentions that a person's self-esteem and self-image are validated by significant others who provide emotional and social support in culturally patterned ways, and that moving to a different culture deprives a person of these support systems: "A normal response to the withdrawing of support is anxiety, ranging from irritation and mild annoyance to the panic of extreme pain and the feelings of disorientation which accompany being lost" (p. 12). Furthermore, Belenky, McVicker, Rule and Mattuck (1986) say that, "If one can see the self only as mirrored in the eyes of others, the urgency is great to live up to other's expectations, in the hope of preventing others from forming a dim view" (p. 48). Affective factors encompassing the students' personal realm (e.g., family-related worries, illnesses, economic constraints and so forth) are likely to affect their studies, especially where there is little or no understanding and support for these concerns. As Young and Bagley (1982) notice, "identity and identity problems change as the individual gets older and experiences 'crises' associated with biological, social and role changes" (p. 58).

Among the difficulties that might delay their growth and adaptation, international students are most afraid to disclose their concerns and anxieties before strangers and consequently affect their adjustment to a foreign country. As described by Torrey, Van Rheenan and Katchadourian (1970) and Pedersen, Draguns, Lonner and Trimble (2012), "Relationships with co-nationals become an extremely important resource for success, with international students far more willing to disclose a 'personal problem' to a co-national than to any other counselling resource on campus" (p. 21). Counsellors and advisors are therefore challenged to help students work through their modified self-image, their changing self-esteem, the loss of social support experienced as the result of studying abroad and the academic requirements in order to succeed. Further, they must help students develop the necessary social networks to support them both personally and academically. Steinglass, DeNour and Shye (1985) suggest that the size of the social network is the best predictor of social adjustment; the establishment of a cultural subgroup might provide a place where international students can establish new relationships that will help them create a sense of belonging and a place to share familiar traditional values and belief systems. Further, counsellors can also help faculty and staff increase their knowledge and ability to work with international students, emphasizing some of the most difficult barriers to overcome, such as language.

Language Limitations

In addition to the loss of social support is the student's in/ability to communicate in the host culture. Unsurprisingly, English proficiency has also been found to be an important factor in social interaction and adjustment (Meloni, 1986; Pedersen, 1991; Schram & Lauver, 1988; Surdham & Collins, 1984). Research has shown that language restrictions and other affective and situational factors are detrimental to academic performance (Luzio-Lockett, 1995) and affect the overall educational experience. Although studies suggest the need for social contact with host nationals, such contact among international students seems limited by their language proficiency level, which in turn deters communication with peers, teachers and counsellors (Bochner, Hutnik & Furnham, 1985; Furnham & Alibhai, 1985). Many studies support the finding that the inability to speak the host language fluently is a primary inhibitor to becoming socially involved in the host society (Furnham & Alibhai, 1985; Heikinheimo & Shute, 1986; Meloni, 1986; Ray & Lee, 1988). In these situations, it is not difficult to perceive how one variable (language barrier) impacts another one (lack of social networks) and how spirals that lead to depression and stress may be created.

Dryden and Ellis (1987) declare that language is a fundamental characteristic due to "the powerful effect that language has on thought and the fact that our emotional processes are heavily dependent on the way we, as humans, structure our thought by the language we employ" (pp. 130–131). Moreover, Albert and Triandis (1991) maintain that language is "intimately connected with the way in which experience is interpreted and with the cognitive and affective categories which are used to conceptualize the world" (p. 412). Tasks such as taking notes and asking questions in classes can be different for international students. Students' limited ability to express opinions orally might lead teachers to perceive students as passive and shy. Further, Lin and Yi (1997) noted that students for whom English is a second language might have difficulty in articulating their knowledge on exams or papers due to their limited vocabulary, while Yeh and Inose (2003) found that lower levels of English fluency, among other indicators of social concerns (e.g., social support satisfaction and social connectedness), were significant predictors of acculturative stress. They also found that connectedness and relationships were essential aspects of the students' self-identity, values and ways of interacting. Consequently, it is important to keep in mind that close connections and social support networks can be critical to dealing with stress and mental health concerns. Counsellors working with international students need to remember that their own desire to work with the students and the quality of their contribution to the conversation and exchange of trust and empathy are most significant to the relationship.

Differences between Male and Female Students

Manese, Sedlacek and Leong (1988) conducted a study to examine differences in the needs and perceptions of male and female undergraduate international students from a variety of countries. The results reported sex differences, with women expecting to have a harder time, being more easily discouraged and questioning their self-efficacy more than men. Mallinckrodt and Leong (1992) conducted research to examine the level of stress symptoms and sources of social support in male and female international graduate students. They found that female students exhibited more stress symptoms, experienced increased stress and were less satisfied with social support received from family and academic departments. Since women are generally encouraged more than men to develop greater sensitivity to the needs of others (Gilligan, 1982), women are expected to have superior support resources. Even though research results demonstrate a reality different from the expectations, it is generally those individuals with an expressive orientation (i.e., warm, compassionate and nurturing) who seem to have more social support and are more likely to use these resources in times of need (Burda, Vaux & Schill, 1984). These notions have provided some insight for counsellors and academic advisors, alerting them about the impact of stress and stress-related issues that international students face. One additional implication is that men, who are less likely to be seen by others or themselves as needing support, are most likely to need it and least likely to know how to get help or be willing to take the steps necessary to get it.

Despite these differences, the literature demonstrates that the more the student's cultural background differs from that of the host culture, the more likely the student will develop emotional problems of adjustment (Domingues, 1970). Alexander, Klein, Workneh and Miller (1981) researched the adaptation of international students from developing countries to life on a US campus. Their findings demonstrated that the students experienced stress and feelings of vulnerability throughout their time of study. An important variable in this group of students was the lack of a familial support system, which is frequently found in people from such countries (Arredondo-Dowd, 1981). For these students, initial expressions of happiness about studying abroad can soon turn to feelings of sadness and even disappointment (Arredondo-Dowd, 1981). In another study, Ying and Liese (1990) used a longitudinal perspective to examine the process of adaptation in a group of Taiwanese international students where adaptation was conceptualized as a subjective sense of adjustment (result oriented, cognitive appraisal of one's life) as well as emotional well-being (process oriented, level of distress experienced while engaged in the process of making the adjustment). The researchers wanted to know what differentiated international students who benefitted and grew from the experience of studying abroad from those who were overburdened and unable to cope with the experience. Their findings showed that superior adjustment after arrival was significantly correlated with post-arrival emotional well-being. Hence, they suggest that it may be possible to predict adaptation to a new culture because it is largely a self-fulfilling prophecy.

The Role of the Helper

Despite similar ethnic/cultural background, degree of language proficiency and other shared experiences, international students need different alternatives to being helped depending on their academic interest, emotional need for stability, development of relationships and other areas of life. Academic advisors and counsellors are two key players in helping international students with their transitions to achieve successful and satisfactory functioning in the host context. Helpers need to remember that not only will students experience problems of adjustment to university but they will also be facing the challenges associated with adjusting to a new culture (Grayson, 2008). For graduate international students, these challenges also involve socialization to the values and culture of a profession (Nesheim, Guentzel, Gansemer-Topf, Ross & Turrentine, 2006); the way in which students cope with these challenges will likely affect their overall life experiences.

The Academic Advisor

As a person who will be guiding the student throughout his/her program, the academic advisor should be committed to possessing a certain amount of information (e.g., on- and off-campus resources) that will assist the student. The advisor is also responsible for developing skills and competencies to help the student during this transition. Differences in how advisors are perceived by international students may be a source of tension in the relationship or might represent a source of relief and trust. These perceptual differences may arise from the ways in which various cultures view males and females in their roles. Depending on their country of origin, for example, male students may feel insulted or find it humiliating to have a woman as an advisor. In other cases, some female international students may find it difficult to look male advisors in the eye (Idowu, 1985), a practice that is normal and even expected in North America. Because of the differences among cultures in the perception of authority figures, some international students may expect a more formal relationship with their academic advisors or instructors than do most North American students. They may be more dependent, demanding or both, believing that advisors or professors should show, tell or even do for them that for which students would be expected to assume individual responsibility in a North American culture. The advisor, in some cases, takes on a mentoring role instead. An empathic understanding toward the transitional experience, which involves a sudden self-re-evaluation (for both student and advisor), is required.

Two of the most fundamental objectives in advising international students are helping them adjust to the demands of their respective academic programs and helping them achieve academic success. The academic advisor serves as a link between the institution and international students to realize these important goals. Given the seriousness with which the students typically view academic achievement (Heikinheimo & Shute, 1986), the academic advisor may be the central figure in their life. Whether or not this is an accurate description of the advisor's role, advisors must be cognizant of certain issues (e.g., administrative procedures, resource availability and so forth) if they hope to be successful in dealing with this special group. The role that an advisor must fulfill goes beyond assisting students with their academic programs, however. It is the cultural diversity among international students that may prove the greatest challenge for academic advisors and counsellors. The challenge comes from the knowledge that, whereas diversity must be understood and addressed, advising must be highly individualized (Weill, 1982). Despite common cultural threads or shared experiences among students with similar backgrounds, each student brings to the context different motivations and needs. If the advisor considers students' cultural/ethnic background and unique needs, the advising process can be meaningful and effective. Academic advisors should be prepared to provide ready access to services, help students cope with and balance their emotions and help them anticipate possible challenges and difficulties (being careful not to predispose students) that form part of the adaptation process.

Wan (2001) noted that learning styles in some ways reflect an individual's process of socialization in childhood. Therefore, students with different home cultural backgrounds may have diverse preferences for teaching and learning styles, and they may have different perceptions of interactions between professor and students, sometimes sending the message that the professor is not prepared or motivated or that students did not treat professors with respect (Poyrazli & Grahame, 2007).

The Counsellor

Despite the recent trend of student mobility, North American institutions still have a long way to go to accommodate the needs of international students. According to Sue (1981), the cultural adjustment of international students follows a developmental course similar to that of members of minority groups: there is an initial sense of a need to conform to the host culture, followed by conflict and disharmony due to resistance toward the values and systems encountered and experienced in the new environment. It is not uncommon, if they are to function successfully in the host culture, for individuals to engage in introspection to develop a sense of awareness. Understanding the stages of this journey and identifying the student's progress along the way will help the counsellor select appropriate intervention strategies for the student's developing needs. In addition, counsellors must transcend their own personal background if they are to be effective in a multicultural society (Heikkinen, 1981; Pedersen, 1991).

International students do have concerns and problems different from those of North American students. As a consequence, North American colleges and universities have a responsibility to international students to provide special services — or customary services in special ways (Locke & Velasco, 1987). After all, counsellors accept a legitimate role in helping international students in the period of cultural transition. However, helping skills must be developed and worked at in order to be effective. Thus, professional counsellors ought to make conscious efforts to increase their cultural awareness and learn the skills and knowledge appropriate to helping students in an international context. Counsellors who accept the challenge to work directly with international students not only are likely to help make international study a fulfilling experience for these students, but are likely to rediscover themselves in the process.

Essential Attributes

Establishing Rapport

Being empathic with international students is much easier when the counsellor has experienced living abroad. In some ways it is easier for him/her to understand the students and be patient with them. Counsellors could initiate conversation by asking students to express how they feel and what they fear. It is less useful for counsellors to lecture about their personal experiences since personal accounts are never similar (although pointing them out might help). Counsellors know that acculturation requires time and interaction with the host culture; therefore, it is fundamental that they promote activities where students feel comfortable and safe to explore their fears, doubts, changes and improvements.

Cultural Sensitivity

Cultural sensitivity is fundamental to helping international students. It requires that counsellors ignore ethnocentric ways of perceiving differences in behaviours and opinions. Given variations in world view orientations, international students may demonstrate cultural differences in terms of their concept of time, their understanding of self, their degree of comfort with physical space, distance and touch (Hall, 1981) and/or their value orientations (Sue & Sue, 1995). Regardless of the differences manifested by international students, counsellors must present an attitude of genuine caring (Bargar & Mayo-Chamberlain, 1983) and express interest in the students as individuals. Cultural sensitivity is a quality that takes time and effort to develop since it involves an opening of the mind (and the heart) to different world views, as well as seeking a deeper understanding of one's own world view as a helper. We must remember that the presence of international students on university campuses represents a commitment on the students' part to achieve academic success. Therefore, counsellors must be similarly committed to helping students adjust to life in the new culture and its academic demands.

Trust

Counsellors need to understand that homesickness, academic goals, obtaining housing, the level of proficiency in the host language, and finances are only some of the problems generally faced by international students (Stafford, Marion & Salter, 1980; Hyun, Quinn, Madon & Lustig, 2007); thus, referring students to different services on campus might be an appropriate response to resolve some of these problems. However, prudence is advised since, although making referrals is standard practice in American culture, simply referring someone to a particular department for specialized services may not be enough or appropriate to meet a student's needs. Developing a sense of trust and credibility might prove to be more helpful since many international students, for cultural reasons, may not be assertive enough to search for help on their own; making a phone call on their behalf or taking them to the department as a way of introduction may be very useful. According to Dillard and Chisolm (1983), some international students may wait longer than the average North American student before seeking professional assistance because of a strong conviction to obtain help through the traditional family system. Therefore, counsellors should maintain close contact with international students in order to follow their progress. Counsellors who do this are more likely to gain confidence and respect, as well as be more effective in helping students to find future help if needed.

Accepting Ambiguity

The cultural dimension of working with international students may create ambiguity that may not exist in counselling relationships with host students. The codes of communication that counsellors may be familiar with, and might even expect in an interaction, may differ from those of their international students for cultural reasons. In instances where these differences create misunderstandings, counsellors must be patient and willing to do everything possible to encourage clarity. The first step in avoiding such dilemmas is likely to realize that limited proficiency in English or a lack of North American social skills is no reflection on the intelligence of international students. Speaking slowly, carefully articulating words and being willing to repeat oneself when necessary could go a long way in helping to promote understanding and avoid conflict. Displays of restlessness or disappointment when students are not sufficiently articulate simply builds barriers in the communication process and may even damage the relationship. However, despite efforts to maximize mutual understanding, there may still be aspects of a particular relationship that may be ambiguous. Counsellors must be prepared to accept this, hoping that as the newly established relationship improves, the level of ambiguity will decrease. It is fundamental that counsellors promote activities where the students feel comfortable and safe to explore their fears, doubts, changes and improvements.

Communication

It is not unusual for students from non-English-speaking countries to have problems with English speech and comprehension. Although they are required to earn scores on the Test of English as a Foreign Language (TOEFL) at or above a level believed to be adequate for them to understand lectures and do their assignments, many still report English to be a problem (Heikinheimo & Shute, 1986). Counsellors could advise students to take an English support course that would help them improve their proficiency level. Moreover, counsellors could examine and help students with their articulation and comprehension skills during encounters. A cross-cultural group could evolve from the counsellor's meetings with other international students. This group could be a safe place to explore feelings and emotions that might otherwise not emerge, and could provide opportunities for international students to talk among themselves about related adaptation issues. The purpose of the conversation group could aim at supporting personal growth and self-exploration, encouraging the expression of students' sense of identity and enhancing self-esteem and confidence while concurrently tending to their learning needs by creating effective conditions. The group could also provide support to other members by establishing new connections based on common needs, creating a learning community where individuals can benefit from the group as an environment conducive to personal and professional development. The group would not only be a resource from international students to raise cross-cultural awareness, but it could also aid host nationals to become more sensitive to the multicultural context of their relationship with international students. Additional activities (for the more advanced) might include providing students with opportunities to act as guest speakers for other classes or groups of people (community organizations such as retirement homes, schools, tourist agencies and so forth). Even though some of these activities might require a certain level of language proficiency, they represent opportunities for international students not only to promote their culture and their country but also to practice English and appear as visible components of the university student body.

Implications for Counselling

International students enrich the educational and cultural environments of universities and colleges; they help local students gain an appreciation of the vast array of human traditions throughout the world and help foster sophistication and a cosmopolitan identity in the student body (Weill, 1982). The field of cross-cultural counselling has already built a considerable frame of research, yielding insights for those concerned with international student support (d'Ardenne & Mahtani, 1989; Eleftheriadou, 1994; Lago, 1996; Pedersen, 1994; Sue & Sue, 2007). In many universities, however, there may be no relationship developing between students and that academic advisor. When meetings take place, the interaction can tend to be related to formalities or external practicalities (Luzio-Lockett, 1995). This circumstance suggests a need for more natural channels to be opened up and incorporated in the context of cross-cultural counselling through more open communication and exchange. The experience of international students cannot be reduced to a purely cognitive journey, but should also allow opportunities for the expression and integration of the personal, emotional and "redefined" self. A support group led by the academic advisor or counsellor could be an effective venue for addressing students' needs for integration, a context in which to establish their sense of belonging and to find a facilitating climate of trust and understanding that will in turn promote personal and professional growth.

Research on groups (Aveline & Dryden, 1988; Henderson & Forster, 1991; Whitaker, 1987) has shown that the commonality of being with people who share an experience is vital in helping individuals feel less isolated, and provides a strong incentive to group members to seek alternative resolutions to common concerns. According to Wolfe, Murgatroyd and Rhys (1987),

> learning is as much an emotional as a cognitive experience. If one follows this line of reasoning, the idea of the learner as a whole person, not just as a detached cognitive entity, is elevated in importance. How people feel about themselves is as important as detached intellectual ability in influencing what progress they make. (p. 2)

If we consider the learning experience in its academic domain as fostering self-actualization and growth, then the process of growth cannot be achieved solely through the academic milieu but has to be accompanied at the same time by the self-perception that an individual achieves as a fulfilled self. The process of growth involves communication, interaction, sharing experiences and being able to display the affective side of a cognitive being. Unfortunately, when it comes to counselling or guiding international students, it appears that attention is directed almost entirely towards their academic experience (i.e., complying with academic requirements and being successful), leaving little or no room for exploring personal growth and the changes that accompany it.

Conclusion

During the past decades, Canadian universities have become a preferred location for foreign students, including American and European students. Nearly 70 per cent of the international students enrolled in Canadian universities are from developing countries (Statistics Canada, 2006), and research has demonstrated they have had to make more substantial adjustments to North American academic and cultural life than their American, European or Caribbean counterparts. Hall (1981) and Mickle (in Heikinheimo & Shute, 1984) mention that foreign students are more likely to have positive academic and non-academic experiences if they enjoy satisfying contact with the host community; such an achievement is more likely if the emotional and social atmosphere is pleasant and the environment congenial. Domingues (1970) described the need for full-time foreign student advisors in universities and colleges; she stated that the more different the student's cultural background is from that of North America, the more likely it was for the student to develop emotional problems of adjustment. Working with international students in small groups could mitigate the feelings of isolation and despair that arise as the result of leaving behind what is familiar and known. Pedersen (1991) warns that by making a special case of international students, counsellors and educators run the danger of isolating and stereotyping them by not recognizing the unique situations international students face.

Although universities often provide counselling services for their international (and local) population, these might not be enough nor completely adequate to assist students from up to 200 nationalities. It is understandable that cross-cultural counsellors are not entirely prepared to handle international students with an individual, exclusive approach regarding their country of origin. Hence, international students should be strongly encouraged to adopt a receptive, intuitive and open view concerning their lifestyle in the host country. Here is what one international student points out:

As a result of having lived in a foreign country, I changed and experienced growth. Facing culture shock, language misunderstandings, monetary constraints (which derived in dietary restrictions, limited resources for academic purposes and traveling) and academic disadvantage (because of the difference in programs and requirements) originated in me the need to express everything I was feeling and what was happening around me, to me and inside me. I found that writing about these events and sharing them with other international students alleviated these happenings. I utilized my writing to talk to my advisor about my feelings and emotions. It was not an easy process, but I thought that if I was to make this experience one of the best of my life, I had to be authentic and true to myself. Being aware of what this meant was not simple nor was it enjoyable at times. Describing to myself and sharing with others what I was feeling, and unveiling my limitations were not easy endeavors. There were many feelings attached to everyday events, and talking about them sometimes meant jeopardizing my own values, beliefs and convictions. However, being specific and authentic about my feelings and emotions thoroughly aided in my adaptation to a new culture. I had to learn how to live in a society that, by being multicultural, shares different world views, ideologies, religions and customs. But this was not all; I also had to be aware of the academic requirements of the university and I firmly desired to succeed. Being an international student was not easy at all; however, this experience allowed my self-awareness to emerge and my self-reflection to develop. I was rendered with the opportunity to concurrently review, analyze, challenge and develop my skills, my knowledge, my abilities, my maturity and my common sense . . . although, according to my mother, it's the least common of all senses.

References

Adler, P.S. (1975). The transitional experience: an alternative view of culture shock. *Journal of Humanistic Psychology*, 15(4), 13–23.

Albert, R.D., & Triandis, H.C. (1991). Intercultural education for multicultural societies: Critical issues. In L.A. Samovar & R.E. Porter (Eds.), *Intercultural communication: A reader* (6th ed.). Belmont, CA: Wadsworth.

Alexander, A., Klein, M., Workneh, F., & Miller, M. (1981). Psychotherapy and the foreign student. In P. Pedersen, J. Draguns & J. Trimble (Eds.), *Counseling across cultures* (2nd ed., pp. 227–243). Honolulu, HI: University of Hawaii Press.

Arredondo-Dowd, P. (1981). Personal loss and grief as a result of immigration. *Personnel and Guidance Journal*, 2, 376–378.

Aveline, M., & Dryden, W. (Eds.). (1988). *Group therapy in Britain*. Milton Keynes: Open University Press.

Bargar, R., & Mayo-Chamberlain, J. (1983). Advisor and advisee issues in doctoral education. *Journal of Higher Education*, 54(4), 407–432.

Belenky, M., McVicker, B., Goldberger, N., & Mattuck, J. (1986). *Women's ways of knowing*. USA: Basic Books.

Bochner, S., Hutnik, N., & Furnham, A. (1985). The friendship patterns of overseas and host students in an Oxford student residence. *Journal of Social Psychology*, 125.

Burda. P., Vaux, A., & Schill, T. (1984). Social support resources: Variation across sex and sex role. *Personality and Social Psychology Bulletin*, 10, 119–126.

Carr, J.L., Koyama, M., & Thiagarajan, M. (2003). A women's support group for Asian international students. *Journal of American College Health*, 52(3), 131–134.

Constantine, M.G., Okazaki, S., & Utsey, S.O. (2004). Self-concealment, social self-efficacy, acculturative stress, and depression in African, Asian, and Latin American international college students. *American Journal of Orthopsychiatry*, 74, 230–241.

D'Ardenne, P., & Mahtani, A. (1989). *Transcultural counseling in action*. London: Sage.

Day, R., & Hajj, F. (1986). Delivering counseling service to international students: The experience of the American University of Beirut. *Journal of College Student Personnel*, 7, 353–357.

Dillard, J., & Chisolm, G. (1983). Counseling the International student in a multicultural context. *Journal of College Student Personnel*, 3, 101–105.

Domingues, P.M. (1970). Student personnel services for international students. *International Journal for the Advancement of Counseling*, 9, 11–22.

Dryden, W., & Ellis, A. (1987). Rational-emotive therapy. In W. Dryden & W.L. Golden (Eds.), *Cognitive behavioural approaches to psychotherapy*. New York: Hemisphere Publishing.

Eleftheriadou, Z. (1994). *Transcultural counseling*. London: Central.

Exum, H., & Lau, E. (1988). Counseling style preference of Chinese college students. *Journal of Multicultural Counseling and Development*, 16, 84–92.

Furnham, A. (1989). Communicating across cultures: A social skills perspective. *Counseling Psychology Quarterly*, 2, 205–222.

Furnham, A., & Alibhai. N. (1985). The friendship networks of foreign students: A replication and extension of the functional model. *International Journal of Psychology*, 20, 709–722.

Gilligan, C. (1982). *In a different voice*. Cambridge, MA: Harvard University Press.

Grayson, J.P. (2008). The experiences and outcomes of domestic and international students at four Canadian universities. *Higher Education Research and Development*, 27, 215–230.

Hall, E. (1981). *Beyond culture*. New York: Anchor Press, Doubleday.

Heikinheimo, P., & Shute, J. (1986). The adaptation of foreign students: Student views and institutional implications. *Journal of College Student Personnel*, 27(5), 399–406.

Heikkinen, C. (1981). Loss resolution for growth. *Personnel and Guidance Journal*, 59, 327–331.

Henderson, P., & Forster, G. (1991). *Groupwork*. Cambridge: National Extension College.

Hyun, J., Quinn, B., Madon, T., & Lustig, S. (2007). Mental health need, awareness, and use of counseling services among international graduate students. *Journal of American College Health*, 56, 109–118.

Idowu, A. (1985). Counseling Nigerian students in United States colleges and universities. *Journal of Counseling and Development*, 63(8), 506–509.

Klein, M. (1977). Preliminary overview: Adaptation to new cultural environments. *The Counseling Psychologist*, 1 (January 1991), 10–58.

Klineberg, D., & Hull, W.F. (1979). *At a foreign university: An international study of adaptation and coping*. New York: Praeger.

Lago, C. (1996). *Race, culture and counseling*. Buckingham: Open University Press.

Leong, F., & Sedlacek. W. (1986). A comparison of international and U.S. students' preferences for help sources. *Journal of College Student Personnel*, 27, 426–430.

Leung, C. (2001). The psychological adaptation of overseas and migrant students in Australia. *International Journal of Psychology*, 36, 251–259.

Lin, G., & Yi, J.K. (1997). Asian international students' adjustment: Issues and program suggestions. *College Student Journal*, 31, 473–479.

Locke, D.C., & Velasco, J. (1987). Hospitality begins with the invitation: Counseling foreign students. *Journal of Multicultural Counseling and Development*, 7, 115–119.

Luzio-Lockett, A. (1998). The squeezing effect: The cross-cultural experience of international students. *British Journal of Guidance and Counselling*, 26(2), 209–223.

Mallinckrodt, B., & Leong, F.T.L. (1992). International graduate students, stress and social support. *Journal of College Student Development*, 33, 71–78.

Manese, J.E., Sedlacek, W.E., & Leong, F.T.L. (1988). Needs and perceptions of female and male international undergraduate students. *Journal of Multicultural Counseling and Development*, 24–29.

Meloni, C. (1986). *Adjustment problems of foreign students in U.S. colleges and universities*. Washington, DC: ERIC Clearinghouse on Language and Linguistics.

Nesheim, B.E., Guentzel, M.J., Gansemer-Topf, A.M., Ross, L.E., & Turrentine, C.G.. (2006). If you want to know, ask: Assessing the needs and experiences of graduate students. *New Directions for Student Services*, 115, 5–17.

Oberg, K. (1957). Culture shock and the problem of adjustment to new cultural environments. In P. Pedersen, J. Draguns, W. Lonner & J. Trimble (Eds.), *Counseling across cultures*. Thousand Oaks, Calif.: Sage Publications.

Paulhus, D., & Martin, C. (1987). The structure of personality capabilities. *Journal of Personality and Social Psychology*, 52, 354–365.

Pedersen, P. (1991). Counseling international students. *The Counseling Psychologist*, 19, 10–58.

Pedersen, P., Draguns, J., Lonner, W., & Trimble, J. (2012). *Counseling across cultures* (6th ed.). Thousand Oaks, CA: Sage Publications.

Powell, L. (1986). Participant satisfaction in second-language conversation. *Communication Research Report*, 3, 135–139.

Poyrazli, S., & Grahame, K.M. (2007). Barriers to adjustment: Needs of international students within a semi-urban campus community. *Journal of Instructional Psychology*, 34, 28–45.

Poyrazli, S., Kavanaugh, P.R., Baker, A., & Al-Timimi, N. (2004). Social support and demographic correlates of acculturative stress in international students. *Journal of College Counseling*, 7, 73–82.

Putney, R. (1981). Impact of marital loss on support systems. *Personnel and Guidance Journal*, 59, 351–354.

Rahman, O., & Rollock, D. (2004). Acculturation, competence, and mental health among South Asian students in the United States. *Journal of Multicultural Counseling and Development*, 32, 130–142.

Ray, M., & Lee, M. (1988). Effects of stigmas on intergroup relationships. *Journal of Social Psychology*, 129, 855–857.

Romero, M. (1981). Multicultural reality: The pain of growth. *Personnel and Guidance Journal*, 59, 384–386.

Schram, J., & Lauver, P. (1988). Alienation in international students. *Journal of College Student Development*, 29, 146–150.

Stafford. T., Jr., Marion, P., & Salter, M. (1980). Adjustment of international students. *NASPA Journal*. 18(1), 40–45.

Statistics Canada (2012). *A changing portrait of international students in Canadian universities*. Retrieved from http://www.statcan.ca

Steinglass, P., DeNour, A., & Shye, S. (1985). Factors influencing psychosocial adjustment to forces in geographical relocation: The Israeli withdrawal from the Sinai. *American Journal of Orthopsychiatry*, 55, 513–529.

Sue, D.W. (1981). *Counseling the culturally different*. New York: Wiley.

Sue, D.W., & Sue, D. (2007). *Counseling the culturally different: Theory and practice* (5th ed.). New York, NY: Wiley.

Surdam, J.C., & Collins, J.R. (1984). Adaptation of international students: A cause for concern. *Journal of College Student Personnel*, 25, 240–244.

Taft, R. (1977). Coping with unfamiliar cultures. In N. Warren (Ed.), *Studies in cross-cultural psychology* (pp. 120–135). London: Academic Press.

Torrey, E.F., Van Rheenan, F., & Katchadourian, H. (1970). Problems of foreign students: An overview. *Journal of the American College Health Association*, 19, 83–86.

Wan, G.F. (2001). The learning experience of Chinese students in American universities: A cross-cultural perspective. *College Student Journal*, 35, 28–44.

Webster's New World Dictionary of the English Language. (2012). New York, NY: Collins World. Retrieved from http://www.merriam-webster.com/dictionary/foreigner

Weill, L. (1982). Advising international students at small colleges. *NACADA Journal*, 2(1), 52–56.

Wheeler, S., & Birtle, J. (1993). *A Handbook for personal tutors*. Buckingham: Society for Research into Higher Education. Buckingham: Open University Press.

Whitaker, D. (1987). *Using groups to help people*. London: Tavistock/Routledge.

Winkelman, M. (1994). Cultural shock and adaptation. *Journal of Counseling and Development*, 73, 121–126.

Wolfe, R., Murgatroyd, S., & Rhys, S. (1987). *Guidance and counselling in adult and continuing education*. Milton Keynes: Open University Press.

Yeh, C.J., & Inose, M. (2003). International students' reported English fluency, social support satisfaction, and social connectedness as predictors of acculturative stress. *Counseling Psychology Quarterly*, 16, 15–28.

Ying, Y.W., & Liese, L.H. (1990). Initial adaptation of Chinese sojourners in Canada. In P. Pedersen, J. Draguns, W. Lonner & J. Trimble (Eds.), *Counseling across cultures*. Thousand Oaks, CA.: Sage Publications.

Young, L., & Bagley, C. (1982). Self-esteem, self-concept, and the development of black identity: A theoretical overview. In G.K. Verma & C. Bagley (Eds.), *Self-concept, achievement and multi-cultural education*. London: Macmillan.

16

The Counselling Profession and the GLBTQI Community

Tracey Coulter & M. Honoré France

Native American concepts usually prefer circles to lines. If one takes the line of a male/female, gay/straight, and bends it into a circle, there are an infinite number of points. Just so there are theoretically an infinite number of possible points of gender and sexuality for an individual that can shift and differ over time and location. (Tafoya, 1997, p. 7)

WHAT THIS INCISIVE QUOTATION DEMONSTRATES is not only how other cultures deal with sexual orientation but also how Western notions of linear thinking have caused so much concern in regards to sexuality. Garrett and Barret (2003) provide an interesting analysis of the Cartesian penchant for classifying people into dichotomous kinds with values like good and bad, and a linear way of thinking that is responsible for creating a static interpretation of gender and behaviour. It is true that over the centuries attitudes toward homosexuality have varied, but it was not until the growth of religions that followed the Judeo-Christian–Islamic belief system that outright persecution of people who did not adhere to strict gender specific orientation grew. In the Aboriginal community, beliefs about gender were very different at the time Europeans migrated to the western hemisphere. Native people tended to "value relationships, contexts, and interactions" (Garrett & Barret, 2003, p. 133) and did not value the individualism that Europeans brought. The term *two-spirited* combines social and spiritual identity in a way that terms such as *gay*, *lesbian* or *transgendered* do not, because these terms are based more in sexual orientation. A two-spirited person possesses both male and female spirits and thus is special with dual ways of being; or, to put it another way, the two-spirited person possesses the ability to transform, suggesting that the duality of life is circular in the Aboriginal way of thinking. Rather than being ostracized, as happened in countries that embraced the Judeo-Christian–Islamic way of thinking, the two-spirited person was seen as a person with special abilities. In essence, two-spirited people were "acknowledged and given the role of sacred persons who represented transformation and change through harmony and balance" (Garret & Barret, 2003, p. 133). Thus, one's world view highly influences the way one views sexual orientation. Understanding this process, including historical and social pressures about what is right or wrong, is paramount if one is to understand and work successfully with gay, lesbian, bisexual and transgendered clients.

When counselling members of the GLBTQI (gay, lesbian, bisexual, transgendered, questioning, intersex) community, we must remember that it is about counselling human beings. This point of course must be balanced with the knowledge and understanding of what it means to be a sexual minority in our culture. One interesting development in North American society is the reclaiming of the word *queer*, which in the past was used as a slur; these days more and more members of the GLBTQI community use it with defiant pride. Since the 1980s gay and lesbian activists have used *queer* as a comprehensive term that includes all GLBTQI people. Not everyone feels comfortable about this use, though, and *queer* is still used as an insult by homophobic people. Like many other reclaimed words, *queer* is not used acceptably by those outside the GLBTQI community.

This chapter explores the social structures that may influence or impact the lives of the GLBTQI, or queer, community; identity development models for this group; internalized beliefs of counsellors and their implications; ways to talk about sexual preference/gender/ sexuality in the counselling setting; some general values of the queer community; and where we as a profession need to develop for the future.

Definitions

Definitions often change with the times, as do social views of what is normal or abnormal. Consider that in Ancient Greece, bisexuality was the norm; centuries from now there will probably be even more categories and definitions. Most of the terms in GLBTQI are well known except perhaps *intersex*, which is a medical term that applies to people whose biological sex is neither female nor male. We would like to use a term common in the GLBTQI community: queer. We use this term to encompass not only those who prefer sexual partners of the same sex as themselves but also those who view their gender as different from their biological sex or who simply do not take gender or sex into consideration when choosing sexual partners; people who are non-monogamous; "transfolk"; and those who do not define their sexual activity or partners in traditional terms of penetration, orgasm or act. This term is meant to be as inclusive as possible and to bring focus not just to the gender of our clients and their partners but to everyone and the ways our identities are a multifaceted reality. We want to challenge our fellow human beings to think more expansively about themselves as sexual beings and not just to accept the definitions imposed by society. It is time, then, for counsellors to follow the queer community and "come out of the closet" on our sexual beliefs and identities.

We would also like to differentiate between the terms *homophobia* and *heterosexism*. Homophobia can be defined as

> the irrational fear of gay people or any behaviour, belief or attitude in self or others which doesn't conform to rigid sex-role stereotypes. It is a fear of homosexuality and homosexual people, of all things associated with homosexuality. Some people who experience homophobia simply avoid gay and lesbian people, places, events and topics of conversation. The extreme behaviour of homophobia is violence against homosexuals. (www.equity.qut.edu.au, 2007)

The definition of homophobia usually focusses on an internal feeling or fear, disgust or hatred in an individual. Members of the queer community may have any number of encounters with homophobes that may leave them with sadness, disappointment or fear for their lives.

The definition of homophobia involves fear or hatred within a person, whereas heterosexism can be defined as

> the assumption that being heterosexual is the only "normal" and "correct" type of lifestyle, and in fact superior to alternative relationships. Heterosexism is the systematic and institutional oppression of the LGBTIQ population. Sometimes, even if individual people are not bigots or homophobes, institutions and cultural norms may be discriminatory or even oppressive by favouring heterosexual people at the expense of non-heterosexual people. Such institutions and norms are heterosexist, and people who do not protest against them or resist them also may be said to be heterosexist. Not all heterosexuals are homophobic, but all homophobes are heterosexist. (www.equity.qut.edu.au, 2007)

This explanation shows that, whereas homophobia resides in a person, heterosexism is a systemic notion and assumption that heterosexuality is the default "normal" sexuality and that institutions, belief systems and society may follow this system. The importance of these definitions and distinctions will be apparent as we discuss counselling members of the queer community.

Identity Development Theories

A number of identity development theories exist. Cass's model (1979) is probably the best known and does not rely on age-group–specific development. However, as Degges-White, Rice and Myers (2000) and Diamond (2005) point out, Cass used primarily gay males as the subjects; thus, the model may not apply to lesbians: "there is some validity to inclusion of several of the stages proposed by Cass. . . . discrepancies exist, however, in the order in which the stages are experienced and with the implied inevitability that all lesbians must pass through each stage sequentially in order to reach synthesis" (Degges-White, Rice and Myers, p. 6). In all fairness, the model does provide a hint of what gay people experience in coming to terms with their sexual identity in a heterosexist society, but the client may not be able to explore his/her sexuality until he/she is older. Cass's model has six stages.

1. Identity awareness: This is the point when the individual, usually as a child or adolescent, realizes he/she has feelings and thoughts different from others and possibly different from what society has taught.
2. Identity comparison: The individual begins to explore his/her feelings alone and to compare them to the beliefs of society, parents and peers.
3. Identity tolerance: During this stage, the individual will often rebel against his/her feelings and attempt to deny them (e.g., nobody wants to be different or gay and lesbian in a heterosexual environment).
4. Identity acceptance: The individual realizes that his/her sexuality is not abnormal. The person explores and embraces his/her sexuality, looking for a place where his/her orientation is accepted and he/she can feel a sense of belonging.
5. Identity pride: The individual's commitment to the homosexual group, or sense of group identity, is very strong. This commitment often leads to activism and purposeful confrontation with the establishment (Cass, 1979). According to Degges-White, Rice and Myers (2000), "one's homosexual identity is the primary identity — superseding all other aspects of one's life. The disclosing of one's sexuality to others is likely to increase; how others' responses are perceived has a great impact on whether or not development continues. When disclosing a minority sexual orientation results in an unexpected positive response on the part of a heterosexual, the individual recognizes the inconsistency of their thoughts and moves naturally into the final stage of development" (p. 1). At this stage, many people go on to challenge laws and other discriminatory social ideas.
6. Identity synthesis: The final stage in accepting the queer identity is not, for example, as a queer person but rather as a person who is queer. In other words, sexuality

becomes *a part* of who the person is rather than the defining factor; thus, the individual is one of the combinations of LGBTIQ (Cass, as cited in Beaty, 1999; Heffner, 2003).

Gumaer (1987) integrated Maslow's hierarchy of needs model with Minton and McDonald's 1983 three-stage homosexuality development model. Gumaer postulates that the three stages occur at every stage of Maslow's hierarchy, making homosexual development a much more difficult process than heterosexual development:

1. Egocentric stage: This stage involves early experiences with beginning awareness of homosexuality in childhood and early puberty. Gumaer says, "this early awareness includes feelings of separateness from peers, a sense of being different, sexual inadequacy, and excitement or arousal with those of the same sex" (p. 144).
2. Socio-centric stage: This stage involves stronger homosexual desires and increasing identity confusion. Gumaer says, "increased awareness of homo-erotic desires and feelings of identity confusion" (p. 144-45).
3. Universalistic stage: This stage involves beginning to evaluate societal norms critically and accepting gay identity. As such, according to Gumaer, "this commitment involves disclosing the gay self to significant others, such as family and friends, and facing the consequences of the disclosure. After the coming out process, gays manage their lives as would anyone else, which includes successful coupling" (p. 145).

In their critique of Cass's model, Degges-White, Rice and Myers (2000) caution that, in deconstructing these models, our concern is with positioning the queer client as the one with the problem. Another way of putting it — and for us this point is important — is that problems occur because the development of queer identity is not nurtured. If social child-rearing practices were open, schools were accepting and homophobia were nonexistent, then the coming-out process would not be an issue. This is why the two-spirited and circular notion of sexual orientation is so appealing. While one may go through various stages of identity development, inherent in these models is how the individual accepts external notions of who and what the individual is. If society had no problem with homosexuality, queer people would have no issues around their sexual orientation and would experience only those developmental challenges and difficulties a heterosexual individual might experience.

Challenges that Queers Face Growing Up

Acceptance in the eyes of the law as an anti-discriminatory practice has brought some measure of tranquility for the queer community, but there is no question that challenges still exist. According to Roberts (2004), queer youth face issues around isolation, family difficulties, violence, sexual abuse and HIV infection. The most frequent feeling expressed by those living in situations or families where a free sense of sexual orientation is not an option is isolation. Living in a family or society where gender is interpreted in a linear way produces confusion; it is likely that one would incorporate society's negative attitudes towards queerness. According to Roberts,

> In adopting a sexual identity that is often considered abnormal, immoral or pathological, many teens internalize the negative stereotypes, thereby believing they are psychological and/or social deviants. Many gay and lesbian youth react by hiding their homosexuality, which contributes to an even greater sense of loneliness, as fear of discovery becomes an integral part of life. (p. 230)

Those who do keep their sexual orientation private live with the consequences of a life that is a lie. They either suppress their feelings or feel less than adequate with the consequence of having no one to talk to and no emotional support. According to Harbeck (1992), 10 per cent to 18 per cent of the school population identify themselves as queer; the numbers are startling. The human cost in school absenteeism, dropouts, depression and suicide is especially high.

Stone (2003) documented the following:

- Students hear anti-gay remarks 25 times per day.
- Twenty-two percent of gay respondents reported they had skipped school in the past month because they felt unsafe.
- The dropout rate for gay students is estimated at three times the national average.
- Suicide attempts by gay and lesbian students are 20 per cent to 30 per cent higher than the national average. (pp. 145–146)

The importance of family in shaping one's identity and self-esteem can never be minimized; in fact, it is well established that family life has the most important effect on a child's development. When the family has homophobic values, then alienation, rejection and even expulsion are real possibilities. Not only do children develop their early sense of trust, acceptance and identity within the family; they depend on their families — especially their mothers and fathers — for emotional, social and economic support. Queer children's fears that they will embarrass their families because they are queer bring not only guilt but also cognitive dissonance from the failure to live up to parental expectations. Interestingly, most queer children do not have the same sexual orientation as their parents and thus are more prone to have family difficulties around their sexuality. Roberts (2004) reports that these fears are real:

- Half of all gay and lesbian youths interviewed reported that their parents rejected them for being homosexual.
- One in four gay and lesbian teens are forced to leave homes because of conflicts with their families about their sexual orientation.
- Most parents of queer youth do not have personal experience in dealing with sexual orientation.
- Parents of queer youth often feel stigmatized for their child's sexual orientation, especially if it is different from their own.

History of Counselling Members of the Queer Community

Homosexuality was removed from the American Psychological Association's *Diagnostic and Statistical Manual* only in 1973; it was only in 1986 that the last politically motivated "ego-dystonic homosexuality" category was removed (Herek, 2008). The fact that homosexuality was considered a mental illness only 35 years ago cannot be lost on us as we approach clients from the queer community, some of whom may have suffered under this homophobia to the extreme of being committed to a psychiatric hospital. Of course, simply because it was removed from the DSM does not mean that the belief that homosexuality is a mental illness was removed from counsellors in practice, professionals in counsellor-training programs or counselling students, let alone from the hearts and minds of members of the queer community.

Consider that even after this removal, we can find articles that speak of the "problems" of counselling the homosexual as late as the 1980s in publications such as the *Journal of Counseling and Development*:

> I have dealt with a variety of clients in my private practice, and no client has been more frustrating to understand and work with than the male homosexual. . . . Their complex personalities and coping strategies are difficult for heterosexuals to understand and create problems in counseling. (Gumaer, 1987)

Rather than see the counsellor's internalized homophobia as the problem, Gumaer places the blame for his own counselling inabilities directly on the shoulders of his gay clients. There is also his sweeping generalization of complex personalities and coping skills: he sees them being specific to clients who are gay, as opposed to every living, breathing human being.

Another example can be found in an article in the *Personnel and Guidance Journal*, which states that "'Coming out of the closet,' wearing 'drag' or in some manner being 'loud' are just several ways for some homosexuals to act out their feelings toward real or imaginary societal pressures" (Haynes, 1977, p. 124). Here we can see the pathologizing of possible pride or enjoyment of sexual or identity exploration. The underlying tone is one of believing that the best thing for homosexuals is to fit into social norms; to do anything else warrants therapy.

Although this is a very small sampling of writings that occurred after homosexuality was no longer considered a mental illness, it illustrates that heterosexism has been alive and well in the counselling field in the past. We say past because in the intervening years, much has changed. For example, the Association for Lesbian, Gay, Bisexual and Transgender Issues (ALGBTI) is one of nineteen divisions within the American Counseling Association. This association sees its mandate to educate "counselors to the unique needs of client identity development; and [provide] a non-threatening counseling environment by aiding in the reduction of stereotypical thinking and homo-prejudice" (American Counseling Association, 2012). As an organization, ALGBTI accepts that homophobia exists in the counselling profession. It educates counsellors about identity development, how labels affect people and how the socio-political construct makes queer people objects of oppression, creating an internalized oppressor and bringing about lateral oppression. If we ensure that counsellors are aware of their own biases, much of the oppression engendered by the profession at an earlier time can be reversed. However, educating counsellors and others about homophobia and issues related to the queer community is an ongoing task.

Counsellor Training in Queer Issues

Many studies have found heterosexual bias and lack of training in queer issues for counselling students in professional graduate programs (Liddle, 1995; Phillips & Fisher, 1998; Pilkington & Cantor, cited in Lidderdale, 2002). These issues can lead to unethical practice when counsellors deal with clients from the queer community. Lidderdale has three suggestions for ameliorating this: include queer issues in every course; require a focussed practicum for all students; offer a specific class focussed on queer issues. These suggestions may be difficult for the educational system to take on, as heterosexism is such an ingrained cultural attitude. Erwin (2006) found that most graduate students in counselling feel that queer issues are irrelevant to their studies and future professional careers. This finding speaks volumes to the values and beliefs counsellors bring into their professional work. To claim that learning about a culturally important group of individuals, such as the queer community, is irrelevant assumes that whatever population these students plan to work with will not include any gay people or transfolk. It implies that the issues of the queer community are greeted, even in a university setting, by beliefs that at best are uninformed and at worse invalidate queer people. At the University of Victoria, for example, a grassroots movement called the Positive Space Network has the aim of "creating a network that supports and connects people working toward inclusion, promotes best practices, links researchers and provides support and resources for individuals" (Positive Space Network, 2012). This is an indication that there is much to be done on university campuses to ensure that GLBTQI people are accepted. Thus, it is no surprise to know that most members of the queer community seeking professional counselling screen potential counsellors carefully and often prefer counsellors who are also part of the queer community (Erwin, 2006).

Erwin states that one of the best ways to deal with counsellor education around queer issues is by providing general education around controversial issues and how to work with them (e.g., perspective shifting, avoidance of simplistic arguments, questioning use of dichotomies, evaluating credibility of sources) and by providing open space for acknowledgment of feelings and concerns. These educational practices will work not only for exploring heterosexism but also for learning about the issues surrounding many "othered" groups in our culture: racial, ability and age, to name a few.

Areas for Discussion When Counselling a Client from the Queer Community

It is important to begin this section by stating that, depending on the topic at hand, a counsellor may never know a client's sexual preference(s). Most literature on the topic seems to assume that a client from the queer community who comes to counselling is there to discuss issues around his/her sexuality. Of course, the client may also be there for grief at a parent's passing, career indecision or a phobia of flying. The recommendations below are intended mainly for situations when the client's sex and sexuality are topics in the counselling setting.

Identity and labels: The best practice here is to follow the client's lead. Whatever term the client uses to describe him/herself is the term the counsellor should use. This is simply following the concept of matching the tone and vocabulary of one's client, a common skill in any beginning helping professional course. If the client's main presenting concern is identity, an exploration of his/her sexuality and connection to a community may be important factors. To be competent, the counsellor must be aware of resources, including pride groups and specific community issues (e.g., resources for ageing lesbians). This way, discussing identity can be a fruitful way to check in with clients around their needs. The vital piece is not to assume that if a client does not overtly identify as queer, that means the client is straight. An important way to display a lack of heterosexism is by using the term *partner* to talk about one's spouse.

Intersectionalities: No one exists in a vacuum, including members of the queer community. A client's sexuality may not be the only major defining feature of "otherness" in our culture. Combinations of race, gender, class, abilities and size may define a client more than his/her sexuality. It would be presumptuous of us not to take all the complexities of life into consideration. The simple question "How do you see your sexuality fitting in with the rest of your life or personality?" is a straightforward way to begin a discussion on this topic. The concept of family may appear very different and may focus on what is commonly called the "found family" as opposed to a focus on blood relatives. This point can be especially pertinent if the client's family of origin has cut the client out of their lives or made it clear that the client is unacceptable to them. Because of societal devaluing, some members of the queer community do not want to bring any negative attention to problems or issues within the community and value keeping any problems within the community. This point is especially true in cases of drug issues or partner abuse (Merril & Wolfe, 2000).

Due to the history of gay rights in North America, and the constant battle for basic human rights, activism at some level is important for many members of the queer community. Because of the many battles still waging (such as adoption rights or partner pension rights, depending on where in North America one is practising), clients may come to counselling to deal with actively battling systemic heterosexism.

The most salient concern that can be seen in the queer community is the suspicion of the medical and helping professionals, because of a perceived lack of awareness or the sense that clients will be negatively evaluated. Because the people who make up these professions come into the setting with the tacit heterosexism from our culture, many members of the queer community do not feel understood or valued by these resources. As we stated earlier, many of these clients will screen counsellors thoroughly and are more likely to see counsellors who are part of the queer community. This problem is not the client's: it is our problem as professionals to work with and for our clients, to gain a greater understanding of the totality of the human experience.

Future Development

Because graduate counselling programs are the basis for the professional education of counsellors, it is imperative that these programs be infused with education around queer issues and the kinds of critical-thinking skills necessary to question unacknowledged values in our culture. Valuing members of the queer community in the counselling setting is no different than valuing anyone who is "othered" in mainstream society, and to begin changing beliefs about one group is to begin to change beliefs about others.

None of this will happen overnight, and it cannot happen in a vacuum. Because counselling happens in culture, it is infused with many of the values of the culture in which it takes place. It is therefore our job as counsellors to become aware of our own assumptions about the queer community and to question our own roles in supporting heterosexist standards. The role of the counsellor, in Rogerian terms, is unconditional positive regard for our clients. If we are carrying around homophobic or heterosexist beliefs, to work with members of the queer community is not only ineffective, but unethical as well.

Conclusion

Every day we wake up and get ready for work.
We drive our cars on the same roads, the same highways.
We park right next to your cars. We use the same bathrooms.
We listen to the same music.
We breathe the same air.
We live in the same society.
So, why do you abhor us when we share so many of the same things?
Okay, so we love differently!
Why does that matter?
There is really nothing to fear from us except the pain that comes from your ignorance!
— Brett, a high school student (in Roberts, 2004, p. 229)

Clearly, society has a long way to go to provide understanding to all its members, whether they are straight, gay, bisexual, transgendered or intersex. The idea of sexual orientation needs to be more like Tafoya's (1997) idea of gender: not linear or one or another, but circular so as to embrace the many variations of sexual identity. In the past, culturally sensitive counselling was often based on ethnicity or race rather than on differences that exist within people. It is true that one could be of colour and yet also be lesbian, gay or bisexual, and that element of the self may be more relevant than ethnicity to one's identity. According to Fassinger (2003), "it is becoming increasingly clear in the present that many multicultural scholars and practitioners are ready to incorporate sexual identity and orientation into their conceptualization of cultural effects on human behaviour, and many LGB scholars and practitioners are acknowledging and exploring the role of racial/

ethnic influences in the lives of LGB people of color" (p. 82). Therefore, counsellors need to have knowledge of the background, concerns, identity development models and strategies that work best with the queer client. Along with this knowledge, counsellors need to understand their own biases and how they affect the way counsellors interact with and treat clients. Research has shown that counsellors are much more likely to pathologize the queer client than racial and ethnic clients (Israel & Selvidege, 2003). It is imperative that counsellors possess the skills to assess clients within their cultural milieu, which, for many queer clients, reflects experiences in a homophobic society rather than internal factors associated with personal problems or issues. In the same way that counsellors fight racism, they also need to fight homophobia and to help clients deal with the effects of homophobia. In our opinion, the counselling process that Garrett and Barret (2003) use with two-spirited people can be helpful to queer clients from other cultural and racial backgrounds. They suggest paying attention to family issues, substance abuse and the way clients see themselves, remembering that the circle of gender is varied. Further, they suggest using the following questions to ascertain clients' experiences:

- Where are you from?

- Where do you live now?

- What experiences have brought you from where you were to where you are now, both literally and metaphorically?

- What do those experiences mean to you, and how are they specifically played out in your life?

- Have you come out, and if so, what was the experience like? How has it shaped who you are right now? If you have not come out, then what is that experience like for you at this point?

- How do family and community of origin play into your life experiences to this point, and how will they shape who you are becoming? (p. 138)

References

American Counseling Association. (2012). ACA Divisions. Retrieved from http://www.counseling.org/AboutUs/DivisionsBranchesAndRegions/TP/Divisions/CT2.aspx

Beaty, L.A. (1999). Identity development of homosexual youth and parental and familial influences on the coming out process. *Adolescence* (Fall). Retrieved December 1, 2008, from http://findarticles.com/p/articles/mi_m2248/is_135_34/ai_60302525

Degges-White, D., Rice, B., and Myers, J.E. (2000). Revisiting Cass's theory of sexual identity formation: A study of lesbian development. *Journal of Mental Health Counseling*, 22 (4), pp. 318–33.

Diamond, L. (2005). What we got wrong about sexual identity development: Unexpected findings from a longitudinal study of young women. In A.M. Omoto & H. Kurtzman (Eds.), *Sexual orientation and mental health: Examining identity and development in lesbian, gay, and bisexual people* (pp. 73–94) Washington, DC: APA.

Erwin, T.A. (2006). Infusing lesbigay research into the counseling research classroom. *Journal of Homosexuality*, 51(3), 125–164.

Gumaer, J. (1987). Understanding and counseling gay men: A developmental perspective. *Journal of Counseling and Development*, 66, 144–146.

Fassinger, R. (2003). Introduction to the special issue. *Journal of Multicultural Counseling*, 31, 82–83.

Haynes, A.W. (1977). The challenge of counseling the homosexual client. *Personnel and Guidance Journal*, 56(4), 243–246.

Heffner, C. (2003). Counselling the gay and lesbian client: Treatment issues and conversion therapy, *AllPsych*. Retrieved from http://allpsych.com/journal/counselinggay.html

Herek, G.M. (2008). *Homosexuality and mental health*. Retrieved December 1, 2008, from http://psychology.ucdavis.edu/rainbow/html/facts_mental_health.html

Israel, T., & Selbidege, M. (2003). Contributions of multicultural counseling to counselor competence with lesbian, gay and bisexual clients. *Journal of Multicultural Counseling*, 31, 84–98.

Lidderdale, M.A. (2002). Practitioner training for counseling lesbian, gay, and bisexual clients. *Journal of Lesbian Studies*, 6(3/4), 111–120.

Merrill, G., & Wolfe, V. (2000). Battered gay men: An exploration of abuse, help seeking, and why they stay. *Journal of Homosexuality*, 39, 1–30.

Queensland University of Technology (2007). *LGBTIQ definitions*. Retrieved December 1, 2008, from http://www.equity.qut.edu.au/issues/sexuality/definitions.jsp

Positive Space Network. (2012). Retrieved from http://web.uvic.ca/psn

Roberts, H. (2004). The invisible minority: The role of the school counsellor. In M.H. France, M.C. Rodriguez & G.G. Hett (Eds), *Diversity, Culture and Counselling: A Canadian Perspective* (pp. 229–238). Calgary, AB: Detselig Enterprises.

Stone, C. (2003). Counselors as advocates for gay, lesbian, and bisexual youth: A call for equity and action. *Journal of Multicultural Counseling and Development*, 31(2), 143–155.

17

Counselling Euro-Canadians

A Multicultural Perspective

M. Honoré France & Steve Bentheim

In a pluralistic and multicultural society, it is vital to make people aware that there is not just a large majority on one side and visible minorities on the other side. In fact the "white" population, which has been referred to in the research literature as the majority, is made up of a variety of peoples with differing cultural practices, values, languages and religions. When many of them came to North America, they were escaping persecution for being different because of their language, beliefs, religion or ethnic identity. They came to Canada in the last 150 years, as many people who immigrate today do, to find justice and a safe place to raise a family. The first wave of European immigration was primarily composed of English and French people. Later, Irish, southern Europeans and eastern Europeans came to the shores of Canada. Today, the primary groups of immigrants come from China, with other large segments coming from such diverse places as Trinidad, Ethiopia and El Salvador. Many of these people have been labelled *allophones*, to show the distinction from both francophone and anglophone. We need to get into our consciousness, and into our counselling and teaching practices, that in a truly multicultural society, every group of people is different.

So what does it mean to be pluralistic or multicultural? It means to become aware of and knowledgeable about every group, regardless of their colour, ethnic background, language or religion. This chapter will cover European immigrants to Canada, including anglophones, francophones and other ethnic groups who originated in Europe. To highlight some of the differences among these groups, we have examined specific aspects of those groups with spiritual differences, including Protestant, Catholic and Jewish. In addition, we have included the examples of Italian Canadians and Jewish Canadians and some of the ways in which they differ.

Acculturation and Assimilation

According to Dyer (1994), the concept of national identity is not only recent but also fluid in nature. The nation-state is historically a recent phenomenon that goes back to a time when people started to live in large groups. Before that, people identified with their families or clans. Nation-states are not permanent but rise and fall according to historical events. Canada is not unique in this regard, having not only a very recent history but also a dramatically diverse population that has changed since Confederation. People who immigrated to Canada have adapted themselves to the new land and over time created a national identity that is changing as the diversity of its people changes. The forces that forged Canadian society can be better understood if we examine the concepts of acculturation and assimilation.

Acculturation

Acculturation is an internal process of accepting the values of the majority society at the expense of one's traditional culture. It often occurs slowly, as one's original cultural values change. According to Berry and Sam (1997), there are four strategies of acculturation: assimilation, traditionality, integration and marginality. These dynamic forces, which have shaped people to become who they are today, should not been seen as negative or positive, but rather as processes that were either chosen (e.g., by the Irish), forced (e.g., on the First Nations) or circumstantial (e.g., refugees from a variety of countries).

Assimilation

Generally, most people, particularly those of European origin, have assimilated into the mainstream of Canadian life with little difficulty. Assimilation is a process where people are absorbed, either passively, deliberately or by government policy, losing their cultural differences and blending into society. For example, people of German ancestry give up the language and customs of their ancestors either by choice or over time and become anglophone in language and culture. In the United States, this process is sometimes positively viewed as a "melting pot" in which everyone blends together to make something new or different.

The Canadian government, on the other hand, has stressed its commitment to encouraging groups to maintain their identities so that a pattern of distinct differences — a cultural mosaic — among people can emerge. In actuality, this view has sometimes been idealized, in that it is not shared by the general population nor by various social institutions. Despite whether the mosaic or melting pot is better, the fact is that many people, when they go to work, must give up what makes them distinct.

Traditionality

Traditionality, unlike assimilation, occurs when people choose to keep their language and culture, often by rejecting or avoiding interaction with the majority culture. Traditionalists, while maintaining their own culture and traditions, have little knowledge or appreciation of the majority culture. Groups like the Doukhobors, who have kept Russian language and customs, or the Mennonites, who kept German language and customs, have maintained these cultural features by keeping themselves apart from mainstream Canadian culture. Interestingly, traditionality is much more difficult to maintain when there is frequent contact with dominant society. For example, by the late twentieth century, Doukhobor society had largely assimilated, unlike the Mennonites. When traditionality is forced on people, it is called *segregation*. Segregation occurs when those in power force separation on the powerless (e.g., apartheid).

Integration

Integration, on the other hand, is a process of maintaining one's language, culture and traditions while gaining knowledge about and an appreciation for the majority culture. This stance is bicultural, and the ideal of integration demonstrates the mosaic philosophy. Berry and Kim (1988) stress that those who have a strong sense of their cultural identity, while being able to function successfully in majority society, are least likely to suffer from mental health problems.

Marginality

Marginality is the process in which the original or traditional culture is not maintained and the majority culture is rejected. Sometimes the process of acceptance or rejection may be determined or affected by historical experience of discrimination. Marginalized people have lost their language and traditions and have not replaced them by accepting the dominant culture's values. In rejecting themselves and others, marginalized people are unsurprisingly led to acculturation stress, sometimes accompanied by alcohol and substance abuse. According to Robinson and Howard-Hamilton (1999), the relationship between marginalization and substance abuse can be seen in some Hispanic and Aboriginal groups, which have been culturally devastated. The case of the Inuit of Davis Inlet is a good example of the effects of people who have been marginalized by majority society.

What we must remember is that dealing with different ethnic groups successfully involves being able to adopt helping strategies that can exist with acculturation differences. Culture — beliefs, behaviours and traditions — plays a fundamental role in people's lives. Effective counselling can occur only when one becomes aware of, accepts and values the differences in others. This is what accepting the diversity in society is all about. It is important to remember that while diversity encompasses the traits that distinguish one group from another group, ethnicity "is the consciousness of a cultural heritage shared with other people" (Bucher, 1999, p. 13).

Anglo-Canadians

The category of *Anglo-Canadians* includes not only those people whose parents originated from English-speaking places but also Germanic and other northern Europeans. It also includes those who were acculturated by English speakers. After the defeat of French forces on the Plains of Abraham in Quebec, Canada became an integral part of the British Empire. Every "white" person born during this period was considered a citizen of the British Empire. The concept of *Canadian* started only after Confederation, and even then Canadian identity was firmly rooted in the Anglo-Saxon tradition. Other early groups, such as Scandinavians and Germanic people, quickly adopted an English national consciousness. Before the turn of the twentieth century, more than 80 per cent of the people who immigrated to Canada from Europe came from the British Isles or from Germanic countries. Later generations of immigrants from other European ethnic groups, regardless of origin, have assimilated to the point that their ethnic identity can be considered Anglo-Canadian.

Immigration and Racial Identity

The English-speaking peoples, who were primarily Protestant, saw themselves as the founding people of Canada. In fact, up until the Pearson years, most elements of Canadian government and cultural practice were primarily English in origin. People from other parts of Europe, particularly southern Europe, were seen as not measuring up to English standards. (Interestingly, though, people of British ancestry are themselves multicultural in ethnic origin. *Anglo-Saxon*, a term often used to describe people of English origin, actually refers to Germanic and Scandinavian ancestors.) When Canadian immigration laws were changed in 1947, with the passing of the Canadian Citizenship law, all citizens of Canada were considered British subjects. In other words, new immigrants were supposed to assimilate, which Fleras and Elliott (1992) call "Anglo conformity." In fact, the nature of Canadian government, laws, social traditions and other aspects of culture were primarily British. Even the Canadian flag had the British Union Jack as its distinguishing feature. Immigration up to this point favoured those from western Europe and discriminated against those from other parts of Europe and the rest of the world. Early immigration laws were not only racist in nature but also assimilationist in content and segregationist in intent (Walker, 1985).

Immigrants from eastern Europe were considered acceptable, but Mediterranean Europeans and Jewish immigrants needed special permits, and Chinese, Japanese and Indian immigrants were largely kept out by exclusionary laws. Economic demand for labour sometimes allowed these groups into Canada to work, but immigration was shut off when labour demands lessened. Immigrants were expected to comply with Canadian (British) culture and values. The government of Canada eventually realized that a "white only" policy was morally and politically indefensible. After World War Two, the Canadian government

> eliminated the preference for suitable minorities from the selection process and introduced a set of universal criteria for entry. Applicants were admitted on the strength of their capacity for self-reliance. (Fleras & Elliott, 1992, pp. 42–43)

In 1967, immigration laws changed. The criteria for entrance were a point system, eliminating ethnic and racial background from consideration. Four classes of immigrants were defined: family, independent, entrepreneur and refugee. These classes of immigrants could apply under three categories: sponsored, independent or nominated. Under this system, discretionary power was given to immigration officers who implemented the plan. Skills, language ability, age and education determined the suitability of immigrants. Under all categories, the core of immigration policy was family reunification, with admission under the independent category being fairly low (e.g., only 4 per cent until 1988, when it was increased to 28 per cent). The laws continue to change to suit the times, and the result was the changing face of the people of Canada. In 1867, at the time of Confederation, only 8 per cent of the population was neither British nor French (Fleras & Elliott, 1992). By 2001, almost half of the population of Canada was neither British nor French.

Despite the change, however, British traditions predominate. Consider that Canada's head of state is the British monarch. Compared to the United States, Canada is very British. For instance, Benedict Arnold is a hero in Canada (in Saint John, New Brunswick, there is a statue to commemorate his deeds), while in the United States, Benedict Arnold is a traitor. With just a few exceptions, Canadian prime ministers have been of British heritage and Protestant. Interestingly, Canadians, unlike Americans, define themselves in relationship to language, in that descendants of Europeans who have been in North America for two or more generations see themselves as Anglo- or Franco- rather than ethnic. (There are some exceptions, e.g., the Hutterites.)

Historical Phases in Group Relations

In order to put the multicultural nature of counselling in perspective, one must understand the relationship of minorities and new Canadians. Historically, there are three aspects to relationships: conquest (differing national groups competing); anglicizing and the two solitudes (assimilation); and finally the cultural mosaic (diversity). According to Axelson (1999), "conflict is especially likely when the dominant group exerts its influence on minority groups for conformity or when misconceptions are perpetuated by both groups" (p. 76). Consider the following historical phases and how they may affect issues of trust and cooperation between majority and minority groups:

1. Initial meeting: This type of situation occurs when people meet as equals and engage in some mutual exchange or interdependence (e.g., during the fur trade).
2. Subjugation: One group exerts dominance over the other through theft of their land, controlling their culture and restricting cultural norms by outlawing or marginalizing their language (e.g., reserves, English-only institutions, covenants against certain religious groups).
3. Melting pot: This idea is based on the notion that Anglo-Saxons would be the dominant cultural group and all other groups would conform to it as the "master" culture. This notion excluded visible minorities.
4. Canadian identity: This phase is based on the idea that a new identity would emerge (derived from the melting pot), accepting all cultural groups, including the so-called founding races (French and English) but still excluding visible minorities.
5. Multiculturalism: This phase was based on the idea that all people — regardless of colour, creed or national identity — are equal partners in the country. Multiculturalism included not only emphasis on bilingualism but also the inclusion of heritage languages (Aboriginal languages, Chinese, Ukrainian, Japanese, Punjabi, etc.) in school curricula and national policies. To redress earlier discriminatory practices, institutions make equal-employment opportunities and advanced educational opportunities available to accelerate groups' social advancement.

Cultural Pluralism and the Process of Inclusion

While the idea of a pluralistic or multicultural society arose officially in 1972 with a bill introduced in the House of Commons by Prime Minister Pierre Elliott Trudeau, people of different cultures have been living side by side in Canada (e.g., French, English, those of African and Asian origin and Aboriginal peoples), maintaining cultural diversity, for centuries. However, there were problems and outright hostilities. Today, laws bring greater protection and have gone a long way toward alleviating past injustices. One way of viewing cultural diversity and ethnicity is explained by Gordon's theory (McLemore, 1980). There are four components to the theory:

1. Secondary structural assimilation: This component consists of the majority sharing with minorities in education, business and other areas of living; it is often imposed or developed because of circumstances. The atmosphere is characterized as cold and impersonal (e.g., desegregated facilities or equal-employment opportunities).
2. Primary structural assimilation: This component involves the mixing of different cultural and racial groups, majority and minority, in social and living situations in which relationships are close, personal and warm.
3. Cultural assimilation: This component occurs when minority groups lose their cultural identity through adopting majority cultural norms (e.g., value preferences, language, religion, family practices and interest in heritage). Interestingly, McLemore (1980) found that among immigrant groups, there is less hostility to the majority and a shorter period of assimilation. However, there is also some cultural resurgence by the third generation. Among conquered peoples, there is more hostility and a longer period of assimilation. There is also a strong tendency toward separation or secessionist activities.
4. Marital assimilation: This component occurs as the final step in the assimilation process as members of the majority and minority intermarry. One aspect of this phenomena not discussed in Gordon's theory involves those who choose one culture over another and those who choose to be bicultural. Research suggests that it takes three generations to assimilate into the majority population.

The Protestant Tradition

According to research (Axelson, 1999; Sue & Sue, 2007), one's views on life stem in part from one's religious beliefs, which in turn influence one's social reality. Protestantism in Canada was largely Anglican when churches were available, but Methodist and other Calvinist churches also had a strong influence. When churches were not available, people conducted their own services by reading the Bible or holding prayer meetings. Before the middle of the eighteenth century, 98 per cent of people outside of Quebec were Protestant (excluding Aboriginals). Their belief system and customs were woven into the fabric of society and culture. There was a deep mistrust of Catholics. The influence of culture and religion is evident in the notion of the Protestant work ethic: "According to the ethic, work and productive activity in the society are an expression of one's spiritual being and one's eventual self worth" (Axelson, 1999, p. 79). If one's life was predetermined, then one had a calling, or a sacred duty, to accomplish certain things. If one was successful, it was because of God's will; if not, then some "sin" one might have committed caused one's failure. Working hard and being productive became important aspects of the work ethic that determined whether one was good or bad. In fact, the notion of being good or bad was an important value preference among Anglo-Saxon peoples. This sometimes translated into seeing situations in black-or-white terms.

If we examine the majority world view, which by and large refers to those with a European ethnic heritage, the world is a place where one must work hard to survive. Even in times of plenty, work is seen as one's obligation to family, society and God. Since the early exploration of the Americas, immigrants had to sacrifice and labour long hours in order to survive. Thus, being productive and advancing personally and economically were duties. An interesting question is, how do these values of productivity and control affect counselling? Obviously a great deal of pressure is put on the individual to succeed. Consider the following quotations from a variety of influential Europeans and North Americans:

- "It is work which gives flavour to life." — Henri Frédéric Amiel
- "To youth I have but three words of counsel — work, work, work." Otto von Bismarck
- "There is no substitute for hard work." — Thomas Alva Edison
- "I look on that man as happy, who, when there is question of success, looks into his work for a reply." — Ralph Waldo Emerson
- "Every child should be taught that useful work is worship and that intelligent labour is the highest form of prayer." — Robert Green Ingersoll

Canadiens and Franco-Canadians

At one time, the largest European ethnic group in the Americas was the French, who first settled in the New World in 1604 along the territory of what became known as St. Croix Island. The harsh conditions motivated the colonists to move to the Port-Royal area of Nova Scotia, which eventually led to the move to Quebec City, the oldest continuous European settlement in Canada. The settlers of New France prospered until the Seven Years' War, in which the British army defeated the French army, ending French rule in North America. The 1763 Treaty of Paris was typical of the harsh treatment toward defeated peoples, but an unusual event occurred in the British colonies south of Canada. A revolt by American colonists forced the British government to make accommodations to the French-speaking people. In exchange for the French-speaking people's support against the Americans, the British passed the Québec Act, guaranteeing *les Canadiens* freedom of religion and maintenance of the French civil code. In effect, it granted them the same territories that they had enjoyed under the French regime and control over their daily lives. The people of Quebec lived their lives in a more or less French world, developing separately from English Canada, with a separate and distinct identity. Their culture and traditions have become unique, with their linguistic survival being paramount. As the balance of power shifted with the growing population of English Canada, French-speaking Quebec felt a greater desire for protection. Over time, their distinctness grew into dissatisfaction with their English neighbours, including numerous cultural and political movements to ensure their survival as a people. It wasn't until the election of the Parti Québecois in 1975 that the dream of a separate nation became a possibility. Consider the words of René Lévesque, founder of the Parti Québecois:

> Being ourselves is essentially a matter of keeping and developing a personality that has survived for three and a half centuries. At the core of this personality is the fact that we speak French. Everything else depends on this one essential element. . . . We are . . . heirs to the group obstinacy which has kept alive that portion of French America we call Québec. More is involved here than simple intellectual certainty. This is a physical fact. To be unable to live as ourselves, as we should live, in our own language and according to our own ways, would be like living without an arm or a leg — or perhaps a heart. (in Handler, 1984, p. 60)

The ensuing political debate about language and separatism in Canada has brought to the surface deep feelings of anger and distrust. From an English perspective, there is a sense that the government has given too much to the province of Quebec, while in Quebec there is a sense that French-speaking people are not accepted. English Canada's traditional view of French Canadians is that they are "obedient Catholics who have large families and never divorce" (Donnelly, 2000, p. 1). However, like most people who live in Canada, French Canadians have adapted over the years to have very different characteristics. There has been large-scale immigration to Quebec, just as in other parts of Canada, except those who settle in Quebec become francophones and thus adopt the culture of the people living there. Donnelly describes some unique aspects of the Québécois perspective, noting that, like all European immigrants to North America, the Québécois have a Eurocentric perspective; however, because they live in what has become a mass of English-speaking people, the natural tendency of the Québécois is to protect their culture and language. There is a historical distrust of anglophone society, which in the past tried to diminish Québécois cultural and linguistic choices; a strong separatist movement still desires a nation separate from Canada. From a cultural perspective, counsellors need to recognize the historical differences that have produced this view of the world. Unless either the counsellor or the client is fully bilingual, the degree of proficiency of languages may colour the degree of understanding. In addition, the Catholic tradition, while weaker today than in the past, is still a dominant force in French Canadian culture. If counsellors accept the distinctness of French Canadians and ensure they proceed from the client's perspective, there will be little difference between counselling French Canadians and counselling other white ethnic clients.

Other Ethnic Canadian Groups

Until the twentieth century, Canada was predominately populated by First Nations and British and French settlers. The nature of the Canadian federation (Upper and Lower Canada) created geographic pockets of cultural acculturation that confronted later European immigrants. As new immigrants from eastern and southern Europe settled in various areas dominated by the traditional founding nations, they often assimilated into either English or French society. However, many kept the cultural traditions that make them distinct. The following are examples of some of these distinctive white ethnic groups in Canada.

The Catholic Experience

The world view of Catholics is different from that of Protestants. According to Axelson (1993), "Catholicism functions as an influence in the adaptive process for many of the new White Ethnic groups, and perpetuation of spiritual and ideological ties with Catholicism in one form or another is an important characteristic of many of the southern and eastern European peoples who migrated in masses to [North America]" (p. 85). Is Catholicism a religion of the heart while mainstream Protestantism is a religion of the rational mind? If so, this may mean that some preferences or ways of acting differ because of differing religious upbringing. For new immigrants and those living in French Canada, the Catholic Church plays a big part in their lives. Politics and where the Church stands on an issue often determine how people vote. The Church was a pervasive influence in the lives of new immigrants in the following ways: conscientious fulfilment of duty; awe of higher powers; deep reflection; inner sacred preoccupation; and a close and lasting relationship with the supernatural (that is, the ultimate structure of the universe, its centre of power and human destiny). As the result of nineteenth- and twentieth-century immigration, the Catholic Church in Canada grew rapidly and was removed from mission status in 1908. Newcomers, however, changed its character. Irish immigration in the early 1800s reduced French Canadians to a minority among Catholics outside Quebec and led to conflict over language and episcopal appointments. Such tension continued in the 20th century with the arrival of southern and eastern Europeans. In the early 1990s, the Roman Catholic Church was the largest religious group in the country, with about 45 percent of Canadians belonging to it. It still receives some government recognition, especially in Quebec and in provinces where Catholic schools receive tax aid.

Persistence of Euro-Ethnic Cultures

The literature presents a number of examples of white ethnic groups that continue to identify with their culture through language, religion or other cultural practices. In Canada, these can be diverse ethnic groups such as Greek, Russian, Ukrainian and Polish, to name a few. A summary of two distinct examples follows.

Italian Canadians

Many of the Italians who came to North America were from southern Italy, where people were poor and often experienced repression. As a result, Italian immigrants identified more with the family and villages than with the Italian nation. Because many were uneducated, immigrants were exploited and most sought refuge in the family or the "village atmosphere" of the communities where they settled (the Little Italy found in many large centres). Their neighbourhoods were close-knit with strong family ties and deep allegiance to the Catholic Church. This probably helped Italian immigrants to maintain their separateness and uniqueness, and lessened their tendency to be assimilated by the larger culture. The family structure often was extended to hierarchical community structures. At the top was the *padrone*, or boss. This is not the same as the various depictions of Italians in organized crime but rather a social system brought over from southern Italy in which those on top helped others in times of need. Making it in Canadian society often meant a clash of cultures in which the individual had to put his or her welfare ahead of the group. According to Axelson (1993), "the mainstream culture emphasizes individuality and material achievement, often at the cost of breaking away from the family, old friends, and the culture of parents and grandparents" (p. 89).

Jewish Canadians

One of the distinguishing characteristics of Jewish immigration to North America is that Jewish immigrants were highly educated and literate and had experience living as a minority society. In Europe, Jewish people had been forced into ghettos and were often restricted to occupations that serviced the larger society (e.g., merchants, bankers, artisans), although in less-restrictive countries they served as doctors, teachers and other professionals. As a people experienced in being persecuted, Jewish immigrants developed coping mechanisms that assisted in their survival, particularly reliance on their faith and their communities: "Jewish devotion to family life was, and is, highly valued, and loyalty to kin, along with a strong spirit of ethnocentrism, offered strength in confronting many environmental obstacles" (Axelson, 1993, p. 91). Historically, this resilience began some 2,000 years ago, with the destruction of Israel's Second Temple in 70 CE and the dispersal of the Hebrew people from the Holy Land. Many of the rituals performed in the Temple were then performed in the family home. The dining table replaced the altar for the eating of ritually blessed foods. The synagogue, as a community prayer centre, was not meant to replace the ancient Temple fully, and the holiest of the rituals, particularly surrounding the Sabbath, always took place in the home.

Immediately after the destruction of the Temple, the great Rabbi Akiva began to offer the written and oral traditions of ancient Judaism in the first academy-in-exile. Rabbi Akiva maintained that one could fulfil the ancient obligations of the Temple through prayer and studying the Torah (scriptures). Interestingly, he argued against his critics that the Song of Songs not be expunged from the canon of Holy Scripture, maintaining that the Song of Songs was akin to entering the "holy of holies." By this, he was referring to the conjoining of the religious couple and to marital couples becoming "doubly blessed" when consummating their love during the evening of the Sabbath (L. Jung in Litvin, 1987). This point illustrates how Jewish ritual is devoted to maintaining the sanctity of couple relations, believing that it fulfills the Creator's very first commandment to man and woman: "Be fruitful and multiply and replenish the earth" (Gen. 1:28). It is taken even further to mean that the sexual urge, as part of the sexual act, was placed in humankind as a blessing, not as a sin. Mystical Jewish teaching then elevates the sexual act, when properly consecrated, into the spiritual dimension, as a joining of the sacred male and female principles.

Jewish people are expected to be married in order to fulfill their generative, social and spiritual life. However, contemporary Jewish feminists, such as Rosa Kaplan, have examined the position of women who are single, divorced or widowed and who then have difficulty integrating into the family-oriented religious community. Kaplan warns the traditional religious community to accept those who are not part of a mainstream family lifestyle, saying: "Unless individuals learn to relate to each other inside and outside the family as human beings rather than as role-occupant, the family that stays together may well decay together" (in Heschel, 1983).

In 2006, Canada had 315 120 self-described Jewish people, living primarily in the major urban centres. Forty percent are religiously Orthodox, forty percent are Conservative and twenty percent consider themselves Reform, the most liberal of the three (Statistics Canada, 2012). Jewish people were not permitted in Canada at all under the French Catholic rule, but entered Montreal with the British soldiers in 1768. A few merchants settled in British Columbia during the Gold Rush, while some Jewish farmers from eastern Europe settled on the prairies during the late nineteenth century. In 1832, full civil rights were granted, but many institutions, including universities, had quota systems to bar most minority peoples. It is now acknowledged that Canada acted shamefully in denying Jews admission to Canada during the Holocaust, but Canada now has the largest population of Holocaust survivors in the Diaspora (Abella, 1990).

Today Jewish people in Canada are a combination of assimilated and traditional individuals and are integrated into the Canadian mosaic. While the strong sense of ethnocentricity has given them certain advantages, it has also made them a target for hate by skinhead and neo-Nazi groups, despite gains over the years. With the current unrest in the Middle East, many Jewish people are concerned that their relatives abroad will be targeted by terrorists, or that religious and political hatreds may flare up here in Canada.

Implications for Counselling

Multicultural counselling is not just about counselling minorities, although counselling did not initially embrace cultural differences in theory and practice. The acceptance of the new reality of diversity in society has changed the nature of counselling. The traditional theories have had to be revamped to reflect the multicultural nature of society, including those theories that deal with anglophone and white ethnic groups. Axelson (1993) defines multicultural as the interface between counsellor and client that takes the personal dynamics of the counsellor and client into consideration alongside the emerging, changing and/or static configurations that might be identified in the cultures of counsellor and client (p. 13). In working with clients who are culturally different, we must consider the following rules, identified by Pedersen (1994):

1. Consider that conflicting cultural views are equally right;
2. Consider that one can have multiple views or even conflicting views depending on the situation;
3. Try "seeing" what the situation is like from another cultural perspective;

4. Listen for the cultural perspective in dealing with another ethnic group;

5. Develop the ability to shift to another cultural perspective by learning behavioural expectations and values;

6. Learn to identify culturally appropriate feelings accurately in specific rather than general terms (i.e., cues, signals and patterns of emotional expression);

7. Explore multiple levels of support that are possible within a given cultural group;

8. Develop the ability to identify culturally learned criteria being used to evaluate alternative solutions;

9. Develop the ability to generate insights for the culturally different client from his/her culturally learned perspective.

Conclusion

According to Alladin (1996), Canadians have to realize that "a serious study of racism in schools and society will inevitably create controversy [since] racist practices have been so integral in our history that they have gained acceptance" (p. 160). However, in a multicultural society such as Canada, all cultural groups add to the cultural mosaic and work as partners in the development and growth of the nation. New cultural groups are increasingly replacing the French and English who originally immigrated to Canada. In major Canadian cities, Chinese and Indo-Canadian groups are becoming the dominant ethnic groups, while in the North and across the Prairies, First Nations groups are becoming the dominant ethnic groups. Immigration to Canada is coming more and more from Asia rather than Europe. However, to help counsellors understand the important contributions that the English and other white ethnic groups have made, we have summarized material from the literature on these groups. While it is easy to generalize and see the majority population as a monolithic group, there is a great deal of difference that we hope this chapter summarizes. We also feel that revisiting the "majority cultural identity" model is a good place to start in order to understand cultural norms and how the dominant culture has shaped many of the political and social institutions. What we have summarized by describing the Anglo-Saxon and white ethnic groups simply scratches the surface. The struggle for national identity is part of being Canadian and is constantly being redefined. However, in light of all this, it might be wise to keep one's sense of humour. Consider this statement by Canadian novelist, poet and critic Margaret Atwood (1990): "The beginning of Canadian cultural nationalism was not 'Am I really that oppressed?' but "Am I really that boring?'"

References

Abella, I. (1990). *A coat of many colours: Two centuries of Jewish life in Canada*. Toronto: Lester and Orpen Dennys.

Alladin, M.I. (1996). *Racism in Canadian schools*. Toronto: Harcourt Brace & Company.

American Jewish Yearbook (2000). Vol 100. New York: The American Jewish Committee.

Atwood, M. (1990). Dancing on the edge of the precipice. In E.G. Ingersoll (Ed.), *Margaret Atwood: Conversations*. Toronto, ON: Firefly Books, 1990.

Axelson, J. (1999). *Counseling and development in a multicultural society* (3rd ed.). Thousand Oaks, CA: Brooks/Cole.

Bucher, R.D. (1999). *Diversity consciousness: Opening our minds to people, cultures and opportunities*. Upper Saddle River, NJ: Prentice-Hall.

Berry, J.W., & Kim, U. (1988). Acculturation and mental health. In P.R. Dasen, J.W., Berry & N. Sartorius (Eds.), *Health and cross-cultural psychology: Toward applications* (pp. 207–236). Newbury Park, CA: Sage.

Berry, J.W., & Sam, D.L. (1997). Acculturation and adaptation. In J. Berry, M. Segall & C. Kagitcibasi (Eds.), *Cross-cultural psychology* (Vol. 3, pp. 291–326). Boston: Allyn & Bacon.

Dyer, G. (1994). *The human race: Tribal identity*. Ottawa: National Film Board.

Donnelly, G. (1996). *Counselling French-Canadians*. Unpublished MA thesis, University of Victoria.

Fleras, A., & Elliot, J.L. (1992). *Multiculturalism in Canada: The challenge of diversity*. Scarborough, ON: Nelson.

Handler, R. (1984). On sociocultural discontinuity: Nationalism and cultural objection in Quebec. *Current Anthropology*, 25(1), 55–71.

Heschel, S. (Ed.). (1983). *On being a Jewish feminist: A reader*. New York, NY: Schocken Books.

Jung, L. (1987). Married love in Jewish law. In B. Litvin (Ed.), *The sanctity of the synagogue: The case for mechitzah: separation between men and women in the synagogue*. New York. Ktav Publishing House.

McLemore, S.D. (1980). *Racial and ethnic relations in America*. Boston, MA: Allyn & Bacon.

Pedersen, P. (1994). *A handbook for developing multicultural awareness* (2nd ed.). Alexandria, VA: ACA.

Sue, D., & Sue, D. (2007). *Counseling the culturally diverse* (5th ed.). New York, NY: John Wiley and Sons.

Statistics Canada (2012). *Ethnic origins of Canadians*. Government of Canada: Ottawa, ON.

Walker, J. (1985). *Racial discrimination in Canada: The Black experience, Booklet #4*. Ottawa: The Canadian Historical Association.

Part III

Application and Practical Approaches

THE FOCUS OF THE CHAPTERS IN PART III OF THIS BOOK is the practical application of multicultural counselling approaches. Our experience with these approaches tells us about the cultures where these distinct approaches developed and in a sense reminds us as counsellors that there are other ways of knowing that developed in other parts of the world. We believe that culture-friendly theories and approaches have not been given adequate attention in most counselling theory courses, and we hope that the selective inclusion of these approaches will highlight the fact that differing cultural approaches have much to offer the counsellor practitioner. Exploring counselling approaches that come from other ways of knowing can help counsellors expand their repertoire of helping responses, in order to address what is meaningful for the client. Effective counsellors with multicultural skills and knowledge of different methods of healing can empower clients in our diverse country.

We believe that the integration of the approaches highlighted in Part III can increase counsellor awareness of personal values and biases, and the "person-in-relation" frame of reference. Such awareness can also help validate a myriad of multicultural world views, leading to more varied and effective strategies, assessment, treatment and research. Another element counsellor educators may overlook in our drive to be scientific is the lack of attention to the spiritual dimension. We believe that when we examine approaches that emphasize spirituality, there is much to gain from including this important dimension of being human. Counselling in relationship to spirituality and using healing methods that are culturally appropriate may be significant for the many people who thirst for this type of counselling practice. Two spiritual approaches to multicultural counselling are discussed in this section, both offering ideas that can be adapted to other types of counselling. For example, Sufism assumes that as people experience the full range of the spirit of God, they acquire insight into their "greater selves." Included in this therapeutic process, which is highly individualized, is meditation, dance, dreams and parables. Naikan and Yoga are two Asian ways of helping and healing with philosophical roots in Buddhist and Hindu spiritual practices, giving the counsellor a more holistic way of working with people. Another important strategy is the inclusion of nature and the way it can be used to improve personal and interpersonal well-being. Our view is that the separation from nature in our modern world increases stress and leaves people with a sense of psychosocial, emotional and spiritual isolation.

We have been largely critical of traditional counselling approaches. Although they may be least helpful with diverse populations, our feeling is that *some* traditional approaches offer value to diverse clients. Among the traditional approaches that have been shown to be adaptable to diverse groups is cognitive-behavioural counselling. Cognitive-behavioral counselling is the least value-laden approach and is one of the more culture-friendly models. Another important, though often overlooked, theory is transpersonal theory. This approach includes awareness, compassion, emotional transformation, ethical training, motivation, meditation and wisdom as fundamental components of the helping relationship. Finally, as an extension of our belief in compassion, tolerance and acceptance as ingredients of sensitive counselling, we have included ideas on restorative justice as an alternative approach within the context of cross-cultural counselling.

Our view is that exploring alternative ways of healing brings another element into differing counselling roles. We believe that the inclusion of the approaches in this section may be only the tip of the iceberg, and we urge counsellors to be open to other approaches from different cultures and any approaches that include differing world views.

18

The Red Road

Spirituality, the Medicine Wheel and the Sacred Hoop

M. Honoré France, Rod McCormick,
& María del Carmen Rodríguez

When I was standing on the highest mountain of them all, around about beneath me was the whole hoop of the world. And while I stood there I saw more than I can tell and I understood more than I saw; for I was seeing in a sacred manner the shapes of all the things in the spirit, and the shape of all shapes as they must live together like one being. And I saw that the sacred hoop of my people was one of many hoops that made one circle, wide as daylight and as starlight, and in the center grew one mighty flowering tree to shelter all the children of one mother and one father. And I saw that it was holy. — *Black Elk Speaks* (1932)

When Black Elk spoke these words almost a century ago, he was expressing the most fundamental belief of all First Nations people of North America: the idea that all living things are related — brothers and sisters. The philosophical essence of this idea can be expressed in one word: respect. Respect for the land, respect for the animals, respect for the plants, respect for other people and finally respect for the self. This is the essential ingredient for living life. According to Duran (2006), the development of respect among First Nations people can be compared to the ideas of love for Christians and enlightenment for Buddhists. The notion of respect is that humankind is not separate from any other thing in the world but just another living, breathing creature among many. Thus, the environment, as a brother or sister, is not something to be exploited or harmed but is an integral part of everyone. When this respect does not exist, then nature is separate. As a separate entity, nature becomes like a machine: something to be mastered, something to be exploited.

Disease is caused when people are out of harmony with the land. This idea of harmony can be seen in the hot–cold belief in curing illness. In the human body, sickness will ensue if an excess of hot or cold foods is ingested. The hot–cold scheme applies to foods, diseases and remedies. The terms *hot* and *cold* do not necessarily refer to the temperature of foods or remedies. Qualities are assigned on the basis of origin, colour, nutritional value and physiological effects of the food or remedy, as well as therapeutic action (i.e., bananas and sugar cane are considered cold, whereas garlic and corn meal are hot). Cold-classified illnesses, such as arthritis, colds and gastric complaints, must be treated with hot foods and remedies. Their hot counterparts are constipation, diarrhea and intestinal cramps, which require treatment with cold substances. First Nations people believe that humankind has a choice of two roads: the road to technology (blue) or the road to spirituality (red).

In this chapter we explore counselling in relationship to spirituality and culturally appropriate helping and healing methods that can be used with First Nations people. It is important to remember that Indigenous people are just as diverse as European ethnic groups in their customs and language. Yet there exist among First Nations people elements of beliefs and actions that are universal. To be successful with First Nations people, counsellors must take the time to find out about their culture and be open to adapting or replacing the models they presently relate to with those that are more appropriate for the First Nations person. Roysircar (2012) suggests that counsellors "should limit abstract labeling of thoughts and feelings because [First Nations] clients are not socialized to think in terms of labels or categories but rather to narrate, disclose experiences and seek harmony" (p. 67). It is our belief that counsellors, regardless of their ethnic background, can work with appropriate elders and traditional healers in situations in which some of the following strategies can be used.

Basic Values Underlying Actions

Among First Nations people exist beliefs about the world that shape how they view themselves and how they interact with majority culture. Hart (2002) lists the following values that are common among First Nations people: "vision/wholeness, spirit-centred, respect/harmony, kindness, honesty/integrity, sharing, strength, bravery/courage, wisdom, and respect/humility" (p. 45). Values not only drive people but also contain important information on how we experience the world. Among the most important elements in understanding values is the exploration of world view, interconnectedness, balance and spirituality. An understanding of these beliefs can help counsellors work more effectively with Indigenous people.

World View

To be effective with First Nations people, the counsellor must understand differing world views and be able to incorporate such understandings into a helping and learning framework. Despite its naïve wish to be seen as value free, the Western educational system makes inherent assumptions that are rooted in philosophical views of human nature and people's place in the world. As a First Nations person and counsellor, Robbins (2012) relates that "because I am educated at times I feel separated from myself as a tribal person" (p. 102). The challenge for many is to learn to walk two paths, or to blend approaches that can coexist with First Nations values.

World view deals with a culture's orientation and ways of seeing and understanding the world in relationship to humankind, nature, the universe and other philosophical issues concerned with the concept of being. Atleo (2004) describes the basis of Nuu-chah-nulth (West Coast of Vancouver Island) world view as a theory of *tsawalk*, which means "one": that is, a way of understanding how the world exists and the intrinsic relationship between the physical and the spiritual world. In this view, by understanding the origin stories of Son of Raven and Son of Mucas, one understands the way the world is balanced and how people come to understand their place in the universe. It is a very different view from what the Western world understands about how things work and what relationship exists among living things. What is similar is that world view helps humanity locate their place and rank in the universe; it influences the sense and understanding of culture at a very deep and profound level since it affects beliefs, values, attitudes, interpretation of time and other aspects of culture. Our world view affects our belief systems, value orientation, decision-making processes, assumptions and modes of problem solving. Lafromboise, Trimble and Mohatt (1990) state,

> Knowledge of and respect for an Indian world view and value system, which varies according to the client's tribe, level of acculturation, and other personal characteristics is fundamental not only for creating the trusting counselor–client relationship vital to the helping process but also for defining the counseling style or approach most appropriate for each client. (p. 629)

An important point made in this statement concerns the need to recognize the diversity among First Nations people. World view and personal value systems vary according to a person's tribe, level of acculturation and other personal characteristics. But how then can counsellors assess world view? Ibrahim (1984) has developed a scale for assessing world view across cultures based on a value orientation scheme developed by Kluckhohn and Strodtbeck (1961). The Kluckhohn framework considers both philosophical and psychological dimensions, including beliefs, values, assumptions, attitudes and behaviour of individuals and groups. She postulated that these conceptions influence human behaviour, motivations, decisions and lifestyles. Kluckhohn proposed five universal or existential categories that pertain to a general, organized conception and understanding of being:

- human nature: good, bad or a combination of both;
- social relationships: lineal–hierarchical, collateral–mutual and/or individualistic;
- nature: subjugate and control nature, live in harmony with nature and/or accept the power and control of nature over people;
- time orientation: past, present or future;
- activity orientation: being, being-in-becoming and/or doing.

An examination of these schemes would further our understanding of any culture or individual's world view. An example of how First Nations people relate to these categories is the orientation toward nature. Traditionally, Indigenous people attempt to live in harmony with nature whereas non-Indigenous people attempt to control nature to meet people's needs. Time orientation also differs among cultural groups. According to Sue and Sue (2008), time orientation in traditional Native culture has always been towards the present, incorporating the past, in contrast with the Western tendency to focus on the future. This is often confusing to those who do not share this perspective.

Balance

The Native medicine wheel is a ready-made model of the First Nations world view. The medicine wheel shows the elements of people's emotional, mental, spiritual and physical being as equal and part of a larger whole. This representation reinforces the concept of interconnectedness and the lesson that one part cannot be the centre of existence but must instead learn to work in harmony with all of the other parts. The medicine wheel represents the balance that exists among all things. The First Nations world view, as represented by the medicine wheel, has balance as a basic tenet of healthy living because this is a paramount value. The medicine wheel represents the all-encompassing cycle of creation, from birth to death, in which animals, nature, humanity and spirits coexist.

Traditional medicine incorporates the physical, emotional, psychological and spiritual being. As a result, it is difficult to isolate any one aspect, because these parts exist in harmonious balance. Indigenous people become ill when they live life in an unbalanced way (Medicine Eagle, 1989). Balance is essential for the First Nations person because the world itself is seen as a balance among transcendental forces, human beings and the natural environment (Hammerschlag, 1988).

Interconnectedness

The collective orientation of First Nations people has been stressed continuously by lead-ing Native mental health researchers (Trimble & Hayes, 1984; Lafromboise et al., 1990). It is unfortunate that Western counsellors still stress the role of individual responsibility when helping First Nations clients. The role of healing in traditional Indigenous society has been not only to reaffirm cultural values but also to consider the individual in the context of the community (Duran, 2006; Lafromboise et al., 1990). Katz and Rolde (1981) found that the goal of traditional healing was not to strengthen a person's ego, as in non-First Nations situations, but to encourage people to transcend the ego by considering themselves as imbedded in and expressive of community. Traditional ceremonies such as the vision quest and the sweat lodge reinforce Indigenous people's adherence to cultural values and help to remind them of the importance of keeping family and community networks strong (Lafromboise et al., 1990).

Traditional helping approaches, unlike Western approaches, usually involve more than just the counsellor and the client. Relatives and community members are often asked to be part of the healing process. Duran (2006) found that First Nations people would usually turn to their relatives and community members when they were experiencing personal problems. This raises serious doubts as to the usefulness of Western approaches such as client-centred counselling with Indigenous clients. The one-on-one interaction characteristic of many Western helping approaches is isolated outside of the context of the community and family, and must therefore be questioned as a valid means of dealing with First Nations clients.

Spirituality

Traditional American Indians believe that mental health is much more spiritual and ho-listic than Western psychology would suggest (Duran, 2006). Many traditional Indige-nous healing ceremonies emphasize the spiritual aspect of healing. It is to the Great Spirit or Creator, perceived everywhere, that Indigenous people turn in times of need. Different ceremonies stress the need for reconnection with one's spirituality. In the vision quest ceremony, First Nations people make contact with their spiritual identity. The medicine wheel, symbolized by the circle, represents spiritual ties that bind human beings to one another and to the natural world (France & Rodriguez, 2011). This spirituality, or holi-ness, is seen as the essence of healing for Native people. It represents the manifestation of wholeness in spirit, bringing it into our bodies, our families, our communities and our world (Medicine Eagle, 1989).

There is a oneness to the First Nations philosophy that is reflected in the Salish belief of the creation of the world. Ashwell (1989) emphasizes that the Salish believe the human soul is characterized by that "indestructible spark, which once departed went to the sunset, where it remained forever, that which was left behind was the earthly body and its shadows — these shadows held a three-part existence and remained on the earthly scene with either good or evil intent, depending on the characteristic of the person in life" (p. 60). This continuity of life is often represented by the circle, which appears in many of the symbols used in First Nations ceremonies (e.g., the drum, the Ghost Dance, etc.). According to Smoley (1992), this idea of spiritual power is conceptualized in "*si si wiss*, which means sacred breath or sacred life" (p. 85). When people respect everything, there is love of all things because in the trees, the animals and all living things, we see and perceive more than our own humanity. Everything has experienced the same sacred breath. When there is respect, which is the essence of the healing spirit, then we appreciate the "love of God we feel in our hearts" (Smoley, 1992, p. 85). First Nations spirituality demonstrates how humanity can harmoniously coexist with the environment.

Various Methods of Helping and Healing

Working with Dreams

According to Duran and Duran (1995), "as early as 1668 there was documentation as to the importance of dreams in Native American culture" (p. 46). People around the world have long used dream exploration because it is a straightforward method of looking at the unconscious. Consider one of the dreams of Black Elk (1932), one of the principal philosophers of the First Nations tradition. He was a Lakota [Sioux] born in the nineteenth century, but he lived a long life, enabling John Neilhardt to record Black Elk's thoughts on his life, the struggles to revitalize Native American culture and his belief in the continual survival of his people after decades of fighting the US army. One of Black Elk's early dreams or visions provides an excellent example of the transcendent experience.

Before one of the battles of the Little Big Horn (1867), the young Black Elk had a vision of two men descending with flaming spears. They kidnapped Black Elk and brought him to a great plain on a cloud, where horses of different colours greeted him: black, white, red and yellow. These colours represent, in First Nations spirituality, the four directions: white is north (cleaning, endurance and courage), yellow is south (growth and healing), red is east (power of the sacred pipe and the power of peace to awaken others through knowledge and wisdom) and black is west (releases water from the clouds). From there, Black Elk went into a rainbow-covered lodge of the Six Grandfathers. These are the powers of the four directions, Father Sky and Mother Earth. The first Grandfather gave Black Elk water to sustain life, and then handed him a bow and said he could use it to destroy.

The second Grandfather gave sage, cleaning power and a white wing, cleaning power of the northern snow. The third Grandfather gave the power to awaken others by bringing wisdom, peace and knowledge. The fourth Grandfather gave Black Elk the power to heal others. The fifth Grandfather, the spirit of the sky, became an eagle and told Black Elk that all living things were his relatives. The sixth Grandfather, who was really Mother Earth spirit, told him that salvation was within the earth (nature). Later Black Elk was shown the hoop of the world, which was made of many hoops, representing all people, but they were one and the same. When Black Elk actualized his dream upon awakening, he spent his life using his powers to help his people. In the end, as an old man, well into the twentieth century, he thought that the dream had failed. He was wrong because much of what was predicted came true, perhaps through his efforts; but the real gift was what he said and did to revitalize the spiritual revival not only of the Lakota but of all First Nations people. It was just a dream that Ed McGaa, Eagle Man (1990), stresses has become a blooming tree with the

> bright rainbow, symbolic of the flowering tree . . . now blooming among the environmental and spiritual gatherings of enlightened peoples that have begun to flourish throughout the land. The rainbow-covered lodge of the Six Grandfathers is a strong symbol of the old holy man's prediction [dream] that, someday, the flowering tree would bloom. The blooming has begun and will continue — if only some blue man (greed, corruption, and user of the land) doesn't push the wrong button. (p. 17)

Among the Ani-yun-wiya First Nation people, dream sharing is a vital part of their lives because it links the real world they experience to the world beyond themselves. It is where the conscious self meets the unconscious self. Thus to talk about dreams after they occur is important, since it is easy for dreams to be gone by the time one awakes. Dreams "talk" about strange actual events that have affected dreamers. And some dreams are not just for oneself but might even foretell the future. These dreams are about unusual happenings; they transcend life as it really is and can provide a sense of awareness about things that might otherwise be unknown. The history of the Ani-yun-wiya people, whose language was one of the first Indigenous languages to be written, shows that dreams are a pathway to other spiritual dimensions. However, not many of the ancient Ani-yun-wiya signs, presages and dreams have pleasant associations; in fact, it seems as if they are fixated on death, illness and misfortune. In the study of such portents and dreams, there are four important characteristics to consider:

- Some dreams are about things that seldom happen; they caused little concern among the observers.

- Through dreams and signs, people found ways in which to deal with and come to terms with unexpected deaths without accusing the Above Beings [the Creator] for being unfair to them.
- Signs and dreams prepared people to accept death as a natural consequence of living. It was better to be ready than to be suddenly seized.
- People were kept from attempting to solve their problems on their own by seeking the help of a priest for cleansing and restoration. They believed that this action pleased the Above Beings.

For the Ani-yun-wiya, dreams and signs were thought to be among the causes of things happening. To see in a dream the sign of death was to cause the death, the illness or any other matter; and even when most dreams defy recall, the Ani-yun-wiya use seven ritual stones to help in this important act, since this is a vital practice in their lives. These are some examples that foretold sickness or death among the Ani-yun-wiya:

- Seeing anyone with an eagle feather in his/her hand or dreaming of possessing such a feather was a sign of death.
- Seeing a person with very clean clothes meant that the person would not live long.
- Dreaming of a living person or an animal that was dead in the dream was a certain sign of sickness to come, and those who dreamed of seeing a woman would have fever.

Other dreams had to do with good fortune, good luck and greatness. If hunters dreamed of having bread, peaches or any kind of fruit, they were told they would kill a deer; and if someone dreamed of flying, it implied that the person would live a long life. In addition, there were dreams and signs that had to do with strangers and visitors. For example, if a little bird called *tsi ki lili* flew over in the direction of someone who was travelling, that person would soon meet a stranger; if a bird flew into the house, it announced that a visitor was coming. There were also signs that had to do with enemies and warfare. If a *tsa wi sku* bird was heard singing very loud and fast, it meant that enemies were in town; and if an owl rested on a peach or any other tree in town and sang, enemies would approach shortly after.

There is a lingering belief that Ani-yun-wiya dreams speak of positive human attributes and of how people must be centred in their spirituality and the Great Spirit. The dream work process works toward understanding the meaning in the dream, and we recommend the following sequence (France, 2002):

1. Hearing the dream with the idea of exploring feelings, thoughts, actions and experiences that can clarify meaning;
2. Exploring the dream structure, elements, symbols, issues and qualities of the dream characters;
3. Dialoging about the symbols by examining one's outer life and, if possible, by expressing the dream in an art form;
4. Amplifying the symbols by analyzing their cultural and personal meaning in one's external life;
5. Bringing resolution and actualizing the message of the dream in everyday life.

In the transpersonal sense, the traditional way that Ani-yun-wiya people embraced dreaming and then incorporated the messages and signs into their everyday life illustrates how the unconscious world can be a part of everyday existence. Essentially, one looks for the message or meaning in the dream by exploring the symbols, story and other aspects of the emotions in the dream. However, Duran and Duran (1995) advise caution because

> The notion of living out dreams is a cross-tribal phenomenon. There are rules and taboos about reporting dreams, which makes the discussion of dreams a concern for the Western therapist who is naïve to this practice. The therapist must become informed as to the different rules of reporting and discussing dreams within the tribal context in which s/he is working. (p. 50)

Working with Stories

Stories have the power to transform and heal by creating images that are as vivid as life itself. These images faithfully mirror one's journeys through the ordinary and the unexpected experiences of daily life, for it is in stories that one discovers eternal truths, clarification, rectification, meaning and, ultimately, purpose. In telling stories, traditional folktales, myths and legends rich in archetypal imagery, we unveil profound spiritual truths to the listener, reflecting the journey of the soul. As a result, the story becomes part of our own personal spirituality. In listening to stories, one discovers eternal truths that seem to escape amidst a rushed life. Stories carry life, history, traditions and culture. It is not surprising, then, that fifteen minutes of storytelling or listening can reveal and clarify fifteen years of living.

Since stories carry universality, people's shared experiences can be found in their qualities, which serve diverse purposes.

- Sharing and creating a common experience in storytelling aids in the development of people's ability to interpret events beyond their immediate experience. Stories can be used as ways to understand one's life through looking at symbols, creating analogies and bringing closure to diverse issues.
- Stories contribute to one's social, emotional and cognitive development through shared experiences (e.g., feeling joy for another's happiness or sadness at another's misfortunes).
- Stories contribute to clients' mental health and help people cope with their own conscious and unconscious self by giving them the structure for their own daydreams and fantasies.
- Stories aid in the development of an ethical value system, helping people appreciate and reinforce their own cultural heritage.

Helping Strategies: Skaloola (An Example)

Among First Nations people, legends, myths and stories are more than just stories or fairy tales. The story of Skaloola, as shared by Shirley Sterling (1997), demonstrates how stories were used in a traditional context by elders or parents to teach their children. Stories maintain continuity from one generation to the next, ensuring that the values and standards are shared and transmitted not only vertically but also horizontally. In other words, while elders and parents might tell the story with a certain purpose (e.g., to teach about personal safety), children share stories with others to strengthen relations among themselves and to share information and life experiences. In this way, the story reinforces values that are relevant to the storyteller and to the listener, thus creating a sense of understanding, caring and acceptance.

> Skaloola was an owl who stole children. He hid watching boys and girls to see if they wandered far from camp or stayed out too late after dark. If they did, Sakloola would grab them, put them into a big basket on his back and run away to the mountains. Although hunters chased after him, for some reason at some point the tracks always disappeared and there was no sign of Skaloola or the children. They were never seen again.

According to Sterling (1997), this story was used by parents as a device for social control and personal safety. It taught children about some social dangers such as abduction, sexual abuse or encountering enemies. Additionally, the story taught moral values and reminded children about the consequences of lying and not obeying their elders. It also provided explanations for existence and respect for all creation based on kinship ties as it allowed people to engage in conversations about taboos, harm and life in general. From the child's perspective, the myth of Skaloola the Owl provided opportunities to engage in conversations about safety and danger issues, ways to respond and be careful and how help and teach the helpless, as well as to comfort and protect each other. Since respect for self and others is the basis for living a healthy life, fearful reaction of loved ones for breaking such balance served as a warning against transgressions of the moral code. In this sense myths become a preventive means of helping keep the family in spiritual, mental, physical and emotional balance.

The myth of Skaloola also provides a powerful analogy with regards to how the government "stole" First Nations children to take them to residential schools; made them adopt different beliefs, values and language; made them live within a different culture; and made them victims of physical, spiritual and emotional abuse. This parallel offers clarity in understanding the seriousness of the crimes committed against First Nations people. In addition to presenting a story orally, one could analyze and respond to stories through journal writing, visual artwork and dramatization. Writing or drawing evokes one's own images, emotions and interpretations, helping create a tangible sense of what was verbalized. Drawing exploration becomes a powerful tool to reveal concerns, difficulties, joy and delight. The counsellor can assist the individual in the search for symbols and signs that might be absent in other forms of exploration and interaction. Journaling offers similar possibilities: by anchoring the images in words that have been transferred to paper, the individual is able to explore feelings and emotions in a different way, find symbols and make meaning of the experiences.

Sweat Lodge

According to Duran and Duran (1996), counselling programs, such as the sweat lodge, that mix traditional methods with therapy have been very successful in the therapeutic process. They say that counsellors should work in collaboration with traditional colleagues.

The sweat lodge ceremony is a basic method of purification. A temporary structure is used to enact the ceremony. The sweat lodge is built out of willows around a hole dug in the centre. The willows are covered with canvas or plastic, and a fire is built to heat the rocks, which are put in the centre of the pit. Essential to partaking in the sweat lodge ceremony is being respectful to the spirits. Before beginning, one prays to the guardian spirit. In fact, all aspects of nature are respected and symbolically represented in the ceremony (e.g., such as the rocks, which are called the bones of Mother Earth). In a sense, the sweat lodge is a symbol of the womb of Mother Earth, while the fire represents Father Sun. The rocks represent the act of conception. As participants enter the sweat lodge, they have the opportunity to experience their own birth or to feel reborn. Thus it is a chance for a new beginning in life. Every action is performed with deference, because the ceremony is sacred. It is essentially a demonstration of respect to Mother Earth and all creation.

Before the ceremony begins, the leader instructs everyone about what is to happen. Once participants enter the sweat lodge, all movement is clockwise and circular. Participants turn to the left and either walk or crawl to where they will be seated. Once they choose a spot, this is where they will sit for succeeding rounds. Upon entering, participants are given a prescribed prayer, which is a method of demonstrating respect and putting participants in the proper state of mind. As participants become closer to the elements, they enter a spiritual space in which insights or messages can be received. The duration of the round depends on the leader of the ceremony, who enters with the participants. The fire person brings the stones, as required by the leader, while the door person brings in the water. Once the door is closed, the leader burns dried sage, sweet grass or pieces of cedar. These herbs clean the lodge, symbolic of the world. It is felt that sage smoke affects all colours of the light spectrum, thus touching everything in the universe. Physically, the sweating cleanses the body of toxic elements and is symbolic of cleansing the mind (i.e., when the body is clean, then the mind is clear). At various times during the round, the leader sprinkles water over the stones while everyone meditates and stays in a respectful frame of mind. The leader explains what the round is for, such as thanksgiving for the earth or the universe. The leader starts by praying for whatever has been chosen. Each person has the opportunity to follow suit. When finished, he or she will say, "All my relations," to acknowledge all creation and the connectedness. After each prayer, more water is sprinkled. Once the round ends, participants leave in a clockwise fashion in the same order that they entered, thus completing the circle. As the participants leave the womb, they are symbolically reborn.

The new beginning creates a new state of mind and a change in attitude. Those who have cleared their minds during the ceremony can now see the power of the animal spirits, and all of the hurt, anger and negative feelings are released. After they have departed from the sweat lodge, participants can enhance the experience by taking a dip in a cold stream or pond. It takes strength to move from heat to cold and back, yet it is thought that the contrast is curative. The complete process is repeated four times. Once again, the symbolic recognition of the four directions, elements and races is enacted as a means of reinforcing the natural cycles in the natural world: "Steam comes up; that's the breath of life. It cleanses out our negative thoughts and fears. Our whole body is crying; it's a very powerful experience. The sweat lodge (*Initi*) is said to 'strengthen the ghost' of a human being and drive away all evil things" (Smoley, 1992, p. 87).

In Lakota culture, a sweat lodge ceremony is undertaken before any major endeavor. The ceremony takes place in a dome-like structure, which may look like a teepee. Large poles are bent and put into the group to match the sacred directions of north, south, east, west, northwest, and so on. Since the sun rises in the east, the door always faces east. The frame can be covered by blankets or mats or even plastic, as long as the sun is blocked out. Inside the structure, a three-foot hole is dug to hold the stones. Outside the sweat lodge, a fire is built to heat the rocks (lava rocks are best). At one side of the fire is a mound of fir boughs for participants to place personal items to be cleansed and blessed. Inside the sweat lodge, cedar or fir branches are placed around the hole for people to sit on. There are also four pieces of cloth to show the four directions, the four races (red, white, black and yellow) and the four elements (air, fire, earth and water). The cloths are usually red, white, blue or yellow. Most often, the sweat lodge is built near a lake, pond or creek to allow participants to immerse themselves in water between rounds. Participants prepare themselves by giving thanks to the boughs, rocks, twigs, water and sage, because these elements are giving themselves up in the ceremony. The ceremony can be for women only, men only, family members only or for mixed company. If the ceremony is for women only, it is led by a woman; if for men only, it is led by a man. The clothing participants wear depends on the occasion or the wishes of the participants. If they choose not to wear clothes, it is fine. The only instruction given to participants is that they remove negative thoughts and open their hearts and minds to any messages they receive during the ceremony. Besides the one leading the ceremony, one person is chosen to be the fire keeper and one to be the door keeper. The door keeper must make sure that no outside light comes inside and must listen to the participants. It is important for the symmetry of the ceremony that, when someone wants to leave, he or she chants, "All my relations." Once the participants have cleansed their minds, bodies and spirits, they are led in a prayer of appreciation and thanks to the Creator, the great-grandfathers, mothers and ancestors. The First Nations people believe that those who have gone on before are watching over all from the spirit world.

The Vision Quest

The vision quest is a method of opening oneself up to the spirit world through a process of isolating oneself in the wilderness. Among the Coast Salish people, it is called a spirit quest (Jilek, 1982). A person might go into the forest alone and stay there without speaking to anyone or even eating or drinking. The seeker wishes to open the self to a vision. Vision quest embodies much of what is most characteristic in First Nations spirituality: exposing the individual to the forces of nature and the supernatural; most crucial perhaps, is the search for one's inner truth (Smoley, 1992). The vision quest resembles an inner journey, where the spirits are confronted.

In all of the dancing, healing or shamanistic ceremonies, the theme of rebirth and restoration is always constant for it is believed that in order to attain personal change, there must be a kind of death. Death, as a metaphor, is always followed by rebirth. Whether the method is the sweat lodge or the vision quest, the process does not fluctuate. When a client approaches the healer, the healer always attempts to look inside and decipher the client's state of existence. The goal is to destroy the patient's faulty and diseased old self — in a sense, a reawakening of what is called the "baby" and the "helpless" part of the self. The initial ceremonies produce a kind of infantile dependence, which helps in rebirth, reorganization and the beginning of a new self. In effect, according to Jilek (1982), there is a revival of a "new human being, [and when] you come back . . . there is not to be evil thinking after they're through with you; all you think is I'm starting life all over again" (p. 66). What happens is a personality rebuilding that facilitates self-exploration in a totally different light.

In the new birth, people have a different, more powerful sense of self. The old self, which might have been addicted, diseased or confused, now with the help of the guardian spirit or animal spirit becomes stronger. The past falls away and only what is new is important. The effect is to teach rules of personal and social behaviour, indirect reinforcement of coercive group suggestion, the reinforcement of cultural pride (ancestral authority) and the reinforcement of cultural supernatural sanctions. However, despite this, there is a sense of equality as a factor in helping First Nations people to be new people.

The Traditional Healer

Those who lead ceremonies are often medicine men or women. A medicine man or woman can be of three types: priests, who perform ceremonies; storytellers, who pass on the legends and wisdom from the past; and healers, who use herbs or psychic medicine. However, only a healer would be a shaman, who is someone who can enter into another state of consciousness to heal or to divine some type of answer. Medicine men or women, as the name denotes, are powerful, but they are still different from a shaman. All shamans are medicine men or women, but not all medicine men or women are shamans. Interestingly, the word *shaman* comes from the Tungus language of Siberia and so is a word that is new to First Nations people of North America (Smoley, 1992). In Coast Salish society, there are two different classes of shaman. The greater shamans are those who have powers of clairvoyance, can cure the sick and control the ghosts and shadows of people. The lesser shamans are those who have the power to heal minor illnesses and deflect negative influences (Ashwell, 1989). Often, the lesser shaman is a woman who also practices midwifery.

Paramount to a shaman's training is an intimate knowledge of First Nations culture, values, traditional modes of conduct and methods of coping with illness. The practices are most often used to alleviate the distress of disease and restore harmony in people who are emotionally ill, physically ill or both. A shaman does not just rely on the past, however, but will introduce new ideas about sickness and healing practices borrowed from traditional or modern medicine. Shamans have an intimate knowledge of roots and herbs and their medicinal properties, knowledge that is gained through a teacher or through birth (Harner, 1980). Some Salish peoples believe that shamanistic skills are not developed but are present at birth. For others, long years of apprenticeship with a shaman is required to develop such skills.

Shamans employ a variety of ceremonies and methods in their repertoire of skills. They are expected to lead an exemplary life and are frequently required to provide demonstrations of their powers. According to Ashwell (1989), a shaman "has an animal helper who had been revealed to him [or her] in a dream during his [or her] days as a novice and this animal becomes his [or her] relative and could be invoked by him [or her] at any time when assistance was needed" (p. 70). Illness, physical or mental, is thought to be caused by an interference of harmony either through external forces (such as the winds, animals and ghosts) or through internal forces (such as the breaching of taboos). Shamans can heal using herbs, through divining or through specific healing ceremonies such as ritual sweat baths, drinking of herbs and so forth. Ashwell's (1989) description of a shaman working with a patient is quite revealing of how the Shaman enters the patient's world:

> The patient lay in a coma on rush mats inside the long house. The Shaman had first to make a diagnosis. He went into a spirit dance calling on his spirit helper to help him see what was afflicting the sick man. Everyone in the village had gathered to beat on the roof with poles to help him achieve his power. The [Shaman], masked and wearing a headdress of cedar bark and shaking his rattle, bounded in and danced around the patient. His helpers followed him repeating a song, until finally the Shaman went into a trance, showing that his spirit was with him. When he came out of it, weary and exhausted, he had full knowledge of what was causing the patient's ailment. (p. 71)

A Caution: Outside Interest in First Nations Helping

Smoley (1992) suggests that it is "natural that whites should look to Indians to revitalize their spirituality. Mainstream Judaism and Christianity have failed to kindle a spark in many earnest seekers raised in those traditions, and Eastern traditions, with roots in foreign lands, are sometimes difficult for Westerners to assimilate" (p. 84). Yet because of the history of exploitation, First Nations people are suspicious of white people's interest.

In particular, Natives have had potent negative experiences with anthropologists and others from the majority culture who claim knowledge about them. Even some Native spiritual leaders, who teach native spiritual ways, have been criticized by many of their own people for selling out to whites (Smoley, 1992). The rationale is that as outsiders, white people can never learn the teachings since the teachings are rooted in culture. To remove the teaching from its point of origin is to bring damage to it. Yet other Native spiritual teachers believe that those who have come close to the Earth can follow some of the teachings (e.g., vision quest and sweat lodge). However, some ceremonies and practices, such as the Ghost Dance or the Sun Dance, should not be open to outsiders. This does not preclude the use of these approaches in therapeutic intervention with First Nations clients. But such intervention should be done by those qualified to do it and done in a way that is respectful.

Conclusion

Many Native American clients have been so acculturated that the focus of therapy may be merely to reconnect them to a traditional system of belief and make sense of their lifeworld from a traditional perspective (Duran & Duran, 1996, p. 89). While reconnecting with culture is vital, Duran and Duran (1996) say that "for the most part the client must be able to adjust and work in a white environment as well as still maintain a sense of identity" (p. 89). Thus, sensitivity to the historical and political struggles of First Nations people is a must for those who are working with Indigenous people or who wish to work cooperatively with elders or traditional helpers. However, at the same time, the counsellor needs to empower clients to cope with the reality of the world. There are a number of healing practices that can be incorporated in counselling, but it is vital that the counselor use them in a respectful and sensitive manner. Consider that when one becomes respectful and sensitive to the land, then one can communicate with the spirits that inhabit the land and everything in it. What distinguishes First Nations helping approaches are the rituals, so full of cultural symbols that they in themselves have a healing affect. Symbols not only provide important meaning in ceremonies but also have a curative effect. Each act in a ritual is a reminder of humanity's relationship with the spirit world. For example, when Black Elk (1961) spoke, he described the four ribbons on his sacred pipe as representing "the four directions of the four spirits (e.g., the black one is for the west whence the thunder beings live to send us rain; the white one is for the north, whence comes the great white cleansing wind; the red one is from the east, whence springs the light and where the morning star lives to give men wisdom; the yellow for the south, whence come the summer and the power to grow). But these four spirits are only one spirit after all" (p. 39). Thus, when the pipe is smoked, the tobacco is smoked not as it is in white civilization, as an amusement or an addiction, but as an offering to the Great Spirit in the four directions.

Chief Dan George said, "there is a longing among all people and creatures to have a sense of purpose and worth . . . to satisfy that common longing in all of us we must respect each other" (1982, p. 11). Among many First Nations people there is the sense of a loss of control over their everyday lives. Many social initiatives that have been taken by the majority society to help them have reinforced feelings of powerlessness. Even many of the counselling methods that are standard in the helping profession are viewed as inappropriate for First Nations clientele (LaFromboise, Trimble & Mohatt, 1990). That is why using appropriate methods is important for counselling to be effective. According to Jilek (1982), what characterizes First Nations helping and learning, such as in the Salish spirit dance, is that it provides participants "with meaningful collective activity, ego-strengthening group support, and an opportunity for socially sanctioned emotional reaction" (p. 159). Yet the power of these ceremonies is that they bring about a sense of renewal or rebirth in their participants. It is not just the healing of a particular problem but the beginning of a new person. Thus, culture is an important ingredient in successful psychotherapy, particularly with those from Indigenous cultures.

Interestingly, the vision of Black Elk (1932) is a wonderful symbol of the re-emergence of traditional culture in the life of First Nations people in North America. The sacred hoop he spoke of is the restoration of the hoop of the nation after seven generations, which is the time we are living in. Finally, the words of Chief Seattle, a Squamish First Nations leader, epitomize what is basic in First Nations helping:

> Every part of this country is sacred to my people. Every hillside, every valley, every plain and grove, has been hallowed by some found memory or some sad experience of my tribe. Even the rocks, which seem to lie dumb as they swelter in the sun along the silent seashore in solemn grandeur, thrill with memories of past events connected with the lives of my people. The noble braves, found mothers, glad, happy-hearted maidens, and even the little children, who lived and rejoiced here for a brief season, and whose very names are now forgotten, still love these somber solitudes and their deep vastness which, at even-tide, grow shadowy with the presence of dusky spirits. Our dead never forget this beautiful world that gave them being. (Ashwell, 1989, p. 6)

References

Ashwell, R. (1989). *Coast Salish: Their art, culture, and legends*. Surrey, BC: Hancock House.

Atleo, U.E.R. (2004). *Tsawalk: A Nuu-chah-nulth world view*. Vancouver, BC: University of British Columbia Press.

Black Elk. *Black Elk speaks* (1932). As told through John Neilhardt. Lincoln, NE: University of Nebraska Press.

Campbell, M. (1979). *Half-breed*. Toronto, ON: Seal Books.

Dugan, K.M. (1985). *The vision quest of the Plains Indians: Its spiritual significance*. Lewiston, NY: Edwin Mellin Press.

Duran, E. (2006). *Healing the soul wound, counseling with American Indians and other native peoples*. New York, NY: Teachers College Press.

Duran, E., & Duran, B. (1995). *Native American postcolonial psychology*. Albany, NY: SUNY Press.

France, M.H. (2002). *Nexus: Transpersonal approach to groups*. Calgary, AB.: Detselig Enterprises Ltd.

George, D. (1982). *My spirit soars*. Surrey, B.C.: Hancock House.

Hammerschlag, C.A. (1988). *The dancing healers: A doctor's journey of healing with Native Americans*. San Francisco, CA: Harper & Row.

Hart, M.A. (2002). *Seeking Mino-Pimatisiwin: An Aboriginal approach to helping*. Halifax, NS: Ferwood Publishing.

Harner, M. (1989). *The way of the shaman*. New York, NY: Harper and Row.

Ibrahim, F.A. (1984). Cross cultural counseling and psychotherapy: Existential psychological perspective. *International Journal for the Advancement of Counseling, 7*, 59–169.

Jilek, W. (1982). *Indian healing: Shamanic ceremonialism in the Pacific Northwest*. Surrey, B.C.: Hancock House.

Katz, R., & Rolde, E. (1981). Community alternatives to psychotherapy. *Psychotherapy, Theory, Research and Practice, 18*, 365–374.

Kluckhohn, F.R., & Stodtbeck, F.L. (1961). *Variations in value orientation*. Evanston, IL: Row Peterson.

Lafromboise, T., Trimble, J., & Mohatt, G. (1990). Counseling intervention and American Indian tradition: An integrative approach. *The Counseling Psychologist, 18*, 628–654.

Locust, C. (1988). Wounding the spirit: Discrimination and traditional American Indian belief systems. *Harvard Educational Review, 58*, 315–330.

Medicine Eagle, B. (1989). The circle of healing. In R. Carlson & J. Brugh (Eds.), *Healers on healing* (pp. 58–62). New York, NY: Jeremy P. Tarcher/Putname.

Newman, P. (1989). Bold and cautious. *Maclean's*, July, 24–25.

Robbins, R. (2012). A Native American voice in multicultural psychology: Finding healing in an interpersonal tapestry. *Journal of Multicultural Counseling and Development, 40*(2), 93–103.

Roysircar, F. (2012). American Indians and culturally sensitive therapy. *Journal of Multicultural Counseling and Development, 40*(2), 66–69.

Smoley, R. (1992). First Nations spirituality. *Yoga Journal*, January, 84–89, 104–108.

Sterling, S. (1997). Skaloola the owl: Healing power in Salishan mythology. *Guidance & Counselling, 12*(2), 9–12.

Sue, D.W., & Sue, D. (2008). *Counselling the culturally different: Theory and practice* (5th ed.). New York, NY: John Wiley & Sons.

Trimble, J.E., & Hayes, S. (1984). Mental health intervention in the psychosocial contexts of American Indian communities. In W. O'Conner & B. Lubin (Eds.), *Ecological approaches to clinical and community psychology* (pp. 293–321). New York, NY: Wiley-Interscience.

Wachtel, P.L. (1977). *Psychoanalysis and behaviour therapy: Toward an integration*. New York, NY: Basic Books.

19

Yoga Therapy

Ancient Wisdom for Today's Body,
Mind and Spirit

Sarah Kinsley

Through the practice of yoga, the impurities of the mind/body/spirit are destroyed and the light of knowledge and wisdom dawns. — Iyengar

Most people have heard of yoga but do not realize its long history, deep psychological and philosophical roots and many specialized branches. This chapter will examine yoga therapy (Sanskrit: *yoga cikitsa*) within the field of counselling psychology. Therapeutic yoga is a holistic form of therapy used in both individual and group counselling sessions. More and more people are coming to know what yoga practitioners have known for millennia: yoga is a holistic way of being that, when practised, creates balance within oneself and allows for reunion with the universe. When Westerners visit India, they are often surprised to see people practising yoga by sweeping the temple floor, serving warm soup to the homeless or showering their *guru* (Sanskrit: weighty one, referring to a teacher) with fragrant rose petals. These traditional aspects of yoga are known as *karma yoga* (Sanskrit: yoga of action or service) and *bhakti yoga* (Sanskrit: yoga of devotion) (Feuerstein, 1997). For many *yogis* (Sanskrit: yoga practitioners), yoga is a way of life rather than something that happens three times a week on a sweaty rubber mat. In mainstream Western culture, yoga is often seen as an act of contorting oneself into a human pretzel in order to gain perfect physical fitness, yet yoga has a depth and diversity that spans across time and space. Powers (2009), yogi and co-founder of the Insight Yoga Institution, has observed that clients are usually drawn to yoga as a way to heal their bodies or minds. She notes,

Coming through the doorway of the body, people will eventually realize they have a mind that needs attention and, coming through the doorway of the mind, they eventually realize they have a body that is going to be either an obstacle or a support. Both directions point to their opposite. (cited in Miller, 2009, p. 53)

This remembering of the body/mind/spirit connection is being acknowledged by more and more clients and clinicians. In the West, many are beginning to understand through personal experience that yoga is not just something else to tick off their packed "to-do" list, but rather an art, a science and a form of psychosomatic therapy to be recognized and respected for its awesome diversity.

Purpose of Yoga

Yoga attempts to create a state in which we are always present—really present — in every action, in every moment. — Desikachar (1995, p. 3)

Yoga is an ancient wisdom tradition that is considered both an art and a science. The word *yoga* has its epistemological roots in the Sanskrit word *yuj*, which translates as "to yoke and to harness"; other applications of the word include *union, sum* and *conjunction* (Feuerstein, 1997). In the East, it is common practice to see farmers harnessing oxen to wagons to optimize their strength. The same concept can be applied to what happens when one practises yoga: one's body/mind/spirit is harnessed for optimal use. Employing various techniques such as meditation, physical postures (Sanskrit: *asanas)* and breathing exercises (Sanskrit: *pranayama)*, the yoga practitioner is able to free her/himself from the ego personality and its suffering. In yogic terms, this process — the ultimate goal of all yogas — is referred to as self-realization (Sanskrit: *atma-jnana)*, in which one attains liberation or enlightenment (Sanskrit: *moksha* or *purusha-jnana)* by transcending dualities and reuniting with the universe, thus realizing the true self (Feuerstein, 1997; Fields, 2001; Marotta & Valente, 2005). Feuerstein (2000), president of the Yoga Research and Education Centre in California, elaborates:

The purpose of yoga is nothing less than the complete transmutation of the subconscious mind though the transcendence of the ego mechanism, called "I maker" *(ahamkara)* or "I-am-ness." This goal, which coincides with enlightenment or liberation, is alien to the world view of modern psychology and psychotherapy. Nevertheless, humanist Abraham Maslow, and especially transpersonal psychology are more sympathetic toward the yogic idea of self-realization and also appreciate that ecstatic states *(samadhi)* are, as the yogis claim, suprawakeful rather than unconscious states. (p. 234)

History of Yoga

For thousands of years, the union within the individual body/mind/spirit and the universe has been sought by yogis who have diligently carried out experiments to investigate the nature of human experience. It is believed these experiments began over 5000 years ago in the Indus Valley, now modern-day Pakistan. Archaeologists have found soapstone carvings, dating between 3000 and 2000 BCE, of human figures in yogic poses designed for meditation, such as the lotus pose (Sanskrit: *padmasana*). Many spiritual practitioners (Sanskrit: *sadhus/sadhakas/sadhikas)* I met in India felt these practices were received by seers (Sanskrit: *rishis/rishikas)* as messages from the divine. Indologists believe these practices later migrated into what is now India and were passed orally among the Vedic priests, who later formalized the practices into rites and rituals (Cope, 2006; Hartranft, 2008).

Alongside the yogic traditions of the Vedic priests, another lineage of practitioners known as the *Sramanas* (Sanskrit: ones who strive) was blooming in the forests and caves of northern India. These seekers rejected the Vedic priests' authority over the sacred rites and rituals associated with yoga (Hartranft, 2008). The Sramanas sought to free themselves from the shackles of the imposed caste system and rule of the Vedic priests by seeking first-hand the meaning of life and what it means to be having a human experience (Cope, 2006; Hartranft, 2008). Over time, both the Vedic priests' and Sramanas' yoga practices began to inform the sacred texts of India. References to meditation, concentration and breathing techniques are found throughout the Vedas, especially in the Upanishads, the last of the Vedic texts, written about 3000 years ago (Cope, 2006; Feuerstein, 1997).

The *Yoga Sutras* by Sri Patanjali

About 2000 years ago, one of the rishis, Patanjali, is believed to have compiled a collection of yogic practices, the *Yoga Sutras* (Sanskrit: threads of yoga), containing centuries of oral tradition based on yogic investigation. The *Yoga Sutras* are a practical handbook for optimal human living aimed at finding liberation from worldly bondage by lifting the veil of illusion (Sanskrit: *maya*). According to the *Yoga Sutras*, the illusion is the perceived duality that believes the "I" is separate from everything else. This collection of 196 pithy aphorisms forms the base of what is known as *raja yoga* (Sanskrit: royal yoga), or classic yoga (Cope, 2006; Feuerstein, 1997; Saraswati, 1976). The definition of yoga is found in the second sutra (1.2): "*Yogas chitta vrtti nirodhah*" (Saraswati, 1976, p. 33), which means that yoga is a discipline that leads to the cessation of the fluctuations of the mind. The fluctuations come and go and include our thoughts, perceptions, feelings, imaginations, knowledge, memories and sensations. The third sutra (1.3) states that the seer will then be established in his or her essential nature: "*Tada drastuh svarupe' vasthanam*" (Saraswati, 1976, p. 42). In other words, by observing the nature of the mind, the yogi experiences that the fluctuations are not the ultimate truth we so often believe to be ourselves (Hartranft, 2008; Saraswati, 1976). The twelfth sutra (1.12) — "*Abhyasavairagy-abhyam tannirodhah*" — describes that one can obtain liberation by freeing oneself from attachment and having a consistent yoga practice (Saraswati, 1976, p. 58).

Over the centuries and across the world, many diverse yoga traditions have developed, but regardless of which guru is worshiped or which asana is practised, many schools come back to the *Yoga Sutras*. Therefore, raja, or classic, yoga as described in Patanjali's *Yoga Sutras* will form the theoretical basis for this chapter (Cope, 2006; Farhi, 2000; Stone, 2008).

The Eight Limbs of Yoga

Patanjali's *Yoga Sutras* contains the Eight Limbs of Yoga (Sanskrit: *ashtanga yoga),* which, when practised with dedication, lead to union with the true self. When one practises all eight limbs together, the practice becomes a complete way of living. The Eight Limbs of Yoga are as follows:

Yamas: Wise characteristics: *ahimsa* (non-violence), *satya* (commitment to truth), *asteya* (non-stealing), *brahmacharya* (sexual maturity) and *aparigraha* (non-grasping);

Niyamas: Codes of living soulfully: *shaucha* (purity), *santosha* (contentment), *tapas* (burning enthusiasm), *svadhayaya* (study of self and scriptures) and *ishvarapranidhana* (celebration of the spiritual);

Asana: Practice of the poses;

Pranayama: Breathing practices to control, move and expand *prana* (Sanskrit: universal life-force energy);

Pratyahara: Directing one's awareness and senses toward inner silence rather than toward things;

Dharana: Concentration or one-pointed focus;

Dhyana: Maintaining awareness in all conditions;

Samadhi: A state of higher consciousness in which the individual self exists in its own pure nature. (Cope, 2006; Farhi, 2000; Saraswati, 1976)

Hatha Yoga

Today, many styles of yoga practised are based on *hatha yoga* (Sanskrit: forceful yoga) (Feuerstein, 1997). In the history of yoga, hatha yoga is a relatively new form. It was not until the ninth and tenth century CE that texts started appearing with descriptions of physical postures (Sanskrit: *asanas).* In the *Yoga Sutras*, only 3 of the 196 sutras ever mention the term *asana,* and traditionally these three sutras referred to static meditation poses. Unfortunately, in the West today, hatha yoga classes are primarily focussed on asanas. These classes often lack emphasis on the practice of mindfulness and breathing exercises. It is paramount to clarify that yoga is a comprehensive practice, not an exercise class based on asanas. Asanas are one limb on the great tree of yoga and should be practised in combination with the other seven limbs. Phillip Moffitt, a senior yogi, reminds students that the one-pointed focus (Sanskrit: *dharana)* in asana practice should be observing the fluctuations of consciousness, such as our thoughts and sensations (personal communication, March 14, 2009).

One of the best-known manuals, *Hatha Yoga Pradipika* by Svatmarama Yogin (mid-fourteenth century CE), seeks to integrate the physical disciplines with raja/classic yoga (Feuerstein, 1997; Muktibodhananda, 1985). Classic hatha yoga contains asanas, pranayamas, *mudras* (Sanskrit: sacred seals or gestures), *shatkriyas* (Sanskrit: six purification exercises) and meditations. Hatha yoga is a strong form capable of purification and, when practised in conjunction with raja yoga, can lead to liberation and enlightenment (H. Lichty & J. Lichty, personal communication, October 4, 2009).

Is Yoga a Religion?

In Hinduism, yoga is one of six orthodox philosophies. Yoga is often linked to Hinduism when in fact many groups from all over the globe have been practising similar techniques that could also be referred to as yoga. Therefore, I believe it is limiting to refer to yoga solely as a philosophy found in Hinduism. I am not implying that yoga does not have strong roots in Hinduism, but rather that it also has diverse, ancient and far-reaching roots. This is an important distinction to make because many clients do not subscribe to a specific religion or spirituality such as orthodox Hinduism and therefore do not want to participate in something with religious or spiritual undertones in individual or group counselling sessions. When we work with clients, it is helpful to explain that yoga practices have been passed down through the centuries by various groups of people and that yoga continues to cross-pollinate the globe. For instance, yogis in China pay heed to traditional Chinese medicine (TCM) and Taoist philosophy, whereas Buddhist yogis in Tibet concentrate on deity visualizations as a means to connect with one's true nature. In many cases, I have observed clients weaving their own spiritual traditions and religious beliefs into yoga therapy sessions. In my experience, this has been successful because as Toew (2009) points out, "the ultimate aim of Yoga is reconnection with the Transcendental Self, which is synonymous with the universe rather than any particular deity, god, or goddess" (p. 3).

Yoga Therapy *(Yoga Cikitsa)* Defined

Do not seek to follow in the footsteps of the wise. Seek what they sought. — Basho

Historically, the practices of yoga were transmitted from guru to student on an individual basis. Yoga has always been inherently therapeutic. According to Sama Fabian, senior yogi and founder of the Aurolab Yoga Project, yoga was never used specifically as a therapy to correct a certain pathology or illness, but was viewed as a holistic practice aimed at reuniting the yogi with her/his inherently healthy, true nature (personal communication, November 26, 2009; Harper, 2001). Recently in the West there has been a rise in yoga geared toward therapy. Desikachar (1995), one of the world's foremost experts on yoga therapy and co-founder of the Krishnamacharaya Healing and Yoga Foundation, comments: "Yoga Therapy is being promoted as the wave of the future by many Yoga professionals, and in Yoga-related books and magazines. But, Yoga Cikitsa is not a new style or branch of Yoga: it is Yoga. Yoga is and always has been a holistic healing discipline" (n.d., para. 3) and has multiple purposes. Brownstein, an American physician who received a diploma in yogic education from the government of India, wrote, "In its ideal application, Yoga therapy is preventive in nature, as is Yoga itself, but it is also restorative in many instances, palliative in others, and curative in many others" (n.d., para. 10).

Ayurveda: *The Life Science of India*

Traditional yoga therapy often wove together the teachings of Patanjali's *Yoga Sutras* and elements of ayurveda (Sanskrit: life science/knowledge), the Indian system of healing (Frawley, 1999; Kraftsow, n.d.). According to Frawley (1999), founder of the American Institute of Vedic Studies, ayurveda is the science of health, awareness and self-realization. It is one of the oldest holistic systems of healing, often considered the sister of yoga, with documented beginnings reaching 5000 years into the past. The underlying principle of ayurveda is the understanding that health and well-being are established and maintained through the balance and counterbalance of the five elements (earth, fire, water, air and ether), which are present in the universe and within each human being. Ayurvedic philosophy believes humans are all part of the same universe, made up of the same elements, yet all have unique characteristics that define the individual. The centring in one's individuality gave rise to seeing human beings in terms of the three *dhatus* (Sanskrit: constitutions or humours) (Frawley, 1999; Feuerstein, 1997, J. Piercy, personal communication, August 17, 2008). The three dhatus are *vata* (air/ether), *pitta* (fire/water) and *kapha* (earth/water). Most people are a combination of all three dhatus with either one or two predominating. By understanding one's dhatu, or disposition, at the moment of birth and in the present, one can choose practices and a lifestyle that will allow for balance in all areas of one's life (Frawley, 1999; A. Olivera, personal communication, September 25, 2006; J. Piercy & A. Walker, personal communication, August, 17, 2008).

Traditionally, the client's prescription would have been based on ayurvedic principles based on the individual's dhatu (Feuerstein, 1997). Practices included pranayamas, asanas, mantras, cleanses, individualized meditations, karma yoga, bhakti yoga and diet and lifestyle recommendations.

Yoga Therapy: A Holistic Healing Practice

The practices of yoga therapy help clients find and maintain balance. The concept of balance is compatible with the Western medical model's concept of homeostasis (Evans, Sternlieb, Tsao & Zeltzer, 2009). Both seek to eliminate human suffering (Levine, 2002; Hamilton, Kitzman & Guyotte, 2006). The goal of these two systems appears similar, but yogis have always measured balance or homeostasis in a broader sense. Feuerstein (1997) clarifies:

> Yoga psychology is therapy, or healing in the broadest sense of the word. However, whereas modern psychotherapy has grown out of the clinical treatment of cases that medicine was unable to help, Yoga from the beginning has been a system of spiritual transformation, intended to restore the individual to primordial wholeness rather than mere physical and mental health. (p. 233)

Yoga therapy acknowledges the multi-dimensional nature of human existence, taking into account the anatomical, physiological, emotional, intellectual and spiritual dimensions of an individual (Farhi, 2006; Kepner, 2003). The ancient yogis referred to these dimensions as the *koshas* (Sanskrit: sheaths): five layers, sheaths or bodies that serve as a road map to human beings. They are the *annamaya kosha* (Sanskrit: physical body), *pranamaya kosha* (Sanskrit: life-force body), *manomaya kosha* (Sanskrit: mental body), *vijanamaya kosha* (Sanskrit: wisdom body) and *anandamaya kosha* (bliss body) (Feuerstein, 1997; Rae, n.d.). Rae, yogi and founder of Samudra: Global School of Living Yoga, comments,

"From the *kosha* perspective, Yoga helps us bring body, breath, mind, wisdom, and spirit (bliss) into harmony. Like a tapestry, the *koshas* are interwoven layers" (para.1).

Researchers are increasingly using the Biopsychosocial (BPS) model of health found in Western medicine to understand the multi-faceted and interconnected benefits of yoga. A recent study done at the University of California gathered empirical evidence of the physical, psychological and spiritual effects of yoga practice. By approaching the study from a BPS perspective, the researchers honoured the ability of yoga therapy to benefit the various layers within one's being (Evans et al., 2009). Many studies on the efficacy of yoga therapy address only one aspect of health — for example, yoga therapy for depression or yoga for back pain — whereas the above-mentioned study bridges the BPS benefits that have been shown to occur simultaneously from the practice of yoga, thus allowing readers to understand the mind/body/spirit relationship among pain, stress and illness (Evans et al., 2009, p. 1).

The ancient yogis observed and experienced the mind/body/spirit connection for centuries. We hope Western medical and psychological studies are now making the same connection as documented in the study by Evans et al. (2009): "Positive psychological functioning is likely to lead to improved physical functioning, especially in patients experiencing chronic pain and illness" (p. 8). The appeal of using a multi-faceted approach to healing echoes a statement in the Old Testament: "Man does not live by bread alone." We are complex beings who crave a meaningful life that involves more than meeting our basic needs of bread and water. Historically, all cultures have had techniques, belief systems and codes for living a meaningful, healthy life. Yoga serves as a worthy example that has stood the test of time and also space as it continues to migrate across the globe.

Yoga: A Mindfulness-Based Therapy

The mind alone is the cause of bondage and liberation for human beings. Attached to things, it leads to bondage. Emptied of things, it is deemed to lead to liberation.
— Amrita-Bindu-Upanishad

Before I describe the practices involved in a yoga therapy session, it is necessary to explore the term *mindfulness*. Mindfulness has been described as "awareness without judgment of what is, via direct and immediate experience" (Sanderson, 2003, p. 34). Yoga as a whole is a mindfulness-based practice (Segal, Williams & Teasdale, 2002). All limbs on the path are geared toward re-awakening to the true nature of things. Through yoga practices, one learns to pay attention without judging the experience. The study by Evans et al. (2009) elaborates: "This focus on body, mind, and breath in the present moment can then free attention to explore ways of minimizing stress, disability, and pain" (p. 9). The concept of mindfulness is not new but has been used for thousands of years. Mindfulness-based practices in the form of active concentration meditations and contemplations are found in many spiritualities and religions. I believe we are hardwired to be mindful, that mindfulness is our natural state of being; therefore, all beings can practise this innate, albeit buried, skill.

The Power of Observation

When examining the concept of mindfulness, we can look into the roots of yoga and Buddhism. The Sanskrit word *cit* connotes awareness or conscience and "refers to the Transcendental Self [Sanskrit: *purusha*] that continuously perceives the contents of the mind without being involved in the mental processes" (Feuerstein, 1997, p. 73). The key when practising mindfulness is to be aware without attachment and judgement. By practising mindfulness, clients can begin to observe the contents of the mind just as they would observe the night sky full of stars. The stars are akin to all the thoughts, feelings and sensations one experiences. The empty, open and clear space of the night sky may serve as a metaphor for the transcendental self, a place of stability, health and connection to all things. By seeing beyond the stars, clients begin to understand they are much more than their thoughts, emotions, memories, sensations and senses. They begin to remember the night sky and the stars are not only made of the same elements but are inseparable. In other words, form (stars and all phenomena) and emptiness (space) are one and the same (L. Heaton & P. Higgins, personal communication, February 5, 2009). At the Kalachakra for World Peace in 2004, His Holiness the 14th Dalai Lama gave a talk on the cultivation of objectivity through mindfulness-based practices and reminded the audience that becoming as objective as possible (i.e., not identifying solely with the stars or fluctuations of the mind) is one of the most important elements to awakening and obtaining enlightenment in this lifetime (personal communication, May 12, 2004).

Self-Awareness and Mindfulness

Mindfulness is a tool clients can use to develop self-awareness. With self-awareness comes a sense of relief from feeling like a prisoner in a self-created and often times delusional view of reality that is fuelled by one's thoughts. Mindfulness teaches us that we do not have to believe everything we think. Clients may experience a powerful metamorphosis when they realize they are not ruled by their thoughts, emotions and sensations. These fluctuations in the field of awareness often include craving and grasping at objects, people or situations to which people are attached (Sanskrit: *raga)* and resisting what they feel aversion to (Sanskrit: *dvesha)* (Feuerstein, 1997). This cycle of attachment and aversion is one of the root causes of suffering in both yoga and Buddhist philosophies. Mindfulness is the first step toward breaking the cycle.

Increasing one's level of self-awareness positively correlates with increasing one's ability to self-regulate in times of stress (Hamilton et al., 2006). This turning inward helps us to awaken. Clients are often operating on automatic pilot and are not aware of their actions and moreover that they have the innate power to choose their actions and reactions (Kabat-Zinn, 1990). Mate reminded an audience that "without consciousness there can be no choice," in reference to those struggling with addiction (personal communication, July 30, 2008). From that place of consciousness, we are able to make choices rather than living on automatic pilot, making the same unhealthy choices we have made for years. We contain within us the power to change and to heal. Kabat-Zinn (1994) elaborates: "Meditation helps us wake up from this sleep of automaticity and unconsciousness, thereby making it possible for us to live our lives with access to the full spectrum of our conscious and unconscious possibilities" (p. 3). Practising mindfulness allows humans to dwell in the here and now (Dass, 1971).

Self-Acceptance and Mindfulness

Inherent in mindfulness-based therapies are the practices of self-acceptance. One of the commonest misconceptions of mindfulness-based practices is that practitioners' ultimate goal is to rid themselves of thoughts; in reality, the goal is to become aware of them. Mindfulness does not imply ignoring or pushing away thoughts, emotions and sensations (the fluctuations); rather, it invites observation that will eventually show that fluctuations will pass in time like all things. The goal of practising mindfulness is not getting from point A to point B but rather dwelling in non-judgemental awareness at point A. Mindfulness creates a space, and within that space lies the freedom to make choices about how to respond to the next craving or the long line at the grocery store or a messy divorce settlement. It is from this place of clear awareness that one can begin to have a different relationship with thoughts that come and go. The attitude of acceptance applies not only to thoughts but also to emotions about both positive and negative events in life. Through psycho-education, clients learn that thoughts and feelings are a normal and natural part of life. Thich Nhat Hahn (1975), a Buddhist teacher and founder of Plum Village, believes awareness enables one to work with the thoughts rather than become overwhelmed by them.

It is helpful to introduce the concept of ahimsa in relation to the self. Mainstream Western society often places high value on pushing oneself, and it is vital that both the client and therapist listen to their intuition and accept themselves just as they are. If one learns to practise compassion and non-violence on the yoga mat, one can learn to practise it in other areas of life. Ahimsa starts with accepting yourself and then can radiate outwards to all your relationships. Miller, a yogi, psychologist and co-founder of the International Association of Yoga Therapy (IAYT), notes, "We are not here to change ourselves but to meet ourselves where we are" (as cited in Raskin, n.d., p. 2). Eventually some practitioners will transcend the ego personality, uncovering their true nature and inherent oneness with the world and reaching liberation, but first there must be acceptance of the present moment. It should be noted that in some rare cases, some practitioners have reached liberation at a very young age during their first experience with yoga. And in other cases, some have reached liberation through a near-death experience; but for the majority of us it will take some time on the mat.

Relationships and Mindfulness-Based Practices

It is by meeting ourselves both on and off the yoga mat that we develop a level of peace within ourselves. That inner peace then has the ability to radiate outward to all we are in relationship with. Sakyong Mipham Rinpoche (2004) teaches, "Meditation practice is the basis of our sanity, of our happiness; it is the basis of sound and fruitful relationships with our friends and family, who themselves will benefit from our personal practice" (p. 11). The importance and interconnectedness of our relationships is echoed in the phrase "all my relations," used in many Aboriginal communities in North America to acknowledge that we are in relationship with each other and the planet. This phrase implies that one's actions and reactions may affect all our sentient and non-sentient relationships (H. France, personal communication, September 6, 2009).

Principle Guidelines of a Yoga Therapy Session

Before we can find peace among nations, we have to find peace inside that small nation which is our own being. — Iyengar

Theoretical Background of Yoga Therapy

Each yoga therapist will structure a session differently depending on the needs of the clients and the style of yoga therapy the therapist practises. The following information is modelled on my private practice of yoga therapy (padma yoga therapy), based on my yoga therapy training in both India and Canada. Padma yoga therapy also includes elements found in Phoenix Rising Yoga Therapy (PRYT), founded by Michael Lee. PRYT combines the tenets of yoga, such as asana and pranayama, with the non-directed dialogue based on the work of therapist Carl Rogers. Roger's (1948) person-centred approach emphasizes the importance of the therapist having unconditional positive regard for the client. Lee explains, "The therapist acts as a sounding board, repeating much of what the student says to allow them to stay with their own train of thought" (as cited in Raskin, n.d., p. 4). PRYT sessions allow clients to recognize their own body's wisdom and get to the source of emotions that may be causing aches and pains on many levels (Raskin, n.d.). By using the Rogerian psychotherapeutic approach, clients are able to become more sensitive and self-aware. Lee comments, "One of the primary ways of speeding up our evolution as human beings is to increase awareness, to become the witness, to observe oneself without being caught up in what one observes" (cited in Raskin, n.d., p. 4). The therapist listens to the witness who observes the fluctuations in the field of awareness such as thoughts and sensations. The therapist then mirrors what the client shares back to the client, allowing for deep reflection. This work is possible only in a loving environment co-created by client and therapist (Weintraub, 2004).

Components of a Yoga Therapy Session

Yoga therapy can be practised on a one-to-one basis or in a group setting. Yoga therapists and clients design therapeutic practices based on the clients' concerns regarding body/mind/spirit. Kepner (2004), executive director of the International Association of Yoga Therapists, describes the elements of a complete yoga therapy session: "Sessions may include, but are not limited to, *asana* (postures), *pranayama* (breath and energy work), meditation, sound and chanting, personal ritual, and prayer. Teaching may also include, but is not limited to, directed study, discussion, and lifestyle counselling" (p. 98). Yoga therapy might also include homework, inviting clients to practise an element of yoga between sessions.

Environment for a Yoga Therapy Session

Yoga therapy should be practised in a clean, calm and quiet space with enough room for both client and therapist to lie down on yoga mats. Some therapists choose to play relaxing music and light candles, while others prefer an environment akin to a Western medical clinic. Regardless, the room should be comfortable and at a suitable temperature for the climate. Yoga therapy can also be practised out of doors, allowing clients to connect to the powerful yet soothing energy of the Earth. If need be, yoga therapy can be practised in a chair, swimming pool or hospital bed. All that is required is the breath of life and an open mind. Clients are encouraged to wear comfortable clothing and refrain from eating a heavy meal at least two hours before class because some asanas involve twisting and inverting the body.

Intake Process

As with other forms of therapy, yoga therapists begin with the assessment to determine the best treatment plan for the client. Many therapists complete an assessment with the client. Working together invites transparency and can empower the client through co-creating the therapeutic goals. During an intake session, the therapist describes the purpose of yoga therapy and its possible benefits and risks. In my experience, with the assistance of a trained therapist, most people are able to participate in yoga therapy to some degree, but it is crucial to note when it is not suitable, especially in a group setting. Despite good intentions of the therapist, the class might simply be too threatening, especially for those who have experienced severe trauma (T. Black, personal communication, May 21, 2009; Weintraub, 2004). In an intake session, it is critical for the therapist to inquire about the client's past physical, mental and spiritual concerns. The intake session is the beginning of an ongoing dialogue and is a perfect time for clients to ask questions and raise concerns. As with other forms of therapy, it is necessary for clients to sign an informed consent form and be aware of the therapist's personal insurance policy, especially regarding issues of liability because physical movement is usually incorporated into a yoga therapy session.

Honouring the Inner Teacher

One of the key premises of this style of therapy is the importance placed on one's internal teacher. Yoga teacher Farhi (2006) refers to this as a client's "internal reference point" (p. 39). Yogis have long believed that wisdom comes from within and knowledge comes from outside sources. Beginning with the intake session, the client is informed that yoga therapy is about shared inquiry. Clients are encouraged to take an active role in their healing process and to make the yogic teachings relevant with the support of a qualified, empathetic yoga therapist.

Yoga Therapy for Individuals

Yoga therapy was historically imparted on an individual basis, allowing the guru to tailor the session to meet the client's needs. Working one-to-one with a client allowed not only for oral transmission of the teachings but also for energetic transmission, which, in my experience, is the more powerful vehicle for knowledge transmission. This form of teacher–student relationship, common in yoga, has the ability to foster a deep relationship between therapist and client. Both participants may enter a deep state of relaxation. This state of being is associated with entering the right brain. The client's right brain and the therapist's right brain can then attune within the present moment where healing may take place. The success of this process demands both therapist and client be rooted in the present moment (C. Traer-Martinez, personal communication, December, 16, 2009). Additionally, studies in the field of counselling psychology have found a positive correlation between a strong therapeutic relationship and successful outcomes in therapy (T. Black, personal communication, October 10, 2010; Roger, 1946).

Each yogic prescription will be unique, based on individual needs; for instance, two clients might self-report symptoms traditionally associated with depression, but one may benefit from vigorous physical activity such as 10 rounds of sun salutations (Sanskrit: *surya namaskar)* to elevate metabolic and heart rates and allow energy to flow, whereas another client might hold an asana for five minutes, directing healing prana into the heart centre (Sanskrit: *anahata cakra)* (Evans et al., 2009; Feuerstein, 1997).

A Padma Yoga Therapy Session for Individuals

The following is an outline for an individual yoga therapy session. It is important to note that sessions with each client will be different based on the unique needs of the client at the time of therapy.

> **Check-in**: Sessions in padma yoga therapy begin by checking in with the client and getting an update on the current health of body/mind/spirit. This can be done through traditional talk therapy, art therapy and drama therapy or with journaling exercises. It can be helpful for clients to set an intention or a goal for the session as positive intentions have shown to be beneficial for healing (Saraswati, 1976). The therapist may simply ask the clients to think about one reason they have come to yoga therapy. The reason may then be simplified into one word, which clients can repeat to themselves throughout the course of the therapeutic relationship and in other parts of their lives when they find themselves in need of self-soothing.
>
> **Pranayama**: In yoga therapy, the breath serves as the connection through body/mind/spirit and is employed throughout the session. Pranayama, the fourth limb on the Eight Limb Path of yoga, contains thousands of breathing techniques. Pranayama is especially useful at the beginning of a session to help clients "arrive" in their body/mind/spirit. Clients are encouraged to stay with the breathing throughout the practice and notice changes in their breath that might serve as a signal for distress, in which case they could modify or further direct their breath into an area of the body using their intuition and the guidance of the therapist. The practice of *nadi shodhana* (Sanskrit: purification of the channels), or alternative nostril breathing, enables clients to alternate breathing out of one nostril while blocking the other. This invites bal-

ance between the left channel (Sanskrit: *ida nadi)* and right channel (Sanskrit: *pingala nadi)*, circulating energy through the body via the central psycho-energetic channel (Sanskrit: *sushumna nadi)* where the seven principal energy centres (Sanskrit: *cakras* — wheels or vortices) reside. Some believe the cakras roughly correspond to the endocrine system in Western medical anatomy (Feuerstein, 1997).

Grounding exercises: Next clients may begin some gentle grounding exercises to relax. These allow clients to settle into the session by practising mindfulness of their inner and outer environments. A common grounding exercise used in mindfulness-based therapies, including yoga therapy, is a body scan. Clients bring awareness to their breath and then systematically concentrate and observe any sensations in each body part as directed by the therapist. This practice has been found to have a calming effect on the body/mind/spirit. The body scan helps clients move into a parasympathetic nervous system response where they are able to rest and digest rather than dwell in the stress fight/flight or freeze pattern (Kabat-Zinn, 1990). In some cases, once the sensation is observed, clients can begin to work with the area or simply release the area, dissolving long-held tension. For example, clients may not even realize they clench their jaws until they take a moment of mindfulness to focus on their face. These releases through asana, pranayama and intention may require additional time to process with the therapist. This can take place within the current session and in future sessions. It is vital that yoga therapists are professionally trained so they are qualified to serve clients when they are processing and also to know when it is not appropriate to process (for example, in cases where clients may be retraumatized by retelling a traumatic event) (T. Black, personal communication, May 12, 2009; Lee, 1997).

Asanas: Once the client is grounded and relaxed, the therapist may suggest practising a sequence of assisted asanas based on the individual's constitution and current life situation. These postures range from extremely gentle and restorative asanas to quite vigorous flowing sequences. The most important thing when practising asanas is the clients' comfort level. Clients should always be invited to modify or ask for modifications/adjustments if anything does not feel intuitively right. It is the role of the therapist to check in with the client to ensure there is no pain. Yoga therapists often encourage clients to find their "edge," a place where they are challenged both mentally and physically, but not strained. Each asana is entered with mindfulness and awareness of breath. Clients are encouraged to tune in and listen to what is present on all levels without judgement. Therapists may ask clarifying questions, following the principles of Rogerian person-centred therapy. These questions can be regarding inner experiences ranging from bodily sensations to thoughts and feelings. In some cases, this work may facilitate deep emotional and physical releases.

Mantras: Along with asanas, a session may include individualized meditations that concentrate on a mind tool (Sanskrit: *mantra)*. A mantra is a sacred sound that may consist of a sound, syllable, word or sentence that has the power to evoke transformation (Frawley, 1999). The mind is known for wandering, so employing a mantra may help clients enter the present moment, not pushing away their thoughts but rather directing their attention to the task at hand. The most commonly used mantra is the sacred monosyllable *om*, symbolizing the Absolute. Yogacharya Vishwas Vasant Mandlik, founder of Yoga Vidya Guruluk in Nasik, India, believes *om* was the sound the universe made when it came into being (personal communication, March 15, 2004). In Hinduism and Buddhism, *om* is often chanted at the beginning and end of practice to help slow down the breathing process while calming the nervous system, providing the body a vibrational massage and uniting the community of practitioners. Some clients choose a mantra to repeat each time they inhale and exhale, such as *peace* on the inhale and *release* on the exhale (J. Lichty, personal communication, December 18, 2009). Some clients choose to repeat a sentence of their choice (such as "I am at peace"), while others prefer a sacred mantra from their spirituality or religion. These mantras often represent one of the many gods and goddesses that make up that plethora of revered beings. Regardless of which mantra is used, it is critical that clients intuitively use a mantra that works for them in and out of sessions as a centring device. I have found it helpful to use the same mantra over time.

Guided meditation and visualization: A yoga therapy session may employ guided meditations and visualizations to help clients relax and become attuned with their inner environment. It can be helpful to establish an image of a safe place with the client. This is a place the client can go in times of stress when she/he requires self-soothing. The safe place can be real or imaginary, and it is helpful if the client returns to the same place each time (T. Black, personal communication, May 25, 2009). Along with safe-place visualizations, many clients benefit from visualizations that concentrate on self-healing, using their innate energy to bring about healing on the physical, emotional and spiritual levels. For instance, a client may visualize a warm, white light being placed on an area of the body that requires healing. This form of visualization can be empowering because clients are reminded they are their own strongest and most effective healer (Weintraub, 2004).

Yoga nidra: *Yoga nidra* is an ancient form of meditation in which the client is first led through a mental body scan of 61 points and is then instructed to set a *sankalpa* (Sanskrit: resolve, determination or good intention) (Saraswati, 2001). Employing a sankalpa encourages clients to think positively, thus helping to rid themselves of negative mental patterns. Clients are encouraged to impregnate their sankalpas with passion, meaning and faith. The sankalpa is stated internally three times in the present tense. It is believed the practice of yoga nidra resonates at a deep level within one's being, allowing for positive change to occur as one taps into deeper layers of consciousness. Once the sankalpa is set, clients are led through a visualization that enables them to journey internally to a certain place or time, or explore extremes such as the sensations of heaviness or lightness (Saraswati, 2001). Yoga nidra concludes by returning to the original sankalpa.

Final relaxation: Yoga therapy sessions close with a final relaxation pose known as *shavasana* (Sanskrit: corpse pose). In shavasana, the client lies still and allows the work of the session to be integrated into all five koshas of their being. It is recommended that shavasana be between five and thirty minutes long. Some therapists might employ gentle ayurvedic or other forms of massage to relax the client or to help alleviate specific complaints. Once clients have completed shavasana, they can return to their original intention. The session usually closes with the chanting of *om* and a moment of mindfulness when clients can observe how they feel in body/mind/spirit.

Debriefing and yogic psycho-education: Debriefing may include various approaches to talk, art, drama and/or journaling psychotherapy. It is also a time when therapists can provide yogic psycho-education regarding how practices may be affecting one's being. This process may be empowering for clients as they begin to understand the art and science behind this ancient wisdom tradition. Therapists trained in ayurveda may also recommend diet, lifestyle and herbal supplement advice. In addition, some therapists recommend keeping a journal of observations, highlighting the client's reactions to the session and any observations between sessions she/he would like to bring up with the therapist in the next session (Raskin, n.d., p. 2).

Integration with daily life: Many therapists encourage clients to integrate mindfulness-based practices into the rest of their lives. For some, this may mean practising deep breathing while on the highway; for others this may involve creating a routine they can practise daily on their own. It is often said that yoga is not something one does but something one practises. The practice on the yoga mat is really preparation for life off the mat.

Yoga Therapy for Groups

> Be enthusiastic about the nobleness of every person and everything will become noble. — Sri Ananda Acharya

Today in the West, yoga therapy for groups is increasing in popularity in many settings, including schools, hospitals, rehabilitation centres, substance withdrawal centres and disordered-eating centres. Yoga therapy is also employed for various groups such as mindfulness-based anxiety and depression groups, and groups for those who have experienced trauma. First and foremost, clients should be reminded of the importance of listening to their body/mind/spirit and not pushing themselves beyond their edge, which is more likely to occur in group situations where they may compare themselves and feel the need to keep up with their neighbours. Group yoga therapy sessions contain many similar components found in individual sessions. There are, however, some components unique to group yoga therapy.

Group Environment

When practising yoga therapy in a group setting, it is vital to review the necessity of confidentiality and its limitations to create a safe container, allowing clients to participate fully in a non-judgemental environment. One of the most important roles of the yoga therapist is to create and maintain an atmosphere of spaciousness (Weintraub, 2004), where all members feel respected. To facilitate the community connection, practise is best done in a circle, either on yoga mats or in chairs. By creating a womb-like environment, therapists acknowledge that the emotional body is as important as the physical body and moreover that the two cannot be separated in the process of yoga therapy. Weintraub (1995) refers to this as a "holding environment" and states how vital this space is when clients are in turmoil. Practising yoga in a group might be the only safe place clients have: being in a warm, loving space where one is able to be authentic in the company of other beings may be more helpful than all the self-help books in the world.

Group Yoga: A Community-Based Approach to Healing

A special element found in group yoga therapy is the importance placed on the cultivation and maintenance of community. When practising the Eight Limbs of Yoga, from asanas to meditation, one is able to connect with other beings on deep and meaningful levels. Many clients report feeling isolated and alienated; therefore, creating a healthy community is a vital element of group sessions. The power of social well-being should not be underestimated, as at our essence we are social creatures.

Practising yoga in a group allows clients to connect on a different level than is experienced within traditional talk-therapy groups. Clients are invited to share space without feeling the pressure or the need to talk about difficult subjects, such as the depression they feel or their latest biopsy report, if they choose not to. At Calgary's Tom Baker Cancer Centre, patients receiving chemotherapy had the opportunity to participate in a study through the University of Alberta, which offered patients gentle yoga sessions with cancer-specific components added into the session. Practices included asanas geared toward relieving nausea (a common side effect of chemotherapy). One participant commented that she looked forward to sessions because they were a place to relax and bond with others (Mick, 2009). In yogic terms, the community feeling created in group yoga therapy sessions is referred to as *sat-sangha* (Pali/Sanskrit: community of truth seekers/in the company of the real), which traditionally occurred in the company of a guru or saint in order for the teachings and blessings to be transmitted orally and more often subtly via the energy body. Today, sat-sangha, or simply *sangha*, has come to mean a gathering of like-minded people, of truth-seekers, with whom one can be completely relaxed and authentic (Weintraub, 2004).

An Example of a Padma Yoga Therapy Session for Groups

Check-in, grounding, pranayama and asana: Before the group session begins, it is crucial for the therapist to provide a space for clients to voice any concerns, in private, that may affect their ability to participate. Group sessions will commonly start with a focussed check-in — for instance, asking clients to share one thing they are grateful for in the past week. After the group has completed some grounding exercises, often using pranayama to tune into the present moment, the therapist then leads the group through some gentle asanas, encouraging mindfulness of movement. It is important that the therapist continually scans the room, looking for any signs of distress and providing assistance when needed. If possible, it would be helpful to have another therapist in the room, ideally one who knows the clients and is familiar with the basic tenets of yoga therapy.

Guided meditation: As I mentioned above, with sessions for individual clients, therapists may use guided meditations and visualizations to facilitate the cultivation of mindfulness and relaxation. *Metta* meditation (Pali: loving-kindness) is often used in group settings because it involves wishing others well. This meditation has roots in Buddhism but is often found in yoga therapy sessions. The object is to cultivate loving-kindness to oneself, friends, family, teachers, strangers and even those one is in conflict with. Finally, loving-kindness is sent to all sentient beings, from the cedar trees to the great humpback whales, and to all spirits in all realms of existence. By practising metta meditation, one radiates loving-kindness toward oneself and the rest of the world. I have found it very useful for clients who are experiencing anger or have self-reported low self-esteem (C. Sled, personal communication, October 11, 2007; Salzberg, 2002).

Final relaxation, debriefing and yogic psycho-education: Once the group has practised the final relaxation pose of shavasana, either in a chair or on a yoga mat, it is time for debriefing. Debriefing is paramount because yoga practices may stir up fluctuations in emotions, sensations and memories. The debriefing may be in the form of a closing circle, in which each group member takes a turn sharing how she/he felt during practice or after the practice. Group members should always be given the opportunity to pass if they do not wish to share. It might be appropriate to ask people to share one part of the session they enjoyed and one part they would like to change next time. Today, the 1970s concept of a cathartic release, or "letting it all out" in group therapy, is usually seen as unproductive and possibly damaging to some clients (T. Black, personal communication, May, 2009). Therapists should either offer time for each client to debrief in an individual session or ensure clients have resources available in the community. The group debriefing provides an opportunity for yogic psycho-education. Clients can also use this time to ask questions and raise any concerns they may have.

Group Yoga Therapy in University and College Settings

Group yoga therapy sessions are becoming common in many university and college counselling centres. A successful example is the Yoga for Stress Management Program (YSMP), a skill-based group offered to undergraduate students at the Central Michigan University's Counselling Centre. The program teaches students self-awareness and self-acceptance through mindfulness-based practices, thus "providing preventive, psychotherapeutic, and developmental assistance to students" (Milligan, 2006, p. 181). Group sessions include asanas, pranayamas, mindfulness meditations and yoga philosophy and psychology.

Group yoga therapy is also being offered as part of self-care courses for graduate students in the various helping professions such as nursing and counselling, as burnout and compassion fatigue are commonly found in these professions. Master's students in the counselling program at Montana State University have had the option of taking for credit a 15-week, mindfulness-based stress-reduction course called Mind/Body/Spirit Medicine and the Art of Self-Care. The course has a two-fold purpose of familiarizing students with mindfulness and its relevance in the field of counselling and providing students with practical tools for self-care. The course includes in-class practices (yoga, meditation and qigong) along with relaxation techniques. A study by Schure, Christopher and Christopher (2008) based on this program found that counselling students enrolled in the course experienced positive physical, emotional, attitudinal or mental changes, increased spiritual awareness and interpersonal changes on both personal and professional levels.

Yoga Practices in Conjunction with Other Psychotherapeutic Approaches

On this path no effort is wasted, no gain is ever reversed; even a little of this practice will shelter you from great sorrow. — *Bhagavad Gita*

Techniques found in yoga therapy can be woven into both individual and group sessions tailored to suit the needs of the client or group. Incorporating a few yoga therapy techniques into counselling sessions may be useful for clinicians who are interested but are not necessarily certified yoga teachers/therapists or practitioners themselves. Thousands of examples of meditation and grounding exercise are available online, on DVDs, in books and in local community settings. There are many useful practices that teach clients tools to manage stress and suffering; examples include, but are not limited to, breathing exercises, simple movements and guided meditations. These techniques may be employed at the beginning of a session to help clients ground and enter the therapeutic space. When working with a group, therapists may use grounding and breathing techniques to create group cohesion by focussing on a common activity that promotes relaxation and comfort in participants. Yogic techniques may also be used at the end of a session to help clients integrate the session on a deeper, more holistic level.

Mindfulness within Therapy Sessions

Therapists may also use the principles of mindfulness throughout the practice; this is especially useful when clients are experiencing intense fluctuations of the mind such as strong emotions. In addition to talking about their experiences, clients are invited to feel the experiences, possibly locating where they sense the emotion, thought or memory dwelling within their being or by labelling the experience with a particular colour or texture. Boudette (2006) points out, "With some eating-disorder patients, words are not enough. Yoga offers a non-verbal, experiential adjunct to talking therapy that provides an opportunity for connection with the physical body and the inner experiences" (p. 170). Ultimately, all therapy should be mindful, as bringing awareness to one's inner and outer environments is, for many, the first step toward reaching therapeutic goals.

Recommendations for Therapists Interested in Yoga Therapy

Therapists should experiment with mindfulness-based practices on their own before introducing them to clients. This may mean signing up for a yoga class at the local community centre, trying out a yoga nidra CD or participating in an individual yoga therapy session. Interested therapists might want to explore the mindfulness-based approaches to psychotherapy such as the Hakomi method, acceptance and commitment therapy, dialectical behaviour therapy, mindfulness-based stress-reduction workshops, mindfulness-based cognitive therapy, somatic experiencing, mindfulness yoga training with the Insight Yoga Institute and integral therapy by Ken Wilber. I would also highly recommend exploring the traditional teachings and practices of yoga through books, classes and/or retreats.

Benefits of Yoga Therapy

> Whatever we're doing could be done with one intention—which is we want to wake up, we want to ripen our compassion, and we want to develop our ability to let go. Everything in our lives can wake us up or put us to sleep, and basically it's up to us to let it wake us up. — Chodron

Many of the benefits associated with yoga therapy have been woven into the chapter thus far; therefore, this section will describe some of the most profound benefits of yoga therapy.

The Bio-Psychosocial (BPS) Benefits of Yoga Therapy

In the study by Evans et al. (2009,), researchers created a conceptual model to demonstrate how

> structural/physiological benefits (musculoskeletal functioning, cardiopulmonary status, automatic nervous system (ANS) response, and endocrine control system), spiritual benefits (compassionate understanding and mindfulness), and the psychosocial benefits (self-efficacy, coping, social support and positive mood) are interconnected to each other and all lead to enhanced functioning (energy and sleep, quality of life, strength and fitness, and reduced pain, stress, and disability). (p. 3)

As yoga therapy increases in popularity, we may well see similar studies documenting the ability of yoga to affect multiple systems simultaneously. The study by Evans et al. provides a perfect example:

Changes in brain chemistry such as GABA (gamma amino butyric acid) levels and stress hormones such as cortisol may be associated with reduction in depressive or anxious symptoms and enhanced physiological functioning. Likewise, increased mindful awareness may promote coping within the psychological domain, providing a psycho-spiritual mechanism for enhanced well-being. (Evans el al., 2009, p. 11)

Yoga Therapy and Spirituality

In addition to the mind–body connection, many are beginning to acknowledge the spiritual aspect of yoga therapy (Welwood, 2002). Working definitions of spirituality include "a system of beliefs or values (which can be religious or not), life meaning, purpose, and connection with others or a transcendental phenomena" (Sessanna et al. as cited in Evans et al., 2009, p. 12). In counselling psychology and integrated medicine, researchers, clinicians and clients are starting to acknowledge spirituality as an integral aspect of health. This is documented in a growing number of quality-of-life assessments, studies, approaches to therapy and techniques that all deem spirituality an important marker of health and general well-being. As mentioned, clients can choose to connect their yoga practice with their religious/spiritual beliefs or can practise secularly. A qualified yoga therapist will ensure all clients are comfortable, not pushing her/his personal beliefs onto clients.

Benefits of Pranayama

Many of the associated interconnected benefits of yoga are related to the practices of the pranayama — the fourth limb. Pranayama is also woven into the seven other Limbs of Yoga (Feuerstein, 1997). In essence, prana is our life force — the deciding factor between life and death. Without awareness of the breathing process, one is not truly practising yoga. The breath, a powerful tool, serves as the sacred bridge within body/mind/spirit, allowing clients to cultivate awareness and acceptance. Some pranayama techniques are used to energize while others have a calming effect and therefore activate the parasympathetic nervous system (Brown & Gerbarg, 2009).

All pranayama practices are designed to facilitate balance and union within the practitioner. The breath is a sacred portal through which imbalances in the stress-response system can be regulated (Brown & Gerbarg, 2009). In order to pay attention to the breath, one must be in the present moment. Well-known practices include "Breathing deep into the abdomen, breathing against airway resistance, breathing into physical postures, holding the breath at different parts of the breath cycle, and breathing alternately through both nostrils or one nostril" (Brown & Gerberg, 2009, p. 56). Stukin (2003) states, "This [being in the present] creates a calming effect because each breath is simply an experience of the moment, acknowledged without judgment. Thus, habitual responses and defences, which patients have established in years of drug use, attempted detoxes, and relapse, are bypassed" (p. 2). By learning to work with the breath through various techniques, clients unleash the powers (Sanskrit: *siddhis*) of yoga (Feuerstein, 1997).

Yoga Therapy and Emotions

Many Westerners have an image of yoga as an experience where one automatically and always radiates bliss and joy, but this is not always the case for many, at least not initially. The term *sat cit ananda* (Sanskrit: ultimate reality is eternal non-changing awareness and bliss) describes the state of being that can be unearthed with yoga practice. Weintraub (1995) clarifies that at first this state may feel like an altered state of being, but in fact, it is all humans' birthright. She reminds practitioners that they come to the mat with years (some believe lifetimes) of stored experiences that yoga can help release. Clients are often unaware that they hold strong emotions until they release them in sessions. Through these releases, transformation may occur and ultimately may reunite clients with their natural, blissful, nondualistic state of being.

Many yoga therapists, counsellors, psychologists and medical practitioners have said that everything one has ever experienced is stored within the koshas in the form of impressions (Sanskrit: *samskaras).* Body-centred psychotherapies, including yoga therapy, acknowledge the presence of psychosomatic reactions and symptoms by incorporating movements and body-centred meditations. Miller believes, "Yoga is an exquisite form of bodywork that eliminates the residue that has become lodged in the tissues . . . deep releases, be they physical, energetic, or emotional, come when the student is ready" (as cited in Weintraub, 1995, p. 20). Miller reminds therapists that it is unethical for the therapist to try to cause an emotional release, which may involve words, tears, sweat, heat or other somatic reactions. He also encourages therapists and clients to remember that change and growth will unfold naturally. In other words, therapists and clients alike should remember to trust the process (Levine, 1997; Raskin, n.d.).

The Power of the Present

Lastly and most importantly, yoga therapy encourages clients to slow down and live in the present moment — quite rare in today's world. It allows individuals and groups a chance to move into a more peaceful natural rhythm where they can become aware of their precious life and the sacred environment we call home. Unfortunately, so many feel disconnected in our fast-paced "iWorld." Yoga gives us a chance to a live up to the label human *beings,* rather than human doings. The peace found in practising yoga on the mat can be transferred off the mat. Clients can learn to practise yoga as a healthy, connected way of being in the world.

Conclusion

> For as long as space endures and the world exists, may my own existence bring about the end of all suffering in the world. — Shantideva

We can learn from the last 200 generations of seekers who have sought wholeness and a life free from suffering (Feuerstein, 2002). Through yoga therapy, human beings can learn to transform themselves and attain the true goal of yoga: union (Chopra, 1997; Feuerstein, 1997). When they learn that they contain within themselves the power to heal themselves, it is an empowering and life-altering moment (Stukin, 2003). Yoga therapy moves away from pathologizing and sticking labels on the client to a more compassionate approach, which believes we are all naturally whole (Duran, 2006; Welwood, 2002). Yogis have a great deal in common with Michelangelo, who believed his role was to free the forms that already existed inside the stones he so gracefully sculpted. With yoga practice it is the same: we are unearthing the wholeness that has been buried under the veil of illusion (Cope, 2006). It is our sole purpose as humans to unveil our true nature and help others and the planet along the way.

> May all beings know their true selves and be free from the suffering and the roots of suffering
> May all beings be free from inner and outer dangers
> May all beings rest in calm abiding
> Namaste

References

Basho, M. (n.d.). No title. Retrieved from http://quotationsbook.com/quote/41518

Boudette, R. (2006). Question and answer: Yoga in the treatment of disordered eating and body image disturbance: How can the practice of Yoga be helpful in recovery from an eating disorder? *Eating Disorders*, 14, 167–170.

Brown, R., & Gerbarg, P. (2009). Yoga breathing, meditation, and longevity. *Annals of the New York Academy of Sciences*, 1172, 54–62.

Brownstein, A. (n.d.). *Contemporary definitions of yoga therapy*. Retrieved from http://www.iayt.org/site_Vx2/publications/articles/defs.htm

Chodron, P. (1994). *Start where you are: A guide to compassionate living*. Boston, MA: Shambhala.

Chopra, D. (1997). *Overcoming addictions: The spiritual solution*. New York, NY: Three Rivers.

Cope, S. (2006). *The wisdom of yoga*. New York, NY: Bantam.

Dass, R. (1971). *Remember, be here now*. New York, NY: Crown.

Desikachar, T.K.V., & Desikachar, K. (n.d.). *Contemporary definitions of Yoga therapy*. Retrieved from http://www.iayt.org/site_Vx2/publications/articles/defs.htm

Desikachar, T.K.V. (1995). *The heart of yoga: Developing a personal practice*. Rochester, VT: Inner Traditions International.

Duran, E. (2006). *Healing the soul wound: Counselling with American Indians and other native peoples*. New York, NY: Teachers College.

Evans, S., Sternlieb, B., Tsao, J., & Zeltzer, L. (2009). Using the biopsychosocial model to understand the health benefits of Yoga. *Journal of Complementary and Integrative Medicine*, 6(1), 1–24.

Farhi, D. (2006). *Teaching yoga: Exploring the teacher–student relationship*. Berkeley, CA: Rodmell Press.

Fields, G.P. (2001). *Religious therapeutics: Body and health in yoga, ayurveda and tantra*. New York, NY: State University of New York Press.

Feuerstein, G. (1997). Shambhala encyclopaedia of yoga. Boston, MA: Shambhala.

Feuerstein, G. (Ed.). (2002). *Yoga gems*. New York, NY: Bantam Books.

Frawley, D. (1999). *Yoga and ayurveda: Self-healing and self-realization*. Twin Lakes, WI: Lotus Press.

Hamilton, N., Kitzman, H., & Guyotte, S. (2006). Enhancing health and emotion: Mindfulness as a missing link between cognitive therapy and positive psychology. *Journal of Cognitive Psychotherapy: An International Quarterly*, 20, 123–134.

Hanh, T. N. (1975). *The miracle of mindfulness*. M. Ho, Trans. Boston, MA: Beacon Press.

Hartranft, C. (2008, July). Hatha raja: Yoga's path to liberation. *Shambhala Sun*, 47–51,100–102.

Kabat-Zinn, J. (1990). *Full catastrophe living: Using the wisdom of your body and mind to face stress, pain and illness*. New York, NY: Delacorte.

Kabat-Zinn, J. (1994). *Wherever you go there you are*. New York, NY: Hyperion.

Kepner, J., Knox, H., Lamb, T., & Zador, V. (2004). *Standards for yoga therapists?* Retrieved from http://www.iayt.org/site_Vx2/publications/articles/standards.htm

Kepner, J. (2004). *Standards for yoga therapists*: Progress to date. Retrieved from http://www.iayt.org/site_Vx2/publications/articles/Yogaprogress.htm

Kepner, J. (2003). Alternative billing codes and yoga: Practical issues and strategic consideration for determining "What is yoga therapy?" and "Who is a yoga therapist?" *International Journal of Yoga Therapy*, 13, 93–99.

Kornfield, J. (n.d.). *Doing the Buddha's practice*. Retrieved from http://www.shambhalasun.com/index.php

Kraftsow, G. (n.d.) *Contemporary definitions of yoga therapy*. Retrieved from http://www.iayt.org/site_Vx2/publications/articles/defs.htm

Levine, P. (1997). *Wakening the tiger: Healing trauma*. Berkeley, CA: North Atlantic Books.

Lee, M. (n.d.). *Contemporary definitions of yoga therapy*. Retrieved from http://www.iayt.org/site_Vx2/publications/articles/defs.htm

Lee, M. (1997). *Phoenix Rising yoga therapy: A bridge from body to soul*. Deerfield Beach, FL: Health Communications.

Marotta, A., & Valente, V. (2005). The impact of yoga on the professional and personal life of the psychotherapist. *Contemporary Family Therapy*, 27(1), 65–79.

Mick, H. (2009). A calm for cancer. *Globe and Mail*. Retrieved from http://www.theglobeandmail.com/life/health/a-calm-for-cancer/article1273796/

Miller, A. (2009). Yoga with insight: A profile with Sarah Powers. *Shambhala Sun*, 49–53, 95.

Miller, R. (n.d.). *Contemporary definitions of yoga*. Retrieved from http://www.iayt.org/site_Vx2/publications/articles/defs.htm

Milligan, C.K. (2006). Yoga for stress management program as a complementary alternative counselling resource in a university counselling centre. *Journal of College Counseling*, 9, 181–187.

Mitchell, S. (2000). *Bhagavad Gita: A new translation*. New York, NY: Random House.

Muktibodhananda, S. (1985). *Hatha Yoga Pradipika*. Bihar, India: Bihar School of Yoga.

Nespor, K. (2001). *Yoga and coping with harmful addictions (Parts 1 & 2)*. Retrieved from http://www.Yogamag.net/archives/2001/esep01/adds1.html

Raskin, D. (n.d.). Emotions in motion. *Yoga Journal*. Retrieved from http://www.Yogajournal.com/practice/1215

Rea, S. (n.d.). You are here. *Yoga Journal*. Retrieved from http://www.Yogajournal.com/wisdom/460

Rogers, C. (1946). Significant aspects of client-centred therapy. *American Psychologist*, 1, 415–422.

Sakyong Mipham Rinpoche. (2004, January). Personal practice. *Shambhala Sun*. 30–31.

Salzberg, S. (2002). *Loving-kindness: The revolutionary art of happiness*. Boston, MA: Shambhala.

Saraswati, S. (1976). *Yoga nidra*. Bihar, India: Yoga Publications Trust.

Saraswati, S. (1976). *Four chapters on freedom: Commentary on the Yoga Sutras of Patanjali*. Bihar, India: Yoga Publications Trust.

Schure, M., Christopher, J., & Christopher, S. (2008). Mind–body medicine and the art of self-care: Teaching mindfulness to counselling students through yoga, meditation, and Qigong. *Journal of Counseling & Development*, 86, 47–56.

Sanderson, C.J. (2003). *Dialectic behaviour therapy: Frequently asked questions*. Retrieved from www.behavioraltech.org.downloads/dbtFaq_Cons.pdf

Segal, Z.V., Williams, J.M.G., & Teasdale, J.D. (2002). *Mindfulness-based cognitive therapy for depression*. New York, NY: The Guilford Press.

Sell, C. (2003). *Yoga from the inside out*. Prescott, AZ: Hohm Press.

Stone, M. (2008). *The inner tradition of yoga: A guide to yoga philosophy for the contemporary practitioner*. Boston, MA: Shambhala.

Stukin, S. (2003). The anti-drug for anxiety. *Yoga Journal*, 3, 1–5. Retrieved from http://www.Yogajournal.com

Toew, D. (2009). *Transpersonal psychology and the chakras*. Unpublished paper, University of Victoria.

Weintraub, A. (2004). *Yoga for depression: A compassionate guide for reliving suffering through yoga*. New York, NY: Broadway Books.

Welwood, J. (2002). *Toward a psychology of awakening: Buddhism, psychotherapy, and the path of personal and spiritual transformation*. Boston, NY: Shambhala.

20

Transpersonal Counselling

A Multicultural Approach

Gary Nixon & M. Honoré France

Now came a rapture so intense that the universe stood still, as if amazed at the unutterable majesty of the spectacle. Only one in all the infinite universe! The All-loving, the Perfect One! (Bucke, 1923)

THE EXPERIENCE OF WHAT MUSLIMS CALL the Supreme Identity is an experience central to every major religion, such as Hinduism, Buddhism, Taoism, Christianity, Islam and Judaism (Wilber, 1977). Maslow (1968, 1971), the founding father of transpersonal psychology, called for the recognition of the higher or transcendent possibilities occurring at the further reaches of human nature. He suggested that, after a person satisfied physiological, safety, belongingness and self-esteem needs, the next step inevitably led to the process of self-actualization. However, Maslow (1968) went one step further by establishing a need for self-transcendence within the process of becoming self-actualized. He called the impulse for self-transcendence a "meta-motivation" that is intrinsic to human nature. In his view, this point necessitated the development of a fourth force of psychology, which he called "transpersonal psychology"; this was "transpersonal, transhuman, centered in the cosmos rather than in human needs and interests, going beyond humanness, identity, self-actualization, and the like" (pp. iii–iv). Cortwright (1997) summarized transpersonal psychology as a blending of the wisdom of the world's spiritual traditions with the learning of modern psychology where "by moving across traditional personal psychology to the larger spiritual context, the individual self moves out of its existential vacuum into a wider dimension to which the world's spiritual teachings point" (p. 10). The transpersonal perspective assumes that our essential nature is spiritual, consciousness is multi-dimensional and humans have valid urges toward spiritual seeking, expressed as a search for wholeness, through deepening individual, social and transcendent awareness.

Transpersonal psychology and counselling have often been referred to as the "fourth force" in psychology in that they are quite different from traditional approaches in orientation, scope and strategies (Sheikh & Sheikh, 1989). The literal definition of transpersonal is quite simple: beyond the personal. In a sense, one might say that it is beyond the traditional constructs of traditional psychology's conception of personality. Walsh and Vaughan (1993) stress that the transpersonal is a developmental process in which one goes beyond the self-limitation of the physical, psychological, social and spiritual, to a point of self-realization of unlimited potentialities. Another important consideration that reflects the holistic idea is expressed by Duran and Duran (1995), who stress that "a postcolonial paradigm would accept knowledge from differing cosmologies as valid in their own right, without their having to adhere to a separate cultural body for legitimacy" (p. 6). Transpersonal experiences may be defined as experiences in which the sense of identity of self extends beyond the individual or personal to encompass wider aspects of humankind, life, psyche or cosmos. Thus, the transpersonal counselling approach significantly moves away from cultural-bound, Eurocentric values to a more multicultural philosophy. In essence, the transpersonal theory moves away from the subject–object split and toward a merging of subject and object. Now there is inclusion, more choices and a radical move away the logic of Rene Descartes, which is embedded in European thinking, and to a more holistic thought embracing a variety of world views. The idea that all things are interrelated makes little sense in a world where a "butterfly in Beijing that flaps its wings and causes a storm on the other side of the world has become a reality" (Coxe, 2003, p. 36). There are contradictions in our institutions, which affect who and what one is; these are in essence a creation of what goes on in the world. Thus, humanity cannot escape the contradictions in the world, just as one cannot escape cultural upheavals that occur a continent away.

Humanity is left with the duality to life that produces energy yet creates problems. There are solutions in the "game of life," but how does one play the game when the fixed order of the world is constantly changing? As counsellors we live with the contradictions in our lives and grope for answers and solutions, which challenge us to go beyond what we have done before. Culture plays a major role in what we are and how we help others cope with the new challenges that face everyone in a world growing smaller and smaller. Approaches that use only a Eurocentric world view cannot explain what happens and are not comprehensive enough to embrace the human condition. Neither can counsellors separate the spirit, mind, emotions and physical world as was customary with previous theories of counselling. The transpersonal theory combines all of these elements with "culture friendly" strategies that can work with a variety of people. Vaughan (1991) stresses that we have mapped transpersonal development beyond what was formerly considered the ceiling of human possibility and have found preliminary evidence of common psychological and spiritual developmental sequences across traditions. (p. 94)

Extensive work has now been done in the area of transpersonal psychology and counselling in Western psychology, integrating wisdom traditions from many cultures with the latest advances of modern psychology. We have seen the development of Ken Wilber's spectrum of consciousness and integral approaches, Michael Washburn's recent innovation centred on Jung's analytical psychology, A.H. Almaas's transformation of narcissism approach, Robert Assigioli's psychosynthesis, Stanislav Grof's holotropic therapy, as well as existential, psychoanalytic and body-centred transpersonal approaches (Almaas, 1996, 2008; Assagioli, 1973; Cortwright, 1997; Grof, 1985, 1988; Hixon, 1978; Small, 1982; Walsh & Vaughan, 1980, 1993; Washburn, 1988, 1994; Whitfield, 1984; Wilber, 1977, 1986, 1990, 1995, 1997, 2000, 2006).

Cortwright (1997) observes that transpersonal psychology has, over time, shifted its emphasis to include not only the high end of human experience but also the personal realms and ordinary consciousness as well. In this way, transpersonal models of development offer the opportunity to recognize the full range of human issues in recovery. Maslow's hierarchy of needs progresses through lower-order needs of physiological, safety, belongingness, love and self-esteem before moving on to self-actualization and self-transcendence (Maslow, 1968). Whitfield (1984) pointed to the hierarchy of consciousness in accordance with the "perennial philosophy," as coined by Huxley (1945), to describe the core areas of agreement between the world's spiritual traditions. Similarly, Small (1982) described seven levels of chakras, or energy centres, based on Eastern systems of growth, that need to be worked through during the journey of transformation.

More recently, Almaas (1996) has developed a model of growth based on a "transformation of narcissism." This model has exciting implications for long-term growth, as typical issues such as self-preoccupation and psychic inflation can be worked through in the counselling process. Pivotal steps of the transformation of narcissism include such themes as discovering the empty shell and fakeness of our typical narcissistic stance; becoming aware of the narcissistic wound; working through the great betrayal of self to self; working through narcissistic rage; and falling into the great chasm of being and discovering, rather than a deficient emptiness that has been long avoided, a place of loving beingness and the realization of the essential identity. Almaas's model, with its focus on moving from reliance on the false self to relaxing into essence, highlights many of the developmental issues of the quest for wholeness and moving beyond ego that are embraced in many spiritual traditions. We will now turn to Wilber's development model of the "spectrum of consciousness" for a more detailed examination of the transformation of self-preoccupation and ego, and the movement toward integration and wholeness.

Wilber's Spectrum of Consciousness Approach

Wilber (1977, 1986, 1990, 1995, 1997, 2000, 2006) has developed a spectrum-of-consciousness developmental model that incorporates both conventional psychology and contemplative traditions. What is exciting about the Wilber model is that it offers a description of growth issues and problems at each level as well as possible interventions to be used. Wilber's (1977, 1986, 1990, 2000) spectrum-of-consciousness model maps out ten principal stages of the psyche in a developmental, structural, holistic, systems-oriented format. Wilber (1986, 2000) synthesized the initial six stages from cognitive, ego, moral, and object relations lines of development of conventional psychology, represented by such theorists as Piaget (1977), Loevinger (1976) and Kohlberg (1981); the final four transpersonal stages come from Eastern and Western sources of contemplative development such as Mahayana, Hinduism, Vedanta, Sufi, Kabalah, Christian mysticism, yoga and Zen. Over time, in reaction to severe criticism and the need to be more comprehensive, Wilber (2000, 2006) has acknowledged limitations to conventional lines of development and integrated alternate perspectives such as Gilligan's work on female moral development (Gilligan, 1982), as well as the spiralling aspect of development through streams and waves rather than levels and lines captured in such theories as Kegan (1982) and Cook-Greuter (1990) and spiral dynamics set out by Beck and Cowan (1996). Spiral dynamics heavily influenced Wilber's later work (1995, 2000, 2006), in which he more readily captured social–cultural aspects through a four-quadrant integral approach integrating singular and plural perspectives with internal and external points of view. While Wilber (2000) has broken the development pathway into more than 20 separate lines of development, we will focus on his main description of self-development across cultures as outlined in a number of his major works (Wilber, 1977, 1986, 1990, 1995, 2000).

Pre-Ego Stages

According to Wilber (1986, 2000), the first three stages of development (each a pre-personal ego stage) are *sensoriphysical*, *phantasmic–emotional*, and *rep-mind*. The first stage — sensoriphysical — consists of matter, sensation and perception. Pathologies at this level need to be treated with interventions at the physical level. In addictions, the physiology of the chemically addicted person is stabilized by sending the person to detox to get the drugs out of his/her system. Treatment at this level can also include medication, an exercise regime, yoga, diet or any other physical remedy.

In the second stage — phantasmic–emotional — the individual begins to develop emotional boundaries of self through the development of a separated–individuated self (Wilber, 1986, 2000). The self–other orientation can be problematic when the self treats the world as an extension of itself (narcissistic) or is constantly invaded by the world (borderline). Psychodynamic interventions focus on structure-building techniques such as in-object relations and psychoanalytic therapy.

The third developmental stage — the rep-mind — represents the development of the intrapsychic representational self (Wilber, 1986, 2000). In Freudian psychology, this is typified by the development of the id, ego and superego and the resulting intrapsychic conflicts between these parts such as inhibition, anxiety, obsession, guilt and depression. Interventions focus on intrapsychic resolution of these internal conflicts through re-integration of repressed, disassociated or alienated aspects of being (Wilber, 1986, 2000).

Ego Stages

The pre-personal stages are followed by *rule/role*, *formal–reflexive* and *vision–logic* stages of development that represent the mature ego developmental phase. The rule/role stage — Wilber's fourth stage of development and first personal ego stage — is highlighted by individual development of rules and roles to belong socially. Because problems at this level are experienced as a fear of losing face and losing one's role, interventions tend to centre on changing dysfunctional rules, roles and scripts (Wilber, 1986, 2000). Therapies at this stage, such as family therapy, cognitive therapy and narrative therapy, uncover false scripts.

The next personal stage, and fifth overall, formal–reflexive, represents the development of the mature ego (Wilber, 1986, 2000). At this stage, identity issues need to be explored and deconstructed. A person needs to move beyond a narrow identity to begin to embrace a global or world-centric perspective. False identities — such as being a "success" or "self-reliant" — and negative identities — such as being a "loser," "victim" or "hopeless case" — need to be let go of. Here, one lets go of one's personal stories to embrace what is essential (Katie, 2002).

The final stage of typical ego development — the final ego stage and sixth overall stage — is the vision–logic, or existential, stage. Here, the integrated body–mind confronts the reality of existence. This level represents the development of the existential self. To deal with an individual's encounter with existence, existential therapy encourages authenticity, coming to terms with one's own finitude, fundamental self-responsibility, intrinsic meaning and self-resoluteness (Wilber, 1986, 2000; Yalom, 1980).

Transpersonal Ego-Transcendence Stages

Wilber (1986, 2000) goes beyond the existential realm to describe four stages of transpersonal contemplative development integrated from Western and Eastern sources of contemplative development. The first stage beyond the mind–body integration of the existential level, and seventh overall, is the *psychic*. This stage symbolizes the level of the yogis (Wilber, 1986, 2000). In this phase, cognitive and perceptual capacities, which used to be narrowly personal and individualistic, can expand to a more pluralistic and universal perspective. There are many potential pitfalls at this stage of preliminary psycho-spiritual development, such as psychic inflation and "the dark night of the soul." People describe experiencing the high of the "pink cloud" syndrome of early recovery and then falling back into depression (Grof, 1993).

The next transpersonal stage, and eighth overall, is the *subtle*, referred to as the level of the saints (Wilber, 1986, 2000). Here, subtle sounds, audible illuminations and transcendent insight and absorption can be experienced. In certain traditions, such as Gnosticism and Hinduism, this is the stage of direct phenomenological apprehension of personal deity-form (Wilber, 1986, 2000). This realm has also been referred to as pseudo-nirvana and refers to the realm of illumination, rapture and transcendental insight (Goleman, 1988). People can have wonderful transformational "white light" experiences at this level, yet struggle to integrate these experiences into everyday life.

The following stage is the *causal*. This is the level of the sages and is the realization of the unmanifest source or transcendental ground of all the lesser structures (Wilber, 1986, 2000). In various traditions, it is referred to as the abyss (Gnosticism), the void (Mahayana Buddhism) or the formless (Vedanta) (Wilber, 1986). People can prematurely experience this level of cosmic consciousness and struggle to integrate this "formless" awareness into everyday life.

The final stage is *nondual* and in various traditions refers to losing one's attachment to the separate self and integrating the suchness of all levels of existence as consciousness reawakens to its prior and eternal abode as absolute spirit (Wilber, 1986, 2000). Here, manifest form is integrated with the unmanifest formless and has been called by various traditions *sahaj* and *bhava samadhi*, the state of *turiya*, absolute and unqualifiable "consciousness" as such, Aurobindo's "supermind," Zen's "One Mind," and *Brahman-Atman*, to name a few of the different traditions' terms for abiding nondual awareness (Wilber, 1986).

Elements of Growth and Transformation in Transpersonal Thought

To develop and stabilize into the higher levels and stages of consciousness, the client will need to use various practices and pathways. Walsh and Vaughan (1993) stress that the transpersonal approach brings a "recognition of old wisdom" (p. 1); what they mean is that the basic concepts and practices are new only to the West. For example, altered states of consciousness have been part of many ancient and traditional approaches from Asia and Native peoples from the western hemisphere. The transpersonal approach embraces and incorporates folk medicines and practices from a variety of traditions. Altered states of consciousness can be achieved by focussing on perceptual sensitivity, thus producing more clarity. As such, perceptual processes vary with state of consciousness in predictable ways. Functionally, this outcome made it possible to achieve specific states of awareness not known in traditional psychotherapy. For example, according to Lueger and Sheikh (1989), higher levels of awareness and consciousness were used in the ancient traditions of "Hinduism, Buddhism, and Sufism [expanded by transcending] in order to connect with the real or cosmic self and to establish a genuine sense of unity with nature" (p. 226). The usual state of consciousness is less than optimal; thus, increasing one's ability to expand one's consciousness increases one's knowledge about the forces in the self and the environment. In a sense, one achieves understanding and insight, or perhaps *satori* (enlightenment), when one's alienated or phony self *(maya)* is discarded. One might even refer to a neurosis as the illusory distortion of perception, which, when one becomes more balanced, is not needed and is discarded. Awakening from *maya* ("illusion") and experiencing liberation is the aim of the transpersonal approach to counselling. Thus, through psychological healing, one can become enlightened. In that sense, the transpersonal approach "is not seen as successful adjustments to the prevailing culture, but rather the daily experience of that state called liberation, enlightenment, individuation, certainty or gnosis according to various traditions" (Fadiman, in Leuger & Sheikh, 1989, p. 227).

The mechanism for achieving higher levels of consciousness is to become more aware of the self and one's surroundings. In addition, meditation helps one recognize the flow of thoughts and fantasies for what they are (this is called dehypnosis). There is insight into how one's behaviour has been shaped by societal forces, and so one can "let go" of any illusions that heretofore have conditioned one to act and believe in a certain way. Consequently, the paradoxical non-goal goal is a release of the conscious self and a new knowledge that might be called "enlightenment" or abiding in "nondual awareness."

In surveying many healing traditions, Walsh and Vaughan (1993) put forth a number of elements that they called "the heart of the art of transcendence" (p. 2). The following is an expanded and augmented descriptive list of elements that intertwine with well-being: awareness, compassion, emotional transformation, ethical training, meditation and refocussing, motivation and wisdom.

Developing Awareness

As a process, awareness sounds similar to introspection, but it is different. The difference is that introspection is a way of looking inward to learn something. It is a process whereby one tries to figure out something or to make sense of it. In doing this, there is a review and analysis of behaviour. In the end, one is perhaps, as Polster (1966) suggests, distracted:

> by expectations of failure or success. We are so prejudiced in favor of one behaviour over another. We are prejudiced . . . in favor of taking over other behaviour, so we are prejudiced in favor of relevance over irrelevance . . . and given these prejudices, we might not be fascinated with people who don't fit those prejudices. (p. 9)

This does not mean that people detach themselves from what is going on around them and become introspective. While detachment from time to time is comfortable and even protective, in the end it is very destructive.

Awareness is a process of noticing and observing what one does, how one feels it, what one's thoughts are and what one's body sensations are. These thoughts and sensations are like passing scenery, which unfurls like a panorama that people experience as it occurs. Consider the following perspectives on what it means to become aware:

> In Freud's narrow view, it meant calling into awareness repressed impulses and instinctual desires. In Fromm's view, the average individual is only half awake; he or she is conscious of fictions but has the potential to become conscious of the reality behind the fiction. Consequently, to make the unconscious conscious means to wake up, to know reality. (Sheikh & Sheikh, 1989, p. 115)

In the ordinary movement of life around one, it is possible to observe the silences, which allow one to hear what is not said and to feel the energy flow around unseen. It is all a pattern or process. In the same way that people listen to what others say to them, people notice how others say it and experience all the sensations, feelings, thoughts and physical reactions. When this happens, there is total contact that allows one to be open to all kinds of possibilities. This contact is the process of awareness.

Two aspects of this process assist in understanding and putting into perspective what is happening: meaning and boundary awareness. Meaning allows one to keep up to date with oneself. At any given time one knows how one feels and what one thinks. Meaning does not have to be processed before one can act. People are people; they act as themselves. Boundary awareness involves the interaction people have with their environment. Boundaries become clear, and one reacts more spontaneously to one's environment. One sees more, experiences more and is aware of more in the surroundings. If people try to split feelings and thoughts, they will find that it is difficult, if not impossible. The focus of the transpersonal approach is to help people to reawaken to the natural rhythm between awareness and the frequent interruptions that exist in day-to-day activities in the environment. When one starts to think and analyze, it is impossible to be aware of what is going on. To attend simultaneously to two things with the same degree of awareness is very difficult: there will always be something missed. If one can just be aware of what is happening and let it flow, one will experience it, not in parts but as a whole.

Arasteh and Sheikh (1989) emphasized that, in the healthy person:

> experience and behaviour overlap and inner and outer expression are the same; but in many cases, behaviour is the rationalization or inhibitor of experience — it is a cover. Experience has an organic and illuminary nature, whereas, behaviour is characterized by conditioning. It is experience, not behaviour, that produces change and, at the same time, strengthens one's sensitivity. (p. 150)

This means that, if people are more aware, they can learn to trust their natural processes. If they ignore these processes or abuse their body, they know that they will destroy it; but if they work with the body and not against it, it will give back to them and help them. As people grow in awareness, they will sense more of the wisdom of their whole being. For example, when people jog, they know that once they overcome the limitations they put on themselves, their jogging takes on a natural rhythm. They seem to glide as they jog. Their mind is not telling their body what to do, for if they let their mind take over, they will feel tired. They will think about finishing. Their rhythm will falter and finally they will want to rest, but when they jog without thoughts, they become aware of all the things around them. They are in a state of awareness, open to new insights, experiences and understandings. In the Sufi tradition, awareness is a final rebirth that starts people on the road to living in a new light:

> Awareness may come to a person suddenly, or it may develop gradually. Yet awareness is not enough. The seeker must cease unsuitable past behaviour: he or she must experience repentance, decide to reform and finally cleanse the self of enmity and cruelty. (Arasteh & Sheikh, 1989, p. 157)

Becoming Compassionate

> To have an open heart that lets the waters of compassion, of understanding, and of forgiveness flow forth is a sign of a mature person. . . . Then we . . . will walk towards greater freedom and let waters flow onto others, healing them and finding healing through them. (Vanier, 1998, p. 102)

From a transpersonal perspective, compassion for others is one of the most empowering characteristics we can wish for. To be compassionate means to wish others not to suffer the indignities of pain and sorrow, whether socially, intellectually, psychologically or spiritually. Compassion that emanates from the heart and embraces all of nature's creatures is the transcendental sense that unites us with everything in existence. When we empathize, we are separate; when we feel compassion that goes beyond ourselves, we are joined with the cosmos. That happens when we realize that we are not a separate ego or self but part of a collective identity that unites us. Brazier (1995) says that:

> Compassion is to understand the other person's subjective world without stealing anything. Stealing means taking over . . . In compassion one sees through the eyes of the other, and feels with their heart, without any private agenda. (p. 195)

In a world that is characterized by oppression, people become burdened by the lack of acceptance; thus they lose one of life's most precious gifts: love. Oppression robs one of opportunities for being compassionate, and without compassion there is no love. When one is compassionate, one gains meaning, lives with purpose and has understanding for the welfare of other living things. This is the ability to see oneself in a context of all living things and to understand that one is related to all of creation. When one is compassionate, every experience is full of meaning, reminding us that even bad experiences help us along the road to greater awareness. That is, one is a part of a great family that loves every member, no matter how small. This is living with the humility that one has survived because another has given to us; it means that to be humble is to receive a reminder of one's humanness. Even disappointments become opportunities for growth. Brazier (1995) says that compassion

> may begin as a set of observational, empathic and caring skills — thoughtfulness, giving time and attention, listening, helping and generous in action — which we can all improve with good effects upon both our professional work and our private lives. As it grows it becomes, inexorably, a challenge to us to overcome the obstacles to life within ourselves and to flow with the boundless Tao in which we lose our attachment to separateness. The world needs kindness. (p. 200)

Emotional Transformation

Consider Dass's (1970) idea on the nature of truth:

> The truth is everywhere. Wherever you are, it's right where you are, even when you can't see it. And you can see it through whatever vehicle you are working with, you can free yourself from certain attachments that keep you from seeing it. The scientist doesn't stop being a scientist, nor does anybody stop being anything. You find how to do the things to yourself, which allow you to find truth where you are at that moment. (p. 2)

The purpose of truth is to sharpen awareness by focussing on senses, emotions, thoughts and perceptions. People are not their different parts but are the sum total of all of them, and by being more aware of the whole they can become more responsible and integrated. The self cannot be examined without looking at the context; it is best discovered by look-ing at the whole — that is, the individual, the group, the environment in which the group lives and the relationship the group has with the cosmos. This is the essence of emotional transformation, or to "nurture those aspects that permit a person to dis-identify from the restrictions of the personality and to recognize his or her identity with the total self" (Leuger & Sheikh, 1989, p. 228).

If people are to live an effective life, they must reduce "destructive emotions such as fear and anger" (Walsh & Vaughan, 1993, p. 4). However, the point is not just the reduc-tion of the negative but the enhancement of positive emotions and the development of optimism. Thus, being accepting, compassionate, forgiving, generous (just to name a few qualities) is not enough. One has to learn to transform one's being to reflect the equilib-rium of water and foster a calm demeanour. In other words, one must be open to expe-riencing things as they are and not as what it is desirable for them to be. Rumi's (1995) eloquent poem describes this attitude:

> Keep walking, though there's no place to get to
> Don't try to see through the distances.
> That's not for human beings. Move within,
> But don't move, the way fear makes you move. (p. 278)

Along with this equanimity, individuals should learn not to put themselves first and must begin unattaching themselves from gross materialism; for only then can they strive to be more humane. Attachment involves those conditionings that keep the human spirit down and create petty emotional reactions. Unconsciously, people attach themselves to "things" without realizing that "holding on" (i.e., identification with external objects) is the cause of suffering. Once this understanding is accepted, then the potential that exists within everyone can be released. In essence, each human being is a miniature universe. Practising generosity and forgiveness helps transform each person beyond his/her material existence. Along with this there must be an acceptance of responsibility and recognition of people's interconnectedness. One way to achieve this is to build a great sense of awareness of that which is inside the self and outside the self.

Ethical Training

The focus on ethical training arises from the observation that unethical behaviour both stems from and reinforces destructive mental factors (e.g., greed, fear, anger). Ethical behaviour undermines these factors and promotes instead factors of kindness, compassion and calm. As transpersonal maturation occurs, ethical behaviour is said to flow naturally from one's identification with all people and life. The simplest technique in a group is to advocate such behaviour by the leader and members, to point out that it is both a group ground rule and a method of development for all, and to discuss when it does or does not occur. Ethical conduct in a group helps create a climate of trust, which enhances risk taking and sincere participation. All of this fosters the transpersonal group community itself and imbeds values and standards that enhance the participants' behaviour in the surrounding community.

   Initial ethical training for a group member involves turning his/her attention inward. In the Sufi tradition, this is considered part of the process of repentance, the first step on the path of integration. One recognizes one's lack of fulfillment in life, observes one's impulses, wishes and deeds, and cleanses oneself of injustice and animosities. To explore this process, a counsellor might create situations in which clients see themselves and are shocked with insight into their true conditions; then the counsellor might offer a variety of practices that move clients along a specific line of development. For example, a counsellor changes the meeting time at the last minute. Perhaps clients would arrive complaining about the abrupt change and the lack of respect it shows them. The counsellor then explains that the change was intentional and describes the difference between seeking respect and seeking knowledge. The counsellor notes that when seeking respect, one often behaves in a manipulative way, acting pious or knowledgeable or with a sense of entitlement. This is a very different posture than that which is effective for seeking knowledge, a posture that demands humility, openness and an absence of manipulations. Real-world changes in one's surrounding community could also produce such reactions in group members. A distinction could be made between personal impulsive reactions (apathy, anger) and deliberate transpersonal responses (e.g., attention, collaboration, secret generous acts). The point is that individuals can observe when they are seeking respect from others. If they are at the stage of ego strengthening, this is important. If they are at the stage of ego transcendence, this gets in the way.

Meditation and Refocussing

Walsh and Vaughan (1993) used the term "attentional training" to describe one of the important elements of the transpersonal approach. Attentional training is the process of cultivating or focussing one's mind on mind, keeping it from wandering. Meditation is often misunderstood in the West. It is often exaggerated either as something that has miraculous properties or as a means for withdrawing from life. But there are different kinds of meditation that have the properties of mystical experiences or the heightened skill of awareness. In some ways, forms of meditation are culturally derived. Yet despite cultural differences, there is a philosophical similarity in the process that goes beyond culture and ends in similar experiences. For example, meditation takes different forms. In Sufism dancing in circles, called dervish, is a form of meditation; in yoga, the constant repetition of a mantra is another form of meditation. In Buddhism, being attentive to one's breathing or contemplating the message in a koan (riddle) is a form of meditation. In all of these examples, the result leads to emptiness or a dulling of one's self and an insight that is quite literally beyond the self. In Buddhism it culminates in nirvana, or a union with the cosmic all. In Sufism and Christianity, it might be a mystical union with God. The idea is indescribable. Perhaps T.S. Elliot (1944) said it best:

Words strain,
Crack and sometimes break, under the burden,
Under the tension, slip, slide, perish,
Decay with imprecision, will not stay in place,
Will not stay still. (p. 12)

Meditation is a natural process in which the aim is to develop awareness. What happens when someone meditates is an altering of his/her consciousness. The aim in developing concentration, just as in meditation, is to increase understanding by realizing and perfecting one's own mind. Yet, paradoxically, meditation strives to release one from the domination of the intellect. According to Humphreys (1968), no person "should go further into meditation who has not found within . . . a faculty superior to the thinking mind" (p. 154). Thinking is important but must be abandoned if enlightenment is to occur and truth is to be revealed. In the Sutra of Hui Neng, there is no real difference between the enlightened and ignorant person; what makes the two different is that one realizes it and the other one does not. Thus, one can become a new person by acting in a natural, mindful and skilful manner. According to Ma-tsu (Hoover, 1980),

> Grasping of the truth is the function of everyday-mindedness. Everyday-mindedness is free from intentional action, free from concepts of right and wrong, taking and giving, the finite or the infinite. . . . All our daily activities — walking, standing, sitting, lying down — all response to situations, our dealings with circumstances as they arise. (pp. 77–78)

The message in meditation is as old as humanity itself. The process of the meditation experience in the East and West is the openness of the soul or self to God or the divine. Depending on one's culture or perspective, this could be identified in different ways. For example, Saint Catherine of Genoa described it as "the moment of that sudden vision of herself and God" (Catholic Encyclopedia), while Jallal-Uddin Rumi described it as "the beloved is all in all, the lover merely veils him; the beloved is all that lives, the lover a dead thing" (1995, p. 27). What is inherent in these ideas is that an inner knowledge exists in everyone. The inner knowledge can be revealed only when one achieves oneness with all things or the total illumination of the self with God. Yet knowledge is not the goal, but the salvation. Thus, the Christian and Islamic mystics suggest that there is a deliverance from a separate self toward a unity with God. Freedom is the key, for

> only one who is ever free of desire can apprehend its spiritual essence; he [or she] who is ever a slave to desire can see no more than its outer fringe . . . all things depend on it for life, and it rejects them not . . . it lives and nourishes all things . . . all things return to it. (Happold, 1963, p. 152)

Notice the themes of humility and love. It seems these elements are required to be receptive, along with a degree of mortification. Mortification involves denial of the self by eliminating all attachments, cravings, pleasures, and self-interests. In other words, the divine within the self can be gained only by losing egocentric impulses and wishing, thinking and feeling. Chuang Tzu (Ramaswami & Sheikh, 1989) emphasizes that a person "without passions . . . does not permit good or evil to disturb his [her] inward economy but rather falls in with what happens and does not add to the sum of his mortality" (p. 447). Thus, meditation is a process of hearing the music of the inner life, which is mystical and creative. The inner life holds the knowledge of the cosmos, waiting to be revealed to us in an entirely new order. Our spiritual world, which is full of symbols, ideas and images, can lead us to enlightenment. The Buddhist mystical experience correlates with the Christian, Islamic and Hindu path. In the *Bhagavad-Gita* (Happold, 1963), Krishna says,

Resign all your actions to me. Regard me, as your dearest loved one. Know me to be your only refuge. Be united always in heart and consciousness to me. United with me, you shall overcome all difficulties by my grace . . . for the Lord lives in the heart of every creature. (p. 158)

Understanding Motivation

In order to create a balanced self that is free from distractions, one must be motivated to be healthier. To be so motivated, Walsh and Vaughan (1993) note that "desires gradually become less self-centered and more self-transcendent with less emphasis on getting and more on giving" (p. 5). But how does one free the self from self-centred urges? Social conditions affect how one performs; so getting beyond this phenomena may go against one's nature. In fact, this is widespread across the animal world. In an early experiment with cockroaches, researchers compared cockroaches running down a runway away from a light, with and without an audience of other cockroaches (Zajonc, Heingartner & Herman, 1969). The study found that the roaches went faster if other cockroaches were present. Among rats, sexual behaviour occurs more often when other rats are present (Baron, Kerr & Miller, 1992). Social psychologists call this phenomenon *social facilitation*, which Forsyth (1999) defines as "improvement in task performance that occurs when people work in the presence of other people" (p. 269).

The social-awareness theory is based on the idea of one's heightened awareness in social situations. When others watch, the performers will become more self-conscious of their actions. In turn, they will become aware of the discrepancies between an ideal performance and their own. Discrepancies cause them to do better or work harder. Mirrors, for instance, are often used in physical training to increase personal awareness, thus producing better results. Social awareness can also cause people to be impaired if they feel they are not doing as well as their goal and feel they cannot come close to achieving the ideal. Physically and psychologically, they withdraw from the task. Thus self-consciousness can improve performance but more than likely decreases performance. How does this translate to redirecting motivation and transcending the need to care about what others think? In Buddhism, this translates into decreasing one's desires as a means of achieving true happiness. Walsh and Vaughan (1993) stress, "the reduction of compulsive craving is . . . said to result in a corresponding reduction in intrapsychic conflict, a claim now supported by studies of advanced meditators" (p. 5).

Wisdom

If a person is psychologically secure, he/she is able to shift from a personal focus to a universal focus. This is what we believe is meant in spiritual practice when people talk about losing one's ego. We believe that if people have a level of personal maturity and ego integration, they can make the shift from "life is happening to me" to "life is happening." It is a happy shift, a shift from an inside-out, me-focussed view to a cosmic or universal overview (Boorstein, 1994, p. 101).

Walsh and Vaughan (1993) make a distinction between knowledge and wisdom, stating that the former is something anyone can gain while the latter is a state of being. Wisdom, then, is a process of growth that occurs as one gains personal insight into the self and the environment. From a therapeutic perspective, Brazier (1997) notes that "each time the therapist dies, a part of the client's prison dies with him [her]" (p. 215). The influence of others becomes less and less as one becomes wise and becomes correspondingly more at one with the self and the world around. While one can become aware of the meaninglessness of objects and material things, there is much more to having wisdom. That is, one transcends the nature of suffering in which the intuitive self becomes more focussed on the cosmos or the power beyond. What may seem solid is only an illusion, and so through wisdom one is liberated from external forces that bind creativity, joy and spontaneity. Brazier (1997) goes on to say that "a deluded person is attracted, repulsed or confused by everything. An enlightened person is enlightened by everything" (p. 222). Walsh and Vaughan (1993) state that this liberating insight is known in many traditions: "in the East as *jnana* (Hinduism), *prjna* (Buddhism), or ma'rifah (Islam), and in the West as *gnosis* or *scientia sacra*. And with this liberation the goal of the art of transcendence is realized" (p. 7).

Psychotherapeutic Approaches

The challenge for practitioners is to practise what they preach or to embody what they share with their clients. The vision they have for others should be developed inside themselves: that is, according to Walsh (1989), "to share and communicate it where we can; to use it to help the healing of our world; and to let it use us as willing servants for the awakening and welfare of all" (p. 136). In an empirical study, Hutton (1993) describes the variables that make a transpersonal practitioner different from other therapists (i.e., behaviour-cognitive and psychoanalytic). Hutton found that transpersonal practitioners used fewer verbal interactions and more action-oriented techniques (e.g., experiments and specific skills promoting action on the part of clients). In addition, transpersonal therapists used meditation, guided imagery (more often with a spiritual focus), dream work and specific books to read more than the other therapists did.

Transpersonal practitioners use a variety of techniques including desensitization, dream work, drama, guided imagery, meditation, nature-connecting experiments and practices that develop ethical personal conduct. That is, they use seven elements — awareness, compassion, emotional transformation, ethical training, motivation, meditation and wisdom — as dimensions for becoming a whole person. The practitioners help clients work toward creating a sense of balance within and without, a greater sense of connectedness to the environment and a desire to be a "good" person (spiritual enhancement). As a result, to practice in the transpersonal method, practitioners must possess

- an openness to the transpersonal dimension, including the belief that contacts with transpersonal realms may be transformative and of greatest healing potential;
- the ability to sense the presence of, or a report of numinous experience, whether it should appear in a dream, a vision, a synchronous event or a contact with a spiritual teacher;
- some knowledge of a variety of spiritual paths;
- an active pursuit of their own spiritual development;
- a degree of openness about themselves and their own spiritual orientation and experience;
- a firm grounding in psychotherapy. (Scotton, in Hutton, 1993, p. 141)

We will now turn to see how a transpersonally oriented counsellor can use Wilber's (1986, 2000) map of spiritual development, combined with some of the pathways of growth previously discussed, to help facilitate transpersonal development in clients. The following case study will show how the issue of releasing the separated selves and moving into nondual being can be worked on in a counselling setting.

A Case Study: Working with Cindy

Cindy worked with one of us over a six-month period that had ended more than a year ago. Now she claimed she was in crisis as she had lost her sense of who she is. She wanted to resume her transpersonal counselling and psychotherapy work. Cindy had an unusual background in that she dabbled in university in management studies after graduating from high school, but then left university and ended up being a traveller for many years in her twenties, living in Australia and coming back to North America to get married and start a family. After a few years as a stay-at-home mom, she returned to university to complete a social work degree. As a child, she had been brought up in the United Church but, like many emerging adults, in her late teens she rejected all religion, calling these paths a crutch.

In her late thirties, after finishing her social work degree, Cindy had come to work with me in transpersonal psychotherapy around her existential crisis (Yalom, 1980) of realizing how much of a people-pleaser she had become. This was making her feel exhausted and resentful, and she was tired of all of the fake posturing. She was perplexed how much time she spent taking care of friends and functions at the kids' school. During our therapy, she came to a significant realization of the need to let go of this other preoccupation, which kept her begging for validation; she needed to be in her own energy and set appropriate boundaries.

She focussed in particular on her relationship with her father. Cindy had desperately searched for validation from her dad for her career, and she began to see that pleading for that validation would keep her in a position of begging-one-down and non-acceptance forever. Her dad always wanted her to be an accountant, something she was not interested in pursuing. Seeing the hopelessness of the situation, she was able to let go of seeking her dad's approval in that this kept her "waiting for Godot." She began to assert herself in her relationship with him.

The psychotherapy work she did with me, coupled with some intense body work she did with an acupuncturist, caused a fairly significant shift in her energy as she settled into her own beingness. This new realization had propelled her journey as a counsellor/ social worker-in-training, and she now could understand many of the therapies and their focus on following one's path and differentiation (Lerner, 1986). At the time of finishing our initial work together, it seemed to me that there was a limit to her surrender, in that it seemed much more of a loosening up of her identity and a letting go of taking care of other people so she could be in her existential beingness. To me, it seemed she was hovering on fulcrum six of Wilber's (1986) spectrum of development. In the future, it seemed, she would have further work to do on her journey.

When we resumed our work together, she reported that in the last month she was feeling very dead — not depressed, but having no energy. She felt she could no longer be alone with herself and found her mind racing all the time. She had just over a month ago started master's studies and had new instructors and fellow students to deal with; she found herself getting anxious and caught up in maintaining a pleasing facade. As this was a counselling course, she felt devastated that even her basic counselling skills seemed to have deserted her; she felt self-conscious for the first time in a long time in her counsellor-training interactions. She even found herself desperately begging for friendship. So, perplexed after so much of her journey, she now was at a place in which her existence had become total misery and suffering. It seemed that she had lost her sense of who she was.

We sat in our chairs together as she recounted her recent woes during our therapy session. She described her total befuddlement at having the sense of a lost self and not knowing who she was anymore. I asked her to be in her awareness and get a sense of how that was experienced in her body. As she relaxed into her belly, she described herself as being suspended over a black abyss, which, if she let go, she could crash into and hurt herself. The abyss did not have the presence of a soft, loving, holding energy but seemed to her to be almost a wall.

I encouraged her to stay with her belly, to be meditative and let go of any judgements of the situation. As Sosan states, she was to have no choice or preferences, just be at one with the situation (Osho, 1994). As Krishnamurti (1954) would say, I encouraged her to accept what is instead of trying frantically to save herself or pick herself up by the bootstraps in some way. I invited Cindy just to "give up," stop trying to save herself and surrender to existence.

She needed to give up the whole gig of her separate self-existence as all she was doing was suffering. As we sat in our chairs, she felt herself clinging and contracting on herself over the black abyss, feeling she could be smashed by its murky bottom. I asked her to relax into the abyss as the deep emptiness is her own energy. It is what Almaas (1996) called the loving black chasm of being:

> When the student finally settles into this experience of deficient emptiness, allowing it without judgement, rejection or reaction, she sees that it is a state of no self, or, more specifically, no identity. When we fully experience this state of an identified self, it transforms naturally and spontaneously into a luminous vastness, a deep spaciousness, a peaceful emptiness. (p. 336)

As she sat there, it was clear from a relaxing of her energy that she was letting go. She described herself feeling like she had broken through the bottom of the blackness, and now she was falling in blackness. Strangely for her, this terrifying, deficient abyss was transforming. She reported that she was feeling held. She described this experience as something very new to her, the vastness of inner spaciousness. As we sat in the meditative stillness of the moment, she reported, "It's like an inner spaciousness has opened up for me."

Cindy also expressed surprise that surrender could happen instantaneously, all in one moment. I responded that that is true surrender in the intensity of the now. We sat there in our chairs, and I invited her to see that she could approach the world from this sense of inner spaciousness and did not have to cling to her separate, egoic self.

We had our follow-up two weeks after this intense session. Her homework had been just to rest in the abyss, even if it felt like deficient emptiness. She was to spend half an hour a day meditating and resting with no judgement. As Tolle (1997) suggested, she was to rest in the present moment. She reported that she had felt she was on cloud nine for the first week, but then slowly some of her old patterns of pleasing and watching others watch her started to drift back. This time, though, rather than allowing herself to get more and more shut down, she found that she was able to recognize the pattern and move instantaneously to surrender her egoic self in the moment through embracing "no judgement" to get back to a place of flowing beingnesss very quickly.

From here, we decided to intensify our work and look into her patterns of fear and anxiety. Her anxiety had been heightened by a major presentation to her graduate class that was looming large in a week. She had already spent a few restless nights.

As the client described her feelings of anxiety about her presentation, I asked her whether there was there any way she could make the future secure. Krishnamurti (1954) would tell her that her separate self is trying to be secure, but nothing works, as it is impossible. The only answer is choiceless awareness in this moment as she realizes that the mind can do nothing.

The invitation was for her to realize that all she can do is surrender now, and in the moment of her presentation surrender her separate self grasping. She sat there and dwelt in the realization that there was nothing she could do. A relaxed light of awareness came over her as she realized there truly was nothing she could do in this moment: all she could do in the next moment or in the moment of her presentation is let go and enjoy the moment without any judgement. We spent a few more minutes immersed in this new realization. This became a pivotal realization for Cindy and helped free her energy up for the demands of her master's program. She did not always reside in nondual being, but was able to catch herself when she got caught up in pursuing the illusion of psychological security in the future and could let go of her mind's obsessive attempts to guarantee her security. This ended up being our last session together, although Cindy did check in from time to time and reported finishing her master's in two years and then working as a family therapist. She continually came back to the realization that she could let go in this moment from all of the ego's demands for validation and security.

Conclusion

The most exciting aspect of all the revolutionary developments in modern Western science — astronomy, physics, biology, medicine, information and systems theory, depth psychology, parapsychology and consciousness research — is the fact that the new image of the universe and of human nature increasingly resemble that of the ancient and Eastern spiritual philosophies, such as the different systems of yoga, the Tibetan Vajrayana, Kashmir Shaivism, Zen Buddhism, Taoism, Kabbalah, Christian mysticism, or gnosticism. It seems that we are approaching a phenomenal synthesis of the ancient and the modern and a far-reaching integration of the great achievements of the East and the West that might have profound consequences for the life on this planet. (Grof, 1983, p. 33)

Some things in life are riddles: paradoxes that may never be answered or resolved through the mind. In the search to find meaning in life, it is easy to despair in this chaotic world. Camus (1947) referred to this as rolling the rock up the hill after it rolls down. In other words, life seems to be a matter of plugging away as a way of transcending the dark forces that pull one down. If nothing else, the plugging away serves as a means for directing energy. However, when self-doubt occurs — and it is inevitable that it will — answers are not easy to find. Camus, like many, dealt with this by romanticizing the absurdity of life; but of course, the tragedy for Camus was that the absurdity of it all was too much, and he drowned himself in the Seine one rainy evening.

The goal of the transpersonal approach is to help others see the impasse as a transformational challenge and an opportunity to move away from the selfishness and contraction of separate self ego preoccupation and to move one's energy toward ego-transcendence, nondual being and selflessness. Life provides each person with the opportunity of transformation to be aware, compassionate and present. Swiss philosopher and poet Henri-Frédéric Amiel said, "it is by teaching that we teach ourselves, by relating that we observe, by affirming that we examine, by showing that we look, by writing that we think, by pumping that we draw water into the well."

It is not surprising that nature is not only used as a metaphor in transpersonal psychology but also as a mechanism for transcendence, for one of the mysteries in nature is that it is not perfect. It is not symmetrical. Nature can never be defined like the ridges of the mountains we have seen at various places in our lives. And if one contemplates the shape and beauty of the mountains, it is impossible to know exactly what it is about them that is so inspiring. And unsurprisingly, nature can bring feelings similar to the ones we feel for someone we love, because they always escape exact definitions. Yet when we let go of the definitions, of the attempt to try to pin down friendship, love and nature, they flow. When we try to define life in our mind, so that we understand and feel in complete control of it, we only get confused. What happens is that we go into our heads, because we base our thoughts on the idea that we are different from it. When that happens, we have limited friendship, love, nature and ultimately ourselves. Perhaps that is an indication that we are trying to master our lives. But everything is leading back to what Adyashanti (2008) described as a spontaneous state of surrender, "letting go of the illusion of the separate self, letting go of the way we think the world is and the way we think it should be" (p. 163). When we let go, life has about it a sense of flowing, like water. So as I close my eyes and see the reflection of the water, I stop thinking, analyzing and just accept what is there. It is the attraction of the river that provided wisdom and peace for Siddhartha; and as people move toward one polarity and back again, they must remember there is no guarantee that there will be no pain in life or in relationships. People will experience pleasure but also pain. And like water, pain and pleasure always go away but they'll always come back. We need to remember that going away and coming back are two sides of the same thing.

References

Adyashanti (2008). *The end of your world: Uncensored straight talk on the nature of enlightenment.* Boulder, CO: Sounds True.

Almaas, A. (1996). *The point of existence: Transformations of narcissism in self-realization.* Berkeley, CA: Diamond Books.

Almaas, A. (2008). *The unfolding now.* Boston, MA: Shambhala.

Arasteh, A.R., & Sheikh, A. (1989). Sufism: The way to universal self. In A. Sheikh & S. Sheikh (Eds.), *Eastern and Western approaches to healing: Ancient wisdom and modern knowledge* (pp. 146–179). New York, NY: John Wiley.

Assagiolo, R. (1973). *Psychosynthesis.* New York, NY: Hobbs, Dorman.

Baron, R., Kerr, N., & Miller, N. (1992). *Group process, group decision, group action.* Pacific Grove, CA: Brooks/Cole.

Beck, D. & Cowan, C. (1996). *Spiral dynamics: Mastering values, leadership, and change.* New York, NY: Wiley-Blackwell.

Boorstein, S. (1994). Spiritual issues in psychotherapy. *Journal of Transpersonal Psychology, 26*(2), 95–106.

Brazier, R. (1995). *Zen therapy.* Boston, MA: Allyn and Bacon.

Bucke, R. (1923). *Cosmic consciousness.* New York, NY: E.P. Dutton.

Camus, A. (1947). *La Peste.* London, UK: Penguin Books.

Catholic Encyclopedia. (n.d.) St. Catherine of Genoa. Retrieved from http://www.newadvent.org/cathen/03446b.htm.

Cook-Greuter, S. (1990). Maps for living: Ego development stages from symbiosis to conscious universal embeddedness. In M. Commons et al. (Eds.), *Adult development. Vol. 2: Models and methods in the study of adolescent and adult thought.* New York: Praeger Publishers, pp. 79–104.

Cortwright, B. (1997). *Psychotherapy and spirit: Theory and practice in transpersonal psychotherapy.* Albany, NY: State University of New York Press.

Coxe, D. (2003, June 9). The new infodemic age. *Maclean's,* p. 36.

Dass, B.R. (1970). Lecture at the Menninger Clinic. *Journal of Transpersonal Psychology, 2*(2), 45–98.

Duran, E., & Duran, B. (1995). *Native American postcolonial psychology.* Albany, NY: State University of New York Press.

Elliot, T.S. (1944). *Four quartets.* New York, NY: Farber and Farber.

Forsyth, D. (1999) *Group dynamics* (3rd ed.). Belmont, CA: Brooks/Cole.

Gilligan, C. (1982). *In a different voice: Psychological theory and women's development.* Cambridge, MA: Harvard University Press.

Goleman, D. (1988). *The meditative mind: Varieties of meditative experience.* Los Angeles, CA: Jeremy P. Tarcher.

Grof, S. (1983). East and West: Ancient wisdom and modern science. *Journal of Transpersonal Psychology, 15*(1), 134–167.

Grof, S. (1985). *Beyond the brain: Birth, death, and transcendence in psychotherapy.* Albany, NY: State University of New York Press.

Grof, S. (1988). *The adventure of self-discovery.* Albany, NY: State University of New York Press.

Hixon, L. (1978). *Coming home.* New York, NY: Anchor.

Huxley, A. (1945). *The perennial philosophy.* New York, NY: Harper and Row.

Happold, F.C. (1963). *Mysticism*. Baltimore, MD: Penguin Books.

Hoover, T. (1980). *The Zen experience: This historical evolution of Zen through the lives and teachings of its great masters*. NY: New American Library.

Humphreys, C. (1968). *Concentration and meditation*. Baltimore, MD: Penguin Books.

Hutton, M. (1993). How transpersonal psychotherapists differ from other practitioners: An empirical study. *Journal of Transpersonal Psychology*, 26(3), 139–174.

Katie, B. (2002). *Loving what is*. New York, NY: Harmony Books.

Kohlberg, L. (1981). *Essays on moral development*. Vol. 1. San Francisco, CA: Harper & Row.

Kegan, R. (1982). *The evolving self: Problems and process in human development*. Cambridge, MA: Harvard University Press.

Krishnamurti, J. (1954). *The first and last freedom*. New York: Harper and Row.

Leuger, L., & Sheikh, A. (1989). The four forces of psychotherapy. In A. Sheikh & S. Sheikh (Eds.), *Eastern and western approaches to healing: Ancient wisdom and modern knowledge*. New York, NY: John Wiley, pp. 197–236.

Loevinger, T. (1976). *Ego development*. San Francisco, CA: Jossey-Bass.

Maslow, A. (1968). *Toward a psychology of being*. New York, NY: Van Nostrund Reinhold.

Maslow, A. (1971). *The further reaches of human nature*. New York, NY: The Viking Press.

Piaget, J. (1977). *The essential Piaget*. New York, NY: Basic Books.

Polster, I. (1966). Imprisoned in the present. *The Gestalt Journal*, 8(1), 5–22.

Osho (1994). *Hsin Hsin Ming: The book of nothing*. Pune, India: Osho International.

Ramaswami, S. & Sheikh, A. (1989). Buddhist psychology: Implications for healing. In A. Sheikh & S. Sheikh (Eds.), *Eastern and Western approaches to healing: Ancient wisdom and modern knowledge*. New York, NY: John Wiley, pp. 91–123.

Rumi, J. (1995). *The essential Rumi*. C. Barks, (Trans.). San Francisco, CA: Harper.

Sheikh, A., & Sheikh, K., 1989. *Eastern and Western approaches to healing*. Toronto: John Wiley & Sons.

Small, J. (1982). *Transformers: The therapists of the future*. Marina del Rey, CA: Devorss & Co.

Tolle, E. (1997). *The power of now: A guide to spiritual enlightenment*. Vancouver, BC: Namaste Publishing.

Vanier, J. (1998). *On being human*. Toronto, ON: House of Anansi Press.

Vaughan, E. (1991). Spiritual issues in psychotherapy. *Journal of Transpersonal Psychology*, 23(2), 105–120.

Walsh, R. (2011). Asian psychotherapies, In R. Corsini & D. Wedding (Eds.), *Current psychotherapies* (pp. 568–603, 9th ed.). Itasca, NY: F.E. Peacock.

Walsh, R., & Vaughan, F. (Eds.) (1980). *Beyond ego*. Los Angeles, CA: Jeremy Tarcher.

Walsh, R. & Vaughan, F. (1993). On transpersonal definitions. *Journal of Transpersonal Psychology*, 25(2), 199–208.

Washburn, M. (1988). *The ego and the dynamic ground*. Albany, NY: State University of New York Press.

Washburn, M. (1994). *Transpersonal psychology in psychoanalytic perspective*. Albany, NY: State University of New York Press.

Whitfield, C.L. (1984). Stress management and spirituality during recovery: A transpersonal approach. Part III: Transforming. *Alcoholism Treatment Quarterly*, 1(4), 1–54.

Wilber, K. (1977). *The spectrum of consciousness*. Wheaton, IL: Quest.

Wilber, K. (1986). The spectrum of development. In K. Wilber, J. Engler, & D. Brown (Eds.), *Transformations of consciousness* (pp. 65–159). Boston, MA: Shambhala.

Wilber, K. (1990). *Eye to eye: The quest for the new paradigm* (rev. ed.). Boston, MA: Shambhala.

Wilber, K. (1995). *Sex, ecology, and spirituality: The spirit of evolution*. Boston, MA: Shambhala.

Wilber, K. (1997). *The eye of spirit: An integral version for a world gone slightly mad*. Boston, MA: Shambhala.

Wilber, K. (2000). *Integral psychology*. Boston, MA: Shambhala.

Wilber, K. (2006). *Integral spirituality*. Boston, MA: Shambhala.

Yalom, I. (1980). *Existential psychotherapy*. New York, NY: Basic Books.

Zajonc, R. B., Heingartner, A. & Herman, E. M. (1969). Social enhancement and impairment of performance in the cockroach. *Journal of Personality and Social Psychology, 13,* 83–92.

21

Sufism and Healing

An Islamic Multicultural Approach

Ava Bahrami & M. Honoré France

I never listen to the cry of animals, or the quivering of trees, or the murmur of water, or the song of birds, or the rustling wind, or the crashing thunder, without feeling them to be an evidence of Thy unity, and a proof that there is nothing like unto Thee. (Nicholson, 1922, p. 12)

There is considerable debate as to what the word *Sufism* means. The most widely accepted meaning is probably derived from the Arabic *suf* ("wool"); therefore, a *Sufi* is a person wearing an ascetic's woolen garment. It is thought that Sufism first appeared in late seventh- and eighth-century Persia as a movement against the worldliness and loose morals of the ruling Umayyad family. The Sufis "denounced the luxury of caliphs, viziers, and merchants, and proposed to return to the simplicity of Abu Bekr and Omar I" (Durant, 1950, p. 258). They denounced not only the government but also the rigid rituals of the mosque. Sufis saw these rituals as an impediment to the "mystic state in which the soul, purified of all earthly concerns, rose not only to the Beatific Vision but to the unity of God" (Durant, 1950, p. 258). One of Sufism's early thinkers was Hasan of Basra (d. 728), who exhorted the Islamic world to return to the strict tenets of the Prophet Mohammad. Hasan taught that people should prepare for judgement day, heed the original teachings of the Koran and remember the transitory nature of life. This emphasis on the love of God brought the transition from asceticism to mysticism. Another early teacher of Sufism was the woman who is considered a saint by Sufis: Rabia of Basra (d. 801), who emphasized the love of God neither out of the hope for heaven nor the fear of hell, but for its own sake.

It is not surprising that Sufism was criticized by traditionalists who feared that the

Sufis' focus on personal experiential knowledge of God might cause people to neglect established religious observances. What bothered these critics most was Sufism's ideal of unity with God as a denial of the principle of the separateness of God. As a result, believers of Sufism who claimed mystical communion with God were persecuted. Later followers, such as Ibn Arabi (d. 1240) and Jili (d. 1428), did teach a kind of theosophist monism. They combined traditional Islamic theological position with a moderate form of Sufism. This led to the wide acceptance of mysticism in the Muslim world. Sufism became more widespread through the mystical poetry of Jalal al-Din al-Rumi and through the formation of religious brotherhoods. These brotherhoods grew out of an intensive study of the Koran by participants under a mystical guide or "saint," who helped them achieve direct communion with God. In addition, Sufism was strengthened through the work of famous Persian Sufis Hujwiri and Ghazzali, who published multiple books about Sufi doctrine (Werbner, 2003, p. 4; Dehlvi, 2009, p. 100).

Another early teacher of Sufism was Farid al-Din Abu Hamid Attar, a Persian poet. Attar was born around 1142 and died around 1221. Attar's works on Sufism are considered definitive and his biographies, composed of delicately balanced rhymed prose, are considered some of the most beautiful in Persian and also the Arab world. His most famous work is the mystical epic *Conference of the Birds*, which created metaphorical stories used by many later poets. According to Attar, the seeker does not submit to God, but becomes one with God:

> And if they looked at both together, both were the Simurgh (a name for the seeker and sought), neither more nor less. This one was that, and that one this; the like of this hath no one heard in the world. (Arasteh 1980, p. 92)

Sufis differed in their living style from Christian counterparts, in that they did not live in monasteries but wandered as mendicant teachers. They advocated mystical practices, which included ecstatic and hypnotic rituals of singing and dancing. One of the most interesting practices of Sufism is the whirling dance. This dance, called *dervish*, has been made famous as the whirling dervish, an extreme ritual, along with howling. The dervishes were generally led by a sheikh who possessed esoteric knowledge. The followers of these sheiks thought they possessed *silsila* ("a chain"), which linked novices to their immediate teacher back through a series of saints all the way to Mohammad himself.

Concept of Unity with God and Sufism

One of the central concepts of Sufism is the relationship between humans and God. Sufis envision humans as the lover, while God is the beloved. This is in contrast with religious establishments that portray humans as servants and God as a kind, invisible lord. According to Sufis, the relationship between the lover and the beloved can grow to the point of unity, where they become indistinguishable. In other words, there is no difference between humans and God. This way of expressing unity with God was first brought to the Sufi world by a Persian mystic called Bayazid Bastami (d. 874): "For 30 years God was my mirror . . . now I say that God is the mirror of myself, for with my tongue he speaks and 'I' have passed away" (Dehlvi, 2009, p. 86).

Given that Bayazid Bastami was from a Zoroastrian family (Dehlvi, 2009), one has to search within the teachings of Zarathustra to understand the context in which Bayazid thrived. Zarathustra was a Persian prophet who lived around the eighteenth century BCE (Kiani, 2009, 22). In Zoroastrianism, the concept of God (Ahura Mazda) and his relationship with mortal beings is one of a Supreme Being that lures the soul mate. The latter is perhaps best described in the work of nineteenth-century German philosopher Friedrich Nietzsche, *Thus spake Zarathustra: A book for all and none*: "I love him who chasteneth his God because he loves his God . . . with singing, laughing and mumbling do I praise the God who is *my* God" (pp. 85, 99). However, Zarathustra's God seems not to be an invisible lord in the skies: "Once blasphemy against God [here referring to an invisible Lord] was the greatest blasphemy; but God *died*, and therewith also those blasphemers" (p. 89). Therefore, Zarathustra teaches a Supreme Being beyond humanization. This is in contrast with the lord in the skies who has many human features; he *watches* one's every action, *asserts* punishment based on one's actions, *helps* one when in need, etc. The concept of unity is also evident in Zarathustra's teachings. In Nietzsche's words: "Lo, I teach you the 'superman' . . . man is a rope stretched between animal and superman" (p. 88). Zarathustra teaches a state of being that Nietzsche calls *Übermensch* ("superman"). Once a man becomes a superman, he is united with the Supreme Being: "Now am I light, now do I fly; now do I see myself under myself, now there dances a God in me" (p. 194). It is this concept of reaching a godly state of being that was introduced to the Sufi world by Bastami and that caused his exile from his hometown.

Bastami's story is not an isolated incident in Sufism. Shortly after Bastami, southern Iran became the thriving place of another Persian Sufi: Mansur the Cotton Processor. "Cotton processor" in Arabic — the official language of the time — translates to Al-Hallaj. Mansur Al-Hallaj, one of the most prominent exponents of Sufism, was born about 858. Al-Hallaj broke early with Sufism; when he began to preach, he publicly revealed his secret experiences after a pilgrimage to Mecca. When he uttered the phrase *An Al-haqq* ("I Am the Truth") in Baghdad, charges of blasphemy were brought against him. He was accused of heterodoxy and charlatanism and was brutally dismembered and finally decapitated in 922 by the Abbasid ruler of the time. Interestingly, Al-Hallaj was also from a Zoroastrian family (Mojaddedi, 2003).

After Bastami and Al-Hallaj, the concept of having a loving relationship with the Supreme Being and uniting with the source of existence became commonplace among Persian and non-Persian Sufis. To reach unity, however, one must first mount various stages of spiritual expansions.

Personality Structure and Stages of Human Development

Stories are often used in Sufism to explain important beliefs and concepts. Consider one of the following stories by Rumi about a group of Chinese and Greek artists (although their nationalities are unimportant to the story). Both groups claimed that they were the best painters, so the king gave both groups a room to paint. The Chinese painters requested hundreds of pigments to paint their room with elaborate colours and intricate designs. However, the Greek painters said they needed nothing and spent all of their time polishing the walls. Finally, their walls shone like a mirror, while the Chinese painters had their walls beautifully painted with elaborate pictures. Both were beautiful, but when the king saw the room that was like a mirror, he determined that it was the most beautiful. This polished room reflects the Sufi idea that one's heart and mind should be clear and reflect openness and the purity of numerous realities. In the same way, each person must strive for the path that has seven stages.

The Sufi Therapeutic Experience

Sufi is at the heart of the helping process that emphasizes the experiential over the didactic. Wholeness is found by developing a spiritual attitude and seeking fulfillment by becoming more aware. Sufism assumes that as people experience the full range of the spirit of God, they gain insight into their greater selves. That is, people must strive for greater spiritual perfection by developing what Kahlil Gibran (1933) calls the larger self. According to Gibran,

> You are not enclosed within your bodies, nor confined to houses or fields . . . that which is in you dwells above the mountain and roves with the wind. . . . it is a thing free, a spirit that envelops the earth and moves in the other. (p. 91–92)

As an experiential process, Sufism values experiencing as the only means for achieving sensitivity to self, others and the world . . . learning and gaining knowledge do not occur through conditioning but through exposure and experiencing something or someone in its totality as a vital living force. To learn about nature, people cannot simply observe it but must experience it by becoming a part of nature. According to Arasteh and Sheikh (1989), experience and behavior overlap and inner and outer expression are the same; but in many cases, behavior is the rationalization or inhibitor of experience — it is a cover. Experience has an organic and illuminatory nature, whereas behavior is characterized by conditioning . . . in fact those who [are] prepared to take the path of Sufism must first "uncondition" themselves. (p. 150)

Once unconditioned, mankind makes the great discovery that part of the Supreme Being is hidden in his body and the only obstacle standing in the way of uniting with the beloved is the body itself. The latter refers to another concept commonly found in Sufi literature: *istishraq* or the "quest for the Orient." This, however, is not a geographic Orient. This is the Oriental location hidden deep in human body and soul. In Sufi terminology, right after birth humans enter *qorbat* ("exile"), usually referred to as the Western exile to contrast the mystical Orient. A Sufi, therefore, is someone who is "conscious of his solitary condition . . . and who ardently desires to his Orient-origins" (Shariat, 1989, p. 99).

The inner experience is not only mystical but is a means that leads to the reclamation of naturalness, or a rebirth. The "inner journey" is a process of transcending the "sinful" self that is caused by living in a materialistic world. Carnal desires, substance addictions, greed, covetousness, selfishness and other worldly desires can be let go if people will it. The process is the identification with the all-knowing power of God as manifested in the creative self-conscious. Arasteh and Sheikh (1989) have described it as being similar to the Gestalt "I–Thou" concept:

Thou can be any object of desire, and "I" can be any person at any stage who is incited by the proper object of desire. In the process of union of I and thou, the essential point is the inner motivation of the seeker. The heart must be motivated from within. The thou, the object of desire, must be worthy enough. (p. 151)

It is the purity of the heart, with the corresponding innocence of intention, that is the most important aspect of the seeker. The heart should become like a mirror, reflecting the attitude of the creator or what is essentially "truth." If this does not happen, then the mind becomes cloudy with negative qualities such as anger, rigidity, selfishness, greed, envy, etc. (Arberry, 1961). The "truth" is always highly personal so it is never explained to another person. Each person must seek his/her own "truth" by total concentration in which the object or state becomes you. The duality results in *An*, or a new state. This is a "situation in which one becomes aware of one's previous states and can communicate symbolically, holistically, and through experiential media" (Arasteh & Sheikh, 1989, p. 153).

The Sufi Therapeutic Process

The "seeker" following the Sufi therapeutic process must approach the process in a completely open and sincere manner. The reason is that the Sufi way is a highly individual process. To transcend one's individual nature, the seeker must be purified (e.g., become innocent). There are three stages of the process: the illumination of the cultural self, qualities of self and self-essence. The process follows two interlocking steps. First, there must be a disintegration *(fana)* of social self, self-intellect and partial soul. Second, there must be a reintegration *(baqa)* of the cosmic or universal self. Everyone possesses the power to be a positive or negative force for personal development. The struggle for everyone is to get beyond either emotion or reason, and harmonize these discordant elements of being. According to Arasteh and Sheikh (1989),

> Disharmony appears most often between (1) *nafs e amareh* (the force with us that commands regressive and evil acts) and reason; (2) reason and *nafs e mutma'ana* (which confirms certainty); and (3) intuition and reason in the final state of personality growth. (p. 153)

Disharmony causes people to act in self-serving ways (e.g., lust robs people of intelligence and reverence, and materialism robs people of growth). The purpose of life is union with all and comes only after the abandonment of the "social self" and the embracing of the "universal self." In a sense, each person has the potential to become godlike. That is, everyone possesses the power for bringing about good if they so choose. Yet it is not so easy for some to understand what is beyond themselves. Understanding may require a great deal of effort or may appear suddenly. The answers are always elusive, but clearly awareness can be found only within and not through someone else. It is important, therefore, to be introspective and remove the mental barriers that have been interjected through socialization. With awareness of the universal self comes a realization of what one is.

The Helper as a Guide

While the answers lie within, Sufis feel that since the journey is difficult, seekers should have a guide *(pir)*. The guide shares his/her experience and acts as a touchstone to measure feelings, thoughts and actions. The guide, as helper or therapist, assists with the traps that befall the seeker (e.g., self-delusions). While the guide has experience of the journey, the guide is not a teacher. Arasteh and Sheikh (1989) stress that the guide cannot teach through instruction but only can set up a situation in which the inspired novice experiences what he or she should. Of course, he or she can experience only those situations that come close to his or her mental state. (p. 156)

The guide should be able to communicate through *tele,* or reciprocal empathy ("heart to heart"). The guide gives and the seeker receives; conversely the seeker gives and the guide receives. The process of change is evolutionary, and as the seeker transcends the social self, there is less need of guidance from the guide: "This guidance promotes rebirth; the guide serves only as a transfer in this path" (Arasteh & Sheikh, 1989, p. 156). As the seeker becomes stronger or more aware, his/her vision (mirror) becomes less cloudy. The stages of rebirth start with

- awareness of the blocks;
- repentance *(tubeh);*
- avoiding behaviours that block (*vara);*
- achievement of piety *(zohd);*
- becoming patient *(sabr);*
- trust *(tavakul);*
- satisfaction *(reza).*

During this therapeutic process, seekers learn to become observers of their psyches or develop the ability to measure self with the object of their search. As they move towards enlightenment, they experience rapturous states of consciousness. The goal of their search intensifies, and they develop a divine state of unconditional love for all. What they feel is an intense state of intimacy with the larger selves. They will spend a great deal of time in contemplation as they become more secure and comfortable with the self. Finally, they achieve a state of unification with the cosmic. In this state, they will desire to live more genuinely, without need for material things.

Therapeutic Methods of Sufism: Meditation, Dance, Poetry and Dreams

"Lamps are many, but light is one," wrote the Sufi poet Rumi. There are a number of methods Sufis use to bring about the realization of one light. With acceptance of that one light, one can gain enlightenment, redemption, unification and rebirth. Methods may range from hypnotherapeutic experiences to meditation. Hallaji (1962) describes one method used by Sufi healers in Afghanistan for inducing hypnotic trances, in which the healers started by leading the clients in chanting and then rhythmically blowing on them. This was followed by more meditation and relaxation training. Both mental disorders and physical disorders are treated. In effect, it is the spirit within that is believed to have curative powers. The practitioner speeds the process and focusses the energy.

Sufi Meditation

One method for achieving self-realization is through meditation. While meditation practices differ from practitioner to practitioner, meditation techniques start with learning to concentrate. According to Shafii (1985), there are three types of Sufi meditation: silent meditation *(zikr)*, mindful meditation and outward meditation *(zikr-i-jali)*.

Silent meditation is basically passive: one focusses on the breath or something else, such as the names of God (e.g., repeating all the names that could be used to call God in Arabic). Mindful meditation is the sense of being free from thoughts, sensations and feelings. Outward meditation uses a poem or music, the names of God or a *pir*, where the goal is to work towards a sense of "emptiness" (Zen) or *kundalini* (yoga), which the Sufis call *fana*.

Consider the Ceremony of Remembrance, which uses these three meditative processes. The Koran emphasizes that by practicing *zikr*, individuals can expand their aliveness, increase spiritual attunement and achieve a peaceful soul. Essential to Sufism is meeting on a regular basis with a *pir* and other seekers. Sometimes, two seekers are matched and asked to meet on a regular basis to study a common theme. The idea is to help everyone become attuned to others or their partner. In the next phase, seekers learn to direct their energy at will with the guide, followed by regular practice with different seekers.

> Sufi meditation may then be seen as a mental approach whose ultimate goal is to allow the seeker to travel from this world of illusion to the Divine Presence. When we visualize our spiritual mentor, the knowledge of the Divine Attributes that operate through him is reflected back upon our minds. With frequent repetition, the mind of the follower reaches the level of enlightenment, acquires the ability to communicate directly with the Mentor, and acquires spiritual awareness of the Mentor. (Sufi Meditation Center, 2012)

Essentially, meditation moves the seeker beyond the self, transcending what is material, and on to the union of all truth. In meditation, the mind becomes empty and allows the seeker to observe mental states, experiences and imperfections. What occurs is an explosion of energy that culminates in a state of rapture and finally the state of emptiness where one becomes "nothing" or above all things, including "God." The seeker might suddenly engage in whirling dances *(sama)*. The Arabic meaning of *sama* is "listening to and hearing." It happens when one reaches ecstasy from singing and hearing music while in a whirling dance.

Sufi Poetry

A surge in poetry is perhaps the most evident manifestation of the growth of Sufism in the Middle East, especially Iran. Many mystical figures turned to words to explain the deep concepts of existence and unity. Hafez of Shiraz was one of these mystics whose poetry created a renaissance in Iranian mysticism. In Iranian tradition, seekers ask Hafez to be their *pir*: with a question in mind, the seeker asks the Oracle of Hafez for guidance, and the poem that comes up is the mirror through which the seeker can see a reflection of his/her own soul.

> Last night, to me, a mystery-knower, keen of sense, secretly spake, saying: "Concealed from thee, one can not hold the mystery of the wine-seller."
>
> Then me, he gave a cup, from whose splendour on the heavens, to dance came Zuhra (Venus), and the lute-striker (player) kept saying: "Drink!" (Wilberforce-Clarke, 1997, p. 563)

In the Western world, the thirteenth-century Persian poet Rumi is perhaps better known than Hafez. Rumi was the son of a famous scholar of Islamic laws and hence had the opportunity to be in touch with famous Persian mystics, in particular Attar of Neyshabur, at a very young age. Rumi became a scholar of Islamic laws himself and after his father's death continued his religious classes, which brought him unprecedented fame. What triggered Rumi to become a famous poet and Sufi, though, was an old dervish named Shams, from the city of Tabriz in northwestern Iran. Shams was a divine spirit who one day ground his way through Rumi's disciples to get to him:

> "I have a question if you allow me!" says Shams. Rumi, who has already realized that Shams is not an ordinary man, awaits the question, looking at the ground. "Who had a higher ranking; Muhammad the prophet of Islam or Bayazid Bastami?" asks Shams. This question overwhelms Rumi. His disciples, who have not understood the depth of this question, become outraged. Rumi replies, "Muhammad, indeed," to calm down the crowd. However, deep inside he knows that Shams is referring to the fact that Bastami was "God" himself; he was united with the beloved.

This incident prompted Rumi to ask Shams to be his *pir*. Shams was later forced out of the city by Rumi's disciples, who saw him as a corrupting force. Nevertheless, Shams's influence on Rumi was everlasting, and it was after his encounter with Shams that Rumi becomes the Sufi figure who sings all the wonderful poetry we know today. Perhaps the most famous verse of Rumi is the opening line of his first book:

Harken to this Reed forlorn,
Breathing, even since 'twas torn
From its rushy bed, a strain
Of impassioned love and pain.
The secret of my song, though near,
None can see and none can hear
Oh, for a friend to know the sign
And mingle all his soul with mine. (Nicholson, 1950, p. 31)

Sufi Dance

"Sama were adopted to actualize these peak experiences" (Arasteh & Sheikh, 1989, p. 158). In fact, movement — particularly circular motion — leads to deeper awareness. Positive energy is "stoked as a fire," and the seeker moves to a different state. Once again it is the experience or passion that remains dominant as seekers move toward rebirth. As emotions peak in the dance, the seeker is filled with love toward all things. This occurs because seekers realize they have become "whole." The separation of mind, body and spirit that society reinforces falls away, and a new sense of power emerges. When seekers realize the wholeness of all things, then conflict is irrelevant. Arasteh and Sheikh (1989) describe the insight as the realization that "the basis of evolution is not conflict (or competition), but rather the positive force of love [and] they discover that the lover and beloved come from love" (p. 190).

According to Ghazzali (in Shafii, 1985), Sufis have used *sama* throughout their history. There is a mystery within everyone, which the seeker must uncover:

Almighty God has placed a secret in the heart of human beings. This secret is hidden like fire in iron. When a stone hits the iron the hidden fire will become evident . . . Sama and listening to beautiful and pleasant music moves the hidden jewel within. It creates a spontaneous situation, which connects the heart of human beings with the Universal and spiritual world. The Universal world is the world of beauty and harmony. Any rhythm, beauty and harmony is the manifestation of that world . . . a beautiful voice and a delightful song are reflections of the wonder of that world. Sama creates awareness in the heart and brings total joy (shauq). If a person's heart is filled with the intense love and total joy of the Beloved, sama will fan the fire within. (1985, p. 155)

Sufi Dream Work

Dreaming is another popular method for achieving understanding. Sufis have always honoured dreams and view them as a means by which the unconscious mind leaves the conscious world (social self) and enters a purer world of the self (true self). Since the true self is uncluttered with the logic and culturization of society, wisdom can be revealed through intuition and messages. As insights increase and knowledge unfolds, seekers experience a renewed sense of consciousness in which

> their minds are illuminated and vision increases . . . now universal trust appears; imagination, perplexity, fantasy, and suspicion disappear entirely . . . they become the mirror of all. All that remains is to become all truth; they grasp truth intuitively . . . thus, they have a direct relationship with evolutionary events . . . they seem unconscious, although they experience a dream-like awareness. (Arasteh & Sheikh, 1989, p. 159)

Conclusion

The traditions of Sufism go back to the very beginnings of Islam; however, Sufism is still evolving as a spiritual force for healing the mind. Sufis exist everywhere in the world that values the spiritual aspect of humanity. While it is important to traditional Muslims who practice Sufism to accept the one true God, Islam as a religion is also tolerant of other religious beliefs. Judaism and Christianity have traditionally been recognized by Islam as important contributors to Islam's beliefs. The traditionalist may say that one must accept Allah (God), while more liberal believers say that one must accept God and whatever one calls God is immaterial: it is more important to seek the truth. Yet Sufism does not have the non-theistic form of mysticism that is Buddhism. The focus of Sufis is always towards the union with the creator (God). Thus Sufism, as a mystical experience, is directly related to the immediate experience of what knowledge is derived from such an experience. Sufism, as a mystical form of healing, is not only highly emotional; it is also highly philosophical. Poetic language, which is a common expressive approach in the Middle East, is frequently the vehicle in the great writings describing Sufism. Not surprisingly, images like fire, the dark, an inner journey, twilight of the soul and knowing the unknown are common descriptions of the mystical experience.

Humanity becomes alienated when people separate themselves from nature, dualistic thinking and fragmentation. The methodology is mystical, yet uses practices that are common to being human (e.g., dance, meditation, music and poetry, just to name a few). However, meditation is the primary technique of the *pir*, or Sufi guide. Humankind has become misguided; by refocussing their energy, people can become more in harmony with themselves, the world and God. In fact, joining with the purity exemplified by God is a primary goal of Sufism. What attracts many healers in the West to Sufism is that Sufism values more than just the emotional and the intellectual. Sufism values the spirit, which Deikman (2012) likens to a house that has been taken over by the servants. In Deikman's view, the servants are the intellect and emotion, while the master/mistress is the spirit. Without the spirit, people are incomplete. In that sense, helping or healing cannot be accomplished without the spirit. The method — whether meditation, dreams or movement — is generally approached with a mystical experience, which becomes the spiritual means for achieving a peak experience. In a sense, one is extending the self beyond the ordinary field of human consciousness. In this state, insight occurs, which a Sufi might call "touching the face of God." For Sufis, the spiritual is a mystical experience and as such is the highest state of human knowing. As a vehicle, mysticism can be approached through meditation, prayer and ascetic discipline. In addition, Sufism embraces experiences of ecstasy, levitation, dreams, visions and power to discern human hearts, to heal and to perform other unusual acts. In these transpersonal occurrences, Sufis report that experience is always immediate, overwhelming and divorced from reality. Yet the experience or knowledge does not have to be justified, because it is highly individual and in fact does not have to be understood outside the experience itself.

But when do people know how they must approach the power that is within? Idries Shah (1981), one of the most articulate exponents of Sufism in the West, uses the metaphor of the limbless fox to explain. In the story, a person observes a fox with no limbs in the wild and wonders how it survives. Through observing the fox, the person discovers that the fox waits for a lion to leave the leftovers from a kill. The man, seeing this as a lesson for living, tries to practise the way of the limbless fox. The person sits and waits on a street corner for the meaning of life. But instead of learning more, he becomes weaker and weaker. Eventually a voice asks the person: "Why should you behave like a limbless fox? Why not be a lion and let others benefit from your leavings?" In other words, the teaching in the story is the understanding that healing must come from the power within and that wisdom is not found from others. Thus, "God provides the food, [humankind] the cooks" (Shah, 1981, p. 188).

References

Arasteh, A., & Sheikh, A. (1989). Sufism: The way to universal self. In A.A. Sheikh & K.S. Sheikh (Eds.), *Eastern & Western approaches to healing* (pp. 146–189). New York: NY: John Wiley & Sons.

Arasteh, A. (1980). *Growth to selfhood*. London, UK: Routledge & Kegan Paul.

Arberry, A.J. (1961). *Tales from the Masnavi*. London, UK: London University Press.

Dehlvi, S. (2009). *Sufism: The heart of Islam*. New Delhi, India: Harper Collins Publishers.

Deikman, A. (2012). Sufism and psychiatry. http://www.australiansuficentre.org/article_sufism_psychiatry.htm

Durant, W. (1950). *The age of faith*. New York, NY: Simon & Schuster.

Gibran, K. (1933). *The prophet*. New York, NY: Alfred Knopf Publishers.

Kiani, B. (2009). *About Zarathustra's life*. In Persian. Tehran, Iran: Jami.

Sufi Meditation Center (2012). What is Sufi meditation? http://www.sufimeditationcenter.com/Whatis-Sufimeditation.html.

Hallaji, J. (1962). Hypnotherapeutic techniques in Central Asian community, *International Journal of Clinical and Experimental Hypnosis*, 10, 271–74.

Mojaddedi, J. (2003). Hallaj, Abu'l-Mogit Hosayn. In *Encyclopedia Iranica*. Retrieved from http://www.iranica.com/articles/hallaj-1

Nicholson, R.A. (1922). *The mystics of Islam*. Cambridge, UK: Cambridge University Press.

Nicholson, R.A. (1950). *Rumi, poet and mystic (1207–1273)*. London: George Allen and Unwin Ltd.

Nietzsche, F. (1883). *Thus spake Zarathustra: A book for all and none*. T. Common, Trans. The Project Gutenberg EBook #1998 release November 7, 2008.

Shah, I. (1981). *Learning how to learn: Psychology and spirituality in the Sufi way*. San Francisco, CA: Harper & Row.

Shafii, M. (1985). *Freedom from the self: Sufism, meditation and psychotherapy*. New York, NY: Human Science Press.

Shariat, A. (1989). Iranian Sufism and the quest for the hidden dimension: Toward a depth psychology of mystic inspiration. *Diogenes*, 37, 92–123. Doi: 10.1177/039219218903714606

Werbner, P. (2003). *Pilgrims of love: The anthropology of a global Sufi cult*. Bloomington, IN: Indiana University Press.

Wilberforce-Clarke, H. (1997). *The Divan-i-Hafiz*. Maryland, DC: Ibex Publishers.

22

Creating Compassion and
Selflessness through Naikan

M. Honoré France

Counselling practices have long been dominated by Western counselling procedures, yet many Asian psychotherapies offer creative and sophisticated strategies that are easily adapted to a variety of theoretical approaches. *Naikan* is one of the simplest yet most elegant modalities that helpers can embrace. Naikan is a Japanese psychotherapy with philosophical roots in Buddhist spiritual practices and emphasizes reflection on past relationships. Like many Asian psychotherapies, Naikan focusses "primarily on existential and transpersonal levels and little on the pathological" (Walsh, 2010, p. 547). The essence of Naikan is revealed in the meaning from its Japanese roots: *nai*, meaning "inner," and *kan*, meaning "observation or introspection." The ToDo Institute (2012), which promotes alternative methods of mental health, provides a more poetic translation: a way of "seeing oneself with the mind's eye" (www.todoinstitute.org/naikan.html). The ToDo Institute uses the analogy of being on a mountain top and looking out over the valley; through practising Naikan one is taught that one's perspective can change by shifting one's focus from a "zoom lens" to a "wide-angle lens." Everything changes, and our perception of reality also shifts and changes.

Consider that personal problems and dissatisfaction are often the result of the discrepancy between the actual self and the ideal self, or between what is and what should be. Buddhism teaches that experience of living is far more valuable than metaphysical speculations. To philosophize too much about existence is a waste of energy, just as is preoccupation with one's condition. Even to focus too much on a problem can lead to attachment. Yet Buddha taught that life should not be seen as a mystery to be figured out. No, life should be lived, simply and practically, accepting events and circumstances as they occur. To emphasize these ideas, consider the wisdom in the words of the poet Chuang-Tsu:

> The purpose of a fishtrap is to catch fish, and when the fish are caught, the trap is forgotten. The purpose of a rabbit snare is to catch rabbits. When the rabbits are caught, the snare is forgotten. The purpose of words is to convey ideas. When the ideas are grasped, the words are forgotten. Where can I find a man who has forgotten words? He is the one I would like to talk to.

Thus, what is natural is lost as people use artificial means to deal with their anxieties and fears. If people will allow themselves to be like water, then they can regain their naturalness and live a more constructive life. There is no pretending, for "water reflects whatever reality brings it" (Reynolds, 1989, p. 181). When people deny reality — whether it is joy or sadness — they fight against the truth of their feelings. "Shoulds" block them and prevent them from making changes to coexist with the changing context in the environment. Like water, which always flows around objects and doesn't fight rocks or other obstacles, people can learn to be more flexible and move at a pace that keeps to the circumstances of existence.

Historical Background of Naikan Therapy

Naikan began as a form of spiritual training for priests of the Jodo Shinshu sect of Buddhism. Jodo Shinshu emphasized the love and self-sacrifice of Buddha and how these qualities were used to help others achieve enlightenment. Through acceptance of life the way it is and giving joyously to others, followers were promised relief from the cycle of birth and death. The early spiritual training consisted of introspective meditation and fasting. In some circumstances priests would go without food, water and sleep, and engage in other forms of self-deprivation. The modern practice of Naikan was modified 50 years ago for lay people by Yoshimoto Ishin: "Nowadays the goal need not be a religious one of an existential confrontation with death; the aim of self-understanding is acceptable" (Reynolds, 1982, p. 50). As the practice of Naikan has grown more popular, it has become more of a rational and scientific method of therapy, yet it has also retained many of the spiritual constructs of Buddhism. Interestingly, it is in the prisons of Japan that Naikan has had its greatest impact. In fact, 60 per cent of the prison facilities in Japan have used Naikan at one time or another. Prison officials reported reduced rates of recidivism among *naikansha* prisoners compared to those who are not following the Naikan approach (Reynolds, 1982). Naikan's popularity is increasing, particularly with those working with juvenile delinquents and alcoholics, in part because Naikan can be combined with a short prison sentence and training during probationary periods.

Theoretical Basis of Naikan

In order to enhance well-being, Buddhism emphasizes self-discipline or self-control, particularly the power to control or modify physical aspects of the body:

> Meditation, the principal psycho-therapeutic tool of Buddhism, also can enrich traditional Western psychotherapy in several ways: 1) by offering insight into self-defeating behaviours by focusing on them and exaggerating them; 2) by severing the tight grip of thinking on behaviour by retraining attention; and 3) by producing an integrated hypothalamic response that decreases sympathetic activity. (Ramaswami & Sheikh, 1989, p. 109)

Through exploring early experiences and present actions, clients using the Naikan approach are helped to let go of selfish attachments and guilt associated with living a self-absorbed life. While the introspection is carefully guided by the therapist, clients share their recollections on what was received from significant others in terms of services, kindness, objects and other important gifts; what has been returned to significant others; and what troubles, inconveniences, deceits, pettiness and the other selfish acts occurred with these people. The rationale is to focus clients on personal actions, past and present, that influenced their present situation. An important goal of Naikan therapy is to assist clients in accepting responsibility for "their selfish and irrational behaviour" (Ramaswami & Sheikh, 1989, p. 108). Responsibility extends not only to significant others in clients' lives, but also to the objects in the environment around the clients. Clients not only have to consider how they have polluted their bodies and relationships, but also how they have polluted their environment.

The Naikan Therapeutic Process

Traditional Naikan therapy consists of two parts: immersion and counselling. The immersion takes place in either a temple or a place where the client can be isolated. Clients are isolated, sleeping and taking meals alone, and are required to undergo meditation training. Meditation, as the primary helping strategy, may last from 4:30 a.m. until 7 p.m. Therapists visit clients at intervals of one to two hours during the day, to instruct them on meditation and engage them in dialogue. In addition, therapists also guide clients in introspection and dialogue by focussing on recurring life themes. For example, clients may explore desires that block constructive living, such as dishonesty, negativity or blaming. In a sense, therapists are "fellow travelers," but with some experience in life. Despite being guides, therapists must show honour to clients and continually reinforce clients' ability to solve personal problems. To empower the client, the therapist will bow his/her "head to the floor, open the folding screen, bow again, and ask clients the topic of [the] current meditation. This ritualized format symbolizes the therapist's humility as he [or she] prepares to listen to the client's confession. The client's response is similarity in ritual form and he [or she] reports the person and time period of his [or her] recollections" (Reynolds, 1982, p. 47).

About 20 per cent of clients' meditation is spent on significant people who have given to them and what the client has returned. Sixty percent of clients' meditation is spent on the trouble or inconveniences that clients have caused significant others. Interestingly, one of the common themes during meditation is clients' relationship with their parents. Since relationships are strongly influenced by parents, this topic is often discussed early in therapy. One of the assumptions is that people develop a distorted sense of self or destructive patterns in the process of growing up. While the traumas or failures of the past cannot be undone, clients' attitudes can be changed. The Naikan therapy process attempts to restructure clients' thinking and provide a moral structure for living life based on the Buddha's ideal of giving. Clients share their idea of past events, working from the past to the present. In the first week of reflection, clients share their remembrances about the themes in their relationships while therapists listen without interpretation or comment. Besides instruction in meditation, the therapeutic process involves rephrasing, recasting and reflecting clients' statements. Once therapists have a solid understanding of clients' issues, they will engage in interpreting and then guiding clients' actions. According to Reynolds (1982), the therapist "directs the client away from abstract or vague descriptions of past events and personal suffering. The goal is [for clients to use] concrete statements about specific personal experiences" (p. 48).

In the second phase, counselling consists of weekly or monthly visits to therapists, during which clients report on their activities and the progress of their meditation. A journal is often used as a means for structuring client–therapist interactions. Clients are also given homework assignments, which may consist of summaries of "good works" (helping others) and saying things that show appreciation to others (e.g., "saying thank-you at least ten times during the day"). Reynolds (1989) describes how a client must also consider how he/she is served not only by people but also by the energy of objects. Clients may be asked to remove objects from a place where they keep personal items such as a drawer: "as the items are returned to the drawer one by one, each item is thanked for some specific service it performed for the [client] . . . conservation of the resources in our world becomes a natural consequence of the grateful recognition of their services they perform for us" (p. 191). Since obtaining a higher state of consciousness and becoming more aware are important goals in living constructively, clients must practise daily meditation at a certain place and time. As an active strategy, meditation is invaluable. Research in meditation has solidly demonstrated benefits in increasing perceptual and empathic sensitivity (Walsh, 2011). Clients are usually instructed to meditate on how someone has given to them, visualizing him or her and letting whatever feelings and thoughts develop. However, in dialogue with therapists, clients share how they can live life by giving back. Clients must develop strategies that do not see others as tools for satisfying personal desires but develop relationships that are open and giving.

Effectiveness of Naikan

According to Sengoku, Murata, Kawahara, Imamura and Nakagome (2010), daily intensive practice of Naikan therapy can reduce depression. Intensive Naikan therapy takes place in a setting where clients are separated from the outside world and practise the introspective techniques with a therapist through a seven-day period; the less intensive form can be integrated with daily activities. In clinical trials intensive Naikan was very effective in helping deal with depression and much more effective than the daily use of Naikan introspective practices. However, it was also found that, although intensive therapy has a more immediate effect, daily use of Naikan is better than doing nothing.

Kresh (2002) provides a more personal reflection on how the daily practice of Naikan changed his outlook on life. Just like meditation, Naikan requires a quiet place for introspection and the ritual of taking time to think about the path. It involves examining our mistakes and how others helped us along our path, even in simple ways and deeds. Once the focus has changed from "What do I want?" to "What do I have to be thankful for?", one looks at the broader picture of life and begins to see that the simple acts of others have helped to move us to a higher level of being. In a sense it is making meaning out of all of life's experiences and seeing our place in the world, while at the same time remembering that we are what we are because of how others have helped us and what we did to help others along their paths. While we let go of attachments, we also need to realize that we have made mistakes and that these mistakes are places where we can learn more about living a more constructive life. Our real power is in realizing that we need others and others need us. Kresh (2002) states that we need to

> study attention by using attention. Let's explore freshness in a candy wrapper and the ancient ritual of who taught us to tie our shoes. Let's watch the film of our lives to see how we have lived and how life lives through us. On this journey we destroy the false myths and we do battle with our ego-centered dragons, get snared in traps of pride, and get stuck in the quicksand of selfishness. Yet even as we travel, our

courage and efforts are gifts, and the unlimited faith we have in ourselves is replaced by a greater faith in life itself. (p. 24)

An Example of Using Naikan in a Western Context

To illustrate how Naikan therapy is used in a Western context, I present the following case of a 35-year-old man trying to come to grips with a relationship breakup. M came to therapy with the desire to reduce stress and overcome a generally "blue" feeling. M reported that he felt a great deal of anger, yet even after expressing his anger, he felt "stuck." After explaining the Naikan form of therapeutic intervention, the therapist invited M to share his feelings. M talked for over an hour about his state of mind and how he thought he had been coping. The therapist listened and asked only clarifying questions. The therapist's sense of M's condition is captured in M's imagery of how he saw his life. M described his existence as "Going down the road of life, minding my own business, and being attacked by colleagues who disagreed with me. The viciousness of their attacks was a real surprise and I felt myself being knocked down in the mud. The sorrow of their attacks seems to have somehow paralyzed me . . . I don't feel that I can get up, yet I see the uselessness of staying and wallowing in the mud."

After M mastered the skill of meditation and practised it for some time, the therapist focussed on significant relationships, positive and negative, in M's life. Of the many people he felt were significant in his life, M chose to "work" on a relationship involving a colleague M felt had treated him in an unfair way. Rather than focussing on the negative aspects of his relationship with the person, M was asked to focus on what he had learned in the encounter with that person. While finding it difficult to explore the positive parts, M did list of number of things he had learned about himself and how the experience had changed his life. After considerable time exploring this experience (two sessions consisting of one-hour each), M was surprised at what he had learned. What predominated was the "little kindnesses" of acquaintances and how much "closer" M had been drawn to his family. The method used to explore these themes was as follows: instruction from the therapist on the topic to focus on; meditation for one hour on the topic; dialoguing the messages in the meditation in a journal; and sharing the messages with the therapist. Generally, the therapist focussed on actions and meaning. In every case M was asked to make sense of what was given and what he did to repay others. While the emphasis was on the positive, M's feelings were honoured. Rather than staying with negative feelings, though, the therapist refocussed M toward the positive. Over the next two sessions, M explored a number of other relationships from the past, including the relationships with his parents, siblings and ex-spouse. In each case, he was asked to meditate on how these people had influenced and given "something" to him. This was followed by an exploration of how he had given back to others.

After tying all these themes together, M was asked to write out how, when, where and with whom he would return the gifts he had been given. In addition to the dialoguing, meditation and journaling, M was asked to consider how he treated pets (cats), plants and objects in his daily life. A clear theme was his pleasure at taking care of his pets and houseplants. In fact, he learned that he was happier in "nurturing" than in controlling his relationships.

The therapist followed a basic Naikan approach in counselling M, with the philosophy and basic strategies remaining constant. However, in adapting the approach to M's cultural milieu, the therapist structured the intervention by teaching meditation skills and encouraging M to focus on the meaning in his actions. The therapist did not engage in interpreting M's actions but in encouraging him to arrive at his own meanings. Finally, the therapist focussed on moving M toward active and positive strategies for living in harmony with himself and his environment. Specific living strategies that gave back were discussed and clarified so M had a clearer idea of what he could do. The two follow-up sessions evaluated how well the strategies were working for him. It was not surprising that a motto M developed and promised to repeat every day consisted of this thought: "The best way to receive is to give."

Conclusion

The beauty in Naikan is the strong reminder that through self-reflection, we have more gratitude for others and honestly make a practice of self-reflection. We can build more loving relationships by showing more attention and thankfulness to those around us on a regular basis and think of all of these people in our lives as gifts. Thus, by embracing the "spiritual" essence of Buddhism and applying it to the human condition, we discover a practical and positive method for living life. Just as M discovered, some things occur in life that cannot be changed or explained. What M learned was to "let go" of his anger and hopelessness about regaining what he had before. However, it was not just a "letting go" but a development of a more constructive way of living in the world. M learned that he had been given a great deal in life; in fact, he said many times he had been fortunate, but he also discovered that he had given very little back. He discovered that in giving, he had a great sense of satisfaction and an outlet for his sadness about the breakup of his marriage. In the process, he learned how to use meditation and "good works" to gain more control over his anxieties and fears. The most difficult strategy was learning how to "let go" of his anger and disappointments, but he realized that survival depended on being more flexible (just like water).

While much can be made of how different Naikan is from many Western forms of therapy, the differences are not in fact as great as they first seem. Take, for example, behaviourism, a very Western approach. One can see many similarities. Both approaches emphasize self-control and avow the intention of helping to modify bodily process to enhance well-being. Both have the objective of teaching clients new behaviours and reducing the gap between the real self and the ideal self. However, they differ in that behaviourism stresses the value of counter-conditioning in undoing neurotic behaviour, while Naikan stresses insight. Naikan views insight and training as the best means for developing a constructive lifestyle. My experience with M and other clients who opt for the Naikan approach reinforces my belief that Naikan is easily adapted into a Western cultural mode. I continue to believe that meditation is one of the best coping strategies to empower clients and provide them with the ability to be more positive. Naikan has a simplicity about it that I can only describe as eloquent and expressive. It is easily adapted to Western culture and the Gestalt therapeutic approach that I normally practise. Naikan respects the dignity of all things. In fact, the Buddhist ideal may not be all that different from the Christian ideal or any other spiritual approach that seeks harmony. I have found that the premises of Naikan, which emphasize the connectedness of all things, the impermanence of existence, the acceptance of suffering and giving to others, have a seductive quality that is quite empowering.

Reality is constantly changing. We are constantly changing. We must receive the Buddha's wisdom, a perspective through which we can discover new meaning in all things. We must learn to have deep appreciation of all the things and people we encounter in our lives. (Nobuo Haneda, 2009, p. 3)

References

Chuang-Tsu: (2012). Retrieved from http://www.katinkahesselink.net/tibet/quotes-zen.html

Haneda, N. (2009). Dharma breeze. ToDo Institute. Retrieved from http://www.todoinstitutebooks.com

Krech, G. (2002). *Naikan: Gratitude, grace and the Japanese art of self-reflection.* Berkley, CA: Stone Bridge Press.

Reynolds, D. (1989). *On being natural: Two Japanese approaches to healing.* In A. Sheikh & S. Sheikh (Eds.), *Eastern and Western approaches to healing: Ancient wisdom and modern knowledge.* New York, NY: John Wiley, pp. 180–196.

Reynolds, D. (1982). *Quiet therapies.* Honolulu, HA: University of Hawaii Press.

Ramaswami, S. & Sheikh, A. (1989). Buddhist psychology: Implications for healing. In A. Sheikh & S. Sheikh (Eds.), *Eastern and Western approaches to healing: Ancient wisdom and modern knowledge.* New York, NY: John Wiley, pp. 91–123.

Sengoku, M., Murat, H., Kawahara, T., Imamura, K., & Nakagome, K. (2010). Does daily Naikan therapy maintain the efficacy of intensive Naikan therapy against depression? *Psychiatry and Clinical Neurosciences,* 64(1), 44–51.

ToDo Institute (2012), http://www.todoinstitute.org/naikan.html.

Walsh, R. (2011). Contemplative therapies. In R. Corsini & D. Wedding (Eds.), *Current psychotherapies* (pp. 568–603, 9th ed.). Belmont, CA: Brooks-Cole Publishers.

23

Reconnecting with Nature

Using Nature in Counselling

M. Honoré France
& María del Carmen Rodríguez

If you extend your mind into Nature, it will extend its mind into yours, meeting you half way, creating common ground, revealing its astonishing beauty to your intuition. (Tuffly, 2010, p. 9)

THE PROCESS OF CONNECTING TO NATURE involves being mindful. You experience everything around you without any evaluation or preconceived ideas. That is, you open to all of the detail and rhythms of nature without judgement, seeing, feeling, smelling and tasting all that nature has to offer. As you open your eyes, seeing all the detail of nature — the trees, the plants and all the living things in the environment — you begin to understand that you are part of the ecology – just another breathing life form among many, dependent on all the life in nature. Thus, the purpose is being in the present without any worries of the past or the future. Tuffly, quoting Hesse, states that

> amongst the thousands [of travellers wishing to cross the river] there have been few, four or five, to whom the river was not an obstacle. They heard its voice and listened to it, and the river has become holy to them, as it has to me. The river has taught me to listen; you will learn from it too. The river knows everything; one can learn everything from it. (pp. 11–12)

Our existence as human beings depends on nature, which we need to respect, preserve and restore if we are to live harmoniously in our environment. Nature is not always benign, and we must accept that we cannot control nature but live with its rhythms, nurturing it and being nurtured in symbiotic embrace. Aboriginal peoples around the world have always stressed the sacredness of humanity's connection with nature, not only for spiritual well-being but also for our physical, social and psychological well-being. Our experiences in counselling reinforce these practices and suggest that humankind's separation from nature in the modern world increases stress and leaves people with a sense of psychological, social and spiritual isolation. Along with relevant case studies, this chapter offers a rationale and description for using nature in counselling to help clients clarify their values, increase personal awareness and self-esteem and reduce stress in everyday life and thus tap into the "higher power" wisdom inherent in each individual.

In *Walden; or, Life in the Woods*, Thoreau showed that connecting with nature could heal the mind and provide people with a sense of meaning; by going out into nature, one could "live deliberately, to feel only the essential facts of life, to see if . . . [one] . . . could not learn what it had to teach, and not when . . . [one] . . . came to die, discover that . . . [one] . . . had not lived" (1970, p. 25). From earliest time, experiencing nature, particularly through what Aboriginal people call the vision quest, has been a common feature. According to Matheson (1996), what happens is that "ordinary boundaries between entities that are defined without question in the Euro-American world suddenly become fluid, interactive, and blurred" (p. 53). Interest in nature and its healing effects continues to grow among all people in the world as people see that the well-being of the planet is directly linked to the well-being of humankind. Salish elder and teacher John Elliot stresses that every place where the First People lived has a spirit, and these places have the memories of those people and their lives. Interestingly, the Siksikaitsitapi (Blackfoot) people believe that

> Knowledge grows through the ability to listen and to hear the whispers of the wind, the teachings of the rock, the seasonal changes of the weather. By connecting with the knowing of animals and plants, we strengthen our knowledge. As in all relationships, consent must given and obligations and responsibilities need to be observed. (Bastien, 2004, p. 111)

There seems to be an estrangement now between humans and nature, giving rise to some speculation that nature is finally rebelling against the pollution and mistreatment of humans. Could it be that the benign aspect attributed by some is not so benign after all? Could it be that nature is a force in the universe that humankind will "fight" as the effects of human endeavours such as development of the land continue? Examples are global warming or the floods in Europe, Asia and North America. Cultural values coming out of the attempt to "conquer" the land have affected North American views. Sue and Sue

(2008) suggest that in regard to nature, Aboriginal people's value preference is one of living in harmony, versus the majority value preference of controlling nature. Berkes (2003) found that Aboriginal people's traditional knowledge of nature is in fact ecologically sound and contributes to environmental sustainability. The relationship between the Cree people in the Hudson Bay area and the environment in which they live has a mutuality to it, benefits their traditional way of life and is ecologically healthy. Perhaps the notion of controlling nature objectifies it rather than sees nature as an extension of life. Taken one step further, people with this attitude also have to control those urges that they feel within themselves. Thus, control becomes a major issue for society and the individual. The way to control nature, it is thought, is not to leave it to its natural cycle, but to bend it to the will of humanity.

The Connection with Nature Enhances Well-Being

Berger and McLeod (2006) stress that healing in nature is not a new phenomenon but goes back eons in human history when shamans incorporated the healing power of nature with traditional medicines of herbs along with rituals as therapeutic forms of healing. The knowledge of the healing power of herbs and the benefit of being in nature were powerful reminders to people living with an intimate knowledge of the land that nature can enhance well-being. As the new science of psychology developed, early European thinkers of the mind, such as Freud and Erickson, routinely sent their clients to nature because they knew not just that being in the natural world was restful from a hectic life, but also that the freshness and beauty of the natural world has a positive effect on well-being.

We have observed a number of positive results in our clients when we use nature either as a background metaphor to express values or as a place to experience something beyond themselves. The latter is particularly powerful in that it immerses clients in nature and helps them move beyond themselves (i.e., moving away from a self-centred attitude). The anecdotal findings in this paper reinforce what Cammack (1996) found in a study of wilderness guides: "the results suggest that there appears to be a movement from egocentrism towards ecocentrism; that is an expansive process that occurs with most people over a period of time" (p. 80).

The following cases provide a rationale for our belief that nature can enhance well-being. Glendinning (1994) states that democracy is encouraged by one's contact with the environment. Perhaps love and a sense of belonging can be reinforced as a means to overcome evil and mean-spiritedness by humankind. What has emerged is the movement called *adventure therapy*, in which the outdoors is used as a basis for moving away from a disruptive and selfish way of being and toward a more cooperative and responsible way of encountering others. The successful use of nature in which people are challenged by hiking and trekking has had a profound way of working with people who have difficulty with authority. However, adventure therapy has not included the spiritual element that makes nature therapy so powerful. Berger (2006) describes nature therapy, a more holistic approach that is a postmodern integration of the elements of art and drama therapy, narrative, eco-psychology and trans-personal psychology, along with adventure therapy.

Two Case Studies Using Nature with Counselling

Case Study One

TR is a young adult female exploring new directions in her life. She is examining her values and experimenting with what she calls "a new way of being." When offered an opportunity to use nature as a means for clarifying her values, she readily agreed. She described the idea as a chance to get "out of her head." At the conclusion of the counselling, TR shared the following from her journal:

> I was going through a rough period in my marriage and felt the urge to run. It just seemed like all the talk in therapy didn't help. . . . Although the change of environment and meeting new people and all the physical activities were pleasant, nothing changed for me internally until a solo two-day wilderness survival trip. It was then that the extraneous and unimportant parts of my life that were obscuring the problem disappeared, and allowed me to focus on my true feelings, followed by a vision of alternatives and possible solutions. When "survival," or aloneness in the wilderness became my social and physical focus, the mental/emotional aspects took on a greater clarity. Now when I feel the need to refocus or recharge, I spend some time with nature in a wilderness situation.

Case Study Two

RG is a professional male who came to counselling reporting extreme stress related to his work. According to RG, the stress of a changing workplace put stress on his professional life and work life. In discussing his issues, RG reported dissatisfaction with the verbal interaction between himself and the therapist. Because of RG's interest in the outdoors, he was encouraged to go out into nature, but to keep a journal and undertake a series of structured activities during his hike. Afterwards, he returned to face-to-face counselling with the therapist where the experience was processed using his journal. The following are some excerpts from his journal that the therapist used to focus the face-to-face encounters.

I want to become more authentic and natural and that means moving away from what is polite and ritualistic. Again, I drank greedily from the pristine stream. The water has such a sparkle and clearness that, when I drank from it, it became like "champagne." My taste buds are used to chlorinated water and were surprised by fresh, natural water. . . . The message is clear: I want to live life in a respectful way, because that is nature's way.

Clarifying Values

Nature is full of metaphors through which people can express their values; for example, the seasons are a cycle of birth, life, dying and rebirth. Both TR and RG began to use the vocabulary of nature to describe their views of how to live a more effective life. In essence, the fixed laws of nature offered them a constant lesson for what was important in their lives. For example, when one looks at the clouds, which are constantly changing, it is easy to see how life too changes. The effect is learning the lessons of nature and applying them to everyday life. Most of our clients, including the two cases described above, readily project their thoughts and feelings onto what they observed in nature. When TR spoke of the comings and goings of the tide, it was quite straightforward to ask her to describe what it meant to her life. Underlying everything she said was an expressed value that could easily be brought out and reflected back to her, thus allowing her to transcribe the metaphors to important values.

Increasing Personal Awareness

The journals of these two clients demonstrate that when their awareness was sharpened, they felt more in touch with their senses, emotions, thoughts and perceptions. The self cannot be examined without looking at the context; it is best discovered by looking at the whole, part of which is being in touch with nature. If people are to live an effective life, they must be open to experiencing things in their immediate environment. The acceptance of responsibility and the recognition of their powers occur through awareness. To this end, being aware involves focussing on what is there and what is not there: what is not there is also a part of what is there. The silence occurring is just as important as our verbal and non-verbal communication. For example, as people go outside and into the forest, they can see only what is in view; yet there exists life beyond that, which cannot be seen nor even sensed, but it is there. Nothing in nature is empty. When using nature to increase awareness, we ask clients to experience all aspects of their environment, including the temperature changes, smells, sounds, tactile awareness and movement around them, to name just a few. It is a discipline of being observant, immediate and open. When they are, clients open all their perceptions to the sensations around them. What our clients expressed is that they can increase their ability to be aware of other aspects in their life at home and work.

Two features related to this process of awareness can help people have more insight into themselves and sharpen their awareness. The first feature is that the process allows them to have a better understanding of the self, because at any given time they can identify their feelings and thoughts at any given moment. Meaning is not something that has to be processed before they can act authentically, as people acting as themselves for themselves. The second feature is the interaction people have with their environment. Boundaries become clear, and people react more spontaneously to their environment. They see more, experience more and are aware of more details in their surroundings. For example, as I walk towards my office, I do not think of my plans, but stay in the present. I keep my focus on my surroundings, looking carefully, without making judgments – just observing what I see in nature. I want to see things as a whole. If people try to split feelings and thoughts, they will find that it is difficult, if not impossible. Our awareness about nature helps us become more in sync with the rhythms that exist around us and helps us stop the frequent interruptions that exist in day-to-day activities as we move about in the environment. In essence, we try to teach our clients not to think and analyze what they see in nature, but just allow their senses to be open to what is going on around them. To attend simultaneously to two things with the same degree of awareness is difficult, because they will always miss out on something. If people can just be aware of what is happening and let it flow, they will experience it — not in parts, but as a whole.

To put it in another perspective, consider the following idea of non-dual consciousness, or what is called the Advaita truth:

> or oneness of Being, has often been thought of as something hidden or difficult to experience, when it is quite ordinary and available in every moment. Non-dual consciousness is the natural state. Of course, a dramatic experience of oneness is a rare event. But why wait for something so rare when this sweet and satisfying oneness is right here, right now? (Waite, 2012).

Increasing Self-Esteem

It has been well documented both anecdotally and quantitatively that being out and involved in nature, whether passively observing it (e.g., sitting in a park) or actively involved in action-oriented activities (e.g., hiking or gardening), brings about a sense of well-being. We have found that there are two important aspects of this phenomenon, which can be described as natural rhythms that reflect life in general (e.g., like one's heartbeat). In addition, our clients report that they have found that being connected to something greater than themselves provides a sense of empowerment.

Part of the sense of well-being is the peacefulness of nature compared to most people's stressful existence in the home and at work. Nature, to most people, seems somehow slower and thus more relaxed, producing a mirror effect in people. When people sit in a natural setting, they physically and psychologically slow down, producing a positive sense of well-being. There is a sense of being connected to something that is greater than oneself — that one's existence is part of a larger self — and an absence of deadlines, commitment and demands.

Stress Reduction

"As I worked in my garden, I felt a sense of relief from the stress of the day," RG reported in his journal. This response to some involvement in natural activities is typical of the kind of responses reported by various people (Debring & Wilis, 1987; Cohen, 1995; Cammack, 1996, Berger & McLeod, 2007). We ask clients, as individual homework or with the counsellor, to go for a walk, sit in a park or go camping as a means of helping them to refocus their attention and energy away from stress in the home and at work. The rhythms in nature are quite opposite the kind of drive and energy that push people to the point of increased stress. Thus, by refocussing on natural rhythms, people can slow down and move at the speed of everything around them.

Nature and Meaning: Walk of Life

As a famous Mexican proverb goes, "There is no path; the path is made by walking." We thought this a fitting theme for using nature as a metaphor for finding meaning in life. The roots of this approach and the rationale came from Carmen Rodríguez in her first year of teaching elementary school. A project was being organized by teachers and volunteer mothers of her Grade 5 students. The activity consisted of taking students on a hike to a nearby mountain called *Chipinque* ("small hill") near the city of Monterrey, Mexico, where students could reflect on the changes and transitions they would go through in the school year. Two large groups of Grade 5 students were divided into smaller groups of seven. Along the hike, there were three stations or posts where students were asked to ponder and reflect on some questions and later exchange views with the rest of the group. As individuals in an important developmental stage of life, the students were invited to look at their present life and reflect on the qualities they have developed, ponder these qualities and consider their spiritual growth.

Being Present — First Station

The goal of the first station was increasing personal awareness and self-esteem. It was important that the students realized that they would soon go from being children to being young adolescents, and thus teaching them to honour the different dimensions of their new self was one of the goals of the project. The definition of spirituality was an individual construction and there were no specific religious affiliations or connotations in this activity. After walking for 15 or 20 minutes, we sat in a circle and the students took turns answering a number of questions that focussed on meaning. Honoré took the approach one step further with counselling graduate students to use it as a framework for counselling outdoors. What we both realized was that the approach worked just as well with elementary students as it did with counselling students. In examining the work of Berger (2007), who used a parallel approach with older adults, we found that the results were the same in assisting clients to understand those challenges in life by using nature as a metaphor, along with counselling strategies like circular questions, refocussing and reflections that reinforced strengths.

As they walked to the first station, participants were asked to pay attention to the sounds (and silences), sights, smells and textures of nature. The following questions were used:

- What do you perceive?
- Is this somehow like you? In what way(s)?
- What does this mean to you?
- How can you represent such meaning?

At this time, participants came up with different representations of their sense of awareness and themselves (e.g., drawings, words or phrases, movements and so forth). Everything was kept or recorded with their permission.

Clarifying Values — Second Station

At the second station, the focus was on all of our relations and on clarifying values. As human beings, our relationship to nature develops and unfolds in diverse ways. Some people see themselves as part of the natural world; some see nature as separate from themselves and as an entity that needs to be taken care of. Others see nature as a force that subjugates humankind and therefore it becomes something feared. Indigenous people around the world have always perceived the land and its creatures as part of their web of life where everyone is interconnected and relies on one another for survival and growth.

"Heal the earth, heal each other" (an Ojibway prayer) embodies the healing process. People need to develop an unfamiliar sense of reintegration of themselves by trying to live in harmony rather than trying to maintain a sense of control in all aspects of life. When this reintegration happens, paralysis and despair can be transformed to a sense of passion and connectedness to the Earth. The primal self (reflected by many Aboriginal and Asian people) can be rediscovered. Healing, through active participation with nature, thus becomes possible. Connecting to nature can help people reach a state of enlightenment, which is non-discriminatory, because no element is valued over any other. In the same way, there should be no separation of self, including the physical, social, psychological and spiritual, from nature. The basic practice of reconnecting with nature starts in the body, for the body epitomizes the natural process of living. It is within this belief that this activity takes place.

Participants are encouraged to "live and breathe" this exercise and relate their life to the metaphors found in nature. The questions posed to the students at this time were as follows:

- List/name three things that are important to you. (e.g., family, friends, education/school).
- Do you feel related/connected to nature? If so, how?
- If you were something in nature, what would you be? Why?

At this point, the participants were asked to exchange and comment on their answers with a partner. Then, each person took some minutes to retell what his/her partner had answered. The goal of this discussion was to make the students feel empathic and closer to understanding other people's views.

Looking Forward — Third Station

At the third station, participants were ask to think about their futures and possible selves. The last station required a deeper understanding of this exploration. Here, students were encouraged to imagine their immediate future by exploring their possible selves. Possible selves are thought to influence an individual's motivation process in two ways: they provide clear goals to strive for and offer clear images to avoid negative outcomes; and they energize an individual to pursue the actions necessary for attaining a possible self (Markus & Ruvolo, 1989). The following questions were offered as a means to reach this goal:

- What personal characteristics do you admire in yourself? Why?
- Which characteristics don't you like? Why?
- Would you change them? How?
- What kind of teenager would you like to be in three years?
- What can you do to achieve it? (Name at least five concrete ways.)

At the end of the exercise, participants were asked to reflect on the overall sensations, feelings, emotions and general thoughts this activity had brought for them. They were asked to cluster the recurring themes they found in their responses in order to share them with the large group. They were surprised at how similar their individual experiences were; afterwards, they were asked to map such experiences in a visual way. Some of them used drawings that represented these ideas; some wrote a poem with the main ideas of their small group, while others represented their outcomes in the form of a story. Once they were assembled as a large group, each group had some minutes to share their creative representation and answer any questions that the rest of the large group had. These final moments provided them with an opportunity to see the common threads and themes of their life at this stage and at the same time offered moments for them to see their emerging spirituality as an element within and not outside themselves.

Discussion and Implications for Counselling

Research by Berkes (2003) and others shows that living in a positive relationship with nature has beneficial results for people and the ecology of a given area. Berger (2009) says that

> nature-therapy's impact upon different populations shows that its creative operation within nature can significantly support people's healing. It seems like the way it relates to the natural elements within this uncontrollable environment can help people develop flexibility and expand their ability to connect to their imagination and body. (p. 1)

The bond with nature demonstrated by those who live according to traditional ecological knowledge not only is adaptive but also is transmitted by cultural practices over time. In an age when society favours technology over culture and traditions, the relationship with nature becomes paramount to maintaining a sense of balance. Further, in the two cases presented above, nature was shown to be extremely useful not only as a metaphor for well-being and healing but also as an arena or environment for personal change. Glendinning

(1994) feels that the first step to healing using nature is very similar to that used by Alcoholics Anonymous: admitting that people are powerless and their lives are unmanageable. This admission creates a sense of being able to direct the next steps in reconnecting to nature, by not denying the trauma, which "is individual . . . is social . . . is historic" (p. 126). Once healing begins, people must be open, focussed and alert to the wealth hidden within and between themselves and the environment. This is a different and more natural way of thinking of oneself, which Cohen (1995) calls "old brain" thinking: "the tearing down of fences and the dismantling of the mechanistic ways that characterized the dissociated state" (Glendinning, 1994, p. 132). Thus, people work towards reuniting with the wildness in nature and in the unconscious self in a holistic way.

How does one reconnect to nature? As we saw in both clients' journals, clients went out to become more aware of nature. This awareness occurs by sharpening the senses, by listening to or witnessing the natural phenomena that occur in nature. As clients became more aware, they gained a greater sense of safety and trust with their environment, which translated to their accepting their place in the ecological process. Values in regards to life were strengthened at the same time, enabling the clients to vocalize important messages of living by what they observed in nature. Client RG's recounting of his hike assisted him in finding connection and meaning in his life. When people start to tell their stories, parts of the trauma will come up while other parts will be suppressed. The task is redefining oneself in relation to the environment, so that we can come into an alignment with the wholeness of the universe (Drebing & Wilis, 1987). According to Glendinning (1994), people are "sitting around the fire" (p. 158) and telling their stories while working through pain and fragmentation (e.g., metaphorically tearing down the chain-link fence and restoring the land to wilderness).

McGaa's statement "if you are going to learn to swim, then you have to immerse yourself in water" (1990, p. 133) is an important challenge for all of us who want to engage in activities in nature. We need to accept the challenge of reintegrating ourselves and those we work with by living in harmony with nature rather than trying to maintain a sense of control in all aspects of life. When this reintegration happens, paralysis and despair can be transformed to a sense of passion and connectedness to the Earth. The primal self (reflected by many Asian and Indigenous people) can be rediscovered. Healing, through active participation with nature, thus becomes possible. Connecting to nature can help people reach a state of enlightenment, which is non-discriminatory, because no element is valued over any other. In the same way, there should be no separation of self, including the physical, social, psychological and spiritual, from nature.

References

Bastien, B. (2004). *Blackfoot ways of knowing: The world view of the Siksikaitsitapi.* Calgary, AB: University of Calgary Press.

Berger, R. (2009). Being in nature: An innovative framework for incorporating nature in therapy with older adults. *Journal of Holistic Nursing,* 27(1).

Berger, R., & McLeod (2006). Incorporating nature into therapy: a framework for practice. *Journal of Systemic Therapies,* 25(2), 80–94.

Berkes, F. (2003). *Sacred ecology: Reassessing traditional ecological knowledge.* Presentation given at the Department of Environmental Studies, University of Victoria, Victoria, BC.

Cammack, M. (1996). *A rite of passage with outward bound: Transpersonal perspective of the solo from 16 wilderness guides.* An unpublished MA thesis, University of Victoria, Victoria, Canada.

Cohen, M. (1995). *Connecting with nature: Creating moments that let earth teach.* Eugene, ON: World Peace University.

Drebing, C., & Wilis, S.C. (1987). *Wilderness stress camping as an adjunctive therapeutic modality.* An unpublished paper presented at the Western Psychological Association, Long Beach, CA.

Glendinning, C. (1994). *My name is Chellis, and I'm in recovery from Western civilization.* Boston, MA: Shambala Press.

McGaa, E. (1990). *Mother earth spirituality,* New York: Harper Collins.

Matheson, L. (1996). Valuing spirituality among Native American populations. *Counselling and Values,* 41, 51–70.

Sue, D.W., & Sue, D. (2008). *Counselling the culturally different: Theory and practice* (5th ed.). New York, NY: John Wiley and Sons.

Thoreau, H.D. (1970). *Walden.* New York, NY: Harper Collins Publishers.

Tuffly, D. (2010). *Communing with nature.* N.p.: Smashwords Editions.

Waite, D. (2012). What is Advaita or nonduality? Retrieved from http://endless-satsang.com/advaita-nonduality-oneness.htm

24

Culturally Friendly?

A Cognitive-Behavioural Approach to Multicultural Counselling

Geoffrey G. Hett, María del Carmen Rodríguez, & M. Honoré France

CENTRAL TO COUNSELLING IS THE QUESTION, What counselling interventions are most likely to effect change with a particular client? Research suggests that client characteristics account for most of the outcome variance (Cormier & Nurius, 2009). This means that the characteristics a client brings to counselling (for example, cultural values) play a pivotal role in the outcome of the counselling program. According to Tanaka-Matsumi, Higginbotham and Chang (2002), multicultural counselling "involves an integration of universal principles and culturally distinctive values" (p. 338). In Canada, most counselling intervention programs and strategies reflect the dominant culture — that is, the white, middle-class, heterosexual male and female. Caution is suggested in the use of these programs for clients not in the mainstream culture. What strategies are then appropriate for culturally different clients? From a theoretical perspective, cognitive–behavioural strategies may offer culturally sensitive approaches. Cormier and Nurius (2009) propose guidelines for identifying intervention plans for culturally different clients:

1. Intervention planning must reflect the values and world views of the client's cultural identity;
2. Intervention planning must meet the needs of the individual client and his/her social system;

3. Intervention planning must encompass the role of important subsystems and resources in the client's life, such as family structure, support systems, local community, spiritual practices and folk beliefs;
4. Intervention planning must address issues of health, recovery and ways of solving problems;
5. The client's level of acculturation and language must also be considered as must the length of treatment. (p. 314)

Cognitive–Behavioural Counselling to Promote Changes in Thinking and Behaviour

Cognitive–behavioural counselling strategies have been used successfully to help children and adults overcome a wide variety of problems. These strategies are designed to produce changes in human performance and thinking. They are problem based; that is, clients are helped to identify individual problems and then taught methods to resolve and overcome these difficulties.

Several assumptions underlie cognitive–behavioural approaches. First, it is assumed that a person's thoughts, mental images and beliefs, as well as the person's external environment, assert a profound influence on human behaviour. A corollary assumption is that a specific focus on a client's cognition and environment is an effective approach to bring about change. As problem behaviours develop from internal processes and external events, both must be the focus for change.

It is believed that most problem behaviours are learned, maintained and modified in the same manner as appropriate behaviour. That is, human behaviour is developed and maintained by external events (antecedents and consequences) and by internal processes such as thoughts, attitudes and world views (antecedents and consequences). As antecedents and consequences are functionally related to behaviour, a change in one or both variables may change the behaviour it is related to. For example, what a parent or teacher says to a child about his/her behaviour (consequence) influences how the child will behave under similar circumstances in the future. What a person says to him/herself about an event or another person (antecedent) will influence how that person behaves during the event or when meeting the other person. An antecedent that precedes a panic attack might be the internal dialogue or self-talk a person engages in such as, "I can't handle this situation" or "I'm going to look like such a fool!" Fleeing from this uncomfortable situation might result in the reinforcing consequence of thinking, "Thank God I'm out of there" and the body sensation of reduced arousal and feeling relief. The functional relationship that exists between the individual's behaviour and the internal and external antecedents and consequences is emphasized in cognitive–behavioural assessment and counselling.

Culture, Functional Assessment and Cognitive–Behavioural Counselling

It is easy to get confused with the terminology of cognitive–behavioural approaches because it appears to quantify behaviour, thus appearing unfriendly and culturally insensitive. However, consider that the way in which a person learns is similar across cultures and that if people basically learn by observing and experiencing, then these are not valued-laden aspects of learning. Cognitive–behavioural counselling does not imply that a person is good or bad or evaluate what constitutes acceptable or unacceptable. It simply focusses on how a person reacts to or learns from a given situation, not whether the stimulus is good or bad. In a sense, the environment determines this, making the environment a relative fact based on the cultural context in which the behaviour occurs. It is the person's cultural milieu that values whether a person is doing the right thing or the wrong thing. A behaviour in which one shows the bottom of the feet or sits with his/her feet on a table in Thai society, for example, is considered insulting, while in England it is seen as sitting comfortably. Thai society ensures, through conditioning, that no one shows the soles of their feet because it is bad, while in England no such thing is done. Skinner (1953) said, "culture is the social environment" (p. 40). In other words, people shape contingencies of reinforcement, and the behaviour they shape, and hence the behaviour they share, is a determinant of evolving environments or culture.

In every society, norms or rules of behaviour evolve that correspond with expected social roles and behaviour. In Anglo-North American society, maintaining eye contact is thought of as a positive behaviour. It is normal for someone to look into the eyes of another when he/she is speaking. It is even thought of as being more honest to look a person in the eyes. However, among some Aboriginal groups, such as the Navaho, looking into the eyes of another person might be intrusive and thus negative. In fact, the Navaho go further and see intense eye contact as a stare or the "evil eye" (Trimble & Thurman, p. 63). Asking a lot of questions is considered rude in some cultures, yet is seen by many European societies as a mark of interest — a positive. Consider the results of a study of differing perceptions of black and white Americans (Matsumoto, 2000) evaluating "the same behaviour by Caucasians as assertiveness, but aggressive for blacks. Blacks are perceived as aggressive by Whites when they express their feelings, raise questions, or are assertive in interracial situations" (p. 56).

One of the main ways in which cognitive–behavioural counsellors work is helping clients see factors that influence behaviours and the consequences of the behaviour. In a multicultural situation, the counsellor helps clients identify those situations and personal variables that control the current problematic behaviours. More specifically, the counsellor calls attention to the events preceding target behaviour. That is, behavioural counselling does not dwell on philosophical patterns of behaviour; rather, it emphasizes its empirical and functional aspects. The essence is using learning techniques to bring about change in the target behaviour. Consider the following example. Among some Hispanics, seeing and speaking with entities from the spirit world is part of everyday life. It is similar to experiencing auditory and visual hallucinations that can occur during religious situations. Majority society would view this behaviour as a sign of mental illness. The cognitive–behavioural counsellor, using functional analysis, would help the client

> identify specific social conditions under which hallucinations can take place and where these may be culturally appropriate, [and set] the stage for establishing environmental control over hallucinations rather than reducing them by the use of drugs or social sanctions. (Matsumoto, 2000, p. 273)

One method, following cognitive–behavioural principles, uses a process called *functional assessment* before engaging the client in actual counselling. It is based on the notion that besides the establishment of positive rapport with the client, counsellors need to have an accurate sense of the client's cultural background and any relevant aspects of culture in regards to behaviour. In addition, the counsellor's understanding and sensitivity towards culture is a preventive measure of the client's early termination of counselling. Clients need to feel that they have the power to make some progress on addressing whatever issue brought them to counselling. Finally, the functional-assessment process attempts to help the client be more active in the treatment of the problem. It means continually ensuring that the client's perception is in sync with culturally relevant ideas of the target behaviours and the counselling. The assessment process has eight steps (Tanaka-Masumi, Higgenbotham & Chang, 2002).

1. Assessment of cultural identity and acculturation: The counsellor should have a sense of what levels the client adheres to in his/her cultural norms (e.g., high acculturation versus low acculturation).
2. Evaluation of the presenting problem: In order not to misunderstand the problem, the counsellor needs to develop a good understanding of the client's cultural norms, levels of discomfort and idiomatic patterns.
3. Causal explanatory model elicitation: The counsellor gathers information on the problem within a cultural context.
4. Functional assessment: The counsellor needs to identify the problem, select the target behaviours and know how the target is achieved based on an accurate understanding of the problem and the client's cultural norms.
5. Causal explanatory model comparison and negotiation: The counsellor needs to explain the treatment process clearly and what the treatment is based on in order to

decrease client frustration and increase client satisfaction.

6. Establishment of treatment variables: The counsellor, in consultation with the client, works with acceptable treatment goals, target behaviours, counselling techniques, et cetera.

7. Data collection: Clients are asked to focus on their behaviour and the antecedents and consequences of that behaviour. The client monitors their behaviour throughout counselling, with the counsellor paying particular attention to issues around social comparison (e.g., the bind a minority culture might have because the appropriate behaviour in one context might mean something different in another cultural perspective).

8. Discussion of ethical considerations and other treatment concerns: This part consists of a thorough discussion with the client and the family about issues relating to the therapy and the consequence of counselling (e.g., confidentiality).

Thus, the counsellor helps the client identify specific social conditions (antecedents) important to him/her, so he/she can feel free to express problem behaviours without negative evaluation (consequences) from someone of a different cultural background. One of the most effective ways of treating culture shock is first to help clients understand what is happening and then to help them learn new responses to culturally new situations. Clients can even rehearse behaviours in order to understand how they fit culturally or value wise. Finally, the cognitive–behavioural approach emphasizes negotiating treatment strategies with clients, rather than imposing them. In fact, the purpose of conducting functional analysis is to give client and counsellor a basis for negotiating plausible treatment strategies to change the target behaviour.

Rarely is a problem caused by one factor, and rarely does one approach overcome most human problems. Cognitive–behavioural assessment and counselling approaches recognize problems as multi-faceted. Included within this model are such strategies as problem solving, modelling, visualization, cognitive restructuring, reframing, stress inoculation, relaxation, systematic desensitization, meditation, self-management and self-guidance procedures. Several of these strategies are discussed below. The case example that follows describes how some of these strategies were combined to help a man with a developmental disability overcome his fears of public places.

Cognitive–Behavioural Strategies

There are a number of useful strategies that can be used with a variety of clients from different cultures. However, counsellors need to be sensitive with these strategies in that they need to be used with culture in mind as well as how the strategy may be perceived by the client. Historically, counselling has been a tool some people have used to manipulate clients into thinking in the "white way"; therefore, the client needs to feel in control of the therapeutic process (Duran & Duran, 1995). Being cognizant of the clashes of expectation could help defuse misunderstanding. Pfeiffer (in Tanaka-Matsumi, Higgenbotham & Chang, 2002) has identified common conflicts to be aware of:

- direct verses indirect therapy style;
- individual-based versus multi-level therapy involving significant others and community;
- a hierarchical versus an equalitarian power base in therapy;
- an intrapsychic versus a functional approach to the presenting problem;
- attention to somatic versus psychological expressions of distress. (p. 350)

Problem Solving

Problem solving is a cognitive–behavioural approach that employs several sequential steps. These steps include identifying and defining the presenting problems, generating multiple solutions, evaluating and selecting suitable solutions to resolve the problems and evaluating the success of the solutions. Problem-solving strategies have shown to be successful in improving social skills, the aggressive behaviour of children, parenting skills, health, stress and the performance of children and adults in a wide variety of other areas. Problem solving also has important implications for school counsellors in helping children develop education and achievement goals. Of the counselling strategies discussed in this chapter, problem solving is one of the most widely used to assist people from diverse backgrounds.

Progressive Muscle Relaxation

Progressive muscle relaxation is a procedure that can help people cope with the stressful events they encounter in their lives. Although stress is a fact of life, in recent years it has become increasingly apparent that chronic and prolonged stress can contribute substantially to physical and emotional health concerns. Stress comes from a wide variety of sources, including human relationships, family problems, finances and even the time of year, the food we eat and the news we watch on TV or read in the newspaper. Stress can also come from loneliness, ageing and threats to our security and self-esteem. It also stems from our thoughts about past and present events and thoughts about the future.

Muscle relaxation involves learning to tense and relax various muscle groups in one's body. This process allows people to note the difference between having a tense body and having a relaxed body. Normally clients are instructed to tense and relax their hand and arm muscles, then various muscle groups in their face, neck and shoulders, torso and finally legs and feet. Muscle relaxation, although not new, has become popular for helping people overcome headaches, depression, panic, hypertension and many other related problems.

Systematic Desensitization

Systematic desensitization is a widely used anxiety-reducing strategy. The premise on which this procedure is based is that one cannot be fearful, anxious and relaxed at the same time. This counselling strategy includes identifying the source of a client's anxiety; developing a hierarchy of anxiety-evoking situations by listing situations from least anxiety-evoking to most anxiety-evoking; teaching the skill of progressive muscle relaxation; and then, beginning with the least anxiety-evoking situation, having clients visualize each situation several times while in a state of complete relaxation. This procedure is repeated for each item on the hierarchy until the situation loses the ability to evoke anxiety. Systematic desensitization is employed when clients have the ability and skill to handle a situation but avoid doing so or perform poorly because of stress and anxiety. This procedure has been successful in helping people reduce their anxiety and improve their performance in a wide variety of anxiety-evoking situations.

Cognitive Restructuring

Cognitive restructuring is a counselling procedure that helps clients recognize how their internal dialogue (sometimes referred to as "self-talk") can profoundly influence their emotions and performance. The goal of counselling is to help people change their self-defeating thinking. This is accomplished by having clients first recognize their negative and self-defeating thoughts. Next, thought-stopping procedures are taught. Finally, clients are taught to recognize and stop their negative thinking and to substitute these behaviours with self-enhancing positive self-statements.

When faced with problems and life's difficulties, people often neglect to consider how their thinking about themselves affects their level of stress, anxiety and performance. The level of stress and anxiety we all experience in any situation is linked to what we think and say to ourselves about the problem situation and about ourselves in the situation. When thinking or self-talk is primarily negative, stress and anxiety levels increase. High levels of stress result in poor performance. Helping clients to "clean up" their thinking can relieve stress and anxiety and enhance performance.

Research suggests that cognitive restructuring has been successful in helping people with a variety of concerns. For example, cognitive restructuring has been used in the treatment of anger, general anxiety, depression, self-esteem, worry, athletic performance and students' test anxiety.

Self-Guidance

Self-guidance is a procedure in which people are taught what to say to themselves to assist in the performance of a desired task. This procedure begins with the counsellor modelling the desired self-talk. Next, the client engages in the appropriate self-talk while the counsellor coaches. Finally, the client performs the task while guiding or instructing him/herself through the task. The purpose of this procedure is to help clients produce the kind of self-talk that demands attention to the task and minimizes distractions. This procedure helps clients concentrate on the task rather than on fears associated with the task.

A Case Example

To illustrate the use of cognitive–behavioural counselling, we will use Thomas, a sixty-year-old Aboriginal (Mohawk) man with a developmental disability, as a case example. Thomas suffered from seizures during childhood and had a growth removed from his brain when he was three. He continued to have seizures, often as many as eight seizures a day. When he was a boy, he was removed from the rural reservation where his family resided and placed in an institution where he remained for many years. When repatriated back to the community 100 kilometres from his reservation, he lived in a succession of group homes and apartments until finding his current basement suite, where he lives relatively independently. The couple who lived upstairs helped Thomas with medical appointments, budgeting, shopping and personal living skills.

Thomas has good verbal skills although his speech is slow and slurred. He did not have the opportunity to attend school past grade three, but he reads at about a grade six level. He is outgoing and personable and has taken up woodcarving, at which he has begun to excel. In addition, he involves himself in self-help groups, the local Native Friendship Centre and an older adult group. He exercises daily by walking around the block with his walker. During several months prior to counselling, however, he suddenly appeared uninterested in his friends and group activities. He remained in his apartment, isolating himself from others. With Thomas's permission, his caregivers referred him for counselling.

Assessment

The observations made by his caregivers were that Thomas was becoming withdrawn and isolating himself from others. Sharing these concerns with Thomas, they learned that he was afraid to go out into public places for fear of having seizures. He stated that his seizures had "control over him" and he could no longer control them. He believed that when he went out into the community, his seizures increased in frequency. Because of this he grew fearful of leaving his apartment. Thomas's caregivers and caseworker believed that his increased anxiety was triggering his seizures. When Thomas was asked to recall his thoughts and feelings, he stated being "scared" and "hot." He remembered thinking that he was going to have a seizure, worrying about how others would react and feeling the need to "get out of there." Thomas's caseworker reported that recently, when Thomas was faced with a new situation, he would stop, appear confused, breathe heavily and often bolt out the door. She recognized that by leaving the situation, Thomas would begin to feel better and this method of reducing his fear and anxiety served to reinforce his escape from and avoidance of these situations. Because of the absence of trained Aboriginal counsellors, Thomas was paired with a white counsellor recommended by the Native Friendship Centre as being culturally sensitive and experienced in working with Aboriginal clients.

Intervention

The counsellor began to work with Thomas as an Aboriginal man becoming more and more in touch with his culture. Thomas had spoken highly of an elder he met at the Native Friendship Centre, whom the counsellor contacted for assistance. In the first meeting, the elder came with the counsellor and together with Thomas performed a smudge. Next, they talked with Thomas about his carving, encouraging him to continue with it and even contemplate sharing his knowledge with others. The counsellor explained that four cognitive–behavioural counselling strategies would be combined to assist Thomas to overcome his fear of having a seizure in public places. These strategies included progressive muscle relaxation, systematic desensitization, cognitive restructuring and self-guidance. It was hoped that if Thomas used these procedures to lower his anxiety, his seizures would also lessen. In addition, the elder suggested that Thomas begin to use cleansing techniques, such as a smudge and a brush-off with an eagle feather. The elder presented an eagle feather to Thomas, who accepted it with great ceremony.

The first step in Thomas's intervention program was to teach him the skill of progressive muscle relaxation. Relaxation training for people with developmental disabilities typically involves five to ten sessions of about twenty to thirty minutes in length. Due to Thomas's difficulty with short-term memory, the counsellor decided that relaxation training should occur three times a week for approximately three weeks.

Thomas was encouraged to wear loose, comfortable clothing to the training sessions. The sessions began with the elder brushing Thomas and the counsellor off with the eagle feather, followed by a traditional prayer in the Mohawk language. Next the counsellor helped Thomas discriminate between having tense muscles and having relaxed muscles. Thomas found it helpful to feel the counsellor's muscles, as they were tense and relaxed, until Thomas could replicate this procedure. Once Thomas became proficient at relaxing his body, he was encouraged to repeat the word *relax* while experiencing the sensation of having a relaxed body. This step was paired with the image of the lake on the reserve where Thomas was born. It was expected that with practice he could use the word *relax* and the image of the lake as cues to induce relaxation during times of anxiety. Thomas was also encouraged to practice relaxation at home. He was provided with an audiotape to guide him in his practice sessions with traditional native music (e.g., Carlos Nakai). His caregivers helped him develop a chart to record his home practice sessions and to rate his level of relaxation. As Thomas became more proficient at relaxing the muscles in his body, he spent less time on alternating tensing and relaxing muscles, and the focus moved to rhythmic breathing and using the word *relax* as a cue to induce relaxation.

The second step in this program was to help Thomas reduce his level of anxiety during visits to the community. To do this his caseworker took pictures of places Thomas visited and that evoked anxiety. These pictures were ranked according to the levels of anxiety they produced. Thomas was then shown each picture in succession, beginning with the situation that evoked the least anxiety, and taught to relax as he visualized himself being in that particular place. During several counselling sessions this procedure was repeated for each picture until Thomas could visualize being in each situation while remaining relaxed.

Finally, Thomas was taught to talk himself successfully through these difficult situations, to replace the negative statements he had previously used with positive coping statements and to use the word *relax* to achieve a state of relaxation whenever physiological signs of anxiety were evident. By having Thomas engage in self-instructional self-talk, the counsellor expected that Thomas would be fully concentrating on the behaviour he was engaging in and therefore not on his feeling of being scared. It was also assumed that the negative self-talk Thomas had engaged in (such as, "I shouldn't be here," "What will people think if I have a seizure?" and "I want to get out of here") was partially responsible for his high levels of anxiety. The counsellor expected that teaching Thomas positive coping statements to replace his negative thoughts would assist him in remaining more relaxed and able to cope with these situations. For example, Thomas was encouraged to brush off with the eagle feather anything negative that would stick to him and then rehearse an internal dialogue such as,

Now I am getting off of the Handi-Dart and going into the Seniors Centre and everything is okay. I am going to walk through the doors and into the cafeteria for lunch. If I meet anyone, whether I know them or not, I will say hello and smile and maybe talk to them. I feel fine; I don't feel as though I will have a seizure. These people are nice and my friends are here. I feel good being here. And if I feel tense I need to repeat the word *relax* several times and relax my body.

To ensure that Thomas was successful at applying these skills, the counsellor, along with the elder, initially accompanied Thomas to each location that had evoked anxiety. The elder modelled the behaviour Thomas had been taught, and then encouraged and prompted Thomas in its use. In addition, the elder gave Thomas a stone from his home reserve to carry with him for strength. This approach was repeated at each location until Thomas was capable of using these skills independently. Thomas was taken to a park and instructed to enjoy the natural surroundings as a means of relaxing. In addition, Thomas was encouraged to attend an increasing number of events at the Friendship Centre and become more involved in cultural endeavours in the community.

An Expressive Behavioural Strategy: IMM

The Imagery in Movement Method (IMM) is a four-step process used as a tool to explore any topic or question of concern or simply to open investigation into the structure of one's consciousness. It is generally a facilitated process, but people can be trained to work alone. Because every client brings to the counselling session a very personal question or topic to work with, the facilitator or counsellor should consider IMM a tool for working individually with clients and not in groups. The main goal is to help the client explore issues having to do with feelings and emotions, thus leading to an awareness and change in his/her life. The counsellor must act as a supporter and make the client feel confident and safe about the issues that will be explored throughout the four steps. The counsellor must also remember that some individuals might feel vulnerable at any of the four stages because they are dealing with private and intimate situations.

Step One: Expression

For this first step, any kind of self-created art may be used; however, drawing is a preferred technique due to the availability of the materials (paper and crayons), the outcome (a tangible product) and the ease of this form of expression. The purpose of tangible expression is to make the implicit explicit and to experience the non-verbal aspects of the issue through images; that "the feeling in my gut," "an intuition," "on the tip of my tongue" or "my sense of things" can be brought into consciousness, transforming the ground of being into a view. Even when the participant thinks there are no images in his/her mind to draw, the feeling quickly fades and everyone is able to create. People must be reminded that this is not art; all they are doing is letting their hand do whatever it wants. It is important that the facilitator does not make any suggestions to participants about what to draw and that he/she does not express his/her own emotional reactions to the unfolding drawing.

Step Two: Mapping

Mapping is an exploration of each element of the drawing and the overall organization of the drawing itself in order to guide the client through his/her inner landscape, revealing the dynamics of the psyche by implying the direction of growth. The facilitator asks the person to look for a particular shape, pattern or colour in the drawing. The person is then asked to report on any body sensations, feelings, images or thoughts that might speak to him/her. The facilitator helps the client to explore the full sensory experience associated with the drawing, in terms of not only visual images but also olfactory and kinesthetic images. Sometimes the client might be asked to "step into the drawing" and report what is happening (i.e., describe whatever the images evoke at any given time). The next step is to encourage the client to be receptive to the symbolic meaning of each element of the drawing by asking him/herself what the symbolic meaning of a particular part of the drawing might be and to pay close attention to the answer. If the client says he/she does not know, we suggest that the facilitator give a simple instruction to access the appropriate mode by saying something like, "That is your verbal mind and it does not know; ask your imagery mind what it means." The facilitator must comment on or interpret the associations (in the drawing) reported by the participant and must be really careful about the kinds of questions used to trigger ideas, thoughts or sensations.

Step Three: Fantasy Enactment

The purpose of fantasy enactment is self-transformation. When memory and waking-dream experiences ("stepping into the drawing") have been accessed, the client understands the source of an issue, has become aware of how the body has participated in sharing that specific issue and has seen the solution to the issue within the larger context of his/her life. First, the participant is asked to identify the most charged part of the drawing. He/she is asked to step into it once again and report what is happening. One major role of the facilitator is to focus the participant's attention on the sensory details that first present themselves. Based on information given by the participant, the facilitator can ask questions such as, "What colour is the floor?", "How does your body feel?", "What do you smell?" or "What do you hear?" As the scene becomes more and more vivid to the individual, it begins to unfold and evoke sensations, feelings and thoughts. It is then that the facilitator might want to begin the enactment process by asking the participant to role-play the scene as it unfolds. The facilitator acts as an aid to the participant by performing any roles that might be requested. Typically, when there is bodily engagement in the exploration process, a dramatic shift occurs in the person's experience: there is an experience of being at a frightening edge and fearing the unknown. The participant often experiences his/her body moving spontaneously, without any conscious forethought. The client becomes the process, becomes the fantasy unfolding itself; and as he or she experiences catharsis and insight that is at once intellectual, emotional and embodied, the experience finds its own path for resolution. It is not unusual for either a memory experience or a waking dream to unfold in this part of the process.

A participant might find him/herself reliving a memory in vivid detail, recalling aspects that have been long forgotten. Once a scene is retrieved in full sensory detail, the entire memory of the event(s) usually unfolds. The fantasy sequence may be a waking dream, although sometimes it is a symbolic dream where reality is remade in ways that resolve the issue expressed in a particular part of the drawing. Waking dreams that emerge when the client enters a particular colour or shape in the drawing express the issue represented by that part of the drawing and attempt to resolve it. On the other hand, symbolic dreams place the issue in a larger context and provide wisdom about its resolution in terms of options, resources and/or actions. With the conclusion of the fantasy-enactment work, the client moves from accessing material to using methods of verbal translation to understand the relevance of that material for use in finding a solution to the issue or simply discovering alternatives for daily life situations.

Step Four: Verbal Translation

The goal in this last step is to help the client in the understanding of the experiences that have unfolded through the drawings and their explorations. Because the participant has experienced very vivid emotions through the enactment of the fantasy, he/she might be in an altered condition. At this stage, the facilitator's role is to ask general questions about the process in order to move the participant back into his/her everyday situations (e.g., "How was that for you?", "How do these images relate to your reality?", "What in your life reminds you of this memory and fantasy?"). Because some participants may be more vulnerable than others, the "bringing-back" process must be subtle and preferably accompanied by a gentle, soothing voice. Typically, the research reports, participants wipe their faces, adjust their clothes and straighten their body posture; all these gestures indicate that they have returned to the "here and now" world. After this last part of the process has been completed, the participant is given a writing task as homework, divided into three major parts. The first part is a section for reflecting on the graphic elements of the drawing and the emerging experiences during the mapping; the next section is dedicated to reflecting on the major events of the fantasy enactment; and the last part includes various summary sections about the impact that the overall experience has in the participant's current life.

The first two sections of the written assignment ask the person to divide the experience into meaningful segments with the only difference being that for the drawing the client is asked to identify the most significant graphic elements, while for the fantasy the client identifies the major events and/or scenes. Next the client notes all the sensory experiences and feelings associated with these elements, recording them below the element, scene or event that triggered them. Then, the client asks him/herself what the symbolic meaning of the event is and pays attention to his/her own answer, which is recorded under the column labelled *symbolic meaning*. All these components (the chunking of the drawing and the fantasy, the identification of the meaningful parts and so on) are preparatory steps to the most important part of the write-up: tracing the analogies. This step is accomplished by using open-ended questioning. For example, the facilitator asks the client, "Why did your imaginary mind choose this particular sensory experience to represent the symbolic meaning?" The client is supposed to use the section of the writing form labelled *analogies* to write an answer for each sensory image that emerged for that element. After this exploration has concluded, the client fills out the summary part of the form; first, he/she identifies the major themes that emerged during the work and then relates them to his/her current life situation. By tracing the themes and discovering how they relate to a present situation, the client is able to see how the inner life and structure are reflected in his/her own daily world. It reveals why the client has done this particular drawing at this particular time of his/her life. Finally, in the summary part of the task, the client enfolds the imagery and the fantasy material that has emanated throughout the process. The client writes an integrated summary of the insights and in this way evokes powerful experiences of greater expansion and wholeness. The client not only witnesses and experiences him/herself in many different levels of being but also sees his/her current life and past life through the symbolic and imagery representations that organize these experiences. Verbal translation returns the client to his/her ordinary life situations with renewed insights; there is a new and expanded sense of self.

Counsellors must consider certain variables when using this method to help clients find solutions to their situations. One of these variables is time; depending on the depth of the problem and how immediate an option is needed, the possibility of going through all four steps will vary. It is not mandatory to deal with all four parts of the method if the issue is a deep one or if the person needs some time to establish a relationship with the counsellor. The average time to go through the four steps is four sessions. It is not recommended that the in-depth exploration (steps one and two) take more than two sessions since this might weaken the emotions/feelings. The latter part of the method might be explored in a more unhurried way once the initial reactions and emotions have been laid out.

Used over time, IMM helps in the development of a "new something" that is felt and experienced differently by each person. This new something appears to be self-healing; it presents key issues, works on those issues and resolves them, and then the new something moves on to present the next issue. As the drawings change, so does the behaviour. Despite the idiosyncrasies in the way in which each person's process unfolds, the process appears to move towards increasing joy, freedom and capacity.

Conclusion

With any therapy, it is vital to keep in mind that "the models of treatment that are the most effective are those in which traditional [First Nations and other minorities] thinking and practice are utilized in conjunction with Western practices" (Duran & Duran, 1995, p. 87). Cognitive–behavourial strategies have proven effective in helping children and adults who are members of our dominant culture. There is growing evidence that these strategies are also useful with people of diversity. The basic assumption this approach makes about people and the way they behave is the least value-laden therapeutic approach. People are not judged but are taught to recognize how antecedents and consequences influence their behaviour. Once clients recognize these influences, they are in a position to make changes in their lives.

Many factors contribute to an effective counselling program. In this chapter we focussed on a number of cognitive–behavourial counselling strategies for assisting a man with developmental disabilities overcome his fear of public places. By the end of a three-month program that combined several cognitive–behavourial strategies, Thomas was able to engage in community activities once again. Although his seizures continued, they appeared to be fewer in number. Thomas had learned to recognize the physiological cues to anxiety and continued to use these cues to remind himself to apply the new skills he learned. Thomas stated that he continues to feel "a bit scared" on some occasions when he is in public places, but he no longer isolates himself from others or avoids social situations. With encouragement from his caregivers, Thomas continues to use these skills to take charge of his life; he has also begun to relearn his own language. The reconnection with culture is an important element in Thomas's recovery, particularly in that he has begun to describe himself as a "warrior," thereby empowering himself beyond the learning of cognitive skills.

In recent years, cognitive–behavourial strategies have grown in popularity. Numerous books and hundreds of articles have been written attesting to their success. More recently, a number of articles have appeared that discuss the use and benefit of these programs with children and adults with developmental disabilities and cultural differences.

References

Cormier, C., & Nurius, P.S. (2009). Interviewing and change strategies for helpers: Fundamental skills and cognitive–behavioural interventions (6th ed.). Belmot, CA: Brooks/Cole.

Duran, E., & Duran, B. (1996). *Native American postcolonial psychology*. Albany, NY: SUNY Press.

Matsumoto, D. (2000). *Culture and psychology: People around the world* (2nd ed.). Belmont, CA: Wadsworth.

Skinner, B.F. (1953). *Science and human behaviour*. New York, NY: Macmillan.

Tanaka-Matsumi, J., Higginbotham, H.N., & Chang, R. (2002). Cognitive-behavioural approaches to counseling across cultures: A functional analytic approach for clinical applications. In P. Pedersen, J. Draguns, W. Lonner & J. Trimble, *Counseling across cultures* (5th ed., pp. 337–354). Thousand Oaks, CA: Sage.

Trimble, J., & Thurman, P. (2002). Ethnocultural considerations and strategies for providing counseling services to Native American Indians. In P. Pedersen, J. Draguns, W. Lonner & J. Trimble, *Counseling across cultures* (5th ed., pp. 52–92). Thousand Oaks, CA: Sage.

25

Pre-Contact Education and
the Role of Storytelling

Wendy Edwards

First Nations people unanimously emphasized a logical and realistic teaching and learning style that relied on looking, listening and learning (Miller, 1997). Despite their differences, the educational system of the First Nations reflected a common philosophical or spiritual grounding, as well as a similar approach. Because all First Nations based their educational instruction in the deeply ingrained spirituality of their world view, it is not uncommon to find striking commonalities, including the total absence of anything resembling the Europeans' punitive, competitive, institutional approach to schooling. The traditional methods of First Nations education involved family and community as teachers and caregivers. Atleo (2004) emphasized that "each story was also connected to ancestral storytellers who had heard the story from the original storytellers" (p. 2). Miller (1997) reminds us:

> The common elements in Aboriginal education were the shaping of behaviour by positive example in the home, the provisions of subtle guidance towards desired forms of behaviour through the use of games, a heavy reliance on the use of stories for didactic purposes, and, as the child neared early adulthood, the utilization of more formal and ritualized ceremonies to impart rite-of-passage lessons with due solemnity . . . . All of these approaches shared enough assumptions, methods and objectives to be described collectively without doing violence to the individualism of the groups as an Aboriginal system of education. All of them relied on looking and listening to learn. (p. 89)

In childhood, appropriate or desired behaviour was encouraged by indirect and non-coercive means, in direct contrast to European child-rearing methods. Discipline more often consisted of embarrassment or warnings rather than hurtful blows or penalizing deprivation. In a similar spirit was the use of storytelling to teach an indirect lesson to a contrary child. Two important values — love and respect — are at the heart of the Nuu-chah-nulth way. For example,

> The family setting for story telling might include the warmth of a winter night's fire, the closeness of loved ones, warm tones of voice, feelings of security, familiar facial expressions, the imaginative gesticulations that evoke mental images, the absolute confidence of little ones in their families, and altogether these bring home some of the meaning of love. (Atleo, 2004, p. 15)

An Illustration

In an oral society, it is an unforgettable lesson to be the subject of an embarrassing story that may be retold for years to come. Such a story might sound like the following:

Big Brother and Little Brother are Coast Salish boys who live in the village of Snaw Naw As on the east coast of Vancouver Island. One fine, sunny day Big Brother asked Grandpa if he would take them fishing at the Bear Pool. This pool was the site of a fine fish camp and there were always big, fat salmon hiding in the dark water. "Yes," Grandpa replied, "it is time we caught some fish for Grandma and your aunties to prepare for winter eating. And we will catch our supper," he said, "and have a tasty feast at the camp."

The boys were very happy and quickly got ready to go. "Grandpa," said Little Brother, "can our cousin Max come too? He knows how to fish and he can help us catch salmon for Grandma and the aunties." "Yes," said Grandpa, "Max can come too. The more hands we have, the faster the work goes." Little Brother ran to get Max, and Big Brother went out in the yard. Looking skyward he called, "We're going to the Bear Pool. Eagle, will you fly with us?" Then, looking in the direction of the Bear Pool, he called, "We're going to the Bear Pool. Salmon, will you wait for us?"

Little Brother returned with Max, who was carrying a good fishing rod and a big net. They all set out for the Bear Pool. It was going to be a fine day. Grandpa and Big Brother and Little Brother fished that pool all day. They walked further down the river, meeting other relatives who were also inviting the fat salmon to come and keep their winter stomachs full. Max left his rod and net on the bank and went off to play among the trees. Several times during the day, Big Brother called to him,

"Max, there is work to be done. Your rod and net sit there alone. Come and help us." Max would reply, "Not right now. There is plenty of time. I want to play for awhile." Big Brother was getting tired and he grumbled to Grandpa, "This is not right — he knows he is supposed to help. If everybody helps, there will be enough fish for everyone to eat during the winter." "Never mind," said Grandpa. "Just do what you know is right." As supper time approached, Grandpa built a good fire on the river bank. He had saved a particularly fat salmon for their feast. The boys were all hungry. With growling bellies they watched Grandpa prepare their meal. Soon the wonderful smell of roasting salmon was in the air. Yum! Now Grandpa said, "Big Brother and Little Brother, you have done a fine day's work. There are many fish to take home to your Grandmother. Come and share in this feast."

"Max," said Grandpa, "you can go and play among the trees. I know that is where you would rather be. Don't worry about us." And Grandpa turned his back to Max. Max was horrified! He was hungry! He could not argue with Grandpa. Slowly, he walked back to his playing ground and sat down. His belly was growling hard and he could smell the roasted salmon. Max was very sad. Grandpa and Big Brother and Little Brother had a wonderful feast. They felt full and very satisfied. It had been a good day's work. When they were finished eating, they began to pack up the fishing gear and the salmon harvest. Still, Max sat by himself among the trees. Grandpa called to him, "Max, come and eat. We saved some of our feast for you. We will not let you go hungry." Although Max was very hungry, he walked slowly back to the fire. Quietly, he ate his delicious meal.

Advantages of Storytelling

Children hearing the story above would recognize the lesson of co-operation immediately. To ensure that knowledge did not get separated from experience, or wisdom from divinity, elders stressed listening, watching and waiting, not asking why. According to Beck and Walters (1997), training began with children who were taught to sit still and enjoy it; they were taught to use their sense of smell, to look when there was seemingly nothing to see and to listen when, presumably, all was quiet. A child who had to ask "Why?" was not paying attention in the approved manner. Storytelling was also an effective means of preserving the origin histories. In these stories, individuals are told where the people came from, how the stars were created, where fired was discovered, how light became divided from darkness and how death originated. Curled up with Grandmother under a blanket, children learned lessons about life through the experiences of the animal characters in the teaching stories. Gently, they acquired the tools and ways of knowledge with which to survive the world. Since there were no books, movies, radios or television, these stories were the libraries of the people and included the human voice, hand movements and facial expressions. The human memory is a great repository that we ordinarily fill with only a fraction of its capacity. The elders knew this, and tested and trained the memory, along with the other senses, so that the history and traditions of the people could be preserved and passed on. Oral tradition was one of the principal means the people had to maintain stability over the years in the tribal community. In each story there was recorded some event of interest or importance, some happening that affected the lives of the people. There were calamities, discoveries, achievements and victories to be kept. But not all our stories were historical; some taught the virtues of kindness, obedience and thrift, and the rewards of right living. Hart (2002) reminds us that storytelling can also be a means of healing and living more constructively:

> Our Grandfathers and Grandmothers — our elders — tell us that it is not enough merely to listen to the stories which they tell: we must make every attempt to understand the truths which are embodied with these stories and myths. The truth must then become part of us, who have stopped to listen to the inner truth out to lead to self-actualization for the man or woman whom the story is told. (Asikinack, in Hart, 2002, pp. 56–57)

Characteristics of a Storyteller

A good storyteller is able to communicate the universality and timelessness of certain themes we know will never change. Sometimes the story is like a code: the more often it is told over the years, the more a person listens and the more it reveals. According to Beck and Walters (1997), the coding of knowledge in stories is like listening more closely to the narration of events that happened; creatures and characters that are encountered may be symbolic of something besides what they appear to be or do. Storytelling is a very flexible method of education in the ways of generational knowledge since the traditional forms — style, delivery, tone, and words — can be employed not only with traditional content and symbols but also with modern themes and content, as well as gradual dimensions of meaning. Knowing when the child is ready, at certain points in his/her life, to be exposed to certain knowledge is the responsibility of the storyteller. It is important to avoid knowing too much too soon, before the child's maturity to handle the information is in place.

Teachers could use storytelling time to achieve their curricular goals and objectives, and to teach students about geography, world literature, vocabulary and so forth. However, a good storyteller must also emphasize the inherent values that lie in each story being told. If teachers take advantage of their students' thirst to learn and if teachers know how to instill a desire for transmitting oral stories, much could be gained in terms of raising students' awareness about the importance of maintaining, valuing and honouring traditions; after all, oral traditions are part of every cultural group. A tradition is something that is lived out and is communicated in its being lived out to those who come within its circle of influence. Moreover, what is traditional should be viewed not as old-fashioned or unenlightened old ways, but rather as a means to find reassurance that, somehow, those who come after us will find common ground in sharing the tradition. It is also indispensable to mention that storytellers are at an advantage if they use their whole body to express the feelings and ideas behind a story (i.e., hand movements, voice pitch, facial gestures and posture). Finally, it must be said that not only teachers can have the abilities to be storytellers; opportunities and acknowledgement must be given to those children who have a family story or an event to share because, at any rate, we all have stories to tell.

Conclusion

The ways people relate to one another and behave toward one another are as important today as they have always been. Consequently, the teaching stories remain viable in today's world of fast-paced technology. Though some stories might be seen as cautionary tales, the outcome of right or wrong behaviour is not always what might be expected, even when the attitude towards good and bad adds a wonderful complexity to the stories. The characters must undertake some form of the classic journey, beset by dangers, challenges and sacrifices that heroes are often called on to make for personal or communal benefit. In the real world, we too make our journeys for personal or common gains. Some journeys gain knowledge for society, and others yield self-knowledge. Like the Haida youths (in traditional stories) who prepare themselves for any feat of will or body, we too test ourselves in the search for perpetually elusive truths.

Transcending time and culture, the metaphors of journeys, challenges, quests and triumphs in stories envision humanity's constant struggle to understand and experience the mysteries of the universe. Storytelling — the ability to tell a story — is a universal practice, a means of passing on a wide variety of skills and knowledge from one generation to the next.

References

Atleo, U.R. (2004). *Tsawalk: A Nuu-chah-nulth world view*. Vancouver, BC: University of British Columbia Press.

Beck, P.V., & Walters, A.L. (1997). *The sacred: Ways of knowledge, sources of life*. Tsaile, AZ: Navajo Community College.

Hart, M.A. (2002). *Seeking Mino-Pimatisiwin: An Aboriginal approach to helping*. Halifax, NS: Fernwood Publishing.

Keitla, W. (1995). *The sayings of our First People*. Penticton, BC: Theytus Books Ltd.

Miller, J.R. (1997). *Shingwauk's vision: A history of Native residential schools*. Toronto, ON: University of Toronto Press.

26

Toward an Integrated Perspective

Restorative Justice, Cross-Cultural Counselling and School-Based Programming

Shannon A. Moore

Restorative justice cannot be categorically defined; rather, it is a major philosophical movement and social construction in contemporary society (Clairmont, 2000). Philosophically, restorative justice processes are focussed on accountability for one's actions, respect for all persons, cooperation, compassion, a focus on human relationships and community. These formative principles often compel individuals to have a degree of insight into their choices and self-reflection, as well as humility and an open heart and mind. Commitment to work toward changing social, economic and political injustices is also germane to restorative practices:

> Whenever I am asked to explain restorative justice or how it differs from the current criminal justice system, I am always torn between the simple and the complex. Restorative justice is simple yet it is complex. It is not a formula or a method but a process by which we view ourselves, others and the world around us. It is grounded in the spiritual being. Simply stated, it's how we choose to live our lives. The restorative justice approach is positive and future oriented. It offers a process that empowers people to search for healing and constructive solutions, as there is a need for victims and offenders to focus on healing and restoring. It is not surprising that victims and offenders begin to explore issues of compassion, forgiveness and reconciliation when dialogue for healing begins. (E. Evans, cited in Restorative Justice and Dispute Resolution Unit, 2000, p. 7)

Restorative justice implies both process and outcome (Umbreit & Coates, 1999) and provides a lens through which we can understand interpersonal encounters as we transform conflicts, hurt and the impact of crime (Zehr, 1995). The most recognizable restorative justice movements include reparative parole, family group conferencing, circle sentencing and victim–offender mediation. Several principles are foundational to restorative justice and facilitate movement toward healing harm. The following are the principles and practices connecting the movements mentioned above.

1. Harm inflicted and crimes committed create hurt that is not merely an act of law-breaking but fundamentally a violation of a human being or human relationships: it tears the social and community fabric.
2. The goal is to repair the harm done and restore relationships among individuals and community.
3. The victims of hurt or crime must have free choice to participate in a restorative process.
4. The perpetrators of hurt or crime must have the opportunity to accept responsibility for their crimes and the harm they have caused and to choose to participate in a restorative process.
5. Victims must be of central concern in all restorative justice processes. (adapted from Umbreit and Coates, 1999)

It is imperative that victims remain at the centre of restorative justice. Engagement and participation in restorative justice initiatives also must be non-coercive and completely voluntary for all involved. The process can be simple or complex and may include information, dialogue between affected parties, mutual resolution of conflict between victim and offender, restitution, reduction of fear, heightened sense of safety, acceptance of responsibility and/or renewal of hope (Van Ness & Heetderks Strong, 1997).

Historical Roots of Restorative Justice

Restorative justice is not a new movement: it is a return to traditional Western and non-Western patterns of coping with conflict and crime that have been present throughout human history (Llewllyn & Howse, 1999). The retributive system that dominates our Western judicial system has in fact governed our understanding of crime and justice for only a few centuries. Zehr (1995) contrasts the retributive and restorative system as follows:

[In the retributive system] crime is a violation of the state, defined by lawbreaking and guilt. Justice determines blame and administers pain in a contest between the offender and the state directed by systematic rules. . . . [In contrast, for restorative justice] crime is a violation of people and relationships. It creates obligations to make things right. Justice involves the victim, the offender, and the community in a search for solutions which promote repair, reconciliation, and reassurance. (p. 181)

The period of justice that predates our current retributive system has been described as an era of community justice (Zehr, 1995) and reflects customary or indigenous approaches to justice (Van Ness & Heetderks Strong, 1997). Analogies have been made between a community justice process of dispute resolution and traditional healing practices. For example, doctors and healers were traditionally charged with keeping the human body in healthy balance, and law was to keep the social body in good health by bringing relationships back into balance (Llewellyn & Howse, 1999). Survival of the community at large depended on the effectiveness of both of these processes. In the contemporary sense, restorative justice emerged from several earlier movements that contributed to its theory over the past three decades. These include the informal justice movement, restitution, the victims' movement, reconciliation and conferencing, and the social justice movement.

Informal Justice

Legal anthropologists distinguish between informal and formal justice movements because virtually all societies facilitate both forms of proceedings. During the 1970s the Western formal legal system was criticized for its legitimacy, which in turn created the possibility for a stronger role for the informal legal structures. These emphasized increased participation, increased access, deprofessionalization, deregulation and the minimization of stigmatization and coercion. In particular, North American Native views of justice, African customary law and approaches found in the Pacific Islands have provided rich insights for Western informal and alternative justice processes (N. Christie, personal communication, October 27, 2000; Van Ness & Heetderks Strong, 1997).

Restitution

The restitution movement emerged from the dawning awareness in the 1960s that compensating victims for the impact of crime was sensible. The rationale for this process of restitution includes the following points:

1. The rediscovery of the victim as the party harmed by criminal behaviour;

2. The search for alternatives to more restrictive or intrusive sanctions such as imprisonment;

3. The expected rehabilitative value of paying the victim for the offence;

4. The relative ease of implementation;

5. The anticipated reduction in vengeful and retributive sanctions that comes when the public observes the offender actively repairing the harm done. (Van Ness & Heetderks Strong, 1997, p. 18)

The rights of the victim are of central concern in restorative justice processes; this is in sharp contrast to justice motivated solely by the examination of the offenders' behaviour.

The Victims' Movement

The "rediscovery" of the victim and the establishment of a centralized role for victims rights was the result of accumulated effort from several individuals and groups. This movement continues to be motivated by the following tenets:

1. Increasing services to victims in the aftermath of crime;

2. Increasing the likelihood of financial reimbursement for the harm done;

3. Expanding victims' opportunities to intervene during the course of the criminal justice process. (Van Ness & Heetderks Strong, 1997, p. 20)

At best, the current formal Western system has been described as alienating to victims. In contrast, the victims' movement demands that the complexities of victimization and the process of traumatization be accounted for and ultimately compensated for by our judicial processes.

Reconciliation and Conferencing

Reconciliation and conferencing is composed of two major activities: victim–offender mediation and a decision for a future action that will help bring restitution and heal the harm done (Van Ness & Heetderks Strong, 1997). Umbreit has written extensively on the subject of victim–offender mediation as a way to improve the current delivery of justice in North America. For the past three decades victim–offender mediation has been active in North America and has spread to South Africa, England, Germany and other Europe-an countries. Victim–offender mediation has moved from the margins to find a place in mainstream Western justice, clearly indicating international interest in restorative justice (Umbreit, Coates & Warner Roberts, 2000).

Critical social theorists Zehr and Claasen have also contributed to the establishment of victim–offender mediation as an integral part of conflict resolution and judicial proceedings in North America. The roots of Zehr and Claasen's practice emerge from their participation in the Mennonite faith. Both Zehr and Claasen stress the importance of community-driven and -funded victim–offender mediation programs, in contrast to programs funded by the criminal justice system (Claasen, 1996; Van Ness & Heetderks Strong, 1997; Zehr, 1995). In 1989 New Zealand and Australia introduced another branch of victim–offender mediation called family group conferencing (Morris & Maxwell, 1998). This form of conferencing is founded on Maori traditional practices and is characterized by the key principles found in restorative justice. What differentiates family group conferencing from victim–offender mediation is the number of parties involved in the conflict-resolution process. In family group conferencing, organizers strive to include all persons affected by crime in the community, rather than solely focussing on primary victims (Van Ness & Heetderks Strong, 1997).

Social Justice

Members of various religious communities and supporters of the feminist movement have shared a common cause: to critique and pressure the retributive judicial system to adopt fundamental changes. Over the past four decades, Quakers have advocated for significantly reduced use of prisons and the complete abolition of the prison system. This standpoint is largely based on the conviction that criminal justice simply cannot be achieved in an unjust society, nor can it be manifest in judicial and prison systems overrun with abuse and human rights violations (R. Morris, personal communication, October 26, 2000; Van Ness & Heetderks Strong, 1997). Other researchers have argued that the current model of retributive justice emerged from the medieval Christian view of sin and punishment, although this particular viewpoint of Christianity is narrowly framed in place and time. Interpretations of Christian doctrine also proclaim values of relationship, restoration, forgiveness, reconciliation and hope. These latter characteristics are the same principles that form the foundation of restorative justice and are promoted by other faith communities, including the Mennonites and Quakers (Hadley, in press; Van Ness & Heetderks Strong, 1997).

Likewise, feminist theory asserts "that all people have equal value as human beings, that harmony and felicity are more important than power and possession, and that the personal is political" (M. Kay Harris, cited in Van Ness & Heetderks Strong, 1997, pp. 23–24). These assertions are fundamentally opposed to the formal retributive judicial system that is founded on principles of power, control and punishment. In this way feminist theorists continue to be vocal opponents to the dominant Western judicial system.

Cross-Cultural Counselling Implications

All interpersonal exchanges, particularly in the context of helping professions, are potentially cross-cultural. The boundaries where people meet are filled with tensions among values, beliefs, world views and other cultural and personal artifacts — including aspects of being and consciousness. All of us are challenged to navigate through this diversity with knowledge of self and openness to others. It is also important that we have an awareness of our own cultural heritage at the same time as being open to the perspectives of others: centred in a personal sense of truth yet open to other ways of knowing. In this way I understand culture as a shared reservoir of knowledge that is both tacitly and overtly known while informing multiple aspects of being.

Cross-cultural counselling is complex as a result of the multiple dimensions of self and environment that influence interpersonal exchanges. The following principles may assist counsellors to navigate through cross-cultural exchanges and the complexities of diversity.

1. Self-awareness and self-knowledge are key. The counsellor must understand his/her own values, beliefs, world views and prejudices.
2. The counsellor must understand the basic world view and value system of the client's culture, and must suspend disbelief and listen without judgement.
3. Counsellors should listen to the client's history, belief system and spirituality.
4. Counsellors must exude respect, genuineness, availability, congruence and humility.
5. Counsellor and client can focus on how they are similar as well as how they are different.
6. The counsellor must create psychological space for the client's individuality and diversity.
7. The counsellor can allow the client to lead or celebrate mutual experiences of meaning and a sense of spirituality. (Matheson, 1996; Pedersen, Draguns, Lonner & Trimble, 1996)

If we use the above points as a template, it becomes possible to facilitate sensitive and effective cross-cultural counselling practice in any context. The next section will specifically integrate principles of cross-cultural counselling in the context of restorative-justice practice.

**Cross-Cultural Restorative-Justice Processes
and School-Based Interventions**

It is vital that people involved with restorative-justice practices be aware of the impact of divergent cross-cultural perspectives on conflict resolution as well as have the self-knowledge to negotiate diversity sensitively (Umbriet & Coates, 1999). This is important in any context and may enhance facilitation and mediation within schools where, beyond traditional bounds of geographic culture, the world of children and youth today is often viscerally different than the experiences of adult facilitators and school administrators. The following key aspects of cross-cultural counselling are important to consider in restorative justice within school programming (adapted from Minster Public Works and Government Services Canada, 1998; Pedersen, Draguns, Lonner & Trimble, 2007; Sue & Sue, 2007; Umbreit & Coates, 1999).

1. Proximity

- Distance between victims, offenders and other people engaged in restorative justice processes.
- Degree of face-to-face interactions.
- Sitting side by side without desks or other pieces of furniture between individuals.
- Sitting in a circle demonstrating equality between the people present.

2. Body Movements

- It is often suggested that the facilitator of a restorative justice process retain a neutral stance so that resolution is negotiated between those affected by whatever harm was committed.
- It is important to be conscious of eye contact and gestures of approval or disapproval such as smiling or frowning.
- Offenders may not show remorse through demonstrations of emotions such as tears.
- Lack of eye contact by an offender or victim does not necessarily indicate avoidance of an issue, lack of attentiveness, submissiveness, guilt or shame.

3. Paralanguage

- Be conscious of vocal cues such as hesitations, inflections, silences, intonation, cadence and projection of one's voice.

- It is important for the facilitator to be comfortable with silence so that the emotive aspects of the process have space to manifest.

4. Density of Language

- People from differing cultural backgrounds vary in the verbal delivery of ideas.
- Some people are concise and sparse with their verbiage, and these qualities should not necessarily be taken as a terse or uninterested tone.
- Some people use many words to express ideas: "The poetry of the story may be more important than the content of the story, and may actually be the point of the story" (Umbreit & Coates, 1999, p. 46).
- People's style of communication may range from low-key indirect to objective and task oriented.

5. Values and Ideology

- It is essential that one is aware of differences in the cross-cultural ideologies of collectivism and individualism, as well as religious and faith perspectives, as these will likely affect the process of conflict resolution and individuals' definitions of justice.
- The difference in ideology may also affect the identification of primary and secondary victims in facilitation processes.

Across Canada and throughout British Columbia, restorative justice is increasingly acknowledged as an important alternative to traditional systems of discipline in schools. In Greater Victoria, community-based initiatives have emerged in conjunction with several community partners, including school districts, the Royal Canadian Mounted Police and the Ministry of the Attorney General. Individual elementary, middle and secondary schools have also begun to explore the use of restorative-justice initiatives founded on the core principles discussed above. The following excerpt describes such a program in Greater Vancouver, Canada:

Students at the Canada Way education centre, a last-chance alternative school for kids with problems, have experienced what is known as restorative justice, a process that has been used in criminal matters for many years but is just now being tested by BC schools anxious to tame schoolyard bullying and violence. While it's too early to predict its overall success, it's not too early for rave reviews. Restorative justice, also called transformative justice, aims to heal relationships rather than punish wrongdoers by bringing feuding parties together to talk about their dispute. Sometimes that meeting is expanded into a "conference" of everyone affected by the row — which in schools could include a sizeable group of students, participants and bystanders, teachers, parents and support staff. They come on equal footing — as people touched by a conflict — not as authority figures ready to make judgments about who is right and who is wrong. They talk about what they believe happened, how it affected them and what might be done to prevent it from occurring again. It's an emotional process that proponents say is much more of a deterrent than traditional punishments such as suspension or expulsion. (Steffenhagen, 2001)

Victims must be at the centre of any restorative-justice initiative within a context of accountability, respect, safety and honesty on behalf of all. These principles may be integrated within a school system to reduce and prevent conflicts, ultimately fostering an atmosphere of non-violence. In this way, detentions and suspensions administered by school officials may be avoided as accountability and responsibility are restored to students. Students are supported to resolve their own conflicts without escalating violence and bullying. The following description of a school-based restorative justice program was adapted from the work of Vincent Stancato (2000) of the Community Justice Branch of the Ministry of the Attorney General:

What Is School Based Restorative Justice?
- Brings together the affected community — those most directly involved in the incident or pattern of behaviour that has caused harm within the school community.
- Provides an opportunity for the affected community to gain insight into the extent of harm caused to themselves, others and the broader school community.
- Provides an opportunity to determine how to best repair the harm, learn from the experience and prevent further harmful behaviour.

Who participates?
- Victim(s) of the harm caused
- Support people for the victim(s) e.g., family, friends and/or mentors
- Perpetrator(s) of the harm caused
- Support people for the perpetrator(s) e.g., family, friends and/or mentors
- Facilitator for the Restorative Justice process
- Anyone else involved or investigating the incident

Reflections

It is imperative that all parties participate as volunteers and that offenders of hurt express accountability for the harm done prior to engagement in restorative processes. Through restorative justice, all participants are given an opportunity to recount what occurred in order to foster a more complete understanding of the incident and determine how the harm caused will be repaired. All parties sign a contract outlining specific actions that will be taken to repair the harm. Finally, it is helpful to have a mentor follow up and support the perpetrator of the hurt to fulfill the contractual commitment within school settings.

References

Clairmont, D. (2000). Restorative justice in Nova Scotia. *ISUMA,* (Spring), 145–149.

Classen, R. (1996). *Restorative justice primary focus on people not procedures* [on-line]. Retrieved from http://www.fresno.edu

Llewllyn, J., & Howse, R. (1999). *Restorative justice — a conceptual framework.* Ottawa, ON: Law Commission of Canada.

Matheson, L. (1996). Valuing spirituality among Native American populations. *Counseling and Values,* 41, 51–69.

Minister of Public Works and Government Services (1998). *Community justice forum.* Ottawa, ON: Royal Canadian Mounted Police.

Morris, A., & Maxwell, G. (1998). Restorative justice in New Zealand: Family group conferences as a case study. *Western Criminology Review,* (1) [online]. Retrieved from http://wcr.sonoma.edu/v1n1/morris.html

Pedersen, P.B., Draguns J.G., Lonner W.J., & Trimble J.E. (Eds.). (2007). *Counseling across cultures.* Thousand Oaks, CA: Sage.

Restorative Justice and Dispute Resolution Unit. (2000). *Restorative Justice Week 2000: Basic Resource Kit.* Ottawa, ON: Correctional Services of Canada.

Steffenhagen, J. (2001, August 22). Cooling school violence. *Vancouver Sun,* p. D2.

Stancato, V. (2000). *Restorative Justice in Schools.* Community Justice Branch, Ministry of the Attorney-General, Report.

Sue, D.W., & Sue, D. (2007). *Counseling the culturally different: Theory and practice* (5th ed.). New York: John Wiley and Sons.

Umbreit, M., & Coates, R. (1999). Multicultural implications of restorative juvenile justice. *Federal Probation,* (December), 44–51.

Umbreit, M., Coates, R., & Warner Roberts, A. (2000). The impact of victim–offender mediation: A cross-national perspective. *Mediation Quarterly,* 17(3), 215–229.

Van Ness, D., & Heetderks Strong, K. (1997). *Restoring justice.* Cincinnati, OH: Anderson.

Zehr, H. (1995). *Changing lenses: A new focus on crime and justice.* Scottsdale, PA: Herald Press.

Author Biographies

M. Honoré France is from the Ani-yun-wiwa First Nation and is a professor at the University of Victoria, where he teaches courses in diversity, family therapy, group dynamics, and research methodology. His current research and teaching interests are cross-cultural counselling issues, ecopsychology, counselling residential school survivors, and cross-cultural child development. He currently has projects in China, Ethiopia and Mexico.

María del Carmen Rodríguez is an assistant professor of Indigenous education in the Faculty of Education at the University of Victoria. Prior to her appointment, she worked as an early childhood educator and as an elementary school teacher for 20 years in Mexico. Her research interests are education for diversity, bilingualism and identity development, Indigenous early childhood education, and Indigenous pedagogies. Dr. Rodríguez has published numerous articles and book chapters, and has presented scholarly papers throughout the Americas.

Geoffrey G. Hett is a professor emeritis in the Department of Educational Psychology and Leadership Studies at the University of Victoria. He holds a Ph.D. in counselling psychology and teaches undergraduate courses in this area. His teaching and research interests include cognitive behavioural counselling, managing deviant child behaviour and program development for children of divorce. He is the founding president of the Erma Fennell Foundation for the Relief of Poverty, a Canadian charity that supports the relief of poverty in a small community in Mexico.